Sheffield Hallam University
Learning and Information Services
Adsetts Centre, City Campus
Sheffield S1 1WB

Total

102 040 522 8

SHEFFIELD HALLAM UNIVERSITY
LEARNING CENTRE
WITHDRAWN FROM STOCK

This book is due for return on or before the last date shown below.

D1495184

SHEFFIELD HALLAM UNIVERSITY
LEARNING CENTRE
WITHDRAWN FROM STOCK

Total Facility Management

FOURTH EDITION

Brian Atkin
The Facilities Society, UK

Adrian Brooks
GVA Acuity Limited, UK

WILEY Blackwell

This edition first published 2015
© 2000 by The Further Education Funding Council
and Blackwell Science Ltd – First edition
© 2005 B. Atkin & A. Brooks – Second edition
© 2009 B. Atkin & A. Brooks – Third edition
© 2015 John Wiley & Sons, Ltd. – Fourth edition

Registered Office
John Wiley & Sons, Ltd, The Atrium, Southern Gate,
Chichester, West Sussex, PO19 8SQ, United Kingdom.

Editorial Offices
9600 Garsington Road, Oxford, OX4 2DQ,
United Kingdom.
The Atrium, Southern Gate, Chichester, West Sussex,
PO19 8SQ, United Kingdom.

For details of our global editorial offices, for customer
services and for information about how to apply for
permission to reuse the copyright material in this book
please see our website at www.wiley.com/wiley-blackwell.

The right of the author to be identified as the author
of this work has been asserted in accordance with the
UK Copyright, Designs and Patents Act 1988.

All rights reserved. No part of this publication may
be reproduced, stored in a retrieval system, or
transmitted, in any form or by any means, electronic,
mechanical, photocopying, recording or otherwise,
except as permitted by the UK Copyright, Designs and
Patents Act 1988, without the prior permission of the
publisher.

Designations used by companies to distinguish their
products are often claimed as trademarks. All brand
names and product names used in this book are trade
names, service marks, trademarks or registered
trademarks of their respective owners. The publisher
is not associated with any product or vendor mentioned
in this book.

Limit of Liability/Disclaimer of Warranty: While the
publisher and author(s) have used their best efforts in
preparing this book, they make no representations or
warranties with respect to the accuracy or completeness
of the contents of this book and specifically disclaim any
implied warranties of merchantability or fitness for a
particular purpose. It is sold on the understanding that the
publisher is not engaged in rendering professional services
and neither the publisher nor the author shall be liable for
damages arising herefrom. If professional advice or other
expert assistance is required, the services of a competent
professional should be sought.

Library of Congress Cataloging-in-Publication Data

Atkin, Brian.
  [Total facilities management]
  Total facility management / Brian Atkin and Adrian
Brooks. – Fourth edition.
      pages   cm
  Includes index.
  ISBN 978-1-118-65538-2 (pbk.)
1. Real estate management.   2. Facility management.
3. Building management.   I. Brooks, Adrian.   II. Title.
  HD1394.A86 2014
  658.2–dc23
                                                  2014020680

A catalogue record for this book is available from the
British Library.

Wiley also publishes its books in a variety of electronic
formats. Some content that appears in print may not be
available in electronic books.

Cover image: Cover photo taken from the Science and
Engineering Centre at Queensland University of Technology,
Brisbane. Cover photo courtesy of Brian Atkin, the author

Set in 10/12pt Minion by SPi Publisher Services,
Pondicherry, India

Printed and bound in Malaysia by Vivar Printing Sdn Bhd
1   2015

SHEFFIELD HALLAM UNIVERSITY
WL
658.2
AT
LEARNING AND INFORMATION SERVICES

Contents

Preface to the Fourth Edition   x

Abbreviations   xii

Introduction   1
   The organization   1
   The customer as end-user   1
   Principles, process and procedures   2

1 **Fundamentals**   3
   Key issues   3
   Introduction   4
   Background   4
   Key concepts   8
   Other concepts   13
   Key roles, responsibilities and accountabilities 15
   Core competence in facility management   16
   Conclusions   17
   Checklist   18

2 **Facility planning**   19
   Key issues   19
   Introduction   20
   Real estate management   21
   The own, lease or rent decision   21
   The totally serviced workplace   22
   Space management   23
   Space utilization and efficiency   24
   Design and facility management briefing   26
   The feasibility study   34
   Design development   35
   Stakeholders   36
   Risks and opportunities   39
   Conclusions   39
   Checklist   40

3 Facility management strategy   **42**
Key issues   42
Introduction   43
The business context   44
Business drivers and constraints   45
Organizational management levels   46
Cross-cultural management   47
Strategy formulation   48
Strategic analysis   50
Solution development   53
Strategy implementation   55
Conclusions   57
Checklist   57

4 Human resources management   **59**
Key issues   59
Introduction   60
Personnel management   60
Conclusions   66
Checklist   66

5 Workplace productivity   **68**
Key issues   68
Introduction   69
Measuring productivity   69
Sick building syndrome   76
Design issues   77
Unconventional working arrangements   78
Conclusions   83
Checklist   83

6 Health, safety and security   **85**
Key issues   85
Introduction   86
Health, safety and security policy   87
Zero accidents   88
Occupational health and safety   88
Compliance   89
Hazard and risk assessment   92
Security and well-being   93
Conclusions   95
Checklist   95

7 The outsourcing decision   **97**
Key issues   97
Introduction   98
Establishing the baseline   99
Attributes of service provision   105

Options for service delivery 109
Evaluating options 116
Conclusions 118
Checklist 118

8 Procurement **120**
Key issues 120
Introduction 121
The procurement process 122
Centralized versus decentralized procurement 123
Procurement policy and procedures 124
Roles, responsibilities and accountabilities 126
Prequalification of service providers 126
Request for proposals or tender 131
Tendering 140
Financial close 142
Conclusions 145
Checklist 145

9 Service delivery **147**
Key issues 147
Introduction 148
The internal customer as end-user 149
Insourcing 150
The in-house team 150
External service providers 151
Mobilization 152
Contract management 155
Conclusions 162
Checklist 162

10 Specialist services and partnership **164**
Key issues 164
Introduction 165
ICT services 166
Health-care services 169
Security and protection services 170
Custodial services 170
Professional services 171
Performance and SLAs 172
Risk, insurance and indemnities 172
Supplier management 173
Collaborative relationships 174
Public–private partnerships (PPPs) 179
Facility management and private-sector participation 187
Conclusions 189
Checklist 190

11 Performance management 192
Key issues 192
Introduction 193
Quality or performance 194
The post-implementation review 194
Post-occupancy evaluation (POE) 195
The service review 196
Updating service specifications and SLAs 199
Performance measurement 199
Benchmarking 208
Beyond benchmarking 214
The quality system 215
Conclusions 216
Checklist 216

12 Maintenance management 219
Key issues 219
Introduction 220
The maintenance strategy 221
The maintenance policy 221
Maintenance planning 222
Maintenance methods 227
Building logbooks 231
Permits and approvals 232
Inspections 232
Building services engineering installations 233
Manuals, registers and inventories 236
Maintenance management system 238
Conclusions 239
Checklist 240

13 Sustainable facilities 242
Key issues 242
Introduction 243
Sustainable development 244
Environmental management 245
Corporate social responsibility (CSR) 247
Zero carbon 248
Whole-life carbon 248
Environmental performance and energy efficiency 250
The building energy management system 251
Managing water resources 251
Managing waste 252
Management and end-user responsibilities 253
Technology-enhanced facilities 253
Innovative workplaces and housing 260
Conclusions 270
Checklist 271

14 **Change management**   273
    Key issues   273
    Introduction   274
    Transition   275
    Managing change   292
    Organizational change   292
    Innovation, research and development   296
    Conclusions   298
    Checklist   299

15 **Information management**   301
    Key issues   301
    Introduction   302
    Managing information   303
    The facility handbook   310
    The facility user guide   311
    Information and data   311
    Information handover   323
    Building information models (BIMs)   324
    Systems and interfaces   327
    Conclusions   329
    Checklist   330

Appendices   332
    A   Glossary   332
    B   Prevention of fraud and irregularity   355
    C   Risks involved in outsourcing   361
    D   Contract provisions   363
    E   Typical sections of an SLA   366

Bibliography   367

References   369

Index   372

Preface to the Fourth Edition

Facility management has progressed by leaps and bounds since we published the first edition back in 2000. In many countries, the subject and discipline could then be fairly described as in a formative stage of development. Defining the scope of the first edition to provide a coherent account of the subject was a challenge. The success of that first edition led to two major revisions and now this fourth edition. It represents a rethinking of our approach and what we presently consider to be within scope; yet, it retains those elements that our readers and reviewers have told us they value most.

The fourth edition consolidates current best practice, defines and develops emergent areas and offers a pathway for the future development of facility management. The body of knowledge that this new edition represents benefits from the publication of several national and international standards, none of which were around for the earlier editions. The structure and content aligns with these standards to provide readers and their organizations with a comprehensive treatment of the subject. Greater emphasis has been given to facility planning, especially the briefing stage in the design of a new or refurbished facility, design for operability, stakeholder management, outsourcing, procurement, transition, performance management, environmental management, sustainability, maintenance management, information management and building information modelling (BIM).

Facility management has become an internationally recognized discipline, a major sector and the means by which organizations are able to *think globally and act locally*. Primarily for this reason, we have adopted a minor change to the title of this new edition; but the ethos and style of our work remains true to the previous editions and our original aim, which was to develop the subject and discipline through a thorough treatment of concepts, practices and issues. We believe this new edition will continue to support individuals at all levels, whether encountering the subject for the first time or looking for answers to questions of strategic importance as well as those of operational necessity.

This new edition has been prepared for a worldwide market. Whilst every care has been taken in its drafting, it is not possible to cover or anticipate legislation, or indeed other requirements, prevailing in the reader's location. It is for the reader to ascertain the relevance of any such legislation or other requirements and the need for legal or other specialist advice.

Finally, we must express our appreciation to a number of individuals who have contributed their expertise. Our sincere thanks go to Roine Leiringer, Robert Wing, Rachel Stewart, Martin Hooper and Stefan Olander.

Brian Atkin
Reading

Adrian Brooks
London

Abbreviations

AEC	architecture, engineering and construction
ASHRAE	American Society of Heating, Refrigerating and Air-Conditioning Engineers
BIM	building information modelling
BIMs	building information models
BEMS	building energy management system
BMS	building management system
BPR	business process re-engineering
BREEAM	Building Research Establishment Environmental Assessment Method
CAD	computer-aided design
CAFM	computer-aided facility management
CAPEX	capital expenditure
CCTV	closed circuit television
CO_2-eq	carbon (dioxide) equivalent
CMMS	computerized maintenance management system
COBie	Construction Operations Building information exchange
CPD	continuing professional development
CPE	continuing professional education
CREM	corporate real estate management
CSF	critical success factor
CSR	corporate social responsibility
DBFO	design, build, finance and operate
EDI	electronic data interchange
ERP	enterprise resource planning
FM	facility management or facilities management
GPS	global positioning system
HRM	human resources management
HSSE	health, safety, security and the environment
HVAC	heating, ventilating and air-conditioning
ICT	information and communications technology
IFC	Industry Foundation Classes
IFMA	International Facility Management Association
KPI	key performance indicator
LEED	Leadership in Energy and Environmental Design
MVD	model view definition

OLA   operating level agreement
OPEX   operational expenditure
PEST   political, economic, social and technological
PPE   personal protective equipment
PPM   planned preventive maintenance
PPP   public–private partnership
RASCI   responsible, accountable, supported, consulted and informed
RCM   reliability centred maintenance
RFI   request for information
RFID   radio frequency identification
SBS   sick building syndrome
SLA   service level agreement
SMEs   small and medium-sized enterprises
SPV   special purpose vehicle
SQL   structured query language
SWOT   strengths, weaknesses, opportunities and threats
TCO   total cost of ownership
TFM   total facility management
TPM   total productive maintenance

Introduction

Effective management of non-core business (i.e. support services) enables an organization to function at its most efficient level. The focus is facility management, which was once regarded as the poor relation among the construction and real estate disciplines. The significance of facility management is nowadays far more widely recognized. In support of the further development of the discipline, this book offers a comprehensive treatment of what facility management means to owners, operators, tenants, facility managers and professional advisors. The book contains advice on how facilities can be better managed from a number of perspectives, although the approach is not intended to be prescriptive.

The organization

This book is directed at organizations within the private and public sectors acting primarily as owners and/or operators of facilities and tenants, as well as facility managers and professional advisors. The types of organization addressed might range from airport authorities and manufacturers to colleges and financial services firms. The structure, management and facility-related needs of these organizations will vary widely; however, the information contained in this book is intended to have a correspondingly wide application. It is necessary, of course, for each organization to consider the relevance to itself of the issues and points raised.

The customer as end-user

In the broadest sense, the customer is the organization in acting as a purchaser of services. These will sometimes be insourced (in-house) and sometimes sourced from external service providers (outsourcing). Although the distinction between purchaser and provider is more obvious in the case of outsourcing, it is important that the same distinction is recognized with insourcing. The customer in this instance might be an internal department being served by the organization's in-house facility management team, with a financial exchange between the

Total Facility Management, Fourth Edition. Brian Atkin and Adrian Brooks.
© 2015 John Wiley & Sons, Ltd. Published 2015 by John Wiley & Sons, Ltd.

two different cost centres. The relationship between the two parties therefore remains a formal one, requiring guidelines and procedures for its formulation and implementation.

In many organizations, customers will be the internal departments and their personnel as the principal end-users of the facility and its services. In some, such as leisure centres, entertainment complexes or department stores, the external user of the facility becomes an additional type of customer whose needs must be considered within the scope of facility management, as far as is practicable. This book generally refers to the former type of customer (internal user), with these users typically providing the interface between the external user and the service providers. For the most part, it is unnecessary to draw a distinction between internal and external customers and so the all-embodying term of *end-user* is used.

Principles, process and procedures

Many fields and disciplines are subject to guiding principles, defined processes and supporting procedures. Facility management is no exception; however, authoritative guidance has been lacking until fairly recently. The publication of a significant number of national, European and international standards has begun to inform practice through greater clarity and consistency of application on both the demand and supply sides. In an increasingly global context for facility management, the relevance of standards, at whichever level, ought to be recognized. The bibliography lists the most relevant standards together with others that help to define the overall framework within which facility management is undertaken. These cover the subjects of design briefing, operability, outsourcing, procurement, transition, asset management, maintenance management, quality management, environmental management, sustainability, business continuity management, risk and opportunity management, information technology, information management and building information modelling.

1 Fundamentals

Key issues

The following issues are covered in this chapter.

- There are a number of definitions of facility management. One that is commonly used is an integrated approach to operating, maintaining, improving and adapting the buildings and infrastructure of an organization in order to create an environment that strongly supports the primary objectives of that organization.

- In any discussion of facility management, it is necessary to stress the importance of integrative, interdependent disciplines whose overall purpose is to support the organization in the pursuit of its business objectives.

- The correct application of facility management techniques enables the organization to provide the right environment for conducting its core business to deliver end-user satisfaction and best value.

- If a facility is not managed properly, it can impact upon the organization's performance. Conversely, a well-managed facility can enhance performance by contributing towards the provision of the optimal working environment.

- Facility management covers a range of functions, including real estate management, financial management, human resources management, health, safety, security and environment (HSSE), change management and contract management, in addition to maintenance, domestic services (such as cleaning and catering) and utility supplies.

- There is no universal approach to managing facilities. Each organization will have different needs. Understanding those needs is the key to effective facility management measured in terms of providing end-user satisfaction and best value.

Total Facility Management, Fourth Edition. Brian Atkin and Adrian Brooks.
© 2015 John Wiley & Sons, Ltd. Published 2015 by John Wiley & Sons, Ltd.

- Quality of service or performance is a critical factor in any definition of value, and the relationship between quality (or performance) and cost (or price) has to be properly understood.

- Cost savings cannot be looked at in isolation from value. The organization must be able to demonstrate what it is getting for its money and should not assume that paying less today is proof of better value for money.

- The many risks involved in the search for best value should be recognized and allocated to those who are able to manage them effectively. This means that all options should be carefully examined and those that are most likely to achieve best value, whilst achieving and maintaining end-user satisfaction, should be considered.

Introduction

This opening chapter sets the scene, by discussing the importance of a facility to an organization (as the owner, operator or tenant acting as a client[1]) and how approaches to facility management can differ between organizations even within the same sector. There is no single formulation of facility management that will fit all situations. Nonetheless, the concept of the informed client function is common to all situations and is described and discussed in this chapter – see Key concepts. It is a theme that stands behind this book and one that reflects an organization's perspective, its values, culture and needs. This chapter also discusses the necessity of securing best value in the delivery of services and examines some of the attendant risks – more are to be found in Appendix C. The context for facility management is first described and an overview follows in the form of a simple functional model. This is developed in the text to show the distinction between core and non-core business – something that is essential to understanding the focus for facility management.

Background

Origins of facility management

Facility management – the operational environment needed to support and enhance an organization's core business processes and activities – has evolved over the past 150 years or so. It originated at some time in the 1800s, when the American railroad companies thought it better to provide the utility of *facilities* and not merely buildings. This broader interpretation of *facility* is reflected in this book.

---

[1] An organization that procures facility services by means of a facility management agreement (EN 15221-1:2006).

It was not until the late 1950s that facility management became associated with the effective and efficient coordination of services applied holistically to enhance the performance of the organization. The collective practices that we recognize today have therefore evolved fairly slowly.

Forty years ago there was only brief mention of facility management. Buildings were maintained, serviced and cleaned: that was about it. Building maintenance management was arguably the term most commonly identified with these tasks, yet it explicitly excluded a role that embraced the *softer* side of an organization's support services and concern for the well-being of personnel.

A unified concept for facility management was far from attracting broad acceptance in the real estate (or property management) world. Few common procedures were in circulation and it was left to innovative organizations – many of them in the fast-growing financial services, ICT and media sectors – to devise ways of more effectively managing their facilities. Today, facility management is a service sector in its own right and has helped to establish a new professional discipline with its own principles, processes, standards, codes and technical vocabulary.

Definitions

Facility management has been regarded as a relative newcomer to the real estate and AEC (architecture, engineering and construction) sectors. This is because it has been seen in the traditional sense of cleaning, janitorial services, repairs and maintenance. Nowadays, it covers real estate management, financial management, human resources management, health, safety, security and environment (HSSE), change management and contract management, in addition to minor building works, building maintenance, building services engineering maintenance, domestic services and utility supplies. These last three areas are perhaps the most visible. The others are subtler, although of no less importance. For facility management to be effective, both the *hard* issues, such as building services engineering maintenance, and the *soft* issues, such as managing people and change, have to be considered.

The International Facility Management Association[2] has defined facility management as *a profession that encompasses multiple disciplines to ensure functionality of the built environment by integrating people, place, process and technology.* This definition clearly underscores the holistic nature of the discipline and the interdependence of multiple factors in its success. Elsewhere, it has been defined as *the integration of processes within the organization to maintain and develop the agreed services that support and improve the effectiveness of its primary activities.*

An oft-cited definition is provided by Barrett & Baldry (2003), who see it as *an integrated approach to operating, maintaining, improving and adapting the buildings and infrastructure of an organization in order to create an environment that strongly supports the primary objectives of that organization.* They continue by reminding us that the scope of facility management is not constrained by the physical characteristics of buildings. The behaviour and efficiency of personnel and the effectiveness of ICT are important too. Whatever is adopted as a definition,

---

[2] www.ifma.org

either in this book or by personnel within the organization, it should stress the importance of integrative, interdependent disciplines whose overall purpose is to support the organization in the pursuit of its business objectives.

Rationale for facility management

Most facilities represent substantial investments for their organizations and usually have to accommodate and support a range of activities, taking into account competing needs. Within those activities is the organization's core business, for which an appropriate environment must be created in a facility that might not have been designed for the use to which it is now put. Yet, no matter how well focused an organization is on its core business, it cannot lose sight of the services needed to support it; that is, non-core business. The relationship between the two and the place of facility management is shown in Fig. 1.1.

The organization might have already considered the distinction between its core business and non-core business (e.g. security, waste management and cleaning) as part of the drive to achieve end-user satisfaction and best value. Since operational expenditure accounts for a significant part of annual expenditure, there is bound to be pressure to look for savings in non-core business areas. Cutting operating budgets can be financially expedient, but might not help the organization's long-term development. Since operations can involve complex, coordinated processes and activities, it is necessary to take an integrated view. A piecemeal approach to cutting costs is unlikely to produce the required savings and can impair the organization's ability to deliver high-quality services. For this and other reasons, we should be able to see why facility management is a more powerful concept than real estate management (or property management), because it takes a holistic view of the dynamics of the workplace – between people and processes and between people and their environment.

Facility management can thus be regarded as creating an environment that is conducive to the organization's primary processes and activities, taking an

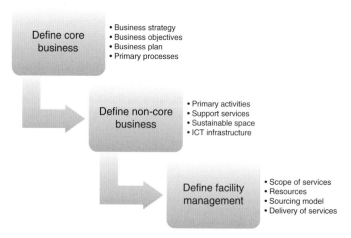

Fig. 1.1   The relationship between core business, non-core business and facility management.

integrated view of its services and support infrastructure, and using them to achieve end-user satisfaction and best value through support for, and enhancement of, the core business. We can develop this definition to describe facility management as something that has a number of distinct goals, and that will:

- Support people in their work and in other activities.
- Enhance individual well-being.
- Enable the organization to deliver effective and responsive services.
- Sweat the physical assets; that is, make them highly cost-effective.
- Allow for future change in the provision and use of space.
- Provide competitive advantage to the core business.
- Enhance the organization's culture and image.

The broad approach to facility management

There are common themes and approaches to facility management, regardless of the size and location of facilities, although these might not necessarily result in common solutions to problems. In some cases, services are contracted out – a form of outsourcing – and in others they are insourced, and for good reason in both cases. Many organizations operate what might be described as a *mixed economy* where some services, even the same services, are co-sourced. Whichever course of action has been taken, the primary concern is the basis of the decision. Where the decision has been arrived at for the right reasons, such as demonstrating better value for money from one approach as opposed to others, facility management can be regarded as working effectively. In order to reach this state, a basic plan for facility management (see Fig. 1.2) should be prepared to incorporate the following steps as a minimum:

1. Develop a strategy for facility management.
2. Determine the most appropriate model for sourcing services.
3. Procure the services, where outsourcing or co-sourcing applies.
4. Deliver the services, including mobilization and contract management.
5. Manage the performance of service providers and/or the in-house team.

This plan for facility management is something of a simplification to highlight key considerations. These and other relevant matters are elaborated in subsequent chapters.

Risks and opportunities

There are innumerable factors and events that can impact an organization's business objectives, planning and operations. Downside risks have the potential to hinder, even negate, attempts at achieving best value. Table 1.1 identifies some downside risks that the organization can face in its facility management. The chapters in which the underlying issues are considered are indicated in Table 1.1. Some of these risks might be easier to address than others. In certain cases, the organization will have to acquire new skills or insights into how problems can be solved.

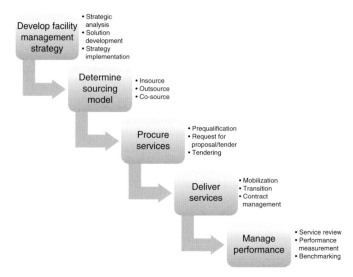

Fig. 1.2 A basic plan for facility management.

In pursuing more efficient and effective facility management, the organization should also be aware of opportunities (upside risks). Some upside risks do, in fact, mirror the downside risks to counter their influence (see Table 1.2).

Key concepts

The informed client function

The organization needs to act as an informed client if it is to be sure of achieving end-user satisfaction and best value. The informed client function is a requisite irrespective of how services are procured – see also the later section in this chapter on Key roles, responsibilities and accountabilities.

The following outlines the scope of the informed client function:

- Understanding the organization, its culture, end-users and their needs.
- Understanding and specifying service requirements and targets.
- Brokering services with, and amongst, stakeholders.
- Managing the implementation of outsourcing.
- Minimizing uncertainty and risks through proactive risk and opportunity management.
- Agreeing standards for control purposes.
- Managing service providers and monitoring their performance.
- Benchmarking the performance of services.
- Surveying end-users for satisfaction with service delivery.
- Providing management reports.
- Reviewing the scope of services and service levels against end-user requirements.
- Developing, with service providers, delivery strategies for services.
- Agreeing, with service providers, changes to service requirements.

Table 1.1   Risks (downside) faced in facility management.

- Inadequately resourced or inexperienced client function (Chapters 4, 7, 8 and 9).
- Inadequate planning of implementation – limited preparation and/or allocation of responsibilities (Chapters 7, 8, 9, 14 and 15).
- Misapplication of transfer of employment of personnel (Chapters 4, 8 and 14).
- Poor relationship between service provider and facility/contract manager (especially if the latter was once involved with preparing an in-house tender) (Chapter 9).
- Conflicts of interest when dealing with in-house tenders, arising from inadequate split between purchaser and provider personnel (Chapter 4).
- Unclear or imprecise roles, responsibilities and targets for effective teamworking (Chapters 7, 8, 9, 14 and 15).
- Possible loss of control over the facility management function and ownership of, and access to, documents and knowledge (Chapters 8, 9, 10 and 14).
- Lack of standard forms of facility management contracts or inadequate conditions of contract (Chapter 8 and Appendix D).
- Inappropriate allocation of risks and rewards between the organization and service providers (Chapter 7).
- Inadequate definition of the scope and content of services (Chapters 7, 8, 9 and 14).
- Lack of consideration of all stakeholders in the facility management sphere (Chapters 2, 3, 7, 8 and 14).
- Specifications that are overly prescriptive and/or concentrate on procedures, not outputs (Chapter 8).
- Stakeholders' *gold plating* of requirements (Chapter 8).
- Poorly controlled changes to end-user requirements (Chapters 8, 9, 10, 11 and 14).
- Excessive monitoring of service provider performance (Chapters 9 and 11).
- Absence of, or a poor system for providing, incentives to raise performance (Chapters 8, 9 and 11).
- Inflexible contracts unable to accommodate changes in end-user requirements during the contract and work outside scope/specification (Chapter 11).
- Failure to take account of relevant health and safety legislation at the correct time, leading to penalties and later excess cost (Chapters 6, 7, 9, 12 and 14).
- Redundancy in the supply chain where cost is added without necessarily adding value (Chapters 7, 8 and 9).
- Poor bundling/grouping of services to be outsourced (Chapters 7, 9 and 10).
- Absence of shared ownership of outcomes (Chapter 10).
- Poor cash-flow position for the organization and/or service providers (Chapters 8 and 9).
- Financial failure of chosen service provider during the contract period (Chapters 8, 9, 10 and 14).
- Absence of benchmarks against which to measure performance and improvement (Chapters 2, 4, 8 and 11).
- Lack of education and training in facility management (Chapters 3, 4, 6, 9, 11 and 14).
- Fraud or irregularity in the award and management of contracts (Appendix B).

- Maintaining the ability to re-tender as and when required.
- Understanding the facility management market and how it is developing.
- Undertaking strategic planning.
- Safeguarding public funds, where applicable.
- Developing in-house skills through education, training and continuing professional development/education (CPD/CPE).

A distinction does need to be drawn between types of organization. Differentiation between them can be based on various criteria and terms; for instance, the *not-for-profit* and *for-profit* sectors. For our purpose, the distinction is based upon the applicability and extent of regulatory control over decision-making and accountability. In most countries, the public sector is therefore clearly defined and, by the presence of far fewer regulatory controls, so too is the private sector to a large extent.

Private-sector organizations

Whilst organizations in the private sector appear to be able to set their own agenda for their affairs, the requirements of corporate governance, including compliance with various legislation and standards (especially financial), mean that greater

Table 1.2   Opportunities (upside risks) arising in facility management.

- Enhancing organizational capability and quality of service delivery, and proper assessment of requirements in the scope of services (Chapters 7, 8, 9 and 14).
- Identification and allocation of risks on a rational basis to help clarify relationships between service providers and the organization (Chapter 7).
- Proper separation of duties between purchasers and service providers (Chapters 8 and 9).
- Clear roles, responsibilities and targets for effective teamworking (Chapters 7, 8, 9, 14 and 15).
- Proper contract documentation with appropriate conditions of contract for insourced as well as outsourced services (Chapter 8 and Appendix D).
- Proper allocation of risks and rewards (Chapter 7).
- Improved response to end-user requirements (Chapters 8, 9, 10, 11 and 14).
- Improved performance with proper incentivization (Chapters 8, 9 and 11).
- Health and safety legislation incorporated into facility management policies and procedures at the appropriate time (Chapters 6, 7, 9, 12 and 14).
- Shared ownership of outcomes (Chapter 10).
- Proper monitoring of contract performance (Chapters 9, 11 and 14).
- Improved cash-flow forecasting and budgeting (Chapters 2, 3, 8, 9, 11 and 14).
- Opportunity to build up benchmarks against which to measure performance and improvement (Chapters 2, 4, 8 and 11).
- Properly focused education and training for in-house personnel in facility management (Chapters 3, 4, 6, 9, 11 and 14).
- Proper assessment of services to be grouped/bundled for outsourcing (Chapters 7, 9 and 10).

transparency is now expected in commercial dealings. Growing recognition of the importance of being a *good* organization extends to facility management, where it is likely to be judged on how well it satisfies or not the end-users of services. Corporate social responsibility – see Chapters 8 and 13 – is now a feature of corporate life and with it come particular responsibilities for facility managers. The direction of travel for the private sector is, consequently, likely to be towards increasing standardization of processes, procedures and practices for its non-core business. In this regard, there is much the private sector can learn from the public sector, where accountability is a given and openness and transparency are the norm.

Public-sector organizations

The imperative of openness and transparency in commercial dealings has been a long-standing preoccupation of the public sector. Often derided for its unimaginative approach to new ideas and novel practices, most public-sector organizations nowadays have both the competence and confidence to devise more effective, cost-efficient and value-adding methods of working. Fixed capital investment in the public sector brings with it responsibility to extract best value for taxpayers. The public sector has, in many countries, become adept at understanding the inherent risks in delivering facilities and the impact their operation would have if they fall short on requirements. For these reasons, we are witnessing something of a renaissance in the role of the public-sector organization and one that can be as informed as the best in the private sector.

Stakeholder engagement

Effective management of those individuals and groups with an interest in a facility is a key factor in the success of facility management. These individuals and groups are referred to as stakeholders and collectively will determine the nature of facility management, including its processes and activities and the extent to which they are able to satisfy their (i.e. stakeholder) interests (see Chapters 2 and 7).

End-user experience

Both inside and outside the organization, the individuals or groups that will experience the impact of facility management are appropriately termed end-users. As the ultimate customers of facility management, their needs and expectations must be properly counselled and managed. They exist for both private- and public-sector organizations. Examples include:

- hospitals;
- financial services companies;
- airport authorities;
- manufacturing companies;
- colleges and universities; and
- entertainment complexes.

As the above examples might suggest, the structure, management and space requirements of organizations can vary widely, but the most important point is to realize that the implementation of best practice facility management is relevant to all. Undoubtedly, some aspects and requirements will be more significant than others, depending on the type of organization and its business objectives and drivers.

The following are examples of individuals or groups as end-users of facility management:

- A *procurer of services* – the general definition of a customer and also the recipient of services.
- An *internal department* – an organizational unit served by the facility management function (perhaps operating as a separate unit) with financial exchange between the two and *internal end-users* as the recipients of services.
- The *external end-users* of the organization's facility and services, as would be found in the customer service sector.

Best value

Value for money is a term long used to express the relationship between the cost of a good or service and its quality or performance. The term *best value* extends the concept of value for money to imply the need to strive continually for something superior at the lowest practicable cost. The organization might not be aware of the extent to which value for money in facility management can be improved; that is, through the search for best value. This would suggest that it is not the outcome that needs to be scrutinized, but the decision-making that leads to it and the assumptions upon which it is based.

The best value decision is generally cited as the determinant of whether to outsource a service or not. Whilst value is about the relationship between cost and quality, it is often equated with achieving a reduction in cost. The organization might believe it is achieving best value if it is paying less for a given service this year compared with the previous year. Whereas cost is easier to measure, best value is concerned with the quality of a service and the efficiency and effectiveness with which it is delivered. The organization should therefore set itself cost and quality objectives for the management of its facility, with the cost objective taking priority only where financial necessity dictates.

When choosing options for service delivery and service providers, there needs to be an assessment not only of cost implications but also of quality (see Chapter 8 on Tender evaluation). The organization should choose the approach and service delivery that offers best value, not simply lowest cost, and measure performance against both cost and quality. Benchmarking can help in checking performance (see Chapter 11).

Normally, the achievement of best value is demonstrated by acceptance of the lowest tender price in a competition where all other criteria (quality, performance, terms and conditions) are equal. Best value can also be achieved through collaborative arrangements with suppliers and service providers. Economy of scale offered by bulk purchasing of utility supplies – see Chapter 8 – is an obvious example. An additional benefit from collaboration is that risks are also shared.

Operability

The success of a new or refurbished facility depends to a certain extent on ensuring that design takes proper account of operational requirements through a thorough process of briefing. Like all *good* decisions, those in design have to be based on the correct information and data, and the impact of a design on operations has to be understood before it is committed to construction and/or installation. Once the facility is operational, it is too late to take issue with the *fitness for purpose* of the design. The principle of constructability is widely applied by designers and design teams; however, the principle of design for operability is not necessarily recognized to the same extent. Designing a new or refurbished facility without understanding the requirements of operability is likely to have negative consequences for both its operational efficiency and energy performance (see Chapter 2 on Design and facility management briefing).

Other concepts

Facility planning

Changes in the use of a facility, whether at the level of routine minor adjustments or as part of a major restructuring of the organization, have to be planned. As a stage within the life cycle of a facility, facility planning serves to determine if the organization has the most appropriate facility to support its core business into the future, providing a formal basis for initiating a process of managed change where found necessary (see Chapter 14).

Sustainability

The organization might have, as an objective for its facility, the requirement to optimize operational cost over the life cycle. The facility might have to sustain operations over many decades in an environment in which pressure to reduce energy consumption and, by implication, carbon emissions is likely to increase significantly. A long-term view of the operability of any facility should be taken so that the organization is aware of its obligations and liabilities into the future. Important in this regard is an understanding of a facility's carbon footprint (see Chapter 13).

Decisions in design have of necessity to take account of the carbon embodied in the manufacture of components and materials and in the construction or refurbishment of a facility (see Chapter 2 on Design and facility management briefing). Account must also be taken of carbon produced during the operation of the facility. Patterns of use over the life of a facility will affect the overall carbon load and will be influenced by the actions of all stakeholders, not just occupants and other end-users. A refurbished facility can be designed for zero carbon, but decision-making might inadvertently ignore the longer-term sustainability of the facility; for instance, occupants and other end-users, together with suppliers of various goods and commodities, will contribute to the facility's carbon footprint throughout its operational life. The result could be a significant underestimation of the carbon impact of the refurbished facility. A whole-life perspective has to be taken, which involves understanding the stakeholders who will be influential in this regard; in particular, their interest in, and impact upon, the facility (see Chapter 13).

Outsourcing

The process by which services are delivered to an organization by an external provider is known as outsourcing and is based upon a sourcing decision. Outsourcing is the alternative to obtaining services from within the organization (i.e. insourcing) and can involve highly prescribed procedures, especially within the public sector. Co-sourcing is where outsourcing and insourcing are combined. Chapter 7 considers the outsourcing decision.

Procurement

Procurement concerns the acquisition of goods and services from an external source and so is the practical manifestation of outsourcing. It is, however, necessary to regard procurement as more than the activity of obtaining quotations from service providers and placing orders. A range of issues has to be taken into account and that normally requires technical knowledge of the services in question. Chapter 8 considers the procurement of services.

Performance management

Services are provided according to agreed performance levels. Measuring actual performance and comparing with stipulated performance levels will show if the service is being provided as agreed or if some action needs to be taken to correct performance (see Chapter 11).

Management of change

Facility management is concerned with routine, minor change arising in the course of day-to-day operations and should be capable of minimizing disruption as well as safeguarding business continuity. Larger and more complex change is better handled outside the normal routine and constituted as a defined project with clear objectives and supporting plans (see Chapter 14).

Human resources management

Managing the delivery of services involves, to a large extent, managing personnel: these might be internal or external to the organization. It means ensuring that services are delivered safely, efficiently and cost-effectively by those involved. Facility management embodies human resources management to an extent that procedures should both reflect and be sensitive to the broader issues and requirements facing the organization. A close working relationship between the human resources manager and the facility manager is desirable to ensure that matters affecting personnel are adequately addressed and that there are no ambiguities.

There is considerable legislation in this area. One fast-moving aspect is equality, which covers issues around the subjects of age, disability, gender reassignment, marriage and civil partnership, pregnancy and maternity, race, religion or belief, sex and sexual orientation. Regular updating on the part of the organization will be necessary. Chapter 4 considers human resources management.

Maintenance management

The origins of facility management included, amongst other functions, building maintenance management. In its modern context, facility management covers the maintenance of the structure, fabric, building engineering services installations, fittings and furnishings that collectively form the facility (see Chapter 12). Maintenance is an integral part of facility management and requires clear definition of arrangements to prevent and deal with failure or breakdown of parts, components, systems and other elements. Business continuity is likely to be a key concern and plans for dealing with any impact on operations should be prepared and kept up to date (see Chapters 9 and 14).

Information management

Proper management of information and data is necessary to comply with statutory obligations and duties, as well as enabling the organization to derive optimal use and benefit from its facility. The breadth and depth of information to be managed can be substantial and requires a structured approach for its collection, analysis, exchange, storage, updating and control. Despite the growth in ICT, much information and data are likely to be paper-based and of variable quantity and reliability (see Chapter 15).

Key roles, responsibilities and accountabilities

There will be changes of personnel and other aspects of an organization's management over time. Arrangements and agreements, with respect to facility management, might well outlast the employment of key personnel. It is important, therefore, that there is recognition of the need for:

- The organization to be an informed client and to develop this function into the future.
- A procurer–provider relationship to develop between those procuring services within the organization and service providers (internal and external).

In coming to terms with these needs, the organization might benefit from a better understanding of the new tasks this role as an informed client represents. This function will demand a significant degree of operational knowledge and experience, not only of the organization's own business, but also of the services being provided. Since little remains the same for long, change is an ever-present condition that has to be managed as part of any facility management remit.

In particular, the success of a change initiative in the delivery of services will depend on two main parties:

- The organization's representative (typically the facility manager, but sometimes the estates manager or other senior manager).
- Service providers, whether internal or external.

Both parties should share the common goal of delivering best value. To be successful in achieving this goal, any divergent interests between the two parties also have to be recognized. A cooperative approach, which recognizes individuals' interests and aligns efforts with business objectives, has the potential to deliver the greatest benefit. A cooperative approach – for example, partnering – is also one of the recommended arrangements for managing external service providers (see Chapters 4 and 10).

Owner

The organization that holds legal title to the facility and that is the ultimate authority in decisions affecting its acquisition, use, alteration, abandonment and disposal is the owner for our purpose in this book.

Operator

The organization that is responsible for the day-to-day operation of the facility and that has legal and financial responsibility for ensuring the safe, efficient and cost-effective operation of the facility is the operator for our purpose in this book.

Core competence in facility management

Successful facility managers are likely to be those who are able to combine knowledge and skill in facility-related matters with an understanding of organizations, people and processes. An accomplished designer does not necessarily make a competent facility manager. Understanding how to design a facility is not the same as ensuring that it is safe and secure in operation. Knowing how people within an organization make use of a facility – moreover, how they can work safely, comfortably and efficiently – goes a long way to becoming a successful facility manager.

Setting aside the historical background to the development of the discipline and, therefore, the particular competences that have been assimilated over the years, we can see that facility management draws on a body of knowledge that spans science, engineering and social science. Even so, facility managers need to be able to take a physiological view of facilities rather than a purely anatomical view. This implies greater familiarity with *softer* issues than those of a purely technical or engineering nature. In practice, this means that facility managers have to understand how facilities behave and function as environments to support people in their work (and in other contexts). A fundamental characteristic of the environment is change and so one of the main competences that facility managers should have is an ability to manage change.

Other competences include organizational management, financial management and end-user service. It is the interaction of these that establishes facility management as a unique discipline. Traditionally, it might have been considered that a sound education and training in an established discipline such as architecture, engineering or surveying was enough; however, aspiring facility managers might lack sufficient understanding of organizational behaviour and human resources management, and how innovation and change can be managed effectively. Core competence in facility management can therefore be said to cover the following, amongst others:

- *Real estate management* – building performance, building services engineering and workplace design.
- *Financial management* – accounting, finance, purchasing and supply, and legal aspects.
- *Organizational management* – organizational structure, behaviour, processes and systems.
- *Innovation and change management* – processes, technology, ICT and information management.
- *Human resources management* – motivation, leadership, employment law, health, safety and security.

Conclusions

Facility management is about providing support to the organization's core business in the form of services. To benefit most, the organization has to understand that it needs to be an informed client in managing any facility. This requires a focus on service delivery that provides end-user satisfaction and best value in an environment where risks abound – there are so many threats to organizational and human well-being. Effective facility management comes from being able to devise and implement practices that reduce or eliminate the risks and that add value to the core business. This current understanding is a far cry from its origins. Indeed, facility management has emerged from an indistinct past to become a key discipline. It owes its success to the increasing awareness amongst facility owners, their personnel and other end-users of the value that a well-managed facility can bring to the core business. At the same time, the discipline of facility management has evolved to embrace *softer* issues, but without ignoring the science and engineering base that remains a cornerstone of the discipline. In an ever-changing world, facility management is likely to evolve in line with changes in corporate real estate management, legislation affecting employment and the workplace, especially health, safety, security and environment, and change management. Whatever happens, distinct core competences must be present for those managing a facility. Where they are not, retraining or recruitment of appropriate human resources will be necessary.

Checklist

This checklist is intended to assist with review and action planning.

	Yes	No	Action required
1. Does facility management have a sufficiently high profile, i.e. is it connected to the organization's business objectives?	☐	☐	☐
2. Have senior managers articulated a workable definition of facility management?	☐	☐	☐
3. Has a formal risk assessment of facility management been undertaken?	☐	☐	☐
4. Could the organization be considered an informed client?	☐	☐	☐
5. Is the role of stakeholders in facility management fully recognized?	☐	☐	☐
6. Have end-users of services been recognized as a distinct group of stakeholders?	☐	☐	☐
7. Is the organization able to determine whether or not it is achieving best value from its facility management, however it is provided?	☐	☐	☐
8. Is the concept of design for operability explicit in all design work?	☐	☐	☐
9. Is facility planning a recognized concept and one that is practised?	☐	☐	☐
10. Is there a practical interpretation of sustainability and is it reflected in the approach to facility management?	☐	☐	☐
11. Is the role of facility management in dealing with routine change recognized?	☐	☐	☐
12. Is the organization aware of the competences that must be instilled in its facility management personnel?	☐	☐	☐
13. Are there arrangements in place for continuing professional development/education (CPD/CPE)?	☐	☐	☐
14. Is the organization aware of the likely *direction of travel* for facility management?	☐	☐	☐

2 Facility Planning

Key issues

The following issues are covered in this chapter.

- Traditionally, real estate management was where responsibility for managing facility-related services was to be found. The emergence of facility management as a distinct discipline has meant that responsibility for real estate – in organizations without a prior interest in it – has become part of facility management.

- Organizations today have many options for meeting their space requirements. These range from the highly formalized, such as the acquisition of a new facility, through to renting temporary space (either serviced or non-serviced).

- For organizations in the early stages of business growth, totally serviced workplaces have much to offer in terms of convenience and economy. For more established organizations, there could be need for readily available workplaces to help mobilize a new operation, relocate an existing team or recover from an incident.

- Space efficiency can be a key factor in the success of the organization. The drivers for space and demand into the future have to be understood. A balance has to be struck between what the organization needs and what it can afford, and this is referred to as its sustainable space provision.

- Planning for change in the use of a facility can arise from the ongoing management of the existing facility; it might otherwise arise from a business decision that has identified a need that is best satisfied by a new or refurbished facility.

- Briefing is the process for engaging the organization in a structured discussion about the functions and other characteristics it requires in a

Total Facility Management, Fourth Edition. Brian Atkin and Adrian Brooks.
© 2015 John Wiley & Sons, Ltd. Published 2015 by John Wiley & Sons, Ltd.

new or refurbished facility. A number of defined steps should be followed to ensure that the facility's design takes full account of operational requirements – the principle of *design for operability*.

- Two important aspects of briefing are defining a *statement of needs* and a *functional brief*. Both should take active account of the operational requirements for the facility and plans for handover and flawless start-up of operations. A facility management brief should be prepared with input from the facility manager to support this process.

- The use of building information models (BIMs) to manage facility information and data is growing. BIMs provide a means for maintaining a current data model of facility assets that can be used to support facility planning and facility management.

Introduction

Facility management is generally regarded as having ongoing responsibility for the delivery of services in support of the organization's core business. It is important, however, to stress the significance of facility management in a more strategic role – see Chapter 3 – and to understand how it can make a more complete contribution to the success of the organization. If we adopt a life-cycle perspective then it is clear that planning for, and of, a facility precedes its realization and operation; however, we have to consider how the need for that facility arises – which comes first, facility planning or facility management? Much depends on where the organization is in the business cycle and how present arrangements satisfy needs. Whatever these are, a holistic approach must be adopted, because planning for a new facility might be based to a great extent on what is currently being managed and experienced. This chapter deals collectively with the issues that enable us to complete the cycle and in so doing realize that the output from one process – that is, facility management – is the input to another, namely facility planning. It is acceptable to argue that planning is part of management and so it is; but we need to have a way of linking the facility to the business objectives of the organization and vice versa. Understanding how a facility is measuring up to expectations about its performance provides valuable feedback to planners, designers and decision-makers, and how information needed to drive the planning and design process forward can be best utilized. We also consider the options that are available in terms of how space can be provided from, at one extreme, the procurement of a new facility that could take several years to complete through to the relocation of personnel overnight in a totally serviced workplace. In the case of a new or refurbished facility, there is now important guidance available within standards. In particular, the provisions of BS 8536, which are reflected in this chapter, cover design briefing and the related concept of *design for operability*.

Real estate management

The relationship between real estate management and facility management, and their link to business strategy, are often debated. For certain organizations – perhaps those with a relatively short history and a rapid rate of growth – facility management might be where responsibility rests for all matters of real estate. In other cases, there might be a long history of real estate acquisition and disposal. Moreover, the discipline of facility management might have emerged from building maintenance management, domestic services or a combination of the two. Given that background, it would be easy to accept real estate management as the natural home for facility management. Without that background, however, the organization might regard real estate as a part of facility management. Buildings are acquired and disposed of according to the need for space. This would make sense in a market where there are options other than taking a long lease on a building. Moreover, the work in acquiring and disposing of buildings might take the facility manager outside his or her core competence. If this extends to procuring the design and construction of a new office building, for example, we are in a new situation altogether and one in which real estate managers would also need to bring in additional expertise.

When the organization has a view of real estate as an asset for investment purposes, the facility management function will likely fall outside its remit and would, therefore, report separately to senior managers. Corporate real estate management (CREM), as a discipline and practice, has the objective of making a return on investment from real estate without changing the organization's core business. CREM should be handled in such a way that it helps to secure and strengthen the competitiveness of the organization. The intention is that strategies for, and methods of, CREM should contribute to the attainment of the organization's business objectives. The gains are that resources can be better utilized, costs can be reduced and potential synergies realized to add value to the core business.

The own, lease or rent decision

The options available to the organization in terms of its needs in real estate and facilities cover a broad spectrum, from procuring the design and construction of a major new facility to *hot-desking* in an externally provided, totally serviced workplace. In terms of a new facility, there is the option of procuring the services of a designer and then awarding a contract to a construction company. This traditional approach might suit some, but for others a management style of contract or a single point of responsibility, such as design and build, might be preferred. Whilst these are important considerations, there is insufficient space here to discuss the advantages and drawbacks of the different approaches to the procurement of a facility; besides, there are many books that deal adequately with the subject.

More important is that the organization is aware of the periods of occupancy that are appropriate for each of the options and, therefore, the nature of the commitment that is being made. Table 2.1 illustrates the periods that might apply to the options available. Actual periods will vary according to location

Table 2.1   Real estate and space provision options and occupancy periods.

Option		Occupancy period
New building	(purpose-built)	25 years or more
Leased building	(long lease)	between 7 and 25 years
	(short lease)	up to 7 years
Rented space	(tenant fitted-out)	between 5 and 15 years
	(furnished)	between 1 and 5 years
	(totally serviced workplace)	up to 1 year

and prevailing market conditions, but they should help to focus attention on the option that best satisfies needs.

It is necessary to recognize that several different life cycles might be imposed on a single building or facility and that the organization will have to plan for refurbishment at intervals to maintain an optimal working environment, as well as to fulfil any leasehold or other conditions imposed by a landlord or owner. In the example of office buildings, it is accepted that the design life of the structure will exceed 60 years, major items of plant and equipment (i.e. building services engineering installations) might last no longer than 15 years and internal partitioning can last between five and ten years, whilst individual workstations and sets might need replacing, upgrading or redecorating every three to five years. No hard and fast rules apply, so the organization would be wise to examine the likely refurbishment and renewal cycles for any facility where it is responsible for maintenance (see Chapter 12). Furthermore, returning a facility to an as-new condition upon expiry of a lease could result in unforeseen cost and disruption if not taken into account.

The totally serviced workplace

Increasingly, there are novel solutions for the organization in wishing to outsource all or part of its facility's requirements or to support new business development. Common amongst these solutions is what is termed the totally serviced workplace. The idea is that an organization seeking a temporary solution to a space problem can rent fully serviced office space from as little as one month up to a few years. In some cases, the serviced workplace might be intended as a permanent solution or at least one that does not have a defined time horizon. For organizations looking to expand their business internationally, the availability – at short notice – of this kind of solution can be attractive, even though it attracts a cost premium.

In one case, a major telecommunications company has secured several thousands of workplaces for its international operations. Moreover, it has an arrangement that is simplified to the point of its paying a lump sum fee based on the number of workplaces multiplied by a unit rate per month. Reducing transaction costs is another benefit from the arrangement, alongside low risk exposure and a high level of flexibility. Of course, the organization in this case has to be certain of the financial standing of the service provider and the status of the underlying property title, and the service provider has to be certain that the organization will not default on payment. In one sense, this is an interesting reversal of the roles.

High-quality, fully serviced space can be available in a variety of forms to suit different organizational demands. The broad categories are:

Office space – serving a full-time, part-time, branch, project, start-up, team or hot-desking need.

Virtual office – offering call handling, a business address, messaging and mail forwarding, and space when required for meetings and private office work.

Disaster recovery – providing workplace recovery to support business continuity in the event of an incident (see Chapter 9).

Space management

An important function of facility management is to ensure the efficient and cost-effective use of space. This purpose presumes that the space provided will satisfy all requirements; often, it does not. Considerable time and resources could be spent in redefining the use of space only to find there is no real improvement. Chapter 14 discusses a number of issues concerning the management of people during periods of change. For now, we will concentrate more on ways in which the organization can be sure it has the most appropriate space for its needs and if it does not, how it intends to make good that shortfall. Consideration of owned space includes operating, maintenance and depreciation costs.

In terms of the design of a new or refurbished facility, recommended practices for *ensuring* space efficiency include (SMG, 2006):

- Maximizing space on the footprint of a new facility.
- Matching new uses to a refurbished facility.
- Increasing the ratio of usable to gross floor area.
- Incorporating design features to support different activities at different times.
- Providing space, furniture and fittings that can be adapted for different activities.
- Creating space that mixes open-plan, meeting and quiet spaces.
- Providing wireless data access to enable maximum use of common space.

Likewise, recommended practices for *promoting* space efficiency include (SMG, 2006):

- Appointing a champion for space management and operating costs.
- Systematically collecting and updating space utilization and cost information.
- Agreeing targets and monitoring their achievement.
- Incorporating space efficiency concepts into the facility management strategy (see Chapter 3).
- Incorporating the need for space efficiency into project design briefs, feasibility studies, option appraisals and design reviews.
- Developing and maintaining a clear decision and communication structure for facility-related projects and their stakeholders.
- Promoting the benefits of adaptable spaces and furniture.
- Assessing space efficiency through post-occupancy evaluations (see Chapter 11).

Space utilization and efficiency

Details of space utilization should be known at all times and recorded in an accessible form (see Chapter 15 on the Facility handbook). In addition to understanding current efficiencies and inefficiencies in the use of space, the organization should be able to measure and forecast the costs of servicing its space, including those relating to energy, and be able to determine the effectiveness of energy-saving measures. Where a policy of sustainable space provision has been adopted – see below – the organization should consider the options for the most effective use of space in future years. In some cases, it will mean a controlled reduction in space and the opportunity to release it with a commensurate cost saving. In others, it could amount to the more effective use of existing space through initiatives that maximize occupancy and/or productivity, whilst maintaining an acceptable work-place environment.

Sustainable space provision

The need to justify available space is obvious and few organizations would seriously hold on to any they did not need or for which there was no likely future demand. Space efficiency is a key factor in the successful use of a facility and has implications for the wider business interests and financial well-being of the organization. A facility that fits needs exactly confers an advantage in the marketplace, because of higher productivity and lower operational costs than would otherwise be the case.

Current practices should rightly concentrate on squeezing greater efficiency out of existing space by building flexibility and adaptability into the internal design. Measures such as reconfigurable space have proven popular over decades and have helped to boost space efficiency rates. Similarly, the incorporation of features to support different activities at different times and the provision of space, fittings and furniture capable of adaptation for a range of purposes raises utilization and, hence, efficiency, leading to higher returns on investment. Considerable effort has gone into the design of more productive workplaces. Commercial offices are a prime example, but not the only one. In many countries, huge effort and investment has gone into designing schools that enhance the learning experience. Increasing the use of ICT and related concepts, such as flexible working, has generated worthwhile gains and will continue as technology converges and becomes ever more pervasive. Yet, despite the often impressive results, it should be self-evident that it is possible to increase space efficiency only so far. Efficiency is not without limit.

In parallel with these concepts, commercial imperatives to right-size the organization – a common euphemism for downsizing and de-layering – have reduced net demand for space. This pragmatic action is a common form of restructuring. The overall result is a leaner organization with a sharp focus on the present. Many will, however, lack an informed view of the medium to long term, seeing it as far enough away not to be a pressing concern; besides, all will become clearer in time, or so the thinking goes.

The deployment of new and more advanced forms of technology can release personnel from rigid structures and re-equip them with more flexible and responsive end-user practices. Yet, most of the gains are not from smarter technology, but smarter thinking and working. Through a process of managed change, the organization can respond to shifting and consolidating markets, as well as tighter legislation, by altering the ways in which work is organized – for example, outsourcing, co-ventures and strategic alliances. These are some of the drivers that impact on the organization and its requirement for, and use of, space.

The planning of space requirements is also affected by trends in those drivers and the total cost of providing the required space. There can be many drivers and so a basic objective is to identify the key drivers for space and to determine if they will apply over the medium to long term. Plans must then reflect this understanding as well as provide some degree of flexibility and adaptability.

The drivers for space into the future will therefore have to be understood, with a balance struck between what the organization needs and what it can afford: it has to be realistic. This concept is the organization's sustainable space provision. The idea is not new and applying the principle should be an automatic, integral part of the design process for any new facility. A greater challenge lies in dealing with the enormous stock of existing facilities that will increasingly fail sustainability criteria and render themselves obsolete.

Sustainable space provision is closely aligned with sustainable development. The functional and operational requirements of end-users and other stakeholders must be balanced with affordable space, taking into account environmental impact, energy use and long-term operational costs. Sustainable space provision therefore replaces the practice of right-sizing with a longer-term and more developed understanding of what is needed. Allowance for growth and/or reduction in the demand for space and its phasing over the lifetime of the facility is part of the assessment of sustainable space provision. It will also be necessary to take account of the space required to achieve an inclusive design that anticipates the needs of disabled people and others with equalities-related needs in line with applicable legislation.

Space is rarely, if ever, provided for free, even if some organizations choose not to charge for its use. Evaluating total cost, which includes facility-related services, is necessary for identifying those spaces offering best value and those that do not. Organizations with a geographically dispersed portfolio have looked at where they generate best value and have acted accordingly. In some cases, this has meant large-scale restructuring and moving operations from one country or continent to another.

Despite the limitations, many organizations will continue to measure space efficiency – or effective density (BCO, 2013) – and use it as a benchmark. Knowing that certain space is utilized, on average, 69% of the time is a measure of value received; but what else is it telling us? If the aim is to drive up levels of utilization, then comparing like with like within and outside the organization – a simple form of benchmarking – should help to pinpoint issues worth investigating. The trouble with this approach is that it is bottom-up and it says that 'This is the space we have and this is the extent to which it is used.' The bigger questions of 'Do we really need it?' and 'Can we afford it?' are not necessarily being addressed.

The problem is, more often than not, the wrong kind of space for the intended functions and activities. A facility designed for a purpose other than its present use is commonplace and the only way forward might be to dispose of it quickly. Of course, that merely succeeds in passing on the legacy of inefficient space to someone else. The questions that have to be asked therefore are: 'What do we need to sustain us into the future?' and 'What can we afford?'

Design and facility management briefing

Decision-making that identifies the need for an additional facility or facilities – new or refurbished – is not something to be taken lightly. Not only is the process of delivering a facility likely to consume much time and expense; it is also essential that as an operational asset it delivers its promise. For the organization as owner, operator or both, there is plenty to consider, conflicts to resolve and forecasts to make about a future some years away. A structured approach will have to be adopted and one that manifests in a transparent plan of work capable of taking the organization from where it is today to where it needs to be in the future. Design and construction are obvious activities and processes, but ensuring that both take account of operational requirements is paramount. Delivery of the facility is merely the beginning of the phase in which the return on investment or the realization of value in business can be secured; often, it is going to happen over a period of many years.

Briefing is the process of communicating the objectives and needs of an owner, or prospective owner, of a facility to a designer or design team in order for them to prepare the design of a new or refurbished facility. The process includes clarifying and confirming the intentions of the owner and documenting the resulting provisions for the facility to support efficient and effective decision-making in design, construction and/or installation, testing and commissioning, handover and start-up of operations. Whilst design is where briefing takes place, the latter is not a discrete activity; rather, briefing must support design decision-making across all life-cycle phases. The main phases are illustrated in Fig. 2.1. In this respect, it is important to move away from the notion that design and construction are all-important, and to recognize that other phases are crucial to the successful delivery of an operational facility.

Briefing is concerned with ensuring that the facility can be operated safely and correctly and so these requirements must be considered uppermost during

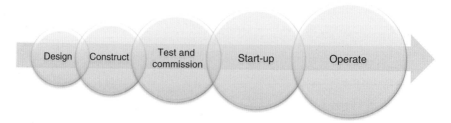

Fig. 2.1   Phases in the life cycle of a facility.

design. Decisions have to be based on the most reliable information and data, and their impact on operations has to be understood ahead of construction and/or installation. Once the facility is operational, it is too late to do anything about the design. The principle of constructability is widely applied in design; however, the principle of design for operability is not necessarily considered to the same extent.

Briefing must therefore reflect a whole-life perspective on the facility and not just its design or construction. For the owner and/or operator of a facility, a business objective might well be to optimize operational cost over the whole life cycle. The facility might also have to sustain operations over decades in an environment in which the requirement to reduce energy use and, therefore, carbon emissions is likely to become ever more challenging. Clearly, these factors will be influential in shaping outcomes.

At the heart of briefing is the objective assessment of needs so that the feasibility of what is being proposed can be determined. The successful outcome of a feasibility study will lead to a scheme design supported by cost, time and environmental information and data. The steps involved in briefing should follow a logical sequence:

1. business case;
2. statement of need;
3. development of design brief(s);
4. functional brief;
5. feasibility study; and
6. scheme design.

The business case and statement of need are the primary inputs to development of the design brief(s) and the remainder are the outputs of the brief(s) to be reviewed and refined as progress is made in developing the design. Where a business case has been prepared by the owner, it should be summarized in, or be appended to, the statement of needs and might typically include strategic fit, initial investment cost, budgets, cash flow, revenues and/or benefits, grants, subsidies and criteria for measuring success, as well as the owner's polices on health, safety, security and the environment (HSSE) and corporate social responsibility (CSR).

It is worth emphasizing the distinction between the statement of needs and the functional brief. The former embodies the organization's business objectives and the extent to which they are likely to be satisfied by the facility. The latter is the interpretation of the statement of needs in the form of a defined scope of work as the basis for design. Each of these concepts is discussed in more detail below.

The briefing process

Before commencing briefing, it is essential to define a process that will ensure that the organization's business objectives are achieved and that the emergent design, in particular, will be subject to appropriate review and alignment with operational requirements, amongst other criteria. Typically, this should follow the form of a phase-gated process in which phases, decision gates, deliverables and criteria for determining progression are clearly defined. With these conditions in mind, a plan of the briefing process should be prepared to cover:

- Phases and decision gates.
- Criteria required in order to pass through decision gates.
- Major activities within phases and their logical sequence.
- Sources of information and data to be used in activities.
- Individuals and entities to be involved directly in activities and their roles and responsibilities.
- Other stakeholders who might be consulted or involved in some other way.
- Deliverables in each phase and at each decision gate and the form they should take.
- Plans for the next phase.

Stakeholders, of one kind or another, are clearly visible in the above and are deserving of separate and more detailed consideration. Later sections in this chapter describe a stakeholder management process that would be appropriate in briefing for the design of a new or refurbished facility and as part of the consultative process that supports procurement (see Chapter 8) and transition (see Chapter 14).

Statement of needs

The organization's primary processes and activities have to be defined if the designer is to understand how the facility can accommodate them. Known and anticipated conditions affecting the organization's ability to sustain these processes and activities, including the space required for this purpose, have to be determined. The statement should express the needs of the organization in general terms – as valuable context-setting information – and specifically in relation to the facility. Criteria for measuring success should be included in the statement of needs and should be revisited regularly so that no one loses sight of the original purpose of the exercise. In addition, a stakeholder impact analysis should be used to determine stakeholder interests in the facility. The results should show the nature, extent and relative importance or weighting of all expressed needs, with any prioritization made clear – see the later section on Stakeholders. Collectively, this information forms the statement of needs and is a key deliverable in the briefing process.

The design brief

A design brief is a comprehensively written document developed jointly by the organization, its professional advisors and the designer or design team, based on the statement of needs, including the business case for the new or refurbished facility. The brief articulates the case for the facility in terms of its functions, performance requirements, sustainable space provision and overall design concept, amongst other aspects. Detailed aesthetic treatment normally falls outside the scope of the brief. Typical of the brief's content are:

- Summary of the business case (strategic fit, objectives and prioritized needs, criteria for measuring success, grants, allowances, subsidies and taxation).
- Studies or briefs previously undertaken.
- End-user requirements.
- Functional, operational and quality standards for the facility.
- Health, safety and security policy.
- Environmental management policy.
- Corporate social responsibility policy.
- Project execution strategy or plan.
- Project delivery schedule including phasing and milestones.
- Capital cost estimate (for CAPEX).

In addition, operational matters should be considered in terms of:

- Operations.
- Start-up provisions.
- *As-built* information.
- Health, safety and security.
- Life expectancy of structure, fabric, fit-out and finishings.
- Life expectancy of building services engineering installations (i.e. systems, components and parts).
- Maintenance strategy and policy.
- Emergency evacuation provisions.
- Inclusive management strategy.
- Operating costs (for OPEX).
- Indicative budgets for services (e.g. security, cleaning and waste management).
- Energy efficiency.
- Carbon management.

The facility management brief

The design brief might not be in fact a single, stand-alone document. Instead, several briefs might have to be prepared depending on the scale, complexity and particular requirements of the organization or challenges in the project for delivering the facility. Separate briefs might cover:

- finance;
- procurement and contracts (see Chapter 8);
- stakeholder management;
- design (as noted above);
- construction management;
- testing and commissioning; and
- facility management.

The place of facility management in the life cycle of a facility is such that it should be seen as a bridge between the end of construction (or more precisely, testing, commissioning and handover) and the beginning of design (for a change of use or the construction of a new facility). In practical terms, it is likely to mean that the facility management brief is the result of an iterative process in which the facility manager analyses the owner's statement of needs to provide advice during development of the design brief on the most appropriate strategy for managing the facility. The results are then embodied in a set of performance requirements, either as a part of the design brief or as a separate document. Without this concern for performance, there would be no objective basis for understanding how the facility was measuring up to requirements during operations.

This process can become quite complicated, as some notion of the emerging design will be needed to confirm any original hypotheses about how the facility will be managed. It will mean retaining some flexibility over the likely management of the facility at least until a scheme design has emerged. The purpose here is to establish a strategy or framework to guide scheme design – followed by outline design and detailed design – rather than being prescriptive and, thus, putting an unnecessary restraint on the designer or the design. Even so, design must take account of how the facility will be managed; but, equally, facility managers must respond positively to owner and designer needs and help turn them into reality. In short, the facility manager has a pivotal role in preparing or contributing to the brief and then retaining a role during feasibility and subsequent design stages. A similar approach applies to other consultants and specialists, who must be able to engage with the (lead) designer and be prepared to look for the most practicable outcome. A potential weakness in this approach is that it needs both the organization, as owner, and the designer to recognize the value of the facility manager's input, rather than viewing it as an inhibitor to the development of novel concepts or designs.

Another issue to address here is the growing importance of extracting the correct information from the design process to verify or evaluate design decisions from an operational perspective. An example is the case of *build, operate and transfer* (BOT) projects under a public–private partnership (PPP), where the operator has a fixed budget for the operations over the term of the concession and is, therefore, attempting to optimize operational costs over the lifetime of the facility (see Chapter 10). Put another way, the operator is taking a calculated risk that has to be based on as an objective assessment as possible. If the means by which that assessment is made are denied or impaired, there is the likelihood of an ill-informed commercial decision that serves no one's interests. Operators not only have to carry risks; they must do so based on the decisions of others and often very early in the facility's life. Being locked out of decision-making raises the prospect of a later failure that could so easily have been avoided.

Information and data for facility management briefing can be grouped under three headings:

- *Description of operations and activities* to be performed in the facility – this information is necessary for planning the layout and arrangement of spaces and functions – see Functional brief below.

- *Information required from the designer* and deemed critical for the operations team to evaluate design solutions, taking into account long-term operational costs including energy use and carbon equivalent.
- *As-built* information – records of the facility's construction are vital for its safe and correct operation and must be kept from the earliest point and then embodied in the facility handbook – see the later section in this chapter and Chapters 12 and 15 – for handing over to the organization as owner and/or operator.

The functional brief

The statement of needs should be used to define the functions that the facility will be required to offer, including details of operational demands and support processes for end-users. These details should be accompanied by proposed technical solutions, including the evaluation of options for satisfying end-user requirements. This information is required when planning the layout and arrangement of spaces and functions within the facility. There could be different ways of satisfying an identified need and these have to be made explicit and supported by appropriate information and data. The following considerations should be addressed when preparing the functional brief, but they should not be regarded as exhaustive.

Description of activities and processes

Overall concept
- The vision and image of the organization and the extent to which these should be reflected in the appearance and general design of the facility.
- The impact of the design on occupants and other users as they approach, enter and move about the facility; in particular, the internal environment and provisions for assuring the health, safety and security of personnel.
- Inclusive design principles applying to the facility, incorporating the needs of disabled people and others with equalities-related needs.
- Design for reduced environmental impact, including choice of principal materials and their ultimate reuse, recycling or disposal, and the extent, if any, of passive systems; for example, natural lighting, cooling and ventilation.

Internal considerations
- Zoning, internal circulation and transportation (e.g. offices, service cores, lifts/elevators, stairways and lobbies).
- Demands for space supporting functions and activities (e.g. production, creative areas, private spaces, meetings and conferences, safety areas, social areas, dining and refreshment areas) and for ancillary services (e.g. waste segregation, recovery, reuse and recycling, and rainwater harvesting).
- Organizational structure (e.g. departments and other subdivisions), including the anticipated number of personnel and their roles.
- Communication across departments.
- Descriptions of the functions, activities and processes supported in the facility, including provisions for the separation of space, by zone, by level and so on.

- Arrangements for enabling access, use and emergency evacuation for all occupants and other users, including disabled people.
- Flexibility/adaptability in the internal design (e.g. reconfigurable space and expansion/reduction potential).
- Energy use, water management and waste disposal (i.e. environmental management).
- Security, safety, fire and resilience (e.g. responses in the event of a failure in an installation or system, or other incident, and arrangements for business continuity).
- Carbon footprint, including calculation of the carbon equivalent.
- Services (e.g. security, waste disposal and cleaning) and supplies such as consumables.

External considerations
- Zoning of external areas and associated security; for example, landscaping, parking, emergency assembly points, fences and gates, lighting, signposting, security and surveillance.
- Entry to and from the facility for different categories of user and visitors, including emergency access and escape routes.
- Access to modes of public transport and their distance from the facility.

The functional brief is a prime deliverable within the briefing process and should define the scope of work as a basis for design. The scope of work covers design, construction and/or installation, testing and commissioning, and start-up activities necessary to deliver an operational asset.

Evaluating design solutions

The designer or design team should present specific information when alternative solutions (e.g. designs, materials, products and systems), prepared from the collective perspectives of operations and inclusiveness, are available. From this information, it is necessary to identify the solution (or combination of solutions) that minimizes energy consumption, carbon equivalent and whole-life cost. Consultation should be in advance of a decision on any matter that could impact on safety, efficiency and cost-effective operations.

Where necessary, information should be sought from manufacturers on the costs of operation and maintenance, breakdown frequency, life expectancy of systems, components and parts, and energy efficiency. The facility manager is arguably best placed to assist in these matters. Designers will, however, need to retain the option of visiting manufacturers and/or existing operational facilities to verify claims before reaching a decision.

As-built *information*

Strictly speaking, *as-built* information is not part of briefing. It is, however, necessary to ensure that, during design, there is a clear understanding of what must be provided prior to and at the point of handover of the facility: it is too late to think about it once the design is complete. When a facility asset is delivered, so too are information assets required for its safe, efficient and cost-effective operation. During testing and commissioning and prior to handover, detailed information about the facility, including the operation and maintenance of systems, should be made available to the facility manager. Information should be supplied in digital form, wherever possible, with paper copies (see Chapter 15). Requiring information in this form should be a condition of every contract with designers so that there can be no chance of a later claim for additional costs. In most cases, the information is generated routinely in the course of design and construction and should not represent extra work; it is a matter of good practice in design management. Details should be forwarded to designers at the outset about the information required and its format. Typical of this information are:

- *Drawings* – architectural, structural and building services engineering drawings, including those for operational purposes.
- *Specifications* – materials and finishes used in spaces and rooms, and on the exterior of the facility.
- *Inventory* – a recognized hierarchical classification system to itemize all plant and equipment, fixtures and fittings (see Chapter 12 on Asset register).

Specifying what this information should look like is invaluable from a facility management perspective if it can be incorporated into the tender documentation for the main construction contract. Often, a limited specification is incorporated, which presents the successful tenderer with the opportunity to provide the minimum. The increasing use of building information modelling (BIM) will help to prevent this problem; meanwhile, the facility manager should be involved in defining the required information deliverables (see Chapter 15). Chapter 12 covers *as-built* information in the context of maintenance management and the particular requirement for a facility handbook is covered below.

The facility handbook

The concept of the facility handbook is straightforward enough – it is a collation of legal, commercial, financial, technical and managerial information relating to the facility, which should be easy to access and update. The handbook should be regarded as more than a data repository and should be used as the definitive source of information and data about the facility. If it is to fulfil its role, preparation should begin during design and continue through all life-cycle phases. If it is to be of maximum benefit, it is essential that it is kept up to date. To initiate its preparation, the owner should forward to the designer details of the information needed to be covered in the handbook and its preferred format. *As-built* design information should be regarded as a constituent part of the handbook and be supplied in a digitally readable form. A building information model for the facility should be considered for the purpose of supplying design information – see below.

Approved changes to the design prior to start-up should be incorporated in the facility handbook, which should be made available to the owner at the end of the design phase, suitably marked as a work in progress. At the end of construction work and/or installation, the health and safety file should be incorporated in the handbook. During testing and commissioning, details of the building services engineering installations, their operation and maintenance should be incorporated in the handbook, which should be reissued to the owner. Provision should be made in the handbook for conveying the management implications of design decisions, together with the means for managing the facility and environment inclusively. For a detailed description of the contents of the facility handbook, see Chapter 15.

BIM

Building information modelling (BIM) has been recognized as a key technology and enabler of efficiency and cost saving in the design, construction and operation of a facility. It is concerned with the management of information and data required to deliver facility assets and then to operate them. The potential for BIM to bring about improvement in design is widely argued and supported by a growing body of research findings and exemplars from practice. Specifically, it is seen to offer distinct benefits in design optimization and integrated project delivery (Wong & Fan, 2013) – two concepts that support the principle of design for operability (see Chapter 2).

The adoption of BIM is expected to grow rapidly, especially in relation to new and refurbished facilities. It provides a means for maintaining a current data model of the operational assets that can be used to support facility planning in particular and facility management in general. Its adoption for existing facilities is less certain, not least for reasons of the payback in terms of savings from the use of an as-built model of the facility when compared to the cost of creating the model initially. The term *retrospective BIM* is used to described such situations. For a more detailed discussion on BIM, see Chapter 15.

Soft Landings

The *Soft Landings Framework* (BSRIA, 2009) has been developed to assist organizations in getting the best out of their new or refurbished facility by providing a unified approach for addressing outcomes from an integrated process of briefing, design and asset delivery. The framework aligns with energy performance criteria, building logbooks, building (or facility) manuals, green leases and corporate social responsibility. The emphasis is upon greater involvement of designers and constructors with the facility manager (or in-house team) and end-users before, during and after completion of construction, with the aim of improving operational readiness in the expectation of a flawless start-up and improved performance in use.

The feasibility study

It is necessary that the viability of the design can be established before progressing too far. A study of the facility's feasibility can normally be prepared from the information provided in the statement of needs, functional brief and other data; for example, cost, time and energy. The feasibility study should include an assessment of the facility's environmental impact and energy performance, adopting recognized conventions and/or methods (e.g. BREEAM and LEED). The facility's whole-life cost should be estimated on the basis of the principal materials, components and systems proposed in its design, with the aim of optimizing energy efficiency and minimizing its carbon equivalent. The expected life expectancy of the facility's structure, fabric, components, systems and major fixtures should be made explicit in a whole-life cost estimate.

The feasibility study is primarily used to inform the decision on whether to proceed with the design within the defined scope, to modify the scope or to terminate design altogether. Earlier appraisal of options for satisfying a specific, identified need might lead to an assessment of feasibility prior to the selection of an option. The significance of the feasibility study is that it can be based on information and data for the facility as a whole, reducing the risk of a sub-optimal design or operational solution as would probably occur when undertaking an appraisal in a piecemeal manner. In the past, the focus tended to be on the capital cost, which is just one of a number of criteria used to judge the fitness for purpose of the design and the overall value of the facility. Nowadays, whole-life cost and carbon management are likely to weigh heavily upon decision-making and, therefore, upon the viability of the facility.

Design development

The designer, or design team, needs to ensure that information deemed critical to the operation of the facility is made available to the organization as owner and, where applicable, the operator during design. In doing so, the fitness for purpose of design solutions as well as the safe, correct and efficient operation of the facility can be more closely assured. This information forms an integral part of the defined scope of the work and is the basis of the design for an operational asset. From these can flow design packages including detailed specifications and supporting material.

Design change control

Understanding operational costs is paramount where the organization is acting as an operator and has entered into a long-term contract for a concession based on a fixed monthly or yearly rate – see the earlier section. In the same way that the cost estimator (or quantity surveyor) needs to be kept informed of changes to the design as it evolves, so must the facility manager be aware of anything that could materially affect operational safety and costs. To ensure that change is properly managed (see Chapter 14), a change control system should be implemented so that all proposed changes are correctly identified, classified and evaluated and their full implications known before anything is considered for approval. In this way, the operator is given the opportunity to determine the impact of any change on the facility's operational parameters and to propose an alternative approach if necessary.

It is therefore highly advisable for a change control system to be implemented either by the organization or the designer or design team on its behalf to evaluate proposed changes to the design before they are submitted for approval, so that the full implications for safe, correct and efficient operation of the facility can be verified. This control system should record details of the proposed change, including:

- Description of the proposed change.
- Justification for the change (e.g. the design is considered to be unsafe or inoperable, or there is potential for value improvement).
- Basis of the design (e.g. description and details of the system, component, process or activity to which it relates).
- Impact on occupants and other end-users.
- Impact on the whole-life cost of the facility and time for construction and/or installation.
- Impact on operations and their cost.
- Impact on energy consumption/efficiency and carbon equivalent.
- Person(s) responsible for approving the change.

A change log should be maintained and used to record approved changes to the design, which should be reported formally at intervals depending on the extent and urgency of the change(s) and the likely time required for design or redesign. It will be essential to keep the change log up to date and to record costs and other data against items logged.

Stakeholders

Stakeholders should be identified at the start of briefing and their interest in the facility should be assessed in terms of their likely impact. Essentially, any individual or group with a legitimate interest in the organization is a stakeholder. They can be thought of as individuals and groups that are internal or external to it. Responsibility for taking account of the interests of users of the facility, as well as stakeholders in general, should be determined and made explicit. A responsibility assignment matrix (RASCI chart) can be a useful way of bringing clarity to *who does what* as well as reducing the likelihood of omitting to involve one or more stakeholders in a crucial matter. Statutory duties relating to consultation covering planning, employment and equalities legislation can be handled in this way.

Stakeholder identification

Stakeholders are those parties with an interest in the facility in general and the delivery of services in particular, and can include the following.

Internal stakeholders

- Owners and shareholders.
- Directors and non-executive directors.

- Senior managers.
- Other personnel.

External stakeholders

- Customers.
- Service providers.
- Suppliers (except utilities).
- Utility companies (e.g. energy, water and telecommunications).
- Neighbours.
- General public.
- Community groups.
- Environmental interest groups.
- Other consultative groups.
- Investors.
- Bankers.
- Insurers.
- Local/public authority (planning).
- Local/public authority (highways).
- Building control body.
- Fire authority.
- Police authority.

This split between internal and external stakeholders is more for convenience in determining who they are rather than as a consequence of any thought about their likely impact: it is necessary to start somewhere. Perceptions can be misleading; for instance, internal stakeholders should never be assumed to be favourably disposed towards something that another part of their organization is promoting. Similarly, external stakeholders should not be assumed to be indifferent or, worse, hostile. The purpose of a stakeholder assessment is to differentiate on criteria other than simply where they stand in relation to an organizational boundary. Casting the net far and wide to seek out those with an interest in the facility might seem wasteful of resources; however, overlooking an individual or group that believes it has a legitimate interest could later have consequences that prove distracting and take valuable resources away from where they are most needed at the time. Olander & Atkin (2010) provide a detailed description of the stakeholder management process; in particular, the importance of acknowledging concerns from all stakeholders, with examples of where the process has worked well and where it has not.

Stakeholder classification

Once stakeholder identification has concluded, it is then necessary to classify stakeholders so that an appropriate means of engaging with them can be followed. Differentiation is, therefore, based on something other than if they are internal, external or perhaps standing at the interface between the two. A workers' union with a representative in the workplace might be regarded as standing at the interface.

Stakeholders are said to have an interest if one or more of the attributes of power, legitimacy and urgency are present. Power and urgency are relatively easy to gauge; however, legitimacy might not be so straightforward. An individual or group pressing to be heard would seem, on the face of it, to be acting out of a sense of legitimate interest. The organization might, however, take a different view.

Stakeholder impact assessment

A stakeholder impact assessment can be undertaken to determine how, and the extent to which, stakeholder interests might impact on the facility in terms of its design, construction and operations. In the case of an existing facility, audits and other reviews should be taken into account when assessing and updating stakeholder interests. The attributes of power, legitimacy and urgency can be used to differentiate between those who appear to exert the most influence on design or other key decisions affecting the facility and those who have little or none. Scores can be attached to these attributes to create a rank ordering of stakeholders. In doing so, it is important to recognize that ranking does not help in understanding the magnitude of influence or impact that one stakeholder might possess in comparison with another. Other means for gauging impact include use of a matrix in which stakeholders are located in relation to their perceived power on one axis and interest on the other, where their position indicates the most appropriate basis for engagement (see Fig. 2.2). Whichever means is adopted, it should be recognized that it does not provide a definitive basis for engaging (or not) with particular stakeholders; it can, however, reveal clusters of stakeholders where engagement might be approached in a similar manner. Whilst it might be desirable to regard all stakeholders as justifying individual treatment, there is unlikely to be either the time or resources to do so.

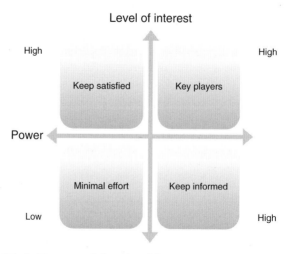

Fig. 2.2   The stakeholder power/interest matrix.

Further stakeholder identification and assessment should take place during design development and before start-up of operations to provide the opportunity to respond to any change in stakeholders or their interests. If a communication plan has been prepared, it should be updated as changes in stakeholders or their interests become known.

Risks and opportunities

Risks abound and can be responsible for ruining even the best laid plans. Any organization embarking on the design and construction of a new or refurbished facility would be well advised to undertake formal risk assessment to identify any factor that could have an impact on design, construction and/or, installation, testing and commissioning, handover and start-up of operations. As part of risk and opportunity management, risk assessment requires that events and conditions having the chance to impact any work in connection with a new or refurbished facility should be identified and assessed in terms of their potential impact and the probability that such an event or condition would materialize.

Risks generally have a negative connotation, but where there is a risk there might also be an opportunity and reward (see Chapter 1). *Downside risks* is a term used for events and conditions (factors) that can have a potentially negative impact on the facility, such as hazards faced in construction. *Upside risks* are factors that can add value to the outcome and are more commonly referred to as opportunities. The latter can arise from a re-examination of assumptions and the possibility of making a better selection now than was the case earlier, when less was perhaps known.

A risk and opportunity register is an essential tool and should be set up and maintained from the outset of briefing to record any identified upside and downside risks, an assessment of their likely impact and the probability of their occurrence. For downside risks, actions should be taken to mitigate their potential impact and monitor outcomes. For upside risks, actions should be actively considered to realize the opportunity. To be effective, the risk and opportunity register has to be kept up to date throughout design, construction and/or installation, testing and commissioning, handover and start-up of operations.

Conclusions

Organizations have many options for their real estate and might not even have to embark upon a process of acquisition. They might also benefit from the totally serviced workplace, which offers a set of options for those that need some flexibility in their space management, perhaps in response to the rapid deployment or redeployment of resources. For organizations in the early stages of the growth cycle, totally serviced workplaces might provide the ideal solution, allowing them to concentrate on growing their business without concern over support services: they are, in effect, outsourcing their facility and its management. Where there is a risk that it could become a distraction, the relationship between real estate management and facility management should be clarified. In all cases, the organization needs to know what space it has and what it can afford; otherwise, it will not achieve a sustainable space provision. Planning for, and planning of, its space requirement is affected by drivers for that space, trends in those drivers and the cost of providing space. Understanding how to provide space, and of which type, falls to the organization and its designers. There has to be an understanding of how space is used, by whom and for what purpose in order to determine if current utilization and, hence, efficiency is appropriate into the future. This information should be used to pinpoint waste (especially energy-related) and non–value-adding services and operations. Design decisions impact directly on the operability of a facility. It is essential, therefore, that adequate briefing takes place for any new or refurbished facility and this should involve the preparation of a facility management brief to ensure that operational requirements are taken into account in design. The brief is the cornerstone of a process for ensuring that identified needs are delivered in the facility. Stakeholders of many kinds exist and their interest in the facility has to be assessed as part of this effort. A process of engagement through communication has then to be initiated. Without this assessment there is the risk that one disaffected stakeholder could later frustrate plans. Stakeholders are one area of risk for the organization, but clearly there are many others. If decisions are to be adequately informed, it will be necessary to consider both downside and upside risks (opportunities). A formal process of risk and opportunity management should be adopted and a risk and opportunity register maintained to support facility planning, not least where a new or refurbished facility is involved.

Checklist

This checklist is intended to assist with review and action planning.

	Yes	No	Action required
1. Is the relationship between real estate management and facility management, including roles and responsibilities, clearly defined?	☐	☐	☐
2. Does the organization envision the need for more or less space in the future and, if so, has it attempted to quantify it?	☐	☐	☐
3. Have the options for providing space been explored and is the organization comfortable with its current arrangements?	☐	☐	☐

	Yes	No	Action required
4. Is information readily to hand on space utilization and efficiency?	☐	☐	☐
5. Has the organization determined if the size of its facility is affordable, i.e. is there a sustainable space provision?	☐	☐	☐
6. Where a new or refurbished facility is planned, has a briefing process been defined?	☐	☐	☐
7. Is the principle of design for operability accepted by the organization?	☐	☐	☐
8. Is there an explicit plan for managing design briefing?	☐	☐	☐
9. Is there a procedure for preparing a facility management brief?	☐	☐	☐
10. Has the facility manager been actively engaged in briefing in regard to handover and start-up of operations?	☐	☐	☐
11. Is the designer aware of his or her obligations for ensuring that sufficient steps are taken to document the new or refurbished facility?	☐	☐	☐
12. Has a procedure for controlling changes to design once approved been defined and is it working?	☐	☐	☐
13. Have stakeholders been identified and classified, and has their impact on the organization and/or new facility been assessed?	☐	☐	☐
14. Have downside risks and upside risks (opportunities) been assessed and are they up to date?	☐	☐	☐

3 Facility Management Strategy

Key issues

The following issues are covered in this chapter.

- Facility management has to encompass a diverse range of matters that influence the success of the organization's core business, mostly set in the context of a dynamic environment. As such, the organization will have to base much of its decision-making on the expectation that change will be a constant feature into the future.

- A strategy for facility management is needed by all organizations to ensure optimal use of facilities over the short, medium and long term. Throughout, it should be aligned with the organization's business strategy, including its business objectives, and be reflected in policies and operational plans.

- The strategy should establish the overall approach to facility management, including maintenance of physical assets, end-user requirements, service definitions, service delivery options and performance management. It should be broad, yet flexible, and remain focused on supporting the organization's core business. Periodic updating will be necessary to ensure that it remains aligned with the business strategy.

- The organization should avoid using the strategy to manage operations directly, but instead should reflect the latter in an approach that can be adapted quickly in light of changes to the business strategy.

- As far as practicable, the strategy should anticipate change and respond with processes and procedures that will ensure the organization has the facility management it requires to meet its current and future needs.

Total Facility Management, Fourth Edition. Brian Atkin and Adrian Brooks.
© 2015 John Wiley & Sons, Ltd. Published 2015 by John Wiley & Sons, Ltd.

- The formulation of the strategy is a project in its own right and must be undertaken rigorously using appropriate methods and tools. Three stages should be followed:

  o Strategic analysis – where all relevant facts are assembled, including the organization's business objectives, needs and policies, reviews/audits of resources, processes, systems and physical assets, together with their attributes in terms of space, function and utilization.

  o Solution development – where criteria for judging options are defined and evaluated against the objectives of the organization to produce the facility management strategy.

  o Strategy implementation – the establishment of an implementation plan that incorporates the key elements of the strategy, notably procurement of services, training, service delivery, review and feedback.

- The extent and detail of the strategy, and the methods and tools utilized, will depend on a number of factors, not least the business context. Smaller organizations – those with modest needs in facility management – should consider scaling their approach rather than simply omitting parts of it.

Introduction

A facility management strategy is the cornerstone of facility management. Managing a facility efficiently and cost-effectively requires the development of a robust strategy that can accommodate change without losing sight of the organization's business objectives and other strategically important considerations. It provides context for the definition, specification and delivery of services. There are basically two ways of looking at the management of a facility. The first adopts a short-term perspective in considering what must be done to maintain services and where it might be possible to enhance them. The second is longer-term and takes into account the potential changes likely to be faced into the future and how these will impact upon the services required. Clearly, a desire to enhance current service delivery is not wrong, but does overlook the inevitability of change and the likelihood that it could easily invalidate earlier decisions. A facility and the demands placed upon it are unlikely to remain static in all but the most unchanging of organizations. An approach must therefore be devised to manage the process of moving from where the organization is now to where it wants to be at some point in the future. In other words, a strategy is used to deal with a dynamic situation in which major business decisions – perhaps affecting the very viability of the organization – are connected with the existing facility and forecasted requirements. The approach is implicitly top-down; otherwise, current operations would, in effect, be dictating the organization's business direction. The key to the development of an effective strategy is a rigorous analysis of needs against existing provisions to determine requirements as precisely as possible. Once known, it is possible to

formulate potential solutions whose suitability can then be evaluated systematically to leave the organization with a clear definition of what needs to be implemented, yet stopping short of being prescriptive in operational terms.

The business context

The single-facility owner-operator

The business context for the organization is a key consideration in the development of a strategy for facility management. Where it has responsibility for a single
facility, it can concentrate upon providing the best conditions and arrangements
for end-users and other stakeholders without worrying about what might be happening elsewhere. Even so, the organization should be aware of what other facility owners and/or operators are doing and achieving. No one organization has a
monopoly on best practices. Knowing how to achieve best value, whilst delivering
end-user satisfaction, is likely to be of interest to most. Even so, one of the tempta-
tions, especially where the facility is relatively modest and involves comparatively
few end-users, is to regard the idea of best practices and continual improvement
as meant for those with larger facilities, responsibilities and budgets. Rather than
make that mistake, the organization should consider the scale of approach that
is appropriate to its needs. Scaling the approach implies active consideration of
the extent to which a set of requirements or recommendations might have to be
adjusted in light of practicalities instead of simply omitting them. In the particular
context of a strategy, the organization can work with a subset of methods and tools
to devise the optimal plan for its facility management. Put another way, the strategy provides a framework within which to work without running the risk of being
needlessly prescriptive and possibly wasteful of valuable resources.

The regional/national facilities owner-operator

Where the organization owns or has responsibility for multiple facilities, there is a
clear argument for ensuring that an equitable approach applies to its facility management across the board. There can be clear benefits from adopting the same approach,
such as economy of scale – for example, from outsourcing to a single service provider
– and the ability to learn from one location or facility and apply the lessons learned
elsewhere. There is also a benefit from understanding how other organizations might
be achieving best value whilst maintaining end-user satisfaction. Doing so is a form
of benchmarking. Knowledge about the performance of all facilities within a portfolio helps to pinpoint inefficiencies, waste and other shortcomings leading to rationalization of space and, where necessary, disposal of facilities that are no longer viable.
Within a region, anomalies are normally easy to spot and explain since custom and
practice, amongst other variables, can be expected to be broadly similar.

The multinational facilities owner-operator

Multinational corporations are more likely than not to outsource their facility
management, including service delivery. They tend to do so with large service
providers that, similarly, have a multinational presence. A less likely scenario is

for a multinational corporation to outsource services to individual service providers in each country or region in which it operates. A typical arrangement is where a region – for example Scandinavia, the Middle East or the United States and Canada – is served by a single provider under a total facility management arrangement. Each location or facility would generally be supported by the service provider's regional or national centre. It is important to have *someone on the ground* to deal with matters that can arise in the normal course of operations and to avoid having to refer to a distant or centralized authority that would otherwise delay responses. In contrast, the organization would be likely to centralize its facility management with local facility managers acting under delegated authority, whilst reporting to local senior managers.

Where the organization operates from multiple locations, differences between facilities in terms of performance and cost are inevitable. Harmonizing processes, procedures and practices across the entire portfolio might seem like a good idea. Unfortunately, this view assumes that everywhere should be the same or can be made the same – it just needs the right kind of management. There is undoubtedly benefit from working to common processes, for example. However, the skill is in setting them at a level that brings conformity and simplicity, but without becoming a slave to detail that might not apply in each and every location.

In the worst case, persistent benchmarking can lead to discord and a lowering of morale as excessive pressure is placed upon teams to cut costs. Differences in national culture and local custom and practice will mean that no two locations are exactly the same and might never become the same. At the highest level, the board or equivalent body might expect to be shown a consistent picture across all locations – although to insist on it would make little, if any, sense. The organization might observe that one location is performing far better than another; for example, one is less costly to service and workplace productivity is higher. These characteristics are, however, a consequence of many factors relating to a facility's location and operations. A capital city location, where competition for space puts a premium on rents, can mean that personnel are squeezed into what is available, so that the cost of space per head is comparable with other locations. The consequences of close proximity to other individuals include lack of privacy, interruption and noise, and can easily lead to stress. Where this situation involves knowledge workers, productivity and creativity can reduce significantly (see Chapter 5). The message is that treating all locations the same, because they are part of one corporation, is likely to prove counterproductive. Attempting to normalize costs that are a direct result of market conditions, workplace practices and culture will simply make matters worse.

Business drivers and constraints

Organizations are driven, and at the same time constrained, by many and diverse factors. Understanding the organization's business drivers and the constraints it faces is fundamental to devising an appropriate business strategy and, in turn, business objectives with which to inform the facility management strategy. There should be no disconnection between these concepts. Examples of business drivers include market opportunities, competition, product launch windows, rationalization of operations and downsizing. Whatever they are, they should be made explicit. In large, publicly quoted corporations, drivers will hardly be a secret and might even be announced far and wide. Constraints, on the other hand, might be more closely guarded because they can reveal weaknesses to competitors. Knowing that the organization might have a looming cash-flow problem or too much space that needs to be released, and quickly, is not something to be bandied around. Nonetheless, those with responsibility for a facility have to know what they are dealing with and any limitations in resources of whatever kind. In many cases, facility management will be used to find ways of reducing operating costs and, in others, to find space to nurture and grow new business.

An appreciation of business drivers and the business objectives that are associated with them helps in understanding what has to be achieved in operational terms if the organization is to succeed. The latter are broadly the organization's critical success factors, where some will be explicitly concerned with facility-related matters (see Chapter 11).

Organizational management levels

Management can be thought of as acting on three levels: strategic, tactical and operational. This generally accepted view of management is evident in most organizations; it is not, however, associated with the most effective outcomes. A weakness is that management levels are often linked with planning horizons that regard *strategic* as long term, *tactical* as medium term and *operational* as short term – no more, no less. This implies that strategy is unconcerned with the immediate future and, similarly, that operations are not considered over the longer term. This is wrong. Investment in a new facility or other major asset has to be considered strategically, tactically and operationally. Moreover, the organization will have to think and act strategically – that is, consider the bigger picture – each time a matter of policy or procedure is reviewed. Likewise, operational requirements run well into the future and must be closely aligned with a policy that reflects the organization's business strategy.

The strategic level

Strategic management is largely about setting the direction for the organization and ensuring that the means for achieving its objectives are in place. As a statement of intent, a strategy is worthless if detached from the financial means to see it through. As noted above, strategy can be regarded as the bigger picture – the broad statement of where the organization is heading and how it intends to get there. It has to provide more than a few clues of what will be needed for the journey. At the same time, the strategy must retain flexibility to deal with changes in the environment that might require a shift in emphasis or direction.

The tactical level

The organization's broad intentions have to be turned into workable plans, and might call for new processes and procedures as well as changes to those that exist. The gap between the strategic and operational levels is too big to be bridged without translation of the strategy into plans that are capable of being imple-mented, monitored and controlled. Policies are synonymous with tactics – a case of *how* something should be done – as opposed to *what* should be done and *why* as embodied in the strategy. Policy-making is, therefore, concerned with procedures that will guide operations towards desired outcomes. This approach generally makes sense, although is not without criticism. From a human resources perspec-tive, there is the risk that procedures prove to be less than effective and, in the worst case, can be unworkable or unsafe. Middle managers can sometimes choose to interpret policy in a way that suits their own agenda, giving rise to operations that are incongruous with the strategy.

The operational level

The primary concern at the operational level is to perform work according to laid-down procedures and not to deviate. At the end of the day, progress towards the organization's business objectives is achieved through actions at the operational level. Ensuring that senior managers know what is being achieved relies on reliable measurement, analysis and reporting. Aside from this obvious role, operations are where there is a sense of *what works*, *what does not* and *what might work* in the future. Tapping into this expertise is essential if the organization is to achieve its objectives. In this connection, communication has to run from top to bottom *and* from bottom to top. In the worst organizations, communication is unidirectional and is not, therefore, communication at all but more a matter of command and control. A flow of information from top to bottom without feedback is likely to result in missed opportunities and unrealized objectives. Middle managers act in an overseeing role and have responsibility for ensuring that the right informa-tion is channelled to senior managers. In the best organizations, the delay between actions at the operational level and reliable information on progress and achieve-ment being in the hands of senior managers is minimal. Success here is due to middle managers who are effective in translating needs into actions and maintain-ing a current understanding of performance and progress.

Cross-cultural management

An organization that is multinational in nature is multicultural in character. Differences between individuals and the groups from which they are drawn add to the challenges faced by managers trying to achieve consistent work practices across the organization. Facility managers who find themselves moved to a loca-tion where they are in many respects the outsider might well observe differences in behaviour, attitude, beliefs and relationships that run counter to their own expe-riences, expectations and outlook. Cross-cultural impact is hardly a recently dis-covered phenomenon (Hofstede, 1991), yet some incoming managers can display a remarkable disregard for the needs of others, religious and other beliefs, local customs and practices, institutions and protocols. When change is attempted, the newcomer might find that it is almost impossible to get anything done, adding to frustration and the potential for conflict. Without a roadmap, navigating unfamil-iar organizational territory can be as confounding as its real-world parallel.

Managers entering new situations have to invest time in planning and preparation. Orientation towards the location, its people, their values, beliefs and behaviour is a necessary step that can take weeks, even months. Most long-serving managers would be able to recall one occasion where someone was *parachuted in* to take charge of a new or tricky situation. It can work out, but often it does not and makes matters worse. Awareness of work relationships, communication and contact, ethics and customs, rules and regulations are necessary prerequisites for the incoming manager. In short, cultural and institutional differences can represent significant obstacles when moving to a new location and one that is unfamiliar.

In a study of the effect of cultural and institutional differences, Koivu *et al.* (2004) identified a number of factors that could improve the chances of success for the incoming manager:

- Acquire as much local institutional knowledge as possible and as early as possible.
- Utilize the knowledge of local partners who have the right connections to the right people and authorities, and who know the correct way of working with them.
- Practice self-reflection – think carefully about your own behaviour and beliefs.
- Pay attention to situational characteristics and not so much to the stereotypes of national cultural differences.

Strategy formulation

The starting point for managing a facility is the organization's business plan, together with its space (or accommodation) strategy. These should encapsulate the business objectives of the organization and make clear what is needed to support its business strategy. The approach advocated here for developing a facility management strategy therefore takes account of the organization's business objectives, needs and policies, as well as the practicalities imposed by its space (see Chapter 2). It considers the successive stages in the process (see Fig. 3.1) and reveals that a wide range of techniques and tools are at the disposal of facility managers to help them in their work (see Table 3.1). The approach is largely one of applying accepted principles of strategic business planning and development to the facility management context.

Fig. 3.1   The process for developing a facility management strategy.

Table 3.1   Techniques and tools to support development of a facility management strategy.

Development stage	Phase	Technique or tool
Strategic analysis	Assessment of expectations and objectives	Political, economic, social and technological (PEST) analysis Strengths, weaknesses, opportunities and threats (SWOT) analysis If … then analysis Mega trends Quantitative analysis Scenario analysis
	Portfolio and space audit	Space analysis Real estate register Maintenance plan Risk assessment
	Services audit/review Resource audit	Performance benchmarking People and skills profiling Service provider audit (existing internal arrangements) Business process modelling Service providers (external)
	Market audit	Real estate availability Market trends
Solution development	Generating options	Insourcing/outsourcing models Business process re-engineering (BPR)
	Evaluating options	Maintenance plan Risk analysis Stakeholder analysis Cost–benefit analysis Life-cycle cost appraisal Feasibility analysis
	Selecting option	Optimization model Sensitivity analysis
Strategy implementation	People and systems	Change management Personnel development and training Business process re-engineering (BPR)
	Communication	Organization's intranet Newsletters, noticeboards, memoranda Instant messaging and corporate social networking Workshops and seminars
	Resource planning	Planning, scheduling and control Resource levelling/optimization
	Procurement/ outsourcing	Service provider selection Market testing Performance benchmarking

This process for developing a facility management strategy, as illustrated in Fig. 3.1, shows three main stages with their contributory elements. The three main stages in the development of a strategy are: strategic analysis, solution development and strategy implementation.

Strategic analysis

The aim of the analysis is to establish a thorough understanding of the present state of the organization's facility or facilities and its approach to facility management. This means assembling all relevant facts under the following headings:

- Organizational objectives, needs and policies – from the business plan.
- Physical assets and space efficiency achieved – from the space strategy.
- Processes, systems and resources – a clear picture of the current provision of services.
- Detailed breakdown of costs – structured in the form of a cost analysis.

The organization should be able to define its objectives and expectations for its facility or facilities with relative ease. For instance, it might aspire to expand its core business into areas for which different types of facility and services will be required compared with those currently provided. It would be useful, therefore, to broaden discussion to identify potential extensions and additions, as well as noting where closure of business operations is necessary or likely. These objectives should be embodied in a formal statement as part of the organization's business strategy, or linked to it, and should relate to needs identified in the business plan. There is an obvious connection here with the organization's sustainable space provision (see Chapter 2).

Portfolio and space audit

An audit of the organization's portfolio should be undertaken to assist in establishing the extent to which the facility (or facilities) requires servicing, noting the nature of services involved. When determining the extent of servicing required, account should be taken of the utilization of space (i.e. space efficiency). Allowance for growth and/or reduction in the demand for space and its phasing into the future should be incorporated, as far as possible, in the assessment of provision (see Chapter 2). The provision of space should reflect an inclusive environment that anticipates the needs of disabled people and others with equalities-related needs. The portfolio should align with space requirements included in, or implied by, the business objectives.

The requirement for maintenance is a particular consideration since it can impact negatively on the beneficial and economical use of space. The nature, extent and frequency of maintenance should therefore be assessed (see Chapter 12) to help determine whether or not space is appropriate to support current and likely future needs. The cost of providing space, maintaining and upgrading it should be considered. Other factors that might impact the organization's use of space negatively and positively should be investigated. Risk and opportunity assessment should be undertaken periodically and a risk and opportunity register kept up to date for each facility (see Chapter 2). An evaluation of the true cost of providing space – that is, the cost of providing support services – must always form part of any assessment. This will help to establish which spaces are providing best value and which are not. In this regard, it is necessary to look at the value (to the organization) of activities against the cost of locating them. For example, it would make little economic sense to house a printing press – no matter how convenient it is – in prime real estate that attracts a premium rent. Chapter 2 discusses space management.

Changes in the use of technology, especially information and communications technology (ICT), can impact upon the type and amount of space required, although not necessarily in terms of a decrease. Even so, space is rarely provided without charge and so superfluous space represents waste. The servicing of space can represent a significant cost item within the overall budget for operating and managing a facility. Comparing the cost of different spaces might reveal situations where some space is inefficient and/or uneconomical. Benchmarking can help to raise awareness amongst stakeholders of the cost of providing, maintaining, upgrading and servicing space. There is, however, the likelihood that perceptions of space utilization will vary within the organization and across regions, with the result that what is regarded as the norm in one location is seen either as extravagant or inadequate by those elsewhere.

Organizations operating in different countries – for example, Sweden and the United Kingdom – are bound to notice differences in the allocation of space per individual. The same company operating in Stockholm and London would probably record quite different figures for space. When looked at from a UK perspective, personnel in Sweden would appear to have generous, even too much, space: the Swedes would likely disagree. Climate and culture can have a significant influence on the amount and quality of space felt to be appropriate.

Attempts to normalize standards across regions could prove counterproductive; even so, it would be wrong to assume that existing standards are appropriate simply because that is what people are used to having. With the emergence of large regional markets, problems can so easily arise and be accentuated by cultural differences, not to mention local customs and practice. Accepting that there are bound to be differences – and that such a situation is fairly normal – is a way to avoid problems. Even so, there are trends that suggest space per individual is decreasing in regions that have previously enjoyed more generous space, largely as a consequence of benchmarking (CoreNet, 2012).

Services audit

The organization should be in the position of having identified and differentiated between its core and non-core business activities. This differentiation is necessary to ensure that effort can be concentrated where it is needed most; that is, in developing the best working environment. In addition to those noted in Chapter 1, examples of non-core business activities include catering, reprographics, vehicle maintenance and conference facilities. It is important in this respect to appreciate that since no two organizations are the same, there is the likelihood that one will regard certain activities as a part of its core business, whilst another would class them as non-core business. The distinction between core and non-core business activities is a matter for senior managers to determine.

Where applicable, the organization should critically review the current delivery of services by considering, as a minimum, the following aspects:

- *Policy* – an examination of existing policy in terms of corporate guidelines and standards, performance standards, quality assurance, health, safety, security and other relevant statutory obligations, human resources, finance and approvals.
- *Processes and procedures* – definition of business processes, including budgeting, procurement, approvals and payments.
- *Service delivery* – audit of all aspects of facility management and the delivery of services, including their cost, as well as relationships with end-users (especially in regard to performance/quality, cost and time objectives).

In carrying out a review of such aspects, the organization should consider making use of benchmarking as a method for measuring current levels of performance and outcomes (see Chapter 11). Measurement is an aid to understanding a process and can provide insights into how it might be improved.

Resources audit

Part of this high-level analysis should include a review of personnel employed in the facility and in delivering services. This will, of necessity, cover both insourced and outsourced arrangements. The organization should also review the extent of available human resources, information about which should be available from its human resources management (see Chapter 4). Additionally, it needs to analyse the processes that are contained within its facility to determine, amongst other things, patterns of use, areas of intensive use and areas of underuse. Methods for determining these factors are increasingly supported by ICT, but should always be based on *good* science and ethical practice. Many organizations now routinely survey their facility using CCTV for reasons of security, and general health and safety. When used for the right motives, this technology can provide proof of a particular need or the lack of it.

The resource audit should concentrate on the following:

- *People* – determine skills' profiles and identify gaps.
- *Providers* – assess capability, scope and terms of engagement.
- *Systems* – establish the status of all procedures and technology by process analysis and systems audit.

Market audit

The organization should consider testing the market at intervals to determine the extent to which current service delivery matches that available, including the cost of services. Frequent attempts to test the market can prove counterproductive and should be avoided. Understanding how the market for services is developing and what trends might be emerging provides the organization with insights into potential opportunities and innovations, as well as alerting it to possible dangers. Discussion with existing and prospective service providers extends understanding by enabling opinions to be formed on the capacity available to meet the organization's planned demand for services.

Appropriate use of the market can include comparisons of current prices and rates for services using published data, indicative cost estimates from service providers and participation in benchmarking clubs. An awareness of the state of the market for services means that at any time an opinion can be formed as to whether or not a preferred option is the most appropriate. Some of the requisite information, however, might already be contained within market audits carried out during the preparation of the portfolio and space audit and services audit.

The terms *cost* and *price* are often used interchangeably. Even so, it is important to distinguish between cost, being a sum that the organization might use for budgetary purposes, and a price, being the sum paid to a service provider for delivery of a service.

The organization should also consider undertaking periodic audits to establish the state of the real estate market (should acquisition or disposal become an option) and the position regarding service providers (see Chapters 7 and 8) in all areas of potential interest. It is possible that this kind of information will be available from market audits carried out when preparing the space strategy and from the valuation of assets for financial accounting purposes.

Solution development

Once information from the analysis stage has been assembled, a structured approach to the interpretation of the information must be adopted. It is essential that this interpretation is open, without bias and allows new ideas and innovative solutions to flow so that the most appropriate arrangement for the organization's facility management can emerge; in other words, its strategy. The recommended approach is:

1. assemble criteria for evaluating options;
2. generate options;
3. evaluate options; and
4. select preferred options.

Criteria for evaluating options

Before any attempt is made to consider the relative merits of options, it is necessary to identify and agree the criteria for judging them. Moreover, there needs to be a very clear separation between the assembly of criteria and their application to options to ensure objectivity. Most importantly, there should be no fudging of criteria to support a preferred option; otherwise, the entire evaluation would be rendered pointless. Criteria should therefore be explicit and open to review, and include likely end-user satisfaction and the extent to which best value might be achieved. Options can therefore be evaluated consistently against the set criteria to ensure objectivity, parity and accountability.

Generation of options

There are many ways in which the organization can establish options; for example, consultation with stakeholders and invitations to external experts. The strategic analysis stage should have highlighted precisely how well the organization's space and other attributes of its facility match up to its needs. This means that options should be considered for bridging identified gaps as well as for aligning innovative solutions with present and future needs. Creativity is a useful commodity to have at this stage and should extend to *thinking outside the box*. Important too is the need to avoid prejudging the merits of any option, as this runs the risk of corrupting the process: evaluation should be left until later. If an option proves unworthy then that will become evident later, so little purpose would be served by trying to work out of sequence.

Evaluation and selection of the preferred options

To a large extent, this can be a fairly straightforward task. If tasks in the preceding stages have been undertaken properly, the preferred option or options will be clear enough. Should the position be otherwise, it is likely that a failure either in identifying relevant criteria or in applying them correctly is to blame. Sometimes the options will not be mutually exclusive and, on occasion, a combination of two or more, or a variation in one, provides a better way forward.

At the conclusion of this stage, all preferred options can be summarized and incorporated in the facility management strategy, which should cover as a minimum:

- Summary of business objectives, main drivers and constraints.
- Relationship between core and non-core business.
- Portfolio and sustainable space provision.
- Significant risks and opportunities.
- Targets for efficiency gains and other improvement.
- Critical success factors and key performance indicators (KPIs).
- End-user and other key stakeholder needs.
- Access, inclusion and equalities-related needs.
- Scope of services.
- Insourcing/outsourcing/co-sourcing (as applicable).
- Human resources.
- Budgetary provision.
- Change management.
- Information management.
- ICT support.

Strategy implementation

Once the strategy has been agreed by senior managers, policy statements should be prepared and then translated into operational plans for realization through a process that is capable of handling change. A change management process should therefore be initiated (see Chapter 14), incorporating best practice in human resources management (see Chapter 4). Implementation should be supported by a time-plan, with milestones, and a risk and opportunity register as it relates to the facility or facilities – see below. Operational plans should encompass people and systems, communication, resource planning and procurement, each of which is discussed below. Senior managers must be committed to the successful implementation of the strategy. Where this involves the decision to outsource (see Chapter 7), attention should be paid to the demands of the informed client function as discussed in Chapter 1.

Downside risks and upside risks (opportunities) from outsourcing should be identified (see Chapters 1 and 7), especially any that might affect core operations, followed by an assessment of the likelihood of their occurrence and potential impact. Allocation of quantified risks should be undertaken on the basis of an understanding of the ability of the party (or individual) to handle the risks in question. Allocation without regard to the capacity of a party (or individual) might lead to increased exposure for the organization instead of successful risk mitigation or elimination.

Typical of the risks that can occur are:

- Unclear definition of roles, responsibilities and accountabilities.
- Insufficient expertise in the drafting of service level agreements (SLAs).
- Lack of definition of requirements before inviting a request for proposals/tender.
- Insufficient time allowed for contract negotiation.
- Too short a transition period between contract award and start-up of service delivery.

Whilst we have yet to consider the position regarding outsourced services, there are some issues that need to be addressed. For example, the effect of a major breakdown in a key service area could threaten continuity of operations for the organization and should be examined at this point. Contingency plans must be drawn up and validated (see Chapter 9). In some cases, it might be necessary to introduce trials or another kind of *run through* to test the efficacy of the proposed arrangements and their ability to cope with certain eventualities.

The organization should also plan and run through the arrangements for managing transition; that is, the move from one arrangement of service delivery to another, as would occur when moving between insourcing and outsourcing, and the reverse situation. For example, the organization should plan the handover of information to any newly appointed service providers. Sufficient time must be allowed for this activity – see Chapters 9 and 14 – as it will generally set the tone of the relationship between the organization and service providers. The accuracy and completeness of information to be handed over must also be verified.

In the transition period before any new contract starts, the service provider should visit end-users (and other key stakeholders, where appropriate) to discuss the new arrangements and what is expected from them; in other words, changed goals and new procedures must be communicated.

People and systems

The most important aspect of implementation, when bringing about any change, is to carry it through in a controlled way. In order to achieve this state, the organization needs to develop the competence and skills of personnel so that they are fully conversant with the meaning and practice of facility management. Education and training, together with the mentoring of individuals, will achieve these aims and enhance capability. Close monitoring and control of tasks will help to ensure that these too develop in the ways intended. This is not a one-off exercise; there has to be a culture of continual improvement, with periodic checks on performance and corrective action where necessary.

Communication

Effective communication between the organization, acting as an informed client, and service providers is essential to ensure that implementation is both understood and acted upon (see Chapters 8 and 9). It is important to involve all stakeholders in the discussion about organization and structure. Failure to do so is bound to lead to complications later.

Personnel and service providers, as appropriate to the arrangement for service delivery, need to recognize that facility management is a proactive process and not one of simply reacting to problems as and when they arise. In organizational terms, this demands a structure that is reasonably flat, so that personnel with decision-making powers are in close contact with end-users to head off problems before they have time to develop. Developing relationships is really only possible by communicating clearly and often.

Resources planning

Planning and controlling the use of resources in an efficient and effective manner is a job in its own right. Where the organization is a large employer of either in-house personnel or external service providers, it makes good sense to plan for the optimal use of resources. When management teams are small and the demands on them appear modest, it is still necessary to take formal steps to plan resources. Even the best managers cannot keep everything in their heads, besides which there will be absences when others have to assume responsibility. ICT can help here through the use of low-cost planning and scheduling software to allocate resources to individual tasks and provide a means for measuring performance and progress (see Chapter 15). Finally, the point is reached when the procurement of services, where appropriate, can be considered (see Chapters 8, 9 and 14).

Conclusions

The organization should regard a facility management strategy as a key component of its business strategy. Without a facility management strategy, the organization will be unable to respond quickly and appropriately to changing circumstances in the marketplace and any consequent need for more or less space. By analysing its portfolio and space provision now and into the future, the organization will be able to quantify any gap that has to be bridged. There are, however, other aspects relating to facility management that have to be considered if the most appropriate strategy is to be developed. Current arrangements for the delivery of services will have to be reviewed in light of business objectives along with resource demands and available budgets. End-user needs and expectations must also be taken into account during the search for a best value outcome for facility management that the strategy represents. Various tools and techniques are available to support a rigorous process of strategic analysis, solution development and strategy implementation, success in which will lead to workable, operational plans for efficient and cost-effective service delivery. The organization would be wise to see strategy formulation and the three key steps that follow it as capable of leading to a workable arrangement, but one that must be revisited should there be a fundamental change in any of the conditions facing the organization's core business.

Checklist

This checklist is intended to assist with review and action planning.

		Yes	No	Action required
1.	Does the organization accept the need for a facility management strategy?	☐	☐	☐
2.	Has a strategic analysis of requirements been completed in the past year?	☐	☐	☐
3.	Is the organization clear about what its business context means in terms of the broad approach to facility management?	☐	☐	☐
4.	Has a distinction been drawn between management at the strategic, tactical and operational levels?	☐	☐	☐
5.	Does the organization have concerns about cross-cultural impacts?	☐	☐	☐
6.	Have sufficient reviews and audits of the current arrangements for facility management been undertaken?	☐	☐	☐

	Yes	No	Action required
7. Has the organization considered its relationship with service providers?	☐	☐	☐
8. Have the criteria for evaluating options been prepared objectively?	☐	☐	☐
9. Do the criteria contain innovative elements?	☐	☐	☐
10. Has the temptation to judge options before they have been systematically evaluated been avoided?	☐	☐	☐
11. Have the most appropriate options been selected and gathered together in one coherent strategy?	☐	☐	☐
12. Has the strategy been translated into operational plans?	☐	☐	☐
13. Have resources been provided to implement the plans?	☐	☐	☐
14. Have outcomes been communicated with key stakeholders in terms of how operational plans will affect them?	☐	☐	☐

4 Human Resources Management

Key issues

The following issues are covered in this chapter.

- Human resources management (HRM) issues should be considered during the formulation of the organization's facility management strategy, as an integral part of managing support services related to the facility.

- The organization's goals for facility management in achieving end-user satisfaction and best value should be shared by all stakeholders, not least directly employed personnel and service providers.

- Personnel fulfilling roles and responsibilities within the sphere of facility management must have competence and skills that are matched to the demands of the tasks in hand. This requirement applies irrespective of whether services are insourced or outsourced.

- Where the organization does not have personnel with the requisite competence, it should acquire them through recruitment, training/retraining or outsourcing.

- Significant changes in the extent of outsourcing will have an impact on the roles and responsibilities of those concerned, potentially requiring changes to HRM policy and procedures.

- Where applicable, the organization must make clear its position on the transfer of personnel to another employer, as would happen when moving from an insourced arrangement to one that is outsourced. Legislation exists in many countries to ensure that personnel are not treated unfairly.

- Performance appraisals are needed across the length and breadth of the organization – there should be no discontinuity between senior managers and operatives – and should be linked to the organization's business objectives.

Total Facility Management, Fourth Edition. Brian Atkin and Adrian Brooks.
© 2015 John Wiley & Sons, Ltd. Published 2015 by John Wiley & Sons, Ltd.

- Remuneration and rewards for personnel should stem from performance appraisal and the overall success of the organization – they should not be detached from it.

- Developing the competence and skills of personnel can be achieved by providing opportunities for them that are identified in performance appraisals.

- There exists a wide range of solutions in terms of education, training and continuing professional development/education (CPD/CPE). The onus is on the organization to make the best use of these opportunities to improve the competence and skills of its personnel – this applies to both insourcing and outsourcing arrangements.

Introduction

Changes to the way in which services are provided will have an impact on the culture of the organization and the nature of relationships with both internal and external parties. This chapter highlights aspects of HRM that need to be addressed when developing a strategy and operational plans to improve the value of support services required by the organization. A key determinant of success for any organization is the performance of its personnel. For this reason, performance appraisal has become the norm; yet it is not always implemented such that remuneration and reward are linked to the overall success of the organization. The needs of disabled people and others with equalities-related needs have to be actively considered too if the organization's human resources are to be properly managed. Talent management and empowerment have become part of the vocabulary, because they reflect an unquestionable concern for the importance and value of people to the organization's success. Developing the competence and skills of personnel is covered in this and later chapters, where the latter are closely linked with specific issues such as health, safety and security. Finally, an area of particular concern for human resources managers and facility managers is the transfer of personnel from the organization to external service providers under an outsourcing arrangement. Legislation exists in many countries to safeguard the interests of personnel to the extent that they are not treated unfairly as the result of their employment being transferred to another organization.

Personnel management

Human resources planning

This chapter does not seek to provide a broad treatment of the subject of HRM, as this can be found in many books. Instead, it deals with issues and questions that arise from changes to the current organizational structure and its direction as would occur if, for example, insourced services were now to be outsourced.

The need for changes in the organization's current HRM practices will depend upon the extent to which services are to be outsourced or insourced, as well as the policies, procedures and practices that are currently in place. Most organizations would probably have already considered many of the issues highlighted in this chapter. The sections that follow act primarily as a check against the main aspects of HRM that have to be reviewed when change is being considered. Of particular importance is the need to seek specialist advice on the current position in regard to the transfer of personnel from the organization to external service providers, which is outlined in a later section.

Any significant change in the number of services that are outsourced (or insourced) will have an impact on the structure of the facility management department (or other unit) and the organization, albeit to a lesser extent. In the case where all services are outsourced, a core management team is required to control and coordinate the activities of external service providers. In this instance, the role of management changes from direct or hands-on management to the management of the output of others; that is, the performance measurement of deliverables. The main management tasks then become the definition and development of policy and procedures and the management of the respective contracts. In this connection, it is essential to ensure that there is a split between purchaser and provider, regardless of whether or not services are outsourced, with the purchaser acting as the informed client in order to monitor the performance of outsourced or insourced service delivery. These policies and procedures, along with relevant standards, are vital if the respective contracts are to meet the expectations of end-users and are not to encourage malpractice or other irregularity.

The most appropriate management structure will be the one that ensures economy and control for the organization over its facility. This means that the organization will need to determine exactly the number of personnel and the functions involved in managing the delivery of services, whether they are outsourced or insourced. Clearly, the management of external service providers is different from the supervision of directly employed personnel and should not demand the same level of resources. It is acceptable that some personnel will have to be retained even where the organization has opted for total facility management by a single service provider (see Chapter 7), since the informed client function must be maintained (see Chapter 1). Under these circumstances, there is a need for someone to be able to manage the interface between the organization and service provider. The duties involved here, in addition to those associated with the procurement of services (see Chapter 8), can be summarized as follows:

- Maintaining and enhancing the informed client function.
- Defining facility-related and space standard policies and monitoring space utilization.
- Understanding and monitoring end-user requirements and keeping senior managers informed of same.
- Planning projects involving new or additional works.
- Managing the approvals process and payments to service providers.
- Measuring the performance of service providers.

Employment obligations

Job markets around the world are subject to varying degrees of control. Increasingly, governments and legislatures are applying more socially minded principles to the matter of employment. The responsibility of organizations for their personnel has come in for serious attention in efforts to safeguard the latter's rights. The organization must establish how legislation affects its policies, procedures and actions to ensure that it complies with the legislation.

Employment obligations, both legal and moral, need to be considered carefully before outsourcing. In the case of directly employed personnel, there should be a consultation period before services are outsourced. In the case of contract personnel, the organization should pass those details to the service providers tendering for the contracts. The scope of actions extends to cover all subsequent situations where the employment status of personnel is subject to change. It is essential, therefore, for the organization to establish how legislation affects its policies, procedures and actions to ensure that it is compliant.

The obligation to consult personnel is a duty to consult with their elected representatives or with any recognized union. If there are no recognized unions and no elected representatives, the organization has a duty to secure the election of representatives. It is not only representatives of personnel subject to transfer who must be consulted, but representatives of any personnel who might otherwise be affected by the transfer. The duty to inform and consult is, therefore, broad and the intention is to involve all stakeholders. The information that must be passed to personnel includes details of the measures that the transferee – that is, the new employer – intends to take in regard to employment.

This is a complex area of legislation and specialist advice should be sought. Consideration should be given both to the management of the process as well as to the inclusion, within tendering documentation, of necessary clauses in order that the mechanism by which the relevant legislation operates can be put in place. In cases where legislation does not apply, a redundancy situation might arise, and different procedures will have to be observed (and, of course, selection for redundancy must be fair too).

Common sense suggests that the best approach for dealing with the transfer of personnel is to involve them fully in discussion about their future employment. There are bound to be cynics amongst those facing potential transfer – many will feel threatened – but the best way forward is to keep to a path that strives for fairness. Failure to do so might not only risk a backlash; it might also incur prosecution for those who have disregarded the correct procedures.

Access, inclusion and equality

The organization should provide information for disabled people and others who might have equalities-related needs or concerns and who are using or visiting the facility. This should be available in advance of and upon arrival at the facility, to explain the provisions for access, movement and emergency evacuation. Equalities-related legislation covers issues around the subjects of age, disability, gender reassignment, marriage and civil partnership, pregnancy and maternity, race, religion or belief, sex and sexual orientation. This is a fast-moving area of legislation, where regular updating on the part of the organization, as well as service providers, is necessary.

Talent management

Organizations whose facilities are amongst the best are likely to find that recruitment and retention of talented personnel is easier than for those that undervalue the importance of either. Attracting and retaining the best talent is, for most organizations, vital to their long-term success. Competition for talent is best fought when the quality of the workplace is unquestionable. The quality of the internal environment and the efficiency of support services are normally highly valued by personnel and can motivate them to higher levels of performance and achievement (see Chapter 5).

Empowerment

In the context of facility management, empowerment can be seen as a way of encouraging personnel to use initiative and make decisions to solve problems and improve service delivery and performance. Endowing personnel with the skills, resources, opportunity and authority with which to undertake their work will, it is believed, motivate them to take responsibility and become accountable for the outcomes of their actions. In turn, it is expected to raise competence and increase job satisfaction. It is far more than delegation, because it is not simply telling a subordinate to do something, but providing resources and other means to make decisions.

There are, however, positive and negative effects of promoting empowerment. Motivating people to face greater challenges than they would normally face and equipping them with the resources they need to accomplish them might work with most people. Empowerment is strongly associated with self-confidence. Increased confidence leads to greater ability to persist in the face of challenges. The overall effect of empowerment, if successfully instilled, is improved levels of end-user service, job satisfaction and commitment to the organization as well as to the team.

The flip side is that, if taken too far, empowerment can result in overconfidence and loss of sight of the organization's objectives. There is the possible additional risk of the individual failing to accept responsibility, or be accountable, for his or her actions. It is essential that personnel empowered to take on new challenges understand the responsibility and accountability that goes with them. In the worst cases, where too many individuals are empowered at once, power struggles can surface, affecting the achievement of the organization's objectives. Empowerment needs to be discussed openly so that everyone can understand what it means to the individual, the team and the organization. Chapter 5 discusses empowerment in the context of workplace productivity.

Job competences and skills

As changes occur in the mode of managing a facility, it is likely that the functions to be performed by personnel will also change. This will mean that job descriptions have to be revised for those with responsibility for managing services. The content of these revised job descriptions will dictate the selection of appropriate personnel for positions. When assigning individuals to positions that require interaction with service providers, including in-house teams, an understanding of operations and performance issues will be required, as well as strong interpersonal skills and knowledge of contracts. In any event, all job descriptions should outline the means for evaluating the performance of the individual. It is important that job descriptions are accompanied by role-evaluation procedures so that the individual and his or her manager are aware from the outset what is expected.

The issues highlighted in this book introduce novel ways of operating in a number of areas. These might require facility managers to develop existing skills further or to learn new skills in order to implement changes effectively. In particular, introducing new information management procedures and systems – many of which are heavily ICT dependent – will require additional training. Difficulties can arise because of the need for personnel to adjust to new working practices. Through sensitive handling, the organization should be able to overcome problems that might arise by using briefings, seminars and training.

Facility managers also need to be aware of the prevailing market for services and what is required to manage service providers effectively. In dealing directly with service providers, facility managers require different skills to those in a typical line management position. This should be recognized so that training and personal development needs can be identified. In fact, the entire organization should be subject to continuing professional development/education (CPD/CPE) as an example of its commitment to lifelong learning and a drive for continual improvement – see the later section in this chapter.

Performance appraisal

Management at all levels should be subject to performance appraisal, including managers employed by service providers. The assessment of the performance of service providers in particular is discussed in Chapter 11. The facility manager should be set performance objectives that reflect the management relationship with service providers, along with the actions taken to monitor performance and deal with any shortcomings. This could, for example, take the form of targets for tasks planned and completed over a given period, the percentage of response times met and the number of tasks needing to be reworked. Where performance depends on the efforts of a group of people, performance at group level should also be addressed, either through individual appraisals or in group sessions.

There are many ways in which the performance of individuals can be measured and used to create incentives and to reward excellent performance. Personnel should have a vested interest in the performance of the organization. With that in mind, personal appraisals should be undertaken annually and based upon core competences and key performance indicators (KPIs), which are aligned with the organization's business objectives. The results of the appraisals have a material bearing on the promotion of individuals and the apportionment of performance bonus payments. These KPIs are in addition to core competences measured as part of a standardized appraisal process. KPIs for senior managers should be customized to suit their specific role and responsibilities.

Generic KPIs can be introduced for other grades of professional and managerial personnel, where they are based on business measures linked to the facility being managed and, thus, to end-user satisfaction. The following example KPIs for professional grade personnel could be applied, where each attracts equal weight:

- *End-user satisfaction* – ISO compliance rating, satisfaction rating and retention/increase in business.
- *Professional management* – ethical behaviour, compliance, upkeep/satisfaction of facility manager's diary and facility inspection report.
- *Company performance* – debtor control rating, audited accounts and participation in business development.
- *Interpersonal skills* – formal/informal communications, turnover of personnel, motivation and goals for self-improvement.

Generic KPIs for personnel in support roles can be based on five fundamental performance areas, where each attracts equal weight:

- *Core skills* – ICT skills, planning and foresight, organization and team participation.
- *Knowledge management* – expertise, consistency, maintenance and time management.
- *Communication* – interpersonal skills and relationships.
- *Technical documentation* – production expertise, adherence to standards and use of multimedia.
- *Standards and codes of practice* – ISO and other compliance.

Personal development

Investing in people is a familiar theme and a necessity if the facility is to be managed safely, efficiently and cost-effectively. Education, training and continuing professional development/education (CPD/CPE) are mentioned in several places in this book, as indeed they should be. In many countries, facility management is firmly established with university degrees at undergraduate and graduate level. Many institutions also offer executive development and similar professional training, and these are joined by innumerable providers of operational training. Opportunities exist for non-cognate degree holders and others with more vocational skills to reskill and retrain as facility managers. Given that core competence in facility management touches many fields – from financial management through health, safety and security to ICT – then it is probably not surprising that there are myriad ways in which individuals can develop themselves. For the organization, it is important to have a clear strategy and formulated policies to support personnel in advancing in their careers. None of this comes without cost and so organizations should be aware of the need to fund education, training and CPD/CPE. Human resources managers, together with facility managers, should identify shortcomings in competence levels and skills gaps, and seek the most cost and time-effective way of overcoming them. If personnel are to acquire and enhance the competence and skills required to succeed within the organization, budgets have to be set at realistic levels. CPD/CPE is a mandatory requirement of virtually all professional institutions and many trade associations. Retention of individual membership is nowadays conditional upon demonstrating commitment to a minimum number of hours of qualifying activities during a calendar year. Achieving this minimum is not difficult and, in many respects, the range of qualifying activities is rather broad.

Conclusions

HRM is a sensitive area for organizations. Increasing legislation has added to the burden on the organization to have clear policies and procedures in place, no more so perhaps than in the case where the transfer of employment of personnel is envisaged. These policies and procedures have to be complete and must apply regardless of whether or not a service is outsourced or insourced. The organization has to adopt a management structure that is appropriate to the type of service delivery and understand its obligations as an employer. Job descriptions, competences and skills requirements must be made explicit and procedures put in place to appraise and reward performance against measurable outputs or outcomes. Where shortcomings in competence levels or skills gaps are identified, action should be taken to overcome them. There is an obvious overlap between HRM in general and the management of personnel in the facility management sphere. Managing and developing talent can improve the chances of successfully delivering services in support of the organization's core business. The organization should accept that competition for talent is best fought when the quality of the workplace is unquestionable. Attracting and retaining the best talent demands a superior facility and the services to match. It also amounts to more than recruiting personnel to fulfil narrowly defined roles; it requires empowerment of individuals who know they will not be punished for using their initiative and who, instead, will be seen as safeguarding the organization's interests.

Checklist

This checklist is intended to assist with review and action planning.

	Yes	No	Action required
1. Is the organization's structure suited to efficient and cost-effective facility management?	☐	☐	☐
2. Have job functions and job descriptions been described for managerial personnel?	☐	☐	☐

		Yes	No	Action required
3.	Where insourcing is involved, have job functions and job descriptions been described for the in-house team?	☐	☐	☐
4.	Do current arrangements properly recognize employment obligations, as well as the relevant legislation?	☐	☐	☐
5.	Is any transfer of personnel to another organization contemplated?	☐	☐	☐
6.	Is the organization aware of the needs of personnel at all levels in regard to disability and equalities, including those of visitors?	☐	☐	☐
7.	Is empowerment of personnel actively encouraged?	☐	☐	☐
8.	Are personnel involved in defining job functions, job descriptions and service requirements?	☐	☐	☐
9.	Is a well-developed method of performance appraisal in place covering all personnel?	☐	☐	☐
10.	Is performance appraisal linked to the organization's strategic business objectives and overall success?	☐	☐	☐
11.	Are personnel provided with the means to develop their competence and skills and are they rewarded when they succeed?	☐	☐	☐

5 Workplace Productivity

Key issues

The following issues are covered in this chapter.

- Productivity in the workplace is a focus of attention for most organizations. If productivity is to be maintained or enhanced, the balance between the demands of work and the well-being of the individual is paramount.

- Realizing that people engage in different activities, and how they do so, then matching the space and facility to the activity is a critical element of an integrated workplace strategy.

- People are generally flexible in most societies and can, within reason, accommodate change. There will, however, be limits to how much flexibility and change can be tolerated. Obsessive organizations will, by definition, find that attempts to raise productivity can push it in the opposite direction. Ground that might have been gained over months or years can be easily lost.

- There are essentially two ways in which the work environment can impact on productivity – enabling it or hindering it. Identifying factors and characteristics that are favourable or detrimental to productivity is essential if progress is to be made.

- Internal environmental factors affect productivity and include air quality, noise control, thermal comfort, privacy, lighting and spatial comfort. Not all of them are entirely negative in their impact.

- Environmental characteristics that influence work at the individual level include architectural properties – size of office, number of walls, ergonomic factors, heating and light.

Total Facility Management, Fourth Edition. Brian Atkin and Adrian Brooks.
© 2015 John Wiley & Sons, Ltd. Published 2015 by John Wiley & Sons, Ltd.

- The issue of control is one that is continually referred to in a variety of contexts. The use of individual environmental control systems can increase productivity, whilst reducing the likelihood of stress-related illness.

- A key factor in realizing productivity is from the increasing use of ICT; however, the organization must be structured to take advantage of the technology and to optimize the contribution of those who use it by providing the necessary education and training.

- Sick building syndrome (SBS) is an ever-present concern, especially where there is any risk of the internal environment not being properly controlled. The incidence of SBS can be exacerbated in the high-tech workplace.

Introduction

Understanding the factors that impact upon productivity in the workplace and acting upon them should be a matter of concern for all facility managers. Workplace productivity is a broadly applicable concept, but is most often taken in the context of the office environment. Here, knowledge workers and support personnel are arguably the most critical of all resources to the success of the organization. There is substantial literature on the subject and a range of issues so diverse that it is hard to summarize succinctly. Nonetheless, many themes and issues recur, not least the difficulty of measuring the actual impact of various factors on the productivity of personnel. Evidence exists of factors that are acknowledged as contributing positively to productivity, though arguably fewer than exist in relation to detrimental or negative impacts. Design-related issues feature strongly in this chapter and some insights are provided as to the kinds of working environment that could bring about useful contributions towards raising productivity. Findings from studies in a variety of specialist fields concerning workplace efficiency tend to be stronger on assumptions about how work should be structured and what future trends suggest than on practical advice as to how these might be addressed. A commonly propagated view, as to the impact of a combination of measures and improvements in areas affecting productivity, is that a substantial gain might be possible, perhaps as much as 50%. The basis of this view is examined. Understanding how productivity is affected by various actions is covered under four headings: the nature of work, the organization, communication and working environment.

Measuring productivity

There is a body of literature on factors affecting productivity in the workplace, with a particular bias towards those factors that impact on decisions regarding the use of space – for a broad treatment of the subject see, for example, Clements-Croome (2000). Most of the factors affecting productivity are consistently identified in literature covering specific and general workplace issues, even where there is sometimes an admission that the particular claim is unsupported by empirical evidence. In some cases it is not possible to amass such evidence, due to difficulties in measurement. In fact, one overriding consideration is the agreement that productivity in the office environment – as opposed to the factory – is extremely difficult to measure. This should not, however, be allowed to be an obstacle to attempts to identify factors affecting productivity because of another issue that is subject to widespread agreement: the possible gains from a combination of improvements in all suggested areas affecting productivity could be substantial, perhaps to the extent of 50%.

Particular difficulties in isolating and measuring the relationship between productivity and the physical setting do not imply that the latter is minor. It is generally agreed that a plan to increase the productivity and effectiveness of office-based work should *employ the design, management and quality of the work environment to maximum advantage* (Aronoff & Kaplan, 1995). The environment is, however, only one aspect. Personnel experience the office as a whole, including the physical, psychological and management setting, with each aspect affecting the others. For this reason, much of the remainder of this chapter is split into sections covering productivity factors relating to:

- the nature of work;
- the organization;
- communication; and
- the working environment.

Most emphasis is given to the working environment, where the issues raised in the previous sections can be seen to impact. This is achieved by reviewing findings in a variety of specialist fields impacting on workplace efficiency and considering the implications for facility management. Unfortunately, the literature tends to be stronger on assumptions about how work is structured nowadays and, therefore, how it can be extrapolated than on practical advice as to how the underlying issues might be addressed.

The nature of work

In today's business environment, personnel are not simply under pressure to *work smarter, not harder* but to do both. Slack time is pushed out as the means for work intensification are sought, not always with a view to quality rather than quantity where the latter is still easier to measure (Thompson & Warhurst, 1998).

There is general agreement that the nature of work has undergone a transformation in the past few decades. Major changes include a shift from a concentration on manpower-intensive manufacturing to a higher proportion of service industry. A majority of personnel are now employed in offices. In some countries, as much as 80% of all personnel are thought to be so-called white-collar workers. This shift immediately highlights a disquieting point: manufacturing industries have been able both to achieve and to measure substantial productivity improvements, whereas performance levels in office work, as far as it is possible to measure them, have lagged significantly in spite of substantial investment in ICT. Given the high percentage of white-collar workers, this picture reveals a disturbing state of affairs and indicates a pressing need to achieve greater productivity. This also explains the growing interest in organizational effectiveness, which becomes of national economic interest when it is shown that the country concerned lags in international competitiveness.

The work that is concentrated in the office sector has also changed. It is generally agreed that the workplace of today is likely to be a high-demand environment, subject to fast and continual change, increasing demands and fewer resources. With moves towards de-layering, downsizing and restructuring, and an atmosphere of near-continuous change prompted by shifts in consumer demands and increasing personnel and space costs, jobs have tended to become less individual and isolated and more multi-activity and integrated. It has become clear that an increasing number of people will also be expected to pursue multiple careers. Advances in ICT have facilitated such changes and many routine tasks have been taken over by computer-based systems. These moves have been paralleled by advanced manufacturing technologies in the factory environment, increasing the psychological or cognitive demands of modern work. There is a move away from non-interactive routine work towards both more collaborative and highly autonomous styles of working. Much routine work is becoming automated or has been exported to lower-cost economies – a case of offshoring as opposed to simple outsourcing. The large number of call centres and other technical functions moved to low-wage countries is evidence of this trend.

In some cases, greater job diversity has been achieved. In other cases, simply greater workload and responsibility taken on by a diminishing number of personnel are resulting in longer hours and/or more intensive work. The technology that has enabled such advances has also supported changes in monitoring some aspects of performance, thus increasing the pressure to perform, which in turn adds to stress (see Chapter 6).

It is often argued and generally assumed that the majority of work now done in offices is *knowledge work* and, consequently, it is the productivity of the knowledge worker that must be maximized. Creative knowledge work demands a combination of highly concentrated individual work alongside interactive teamwork. Knowledge workers tend to pursue their own interests and see their own value. If their needs can be accommodated within the workplace, they can boost productivity within a more collegial form of management, which involves the sharing of information, delegation and the encouragement of upward and horizontal communication. Coordination is now based on collaboration between technical and professional groups, which retain authority over their own work. This is part of the flattening of hierarchical structures and also of the move towards teamworking focused on problem-solving and continual improvement, in a culture of trust and empowerment.

The morale of individuals is of obvious importance to productivity. This has previously been linked to issues such as security, routine and stability in job tasks. While this remains true to a large extent, future demands by personnel in regard to their work are more likely to focus on independence and creativity (see Chapter 4 on Empowerment). Added to this is the increasing flexibility of working patterns and practices that many organizations are now offering their personnel. The following are options open to some personnel, often in combination:

- *Homeworking or telecommuting* – use of ICT and, in particular, virtual private networks.
- *Flexible working hours* – can support a better work–life balance, especially for those with atypical family arrangements.
- *Out-of-office working* – use of satellite centres and the concept of the virtual office (see Chapter 2).

The options have been enabled by technological innovation, which involves not just a change in the way a job is done, but also a social transformation in the nature and/or location of the workplace. This flexibility is seen as being mutually beneficial to individuals and their organizations. This is particularly true of a workforce where female personnel are able to balance work commitments with those of their family. Flexibility in working hours and homeworking means that it is possible to take children to school and later pick them up as part of a normal, daily routine. This has generated significant goodwill and loyalty and, consequently, improved productivity in those organizations where a significant proportion of personnel are female.

There is considerable evidence in various areas of the positive impact of control on the job satisfaction and general well-being of the individual. Conversely, lack of control is detrimental. Given the links seen between satisfaction, well-being and productivity, discussed below, it can be seen that this type of flexibility is beneficial all round. Moreover, there is evidence to suggest that working away from the office leads to higher levels of productivity, subject to the nature of the work, the individual and the alternative environment. It is also most beneficial if conceived as part of an integrated workplace strategy.

There is assumed to be a link between personal satisfaction with one's workplace and the effectiveness of the individual and the organization. The validity of the satisfaction/productivity model is backed up by research findings, which suggest a relationship between the satisfaction of personnel and the factors of absenteeism and turnover, although the relationship to productivity, while consistent, is not as strong as might be expected. A third variable, rewards, seems to determine the relationship. Strong performance might lead to rewards, which in turn can lead to satisfaction; however, this way of looking at it would then say that rather than causing performance, satisfaction is caused by it.

There are two types of reward: extrinsic (e.g. pay, promotion, status and security) and intrinsic (e.g. personal satisfaction). For this reason, it is more important for the organization to look at the match between satisfaction and performance rather than addressing satisfaction in itself. The match seems to depend on the perceived equitable distribution of rewards. This might have an impact on issues of space quality and allocation. Reward is not usually linked to professional achievement, but to managerial hierarchies, on the basis of which enclosed, high-quality spaces are allocated as visible status symbols, as opposed to being allocated according to quality of performance as a means for rewarding productive personnel.

There is a need to focus on the environment in relation to the ease of task performance, rather than in relation to a given job. Ease in accomplishing work affects productivity directly, but also appears to affect motivation and, therefore, performance through its influence on intrinsic rewards. Moreover, *task performance and work satisfaction are optimized when job demands are high enough for the work to be challenging and interesting, but not so high as to be overwhelming* (Aronoff & Kaplan, 1995). Although factors related to job satisfaction might not be the same as those related to job performance, both impact on productivity and are, therefore, of consequence for the organization.

In exchange for the removal of restrictions, personnel are now required to demonstrate their added value and to do whatever is necessary to achieve the organization's goals. We can now look at the impact of the organization on productivity and how this has changed in recent years, as part of changes in the nature and pattern of work.

The organization

The virtual organization is now a reality, but hardly not commonplace. Many changes have been taking place that make the forward-looking organization of the present highly differentiated from the traditional organization. European organizations in particular have experienced a wave of domestic and cross-border mergers, acquisitions and strategic alliances, as well as restructuring from privatization or in response to increasing market competition. Reorganization has an immediate productivity impact in terms of time involved in recruiting or reassigning personnel, moving personnel and/or furniture, re-establishing and resuming work. The traditional hierarchical pyramid has been squashed to accommodate more horizontal communication and empowerment. The move to flatter and leaner organizational structures has increased the workload and demands on the individual. An atmosphere of uncertainty and a need for continual adaptation to new working practices and managerial styles and work cultures, combined with concerns over job security in the move towards fixed-term contracts, have led to increasing degrees of job-related stress. Chapter 6 discusses factors giving rise to stress amongst personnel.

At the beginning of this chapter, we commented on the difficulty of measuring performance in the office environment. The continuing emphasis placed on closely monitoring the performance of personnel, linked to reward and advancement, rests uncomfortably alongside empowerment and participative management, especially if personnel are not consulted on targets or the selection of performance criteria.

Focus on personnel as a resource, particularly the soft approach, sees the potential that can be realized through training and personal development and by cultivating the commitment of personnel to the organization. This last emphasis will require the physical work environment to be more supportive of the human resources strategy adopted by the organization. This is particularly evident in the case of flexibility, where the facility must be able to support the demands of individual and organizational flexibility in order to respond to changes in the marketplace.

Communication

The drive to achieve more efficient realization of office assets and to promote productivity becomes more feasible with ICT and, in particular, networking. The impact of advances in ICT should be self-evident. The effect on productivity is, however, less so, at least in the office environment. Whereas technology has brought about remarkable increases in productivity in manufacturing, it has had comparatively little impact in the office sector and has not provided immediate payback on the high costs of its implementation. Unlike manufacturing, where automation rapidly increases production, technology in the office is likely to increase productivity only to the extent to which users integrate it into their way of working. A key factor in realizing productivity gains is that the organization must be structured to take advantage of the technology and to optimize the contribution of those who use it. The greatest productivity gains are only likely to be achieved when ICT has been used to reform workflows so that inefficiency and waste are driven out.

ICT has been responsible for some important changes, such as removing the functional and spatial division between headquarters, back office and front offices (customer-facing), leading to greater flexibility in work patterns. Adjacency planning has become less constrained by the demands of physical workflow, with emphasis now given to clustering work activities that require similar background environments, services and equipment. Value can be added to office use by improving productivity through the more effective application of ICT and greater flexibility in its use. For example, the organization can choose to manage work in a variety of settings, on multiple sites and even across time zones – the location of call centres abroad is but one example.

With up to 80% of office personnel reckoned to be knowledge workers, perhaps spending a significant proportion of their time on communication activities, they need periods of quiet concentration to allow for creative or complex thought. The group element enhances individual capabilities and it is therefore critical for their success that they are able to communicate and collaborate as necessary. Moreover, people can learn from each other in informal situations, by working alongside those with whom they do not normally share space. Many organizations now plan adjacencies to take advantage of unanticipated opportunities created by social interaction.

The work environment

There are essentially two ways in which the office environment can impact on productivity, either by enabling it or by hindering it. The ways in which the environment adversely affects the satisfaction and performance of personnel are fairly well known and empirically established. Less is known of, or certain about, the ways in which the environment can positively impact on productivity, other than in removing the factors that adversely affect it.

The many issues known or believed to affect production include, but are not restricted to the following:

- Prevention of accidents and diseases, resulting in reduced costs.
- Reduction of sick leave and lower personnel turnover.

- Improvement of communication – consent on the topic of working conditions.
- Commitment of personnel and improvement of industrial relations.
- Enhancement of quality in the internal environment as well as in the job itself.
- Improvement of productivity and efficiency.
- Better position in the job market – more attractive work.

Seven aspects of the work environment have been identified from the perspective of users:

1. indoor air quality;
2. noise control;
3. thermal comfort;
4. privacy;
5. lighting comfort;
6. spatial comfort; and
7. noise control.

In the above context, the physical environment for office work is believed to account for a variation of some 5–15% in the productivity of personnel (Rostron, 1997). These aspects or factors are now discussed. In this connection, it is important to bear in mind the complexity of the factors and the difficulty of uncovering the root cause of most problems affecting personnel. In a book of this kind, we can only hope to provide a summary.

The internal environment

Indoor air quality is one of the major areas of dissatisfaction amongst personnel. It is an umbrella term for a variety of factors that include ventilation, pollutants, moisture, noise and vibration.

Air quality

Stale air is a common complaint and arises from inefficient ventilation. Natural means of ventilation can often alleviate problems caused by a low rate of mechanical (i.e. forced) air changes; however, the subject is complex and cannot be discussed comprehensively here. Indoor pollution sources that release gases or particles into the air are a significant cause of indoor air quality problems. Inadequate ventilation can increase indoor pollutant levels by not bringing in enough outdoor air to dilute emissions from indoor sources and by not carrying indoor air pollutants to the outside. High temperature and moisture can also increase concentrations of some pollutants. In fact, moisture is a widespread problem often linked with mould growth, resulting from spores that drift through indoor and outdoor air continually. When mould spores land on a damp spot indoors, they might begin to grow and digest whatever they are growing on. The way to control the growth of indoor mould is to control moisture.

Noise and vibration

When they occur at high levels, noise and vibration can be both physiologically and psychologically harmful. They can obstruct communication and mentally disturb the individual, resulting in impairment of job performance and/or accidents. When noise distraction is a problem, people rate it as a serious hindrance to productivity, although they do not claim the absence of noise to be an important benefit. Even so, some level of background noise is, in fact, thought to be beneficial to concentration. Noise at inappropriate levels increases mistakes and slows work rates. People also tend to use more simplistic problem-solving methods. Thus, as noise distraction becomes more troublesome, people not only work less effectively but they think differently, leading to a quality cost as well as a productivity cost. Noise causes breaks in concentration, making it harder to address tasks that require sustained concentration and reducing the ability to make creative leaps. It also interferes with the ability to differentiate relevant issues from those that are unimportant.

Lighting

The biological effect of light is significant not only on visual task performance, but also in controlling the physiological and psychological functioning of the human body. As with many other factors, the ultimate effect of light and lighting on human well-being is determined in part by individual perception and satisfaction.

Heating

Thermal comfort tends to receive the highest number of complaints in most end-user surveys. Overly cool conditions make people restless, impairing concentration and increasing error rates, particularly for demanding mental tasks. Being too warm can cause weariness, sleepiness, a reduction in performance and a tendency to make mistakes. Fluctuations in temperature can be even more troublesome.

Sick building syndrome

Factors related to sick building syndrome (SBS) are exacerbated in the high-tech workplace. Offices with more than two symptoms per person of SBS are likely to show general productivity losses. The reported effects of SBS might combine with other job-related factors to produce an overall sense of dissatisfaction. This means that the concentration of research and business efforts and expense on maintenance and cleaning might be misplaced in the search for improved productivity. Moreover, psychosocial problems might actually lead to susceptibility to symptoms through increased stress in working environments.

Minimizing the constraints placed on personnel at their workstations will increase social and economic productivity. The more choice people have, the happier and more productive they are likely to become. The reason why many people underperform is because their behaviour and degrees of freedom are systematically reduced by decisions over which they themselves have no control – decisions usually taken higher up the organization.

Environmental characteristics that influence work on the individual level include architectural properties – for example, size of office, number of walls, ergonomic factors, heating and light – and architectural attributes; that is, people's perceptions of architectural properties. The very design of workplaces might be creating ill health. In fact, health and stress problems are greater in high-demand, low-control environments than in high-demand, high-control environments.

The issue of control is one that is continually referred to in a variety of contexts. It surfaces in connection with the work itself and within the organization, and is a major factor concerning productivity in the context of the working environment. Control of one's working environment includes temperature, lighting and ventilation, as well as choice and configuration of furniture. The use of individual environmental control systems can increase productivity by around 7%. However, the modern office often acts against this, with top-down (or external) control over functions such as heating and ventilation.

Design issues

An investigation into the influence of the working environment on self-reported productivity found that most respondents considered that the office had a direct influence on their well-being and productivity. They felt that productivity in particular would rise by 10% if environmental conditions were improved. Generally, an improved fit between the physical setting and the work process, both at the individual and the organizational level, should improve performance directly; but should also indirectly contribute to future successful job performance by enhancing the intrinsic rewards of the job – performance leads to satisfaction leads to performance.

Aesthetic choices in office design affect human behaviour and job performance, influencing individuals' perceptions of the work environment, how quickly they tire and how tolerant they are of physical stressors. Considerations regarding interior design must therefore take into account the idiosyncrasies of the human visual system. Extremes of contrast are, in particular, visually fatiguing. However, people with certain kinds of visual impairment might benefit from contrasting colour schemes that pick out important objects. For example, white light switches on a white background might not be easily found even if they are located where they are expected to be.

The design of the workspace must address not only an individual's lower-order needs, such as safety, security and physical comfort, but also higher-order needs such as self-esteem. Once environmental needs are satisfied, the individual becomes dominated by the unsatisfied needs and environmental conditions cease to be important to the individual's current concerns. Instead, issues such as amenity, view, décor, space provision and furniture standard come to the fore in the context of status and self-fulfilment.

Whether a better workplace improves individual performance or more productive individuals gravitate to organizations with better work environments is not entirely clear. Yet, there are measurable productivity benefits to be gained by improving the physical working environment. Problems might, however, arise as much from the perception of space, such as open-plan layouts, as from the reality, including its perceived inferiority to enclosed spaces occupied by senior managers. Consequently, interventions that alter such perceptions might be a productive approach.

Whilst open-plan settings are intended to offer greater flexibility, it is often the case that this flexibility is not utilized, as the upheaval involved is itself considered counterproductive. Minimizing the disruption to productivity caused by constant reshuffles can be achieved through such planning measures as the *universal footprint* or the *fixed service spine*. The former limits the number of different office sizes to facilitate movement of personnel; the latter mixes rigidity and flexibility, enabling quick reconfigurations to facilitate different types of activity with minimum disruption. Within the universal footprint, as in other schemes, furniture might also be standardized but with individuals able to choose a personalized combination from a standard range of components. This results in a degree of equity, which is essential to an individual's satisfaction, as well as direct productivity benefits in matching the tools to the task and the individual. Preference for private spaces even for routine tasks and the level of satisfaction achieved by this might be more important to productivity than the benefits of social contact provided in less private spaces. A moderately stimulating setting benefits monotonous or dull tasks, while a non-stimulating setting benefits more complex ones.

Realizing that people engage in different activities, and how they do so, and matching the space and facility to the activity, is a critical element of the new workplace. There are reports of improvements in productivity following reorganization that took place with end-user involvement. The organization can maximize the productivity of its personnel through such a choice of settings that allows individuals and teams to select the one most suited to their task-related needs at any given time. Allocated workspace cannot be optimal for all activities, all of the time.

Unconventional working arrangements

One approach to revising space utilization is to abandon designated spaces or workstations in favour of shared arrangements, within schemes such as *hot-desking* and *hotelling*. This is not always the best way to increase the productive use of office space, in spite of the obvious cost savings. More can be achieved by zoning space, so that, for example, special *touchdown* places, accessible to everyone, are set aside for concentrated, group or specialist work. This can offset some of the problems associated with open-plan offices. In order to maximize the productivity benefits of the non-territorial office, the initiative has to be business-driven rather than cost-driven. The former will involve a fundamental rethinking of organizational structure, performance measurement and business processes.

The productivity increases offered by telecommuting and other non-traditional work arrangements can only be maximized if the right sort of space is provided in the office for the times when personnel are working there. If the office cannot offer appropriate support, then productivity gains might be negated. Appropriate support might involve turning the traditional concept of the office inside out. The primary function of the central office space might become support for communication and interaction. Areas for individual, concentrated work would become the support space for the more team-oriented interactive spaces. A system of loosely coupled settings linked physically by the movement of personnel and the electronic exchange of information could maximize productivity in the organization. The need for an integrated workplace strategy to accommodate and support new modes of work is essential.

One large office might appear an efficient option in terms of running costs, but there is evidence that decentralization and the fragmentation of the organization into several smaller centres is beneficial to job satisfaction and organizational well-being. Hindrances to communication include screening, too little space provided at individual workstations so that impromptu group interactions cannot take place there, and little or no other provision for meetings. Designs that actively support teamwork, collaboration and chance interaction might be highly beneficial to productivity within an organization that values such practices.

The above ideas have come together in the total workplace concept, guided by three principles:

1. Breaking down barriers to encourage functional diversity and mixing people who would not normally mix, increasing stimulating and beneficial exposure to differences and diversity.
2. Access to the physical resources necessary for effective work, with environmental equity.
3. Varying the optimal setting for accomplishing work according to variations in an individual's work over time.

The concept also encourages spatial mobility between office locations and increases the potential for chance interactions. Design features that can contribute to this scheme include suitably located activity magnet areas, such as places for breaks designed to create the right kind of behavioural force fields, shared services and information centres to place the individual's contribution in the wider organizational context and promote contributions to organizational thinking and development.

The concept of the total workplace takes a dual approach to effecting productivity: it accommodates the individual to the greatest extent in some respects, while encouraging mobility and interaction through not making every facility as accessible as possible. Other steps could include dedicated project team rooms, saving time spent on assembling and disassembling materials and amenities before and after each meeting. A combination of such spaces with private workstations to accommodate concentrated individual work, plus the clustering of services, might also bring about higher performance from these potentially productive groups.

For insights into a number of innovative strategies for the future of organizations in regard to the workplace, see Alexander *et al.* (2005).

Case study – global consulting and technology business

A global business was faced with the dilemma of increasing demand for space in a major regional centre whilst, at the same time, experiencing a challenging economic environment with reducing business margins. This case study outlines the actions taken by the senior executives to balance these competing issues in order to achieve a successful outcome.

Globaltech employs more than 200 000 people across the world's major economies. Its annual revenue exceeds £10 billion (roughly $16 billion) and it occupies in excess of 8 million square feet (almost 750 000 square metres) of space. Over the past ten years, its revenue has grown and so has its global real estate footprint. Globaltech estimated that within a year its current space provision would be fully utilized despite the adoption of some flexible working arrangements – *hot-desking* was already in place. It had previously tracked its space efficiency by collecting census data on a weekly basis and adjusting it to eliminate seasonal variations. Experience suggested that when occupancy exceeded 85% for any reasonable length of time, it led to levels of discomfort, through increasing noise levels, excess heat and the non-availability of amenities. The business needed to make some fundamental changes to the way in which it occupied its space. Consistent with other major businesses, the revenue-generating functions operated alongside support functions such as finance, legal, human resources, marketing, secretarial and facility management. These support functions were occupiers of substantial space, primarily office-based, and with a majority operating from the same location.

Globaltech had already invested in flexible working initiatives, providing large areas of open-plan space available on a first come, first served basis. This proved effective for the consulting parts of the business that generally spent large periods of the working week at client locations. These areas were also highly serviced, with customer service representatives providing on-floor support and acting as the first line of fault reporting and resolution. Demand for space continued to increase with this flexible working approach, but there was clearly a limit to the availability of space. A further refinement of the rules of space occupation was required.

The allocation of cellular office space had to be reviewed and, ultimately, reduced both in terms of demand and by sacrificing some of this cellular space for more open-plan areas. Globaltech found that increasing the intensity of use across large open-plan areas also required a modification of behaviour. Noise levels naturally increased in these situations and minor irritations such as leaving a mobile phone unattended soon became major issues. Open-plan areas also acted as conduits for food smells. Hot food with strong odours could no longer be eaten at the desk but in café or breakout areas. Consideration for other occupants became paramount. Storage was also a growing issue, where the ratio of personnel to desks was at least 4:1. Drawers and large cabinets gave way to small lockers for all but senior managers.

One of the most significant changes related to the reduction of dedicated offices. Senior managers, who were welcomed into the leadership of this former partnership, were previously awarded an office as a symbol of their promotion. The increasing demand for space meant that these trappings of success could no longer be provided as an automatic right. A strategy had to be developed and agreement reached with the leadership to manage this change. Certain roles required the privacy afforded by cellular offices, whilst at the same time business leaders needed to be seated in close proximity to their teams. The initial step defined areas of the building dedicated to business units or functions known as neighbourhoods. These allowed personnel who worked together to be seated near one another, with a group of cellular offices dedicated to that neighbourhood. The number of offices and the size of the neighbourhood were in direct proportion to the size of the unit or function and the number of senior managers aligned with it. This initial step proved effective, with personnel feeling a sense of belonging from being seated near to their colleagues, with any conflicts in the use of offices escalated to the head of unit. While demand was flat, this strategy proved effective; but what this strategy provided was a level of inflexibility by dedicating the availability of space to each unit. In addition, external recessionary pressures meant that the footprint had to be reduced further.

In an attempt to increase the level of flexibility, the smaller neighbourhoods were disbanded in favour of larger sector-groups. The number of cellular offices was reduced, giving more space to open-plan areas with the criteria for allocating offices becoming more stringent. The informal office allocation agreed amongst the hierarchy of each neighbourhood would no longer be workable. The senior managers agreed the levels at which an office was a right and where they could be used only if available. During this period consultation took place with a broad cross-section of personnel to understand issues in managing space in this new way. One area of difficulty was the reluctance of personnel to use areas that had been personalized. This was considered to be an invasion of an individual's private space. It was felt more acutely in the case of cellular space, but even open-plan desks that had photos and memorabilia attached to screens often stopped personnel from sitting at desks that were unfamiliar. To achieve further flexibility, personnel were required to use the resources available irrespective of the usual occupants. Basically, this meant that these spaces could no longer be personalized.

It was also recognized that simply increasing the available pool of desks would not solve the demand for more space on its own. In parallel, work would be necessary to implement a *homeworking* initiative. This had been trialled previously with personnel who spent a significant proportion of their time travelling and who would welcome spending one or even two days per week working from home. Investment had already been made to provide secure access to ICT systems remotely, with those covered by the trial having been provided with furniture and equipment argued on a case-by-case basis. To implement this wholesale change would require an investment by the business to ensure that the working environment was appropriate and that access to furniture and so on could be assured where required.

Analysis of work patterns had revealed that personnel in consulting generally visited the main offices on a Friday to meet senior managers, to complete administrative duties and to catch up with colleagues. This was also true of Mondays, although to a lesser extent. However, support functions were generally office-based, creating pinch points on these days. The decision was taken to implement a homeworking initiative across support functions for two days per week. This was not mandatory, since business imperatives might require visits to the offices on these days. Nonetheless, the preferred approach was to work from home on Mondays and Fridays. To assist in effective working, the ICT tools currently used for messaging and conference calling were upgraded, allowing screens and documents to be shared. An allowance per head was claimable to offset the increased costs to personnel of using their homes. Furniture was made available from central sources.

At first, this initiative proved popular and effective, especially with young parents who were available at either end of the day for school runs without the need for any long commuting periods. Surveys carried out post-implementation demonstrated a rising level of personnel satisfaction. The demand for space on these days was significantly reduced and, in fact, created areas of underutilized space. This allowed the senior managers to reduce the footprint in line with lease breaks, which had seemed unlikely just 12 months earlier.

The age profile of personnel has supported the homeworking initiative, since a high proportion is below 30 years of age. This age group is relaxed about the lack of dedicated workspace, with privacy low on their list of important attributes. Even so, a significant negative factor was of concern to the youngest age band (up to 25 years of age). Many in this group have difficulty in working away from the office if not based on a client site, because of a lack of their own dedicated work areas within shared houses or apartments. This matter has not proved to be problematic, but remains a consideration as home ownership becomes less affordable in some cities.

Globaltech continues to challenge its space provision and has resisted the need to expand its footprint despite experiencing stronger growth. The support functions now occupy office space two days per week and these are coordinated between functions so that they occupy space on alternate days. Increasing demand from consulting personnel has led to the implementation of a desk booking system. This provides them with a remote view of availability and increases the flexibility of space, with desks booked only when required and not by default.

Inevitably, such a significant change places a greater burden on the physical attributes of the space as well as its amenities. Soft furnishings, carpets and decoration have to be refreshed at shorter intervals. However, savings in rent, business rates and service charges have allowed the business to make the necessary investments in both the standard of its space as well as the implementation of innovative furniture and ICT solutions. In summary, Globaltech has achieved a reduction of 40% of its footprint over a five-year period, despite increasing the number of personnel. It has made some bold decisions in order to maintain its competitiveness, which has increased its reputation as a well-managed and successful business.

Conclusions

Proper understanding of satisfaction and performance of personnel in the office environment requires examination of a complex set of interacting subsystems, including physical environmental factors, job characteristics, organizational factors, sociocultural characteristics and past experience of personnel. More detailed operational definitions of the variables being investigated (such as noise, space, health, privacy, satisfaction and productivity) must be developed. This has not prevented a considerable amount of literature emerging on these topics as the root problem that must be addressed and which becomes ever more urgent, as also does the need to justify investments in the office environment. Improving one aspect, such as the physical setting, while ignoring others, might send conflicting messages. Moreover, the work environment can only operate productively if all aspects are considered as part of an integrated workplace strategy. The high-performance workplace is much talked and written about, but is not widely established. There are so many factors contributing to productivity that proving a cause-and-effect relationship is bound to be problematic. Whilst it remains elusive to be able to predict reliably the returns on investments in a facility, the evidence that a better work environment promotes better performance is more than superficially compelling. The overriding message is therefore to strike the right balance between maximizing communication and space for quiet reflective work; between group, team and project work, and confidential or individual work; and between group areas and individual access to daylight, aspect and ventilation.

Checklist

This checklist is intended to assist with review and action planning.

	Yes	No	Action required
1. Is there an understanding of the relationship between the quality of facility management and workplace productivity?	☐	☐	☐
2. Has there been any formal measurement of productivity in the workplace?	☐	☐	☐
3. Is there awareness of the factors that can lead to dissatisfaction with the workplace?	☐	☐	☐
4. Is the organization continually monitoring the quality of the internal environment?	☐	☐	☐
5. Are concerns voiced by personnel about the work environment taken seriously and are incidents properly investigated?	☐	☐	☐

	Yes	No	Action required
6. Have steps been taken to minimize negative impacts upon the well-being of personnel?	☐	☐	☐
7. Has the organization taken active steps to ensure that conditions leading to sick building syndrome have been eliminated?	☐	☐	☐
8. Is the design of the facility in general sensitive to the needs of personnel?	☐	☐	☐
9. Where steps have previously been taken to minimize negative impacts, were these successful?	☐	☐	☐
10. Has the organization taken steps to maximize the beneficial aspects of the workplace?	☐	☐	☐
11. Has the organization adopted a flexible policy to the workplace, e.g. working hours, off-site locations and non-traditional office layouts?	☐	☐	☐

6 Health, Safety and Security

Key issues

The following issues are covered in this chapter.

- The health, safety and security of personnel should be the concern of all responsible organizations. The inability of a minority of organizations to act responsibly means that legislation is necessary to force minimum standards of behaviour in all.

- Legislation varies from country to country in terms of its enactment, but all share a common set of principles, the most fundamental of which is that it is unacceptable for someone to be injured in the course of their work. Risk of injury cannot be dismissed as simply an occupational hazard.

- Security is now coupled with health and safety. In some sectors, environmental management, environmental sustainability or, simply, environment is included in a broad concept (HSSE) that focuses on the well-being of people, property and the environment.

- Compliance with health and safety legislation applies to everybody in the workplace. It includes shared parts of a facility and the grounds in which the facility is located.

- A competent person must be appointed or act as a consultant to assist in implementing and complying with health and safety legislation, irrespective of whether services are insourced or outsourced.

- A general policy statement must be produced and communicated to all stakeholders. The management method for implementing the policy must likewise be produced and its effectiveness measured. It is important that the statement *speaks to people* and is not, therefore, regarded as a mere *check-box* requirement.

Total Facility Management, Fourth Edition. Brian Atkin and Adrian Brooks.
© 2015 John Wiley & Sons, Ltd. Published 2015 by John Wiley & Sons, Ltd.

- The organization must not only be aware of its responsibilities, but it also needs to ensure that service providers are equally aware and compliant. Policies, detailed safety rules and safe working practices to ensure compliance with legislation must be devised, implemented and reviewed regularly. In the event of a negligent act by a service provider, senior managers can find themselves culpable.

- Not all health and safety issues have a legislative dimension – a growing area of concern is that of stress at work. The courts are sympathetic to the plight of personnel who succumb to stress-related illnesses. More can be done to ensure that, in all respects, the workplace does not make people ill.

Introduction

The workplace is, to a large extent, defined by a large body of legislation designed primarily to protect the health and safety of personnel. Today, concern extends to security and, increasingly, the environment. The combined subject (HSSE) is extensive and warrants separate consideration of the environment (see Chapter 13). The focus of this chapter is, therefore, health, safety and security, which should be viewed as an integral component of facility management and not as a separate function or, worse, as an adjunct to it. The onus is on the organization – irrespective of type or size – to comply with legislation for the protection of personnel in general. Where services are outsourced, the organization cannot escape responsibility, even if it believes that some legislation might not apply directly to it. Steps must be taken to ensure full compliance. Far from being a minefield – a word sometimes used alongside *begrudging acceptance* – health and safety legislation can be used positively to help define better working arrangements, including those covering facility management. Looked at from this perspective, it is likely to be easier to comply with the requirements than attempt to work around them. Organizations are socially, as well as legally, accountable for their actions and this now extends beyond those of an employer into a wider role in local communities (see Chapter 13). In a practical sense, the facility manager is likely to become a key figure in translating the intentions of the legislation into policies and procedures. This chapter discusses issues that can help the organization ensure that it provides a safe and healthy facility for end-users. It outlines the general nature of legislation and describes the characteristics of a well-managed health and safety regime. Even so, it should not be regarded as a guide to health and safety legislation, as requirements vary from country to country. For this reason, the organization should verify the extent to which legislation applies to it. In all cases, however, an initial review should be undertaken to provide information on the appropriateness, efficiency and effectiveness of existing health and safety management systems. Where no formal, or a minimal, health and safety management system exists (such as when the organization is newly established or when carrying out new activities), the initial review should be used as a base from which to develop a new system.

Health, safety and security policy

The organization must have a general policy on health and safety and this should extend to matters of security. The requirements of this policy are to:

- Provide and maintain, as far as is practicable, a safe, healthy and secure place.
- Take responsibility for compliance with relevant legislation.

The organization needs to be aware that its responsibilities for health, safety and security extend beyond its personnel to the extent that no activity should pose risks to visitors or persons outside the facility. The organization has responsibility for anyone who might be affected by the action of an individual and so the organization's policy statement and risk assessments must reflect this. It is necessary to appoint a person who can be judged to be competent in implementing health and safety legislation and ensuring that the organization complies with it. The organization must therefore have access to a *competent person* (who could be an individual, service provider or managing agent) and must ensure that he or she has adequate training, time and resources to discharge his or her duties under legislation.

It is necessary to identify responsibilities as imposed by legislation at all levels of supervision and management, and not just for those personnel who are directly involved in the day-to-day management of the facility; for example, the purchasing manager and senior managers have roles to play. Care should be taken to apportion responsibility in line with authority, with resources to cover the administrative procedures for dealing with accidents and contingency plans for handling power cuts, bomb alerts, flood and fire. Safety representatives from end-user groups should always be involved.

Regulations limiting the number of hours that personnel can work exist in many countries and are not without criticism. They have proven particularly contentious amongst some organizations and their personnel, but arguably more so in the case of service providers, where greater flexibility in workplace practices is the norm. It is important, therefore, for the organization to check the current situation before offering contracts of employment or renewing existing arrangements. Where services are outsourced, the organization needs to ensure that service providers do not contravene any regulations. If they do, the organization might find itself culpable.

There is also the matter of a minimum or living wage, which is particularly pertinent in the case of work or services that do not demand high levels of skill, as might be the case in general cleaning and porterage. The organization needs to be aware of applicable legislation and any impending changes as might apply to the in-house team or to service providers under contract to it. Regulations aside, the organization cannot turn a blind eye to what it might suspect to be personnel abuses of any kind. Apart from the illegality of what might be happening, there is also the issue of morality, and the health and safety of others who might be affected by malpractice.

Zero accidents

Once, it was acceptable to talk about reducing accidents to a minimum. Nowadays, it is unacceptable and, instead, organizations should be committed to the goal of zero accidents. There are two underlying principles: the first concerns reducing accidents and is largely a matter of trying harder all round, but recognizing that accidents will happen – albeit, hopefully, at a lower rate and with less severity. The second principle is that work should be designed so there are no accidents, by focusing on how work can be performed in a way that is safe and without risk to personnel and property. It is mostly a matter of doing things differently. As one might expect, it demands close attention to how work is undertaken, in its setting, and relies heavily on risk assessment and the continual updating of performance and progress (see the later section on Hazard and risk assessment). Put another way, the aim is to design-out anything that could threaten personal health and safety.

The concept of zero accidents should be properly communicated as an ongoing safety performance expectation for all personnel, including those of service providers. A significant change in the safety attitude of personnel will come from the goal of zero accidents, as everyone realizes that it is no longer acceptable to take chances or shortcuts.

Occupational health and safety

Occupational health is a blanket term that encompasses a variety of issues. It can include minor injuries, such as a cut finger, and can be as severe as a long-term back problem caused by lifting heavy objects. Musculoskeletal disorders top the list of the most common health risks, with one quarter of all incidents believed to be of a musculoskeletal nature. Of those incidents, around one third are for a period of more than three days and contribute significantly to an absence from work of those who suffer from this complaint. It is important to deal with any problem without delay. Damage in the short term can worsen and become potentially disabling if the individual persists with doing a similar task.

A phenomenon called hand–arm vibration syndrome (HAVS), a form of Raynaud's Disease, is a fairly common health disorder. This condition is usually brought on by the use of power tools such as hammer drills. When hands are exposed to vibrating equipment, the individual's blood circulation is affected. Vibration white finger results and is so-called because the fingertips turn white and numb when cold and wet. When circulation does return, the hand will be red and painful. Longer-term damage can result and the whole finger can be affected if there is continual exposure to vibration.

The hazard that continues to top the list of most common health risks is the killer substance, asbestos. Exposure is particularly prominent during the removal of the substance when refurbishing facilities and demolishing structures. Asbestos-related lung cancer is likely to continue as a major health disorder because of the vast quantity of asbestos still present in facilities of one kind or another. Asbestos was used extensively from the 1950s until the mid-1980s. For organizations with even the suspicion of asbestos in their facilities, specialist advice should be sought as a priority, with a view to its removal at the earliest opportunity. In this connection, the organization should be prepared for a costly process, in which any thought of shortcuts should be banished.

Compliance

The organization will need to assess the risks to the health and safety of personnel and anyone else affected by the activities of the organization (e.g. personnel, external customers, other visitors and the general public) and will need to devise means for implementing preventive and protective measures, including arrangements for disabled people and others with equalities-related needs. Assessment should cover planning, organization, control, monitoring and reviews. There is a close link between risk assessment and arrangements specified in the health and safety policy statement.

With a policy and a management system in place, the organization needs to monitor and review arrangements to achieve progressive improvement in health and safety. Improvement is enhanced through the development of policies, approaches to implementation and techniques of risk assessment that place the interests of personnel at the fore. The following checklists should help the organization to monitor its adherence to, and progress against, health and safety legislation. Note that these are minimal requirements and, in all cases, it is advisable to seek specialist advice to confirm the requirements.

Organizational

- Are policy, management and organization, safety rules and procedures in place?
- Are these details available to all personnel?
- Have arrangements been made for consultation with personnel and other end-user groups?

Noticeboards

- Is the health and safety policy clearly displayed?
- Is the health and safety legislation poster displayed, where required by law?
- Is an employer's liability insurance certificate displayed, where required by law?
- Are the names of trained first-aid personnel displayed?
- Are emergency procedures displayed?

Accident reporting

- Is an accident book held in the facility?
- Are personnel aware of the location of the accident book?
- Are accident report forms held?
- Is information for occupants and other users of the facility available about how to behave and deal with any perceived threats to health and safety?

Training

- Have all personnel with health and safety responsibilities received specific health and safety training?
- Have all personnel attended a general health and safety awareness course?
- Are records maintained of training undertaken?
- Are there personnel who have received specialist training; for example, occupational health and safety?

First aid

- How many first-aid personnel are there and how are they spread throughout the facility?
- Is a current list of first-aid personnel and their locations displayed on each noticeboard?
- Does each first-aider have an adequate first-aid box?
- Who keeps top-up supplies for first-aid boxes?
- Who is responsible for inspecting all first-aid boxes for their contents, visibility and availability?
- Who organizes first-aid training?
- Who provides first-aid training?
- Are records of first-aid training adequate and up to date?
- Are treatment record sheets available by each first-aid box or located with the accident book?

Fire precautions

- Has a fire risk assessment been undertaken?
- Is there a fire certificate, where required by law?
- Who has delegated responsibility for fire precautions?
- How often are evacuation drills conducted?
- Are full records of these drills kept, including clearance times?
- How often are fire alarms tested and are full records of these tests maintained?
- How often are smoke and heat detectors tested?
- Are the above practices in accordance with manufacturers' recommendations or the fire certificate?
- Are full records of tests maintained?
- How often are fixed hose-reel and sprinkler systems, if applicable, tested?
- Are full records of these tests maintained?
- Do the drills and tests comply with the conditions of the fire certificate?
- Are records kept of visits from the fire authority?
- Is there a service contract for the maintenance of fire extinguishers and other fire control equipment?
- Are there adequate fire extinguishers of the correct type?
- Is there at least one fire warden for each level in the facility?
- What training, practice or regular meetings are arranged for fire wardens?
- How often is the facility inspected in relation to fire precautions?
- Is there a procedure for notifying the fire authority of alterations to the facility?

Statutory risk assessments

- Have assessments been carried out for all display screen equipment workstations?
- Is there a valid risk assessment for the facility?
- Have all hazardous substances been assessed under relevant legislation?
- Have any other assessments been carried out; for example, lifting of loads and personal protective equipment (PPE)? On this point, see below.
- Are the control measures specified in the risk assessments being observed?

Inspections and audits

- How often does the facility manager or other person with delegated responsibility inspect the facility for physical hazards?
- When was the last inspection carried out?
- When was the last audit of procedures carried out and by whom?

Work equipment

- Who is responsible for arranging annual lift/elevator inspections, where applicable?
- Are the facility's electrical installation and all portable electrical appliances and equipment tested by a competent person, as required by regulations, with the results of those tests and any necessary remedial action properly recorded?
- Are there procedures for inspecting and maintaining all work equipment?
- Is the use of potentially dangerous work equipment restricted to authorized persons and are those persons properly trained?

Personal protective equipment (PPE)

- Have assessments been carried out to determine the requirements of personnel?
- Have records of these assessments been kept?
- Is all necessary PPE available?
- Are records kept of PPE issued?
- Have personnel been trained in the use and maintenance requirements of PPE, if applicable?
- Has adequate storage for PPE been provided?

Off-site

- Have risks associated with visiting other sites or working outside been assessed?
- Is a procedure for lone working defined and in use?
- Are personnel aware of these procedures and have they been trained in them?

Service providers

- Are service providers used for window cleaning, maintenance, electrical instal-lation and so on?
- Is there an on-site policy document that all service providers must read and then sign as evidence of their awareness of their duties and obligations?
- Do service providers carrying out work in the facility complete a health and safety questionnaire before they are engaged?
- Who vets these questionnaires and on what basis is it decided that a service provider is competent to carry out the work?
- What information is given to service providers on emergency procedures, safety rules and access?
- Who is responsible for ensuring compliance with legislation applying to construction operations?

Notices

- Are all necessary compliance and safety signs in place?

Hazard and risk assessment

The organization should assess risks and other hazards at all stages in a facility's life cycle. Identified risks should be monitored and, wherever possible, their potential impacts should be mitigated. The organization should implement a formal system of risk and opportunity management, including establishing and maintaining a risk and opportunity register. Periodic reassessment of risks should be undertaken to update the register and associated risk treatment.

The organization should implement risk control, as an integral part of its risk and opportunity management, to ensure that control measures remain in place and that they remain efficient and effective. The risk and opportunity manage-ment system should cover the following, as a minimum:

- Identification of health and safety hazards arising from maintenance and other work determined by workplace inspections, behavioural observations, safety tours, and formal and informal discussions with personnel.
- Identification of people who might be at risk from maintenance and other work; for example, maintenance operatives, occupants, visitors, passers-by and trespassers.
- Evaluation of the risks to which individuals and/or the organization might be exposed.
- Devising ways of eliminating, reducing and controlling risks; for example, guarding and fencing, method statements, *safe system of work, permit-to-work*, training and supervision.
- Monitoring and recording the effectiveness of risk control measures and systems; for example, inspections, observations, safety tours and checklists.
- Taking coordinated corrective action.
- Providing feedback to personnel and other stakeholders.

- Training, together with health and safety checks, of operatives.
- Auditing and reviewing the system and, therefore, health and safety performance.

The use of access equipment should be assessed to maximize the benefits of its use and to optimize the overall cost of maintenance. Assessment should take into account future requirements for access as would arise under multi-year maintenance plans. The longer-term implications of providing access, particularly the equipment required for this purpose, should be evaluated and permanent means of access should be used wherever possible. In doing so, the risk of operatives taking shortcuts – for instance, making do without adequate access equipment because of the time it takes to erect and dismantle – is avoided. A related issue concerns the planning and scheduling of maintenance work, where sufficient time needs to be allocated for operatives and their supervisors. Realistic schedules are believed to be associated with a lower probability of supervisors being injured (Hon *et al.*, 2014). For a detailed treatment of maintenance management, see Chapter 12.

Security and well-being

Protection of users

The protection of individuals in the workplace has become a common theme within health and safety regimes. In a growing number of organizations, health and safety has already been broadened to incorporate explicit recognition of, and requirements for, the security and well-being of end-users. For some facilities – for example, custodial and other secure environments – protection of personnel is clearly a given. The reality is, however, that all organizations have to take steps to safeguard individual security in the face of threats from known and unknown sources. No facility is insusceptible to potential threat, and so the organization should ensure that it has carefully examined the need for access rights and clearance for each category of occupant and other end-user. Rights and clearance must extend to service providers. In such cases, the organization should make expressly clear any condition concerning prior vetting or clearance of personnel or other matters requiring investigation and, where relevant, involve official bodies, agencies or other authorities.

Stress

Whilst an organization might want to strive for more from fewer personnel, the reality is that people are capable of giving only so much before serious (and sometimes irreversible) damage sets in. At best, this limits organizational effectiveness; at worst, it can lead to conflict, sickness and even litigation. In fact, there is strong evidence to link *organizational ill health* with absences, high turnover and low productivity of personnel. Moreover, stress, which can be directly related to job and organizational problems, is thought responsible for 60–80% of all workplace accidents. Work-related stress is now a common reason for absenteeism. The collective cost of stress to organizations in terms of absenteeism, reduced productivity, potential compensation claims and so on is enormous. Stress-related absences are ten times more costly than all other industrial relations disputes put together. Factors within the workplace causing stress include the following:

- *Unsatisfactory working conditions* – poor-quality internal environment (air quality, light/daylight and temperature), physical location or individual posture.
- *Mental and physical overload from excessive work-related demands* – long working hours, lack of breaks, working weekends and curtailed or cancelled holidays.
- *Role ambiguity and inconsistency in management style* – senior managers who lack leadership skills and whose actions result in confusion and discord.
- *Responsibility for other personnel* – assuming a position for which one is ill-equipped or unsuited.
- *Unsatisfactory working and personal relationships* – conflict or tensions between individuals or groups.
- *Under-promotion or over-promotion* – failing to reward or, conversely, moving personnel to new positions where they are unable to cope.
- *Poor organizational structure/culture* – ineptitude in managing the social infra-structure to the extent that personnel become disillusioned, downbeat and distrustful.

Matters are likely to get worse as reorganizations, relocations of personnel, redesign of jobs and reallocations of roles and responsibilities make changes to the normal way of doing business.

The hidden costs of stress caused by not adequately creating an environment that enhances the well-being of personnel are manifest in a lack of added value to the organization's core business and the costs of rectifying underperformance. Studies of work stress have tended to concentrate upon ways in which the individual can cope with or adapt to stress. Instead, effort should concentrate on how the work environment can alleviate stress. The effort of coping with stress absorbs energy that could otherwise be invested in more productive and satisfying work activities. Williams (2002) discusses the effects of stress on performance and productivity and how to recognize it, manage it and prevent it.

An understandable preoccupation of many facility managers is how to measure performance, especially in an office environment where production line principles do not apply. This might appear to be a legitimate goal and is one area where the use of ICT has led to electronic monitoring (see Chapter 10). This has the capacity to provide fairer compensation for performance through more accurate and timely feedback. The links between performance and reward are such that this should be beneficial to productivity. In terms of stress and health problems, the negative effects of such monitoring can, however, mean a decline in productivity. The stress that stems from performance measurement and monitoring would seem to be associated with lack of control, loss of trust and an increased administrative work-load involved in operating such procedures. Placing emphasis on monitoring the performance of personnel closely can therefore create more problems than it solves.

One workers' union has been reported as dealing with 7000 stress-related claims at one time. Some organizations might approach the management of their personnel by transferring people to more challenging jobs. That view might not, however, be shared by those affected. Moreover, it might bring them into a working environment that damages their health, forcing them into premature retirement and a poor quality of life. Today, courts are more likely than ever to take a sympathetic view of an individual whose quality of life has been ruined by an inconsiderate or unprincipled employer. Awards cover loss of future earnings and the cost of medical treatment.

Conclusions

Providing a safe, healthy and secure place of work for occupants and other users is more than a matter of compliance with legislation; it is a fundamental right for anyone. Health, safety and security cover many common-sense requirements that are generally defined within the law and so ought to be familiar to competent practitioners. Even so, new legislation continues to appear, raising the bar on what the organization must do to safeguard personnel and other end-users. The rights of personnel, in particular, can extend into areas affecting working hours, minimum wages and all-inclusiveness. The potential risk of incident or injury is ever-present and the organization would do well to anticipate the possible events that could give rise to accidents occurring in or around its facility. Hazard and risk assessment provide the means by which the threat to occupants and other users can be minimized. Even so, the only direction of travel for the organization is to have zero accidents as its goal. Adopting this action requires that work is redesigned so that the only job is a safe job. For the organization, there is the additional requirement to ensure that where outsourcing has taken place (or is about to), service providers are not in breach of health and safety legislation. As important is the need to avoid arrangements that become divisive and counterproductive. A further area of concern is the now recognized and growing incidence of stress, which is classed as a major industrial disease. Facility managers should be alert to hidden dangers in the workplace. Guidance in this and other important areas of health and safety cannot be exhaustive and so the organization must take its own steps to ensure compliance. The organization should ensure that it complies with the relevant requirements by seeking specialist advice.

Checklist

This checklist is intended to assist with review and action planning.

	Yes	No	Action required
1. Are the organization and its service providers, where applicable, aware of legislation relating to health and safety?	☐	☐	☐
2. Has the organization elevated individual security to the same level of importance as health and safety?	☐	☐	☐

	Yes	No	Action required
3. Is the organization's health, safety and security policy statement easily accessible to all occupants and other users?	☐	☐	☐
4. Has the principle of zero accidents been accepted and is it reflected in the health, safety and security policy statement?	☐	☐	☐
5. Has a competent person been appointed for the purpose of health and safety compliance and implementation?	☐	☐	☐
6. Have the requirements for implementing a health and safety regime been identified and arrangements made for its management?	☐	☐	☐
7. Have responsibilities for health, safety and security matters been allocated?	☐	☐	☐
8. Has a proper assessment of the risks to health and safety for occupants and other end-users been completed?	☐	☐	☐
9. Have the means for implementing appropriate measures been devised?	☐	☐	☐
10. Is the organization compliant in all respects and can that be easily demonstrated?	☐	☐	☐
11. Is the facility able to accommodate disabled people and others with equalities-related needs?	☐	☐	☐
12. Is the organization aware of the factors that can lead to stress-related illnesses and has it taken steps to eliminate them?	☐	☐	☐

7 The Outsourcing Decision

Key issues

The following issues are covered in this chapter.

- Outsourcing should be the outcome of a decision that has weighed the options for service delivery available to the organization against predefined criteria, with the high probability of achieving end-user satisfaction from a best value solution.

- Stakeholders must be involved from the outset in specifying the kinds of services required and the level of performance that will be acceptable to them.

- Markets for services have to be understood ahead of determining the options for service delivery so that the practicability of a recommended outcome is assured.

- There are several options for service delivery, each of which has its strengths and weaknesses, and these include *managing agent, managing contractor, managed budget* and *total facility management*. The most appropriate option needs to be selected objectively as part of a transparent evaluation involving key stakeholders.

- The organization should identify the key attributes of service provision – both *hard* and *soft* measures – so that a balanced view of needs is established as the basis for evaluating the options for service delivery. The importance or weight given to attributes should reflect requirements embodied in the facility management strategy.

- The degree of flexibility of service delivery desired by the organization will vary with each option and has to be taken into account during evaluation.

Total Facility Management, Fourth Edition. Brian Atkin and Adrian Brooks.
© 2015 John Wiley & Sons, Ltd. Published 2015 by John Wiley & Sons, Ltd.

- Consideration must be given to direct and indirect costs of outsourced service delivery so that a complete financial picture is gained, with comparison of the options made on a like-for-like basis to enable the most appropriate decision to be reached.

- The employment of a *total facility management* service provider – effectively a single point of responsibility – whilst attractive, will not relieve the organization from managing the contract and the interface between the service provider and end-users.

- Novel solutions have entered the marketplace and include fully serviced workspaces of a temporary or long-term nature.

- Since the factors affecting a decision to outsource can change, so the current arrangement for outsourcing might also have to change. Options for service delivery should be re-evaluated against the attributes of service provision at appropriate intervals and should involve market testing.

Introduction

The question of whether or not to outsource services should be answered by a decision that weighs the available options against predefined criteria to indicate the most appropriate solution. A number of options for service delivery are available and each has to be considered carefully if the route that leads to best value is to be followed. It is not simply a matter of outsourcing over insourcing. The choice between outsourced and insourced service delivery is not always clear-cut, which is why there has to be a thorough examination of requirements. If the procedure advocated in Chapter 3 has been followed, the organization will have not prejudged the situation; instead, it will have operated within the limits of its facility management strategy. Nonetheless, it is important to confirm that the organization has assembled sufficient information to establish a firm basis (or baseline) for expressing its needs unambiguously. The next step is to consider the attributes of each service that are regarded as important and the options for service delivery that might best satisfy them. Realism has to prevail, so attributes should be stated in terms that are within range and not over-demanding of service providers to the extent that they are unlikely ever to be fulfilled. Some of the attributes will seem obvious; others will be less so. The issue of cost is bound to be a prominent factor for many organizations; it might have been the primary motivation for considering outsourcing. Finally in this chapter, the organization is presented with the means by which it is able to determine the most appropriate option for service delivery. This step has implications for quality of service, in terms of end-user experience, and cost. Whichever option is adopted, it has to be practicable and affordable. However, it is not a *once and for all time* decision; but one that has to be revisited periodically as conditions change in the market. In arriving at a recommended basis for service delivery, the organization has, in effect, defined its procurement strategy. Important guidance is available within standards in this regard. In particular, the provisions of BS 8572, some of which are reflected in this chapter, cover aspects of outsourcing. The process and procedures for procuring services, including tendering, are covered in Chapter 8.

Establishing the baseline

The question of whether or not to outsource should be based on the best possible information available to the organization at the time a decision has to be made. If this information is sufficient for understanding needs, then later comparison between options for service delivery can be made on an unbiased basis. Outsourcing should not drive decision-making, but should be driven by it. A well-defined baseline for service delivery also supports later comparison between planned and actual performance, enabling the organization to judge the efficacy of its decision-making.

An important starting point is for the organization to adopt a realistic stance in regard to its requirements. It should differentiate between services that are absolutely necessary and those that are desirable or that might, for example, be justifiable or affordable at a later date. For example, a situation could arise where lunchtime catering would be ideally satisfied by a restaurant, but which would require refurbishment of existing space that is either not possible at present or unaffordable from within current budgets. Consideration should therefore be given to any phasing or deferral until a later date when the full scope of a particular service could be delivered. The latter circumstance can also arise where the end-users of services are external customers of the organization and where, for example, present demand or means does not justify roll-out of additional services. A facility can be acquired or built to anticipate future demand for business processes and activities and/or the services to be provided to external customers. As such, these considerations would form part of the organization's sustainable space provision.

The following matters should be considered when defining the baseline for service delivery as part of a decision on whether or not to outsource:

- relationship to business objectives;
- drivers and constraints;
- portfolio and sustainable space provision;
- risks and opportunities;
- stakeholder engagement and communication;
- end-user requirements;
- scope of services and supplies;
- attributes of service provision;
- options for service delivery;
- current arrangement(s) for service delivery; and
- markets for services.

Relationship to business objectives

As a support service to the core business of the organization, facility management has a key role to play in the achievement of its business objectives. A statement on the business objectives and operations, including planned expansion, run-down or closure, should be to hand. The statement should differentiate between core and non-core business. In the case of closure, it is important to provide details on the nature of this decision; that is, the conversion, mothballing or disposal of the facility. Ordinarily, an organization sets targets (or goals) that have to be met, irrespective of whether it is *for-profit* or not. These should be included in the statement, together with key milestones and details that will help to outline the procurement process – see later sections. Milestones, in particular, help in understanding progress towards achieving critical success factors that have been set for the organization in general and its business processes and activities in particular, including facility management.

Where services are procured independently of the facility management function, there is the risk of compromising those objectives. Alignment between the objectives implicit in the delivery of services – an operational matter – and the organization's business objectives is essential to ensuring that the facility supports the core business and that there is no loss of efficiency. The contribution that the facility is expected to make to the success of the organization, in meeting its business objectives, has therefore to be made explicit if informed decisions are to be made and appropriate arrangements are to follow.

Drivers and constraints

The importance of understanding the factors driving or constraining the current and likely future business of the organization has been discussed in Chapter 3. These factors represent external and internal impacts on the business and should be understood before embarking upon the decision of whether or not to outsource. Some drivers and/or constraints will impact more than others at particular points in procurement (see Chapter 8). Internal drivers and/or constraints include personnel, work and information; whereas external drivers and/or constraints include the availability of resources, competition for goods and services, finance and credit. From a control perspective, it is unlikely that the organization can influence external drivers and so should concentrate on those that are controllable, namely the internal drivers, whilst maintaining a watchful eye on those externally. Occasionally, conditions change, enabling some influence to be exerted to the advantage of the organization. Of the many forces acting upon the organization, an increasing number are likely from innovations in technology and changes in society. The organization should be aware of the extent to which these and other factors can impact its core business, operations and support services.

Risks and opportunities

Many factors and events can have a potentially negative or positive impact on the delivery of services. They should therefore be identified, assessed and treated as part of a broader process of risk and opportunity management; moreover, they should have been considered when preparing the facility management strategy. In the case of negative impacts (i.e. downside risks), the organization should establish criteria for judging whether or not they might be classified as significant. Opportunities (i.e. upside risks) that have the potential to improve end-user satisfaction and achieve better value should be subject to their own criteria for determining their worth. All risks – downside and upside – should be recorded in a risk and opportunity register and kept up to date, because the nature and potential impact of risks can change over time.

A serious attempt to identify risks is likely to produce a large number of items in a short time. Risk is embedded in commercial undertakings and it can prove impractical to assess and evaluate all but those that are deemed significant in the time available. The prior establishment of criteria for judging whether or not a risk might be classified as significant can expedite assessment of impact in terms of health, safety, priority, cost, time, performance, productivity, reputation or other factor that is considered important. Some quantification of cost and time impacts is desirable. A service contract is based on a certain amount of risk-taking by the service provider and the organization. Unbalanced risk allocation between the parties, or an attempt by one party to hold a risk that it is ill-equipped to handle, can increase costs needlessly. Understanding which party is best able to handle a particular risk is required. An approach to risk assessment is outlined later in this chapter.

Questionnaires and checklists can be useful tools for identifying potential risks in regard to the delivery of services. A first screening or preliminary assessment can then be made of the probability and consequences of such risks – a qualitative assessment – to determine which might be classified as significant. The evaluation of significant risks – a quantitative analysis – can then take place and appropriate contingency included in budgets and schedules (see Chapter 14).

Stakeholders as qualified end-users

A recurrent theme in this book is that of stakeholders – for a comprehensive discussion on stakeholder identification, classification and impacts, see Chapter 2. In this and later sections and chapters, we shall see how the organization's need to engage with stakeholders should function in practice, not least in the framing of service specifications and service level agreements (SLAs). A key stakeholder group is end-users, who are clearly qualified to specify their needs and the level of performance that will be acceptable to them. The steps involved include the following:

1. Engaging with stakeholders, as far as practicable, to define and detail their needs through, for example, the use of questionnaire surveys and by reviewing service specifications and SLAs.
2. Recognizing diversity in stakeholder needs such as those of disabled people and others with equalities-related needs and then making appropriate allowance for them.
3. Prioritization by stakeholders of their needs.
4. Controlling stakeholder input and changes once the service specification has been agreed to avoid scope creep.

The organization might find that it is defining and detailing its requirements for the first time. In such cases, there is a risk that it unknowingly specifies a higher level of service than is necessary and that, consequently, tender sums might turn out to be higher than forecast. Value management, a technique for ensuring that real needs are addressed, can be used to guard against over-specification, whilst allowing standards to be raised over time. This is a broad philosophy, as opposed to a prescriptive means, for identifying and eliminating excess cost. The organization should consider adopting value management principles on a strategic level and then apply value engineering principles to eliminate elements and attributes of service provision that add cost, but no value. There is ample literature on the inter-related subjects of value management and value engineering – see, for example, Kelly *et al.* (2004). The use of value engineering workshops is generally advocated in the literature and is widely undertaken. What is important is the discipline of questioning the need for, and assumptions embodied in, all attributes of service provision and ensuring that only those adding value, or required to support those that add value, are included. In these ways, stakeholders' interests should be correctly incorporated into service specifications and SLAs. It will be necessary, however, to recognize and avoid attempts by senior managers (or others) to use value engineering as nothing more than a cost-cutting exercise. Failure to do so discredits a perfectly honest attempt to eliminate excess cost.

Stakeholders should therefore be involved in discussion about the arrangements for facility management in general and services in particular to an extent determined by the outcome of a stakeholder impact assessment. Stakeholders should be involved in specifying services if their needs, including those identified during the preparation of the facility management strategy and relating to end-users, are to be properly addressed and communicated (see Chapter 2).

Effective communication between the organization and service providers (another stakeholder group) should be maintained to enable the implementation of a strategy (in the sense of a broad approach to procurement) that is both understood and capable of being acted upon. Clear and regular communication is required to develop relationships. In those cases where the organization has a concern about its ability to deal with myriad stakeholder interests, the appointment of a managing agent or other consultant should be considered. If it is found necessary, then it should be done in sufficient time to allow consultation with stakeholders to take place.

The operation of a facility can affect a variety of interests. Various positive effects include creating better communications, a healthier and safer workplace and higher standards of productivity. Even so, a new or refurbished facility brings change at the operational level affecting end-user interests. Stakeholders, as the representatives of these interests, are an integral part of the process of consultation. Early involvement of all affected stakeholders is necessary to enable views and concerns to be actively canvassed and adequately taken into account.

Since contracts for services involve delivery within occupied environments, the way in which services are delivered and the manner in which stakeholder communication occurs becomes increasingly important as the services embed themselves into day-to-day operations. Maintaining a clear understanding between the organization, end-users and the in-house team and/or service providers of operational requirements, as well as the obligations of each stakeholder group, is a continual process of engagement through communication.

As a key stakeholder group, the end-users of services are in a unique position to be able to provide feedback and make judgements on the extent to which services satisfy or are likely to satisfy needs. They might not, however, be in the best position to know if the organization is achieving best value in the procurement of services. Even so, end-users can offer insights into how service delivery might be performed differently, better and at possibly lower cost.

Questionnaires can be effective tools for eliciting information from stakeholders. Care needs to be exercised when drafting questionnaires to enable respondents to provide information that the organization requires in order to form an appropriate level of understanding of needs as opposed to answers that might be of superficial interest only. Questions that are disingenuous are normally easily detected by respondents. Closed questions that result in simply *yes* or *no* are unlikely to probe deeply enough. On the other hand, questions that require a response to a statement against a scale from, for example, *totally agree* to *totally disagree* can lead to a more robust understanding of needs. Questionnaires that seek opinions and attitudes are therefore preferable to those that attempt to quantify responses. A word of advice is, however, necessary. Too often, questionnaires are put together hastily; they are neither tested nor piloted with a sample of the group to which they will be addressed. In the worst cases, it is a complete waste of everyone's time. If a questionnaire-based survey is worth doing, then it is worth doing properly and should always be drafted from the perspective of those who have to understand what they are being asked.

Prioritization of stakeholders' needs helps to focus on attributes of service provision that are of particular importance. The organization might find it necessary to reconcile different or competing priorities in the interests of economy and practicability. It can do so on the basis of reliable questionnaire responses.

Scope of services

The extent of services and, for that matter, supplies needed by the organization should be outlined, with each service and supply separately identified. The expectations of the facility's end-users and other stakeholders should be summarized for each service and supply. Both should be defined and delimited so that it is absolutely clear *what is included where*. For example, are pest control, waste disposal and sanitary services to be part of the cleaning contract, is there to be separate provision or are any of them combined with another service? Such attention to detail is essential to ensure that all necessary services are provided and that no gaps exist between them that could expose the organization and the facility's end-users to unnecessary hazard or risk. Doing so will help avoid argument later when a service provider's interpretation of the scope differs from expectation. At the same time, the ever-present threat of change might be better controlled and scope creep avoided by having unequivocal scope definitions. The problem of scope creep is best explained by small, incremental changes that, at the time, seem easy to accept. The trouble is that they accumulate over time so that, ultimately, they represent a significant change in scope for which there is no mandate. An oft-quoted expression is 'death by a thousand cuts'.

An all-encompassing statement or expression of needs representing the entire scope of services to be provided should be produced. It should include a definition of the scope of each service, together with its relationship with other services, including shared responsibilities and contingency planning, as well as explicit mention of assumptions and exclusions. The organization's facility management strategy should be used as a continual reminder of the context within which needs and expectations are expressed.

The definition of the scope of a service is almost always bound to resolve to some form of description. Ensuring that each description is coherent and self-contained as far as necessary is paramount. Drafting should be undertaken once a clear understanding of the content of the scope of service has been reached. One way of capturing the content is to use a mapping (or mind mapping) tool. The advantages of creating a map include the ability to pinpoint gaps and overlaps between services, as well as the relationships between them. A challenge in this task is in delimiting services so that they can be defined individually and collectively, as would occur when several services are to be bundled.

Sourcing policy

The organization has to decide on the extent to which, if at all, services are to be provided from within the organization (i.e. insourced) or procured from external service providers (i.e. outsourced). Where co-sourcing is preferred, account should be taken of the need to integrate the two sources of service delivery and the resources and costs that are involved in its management. Due consideration will have to be given to the interfaces between individual services, including any that are insourced, so that end-users experience seamless delivery. Put simply, end-users should not have to think about who is delivering the service, but should be entirely satisfied with the experience they are receiving. In some organizations, policy might be to have all services delivered on the same basis; that is, all outsourced or all insourced. It can mean, therefore, that what appears to be the best option or balance of options might not match the corporate view.

Since conditions within an organization change as do those outside, a review of outsourcing in terms of satisfying current and future needs should take place. Normally, the decision to outsource should be revisited not less than every three years. A longer period might be appropriate depending on the extent to which internal and external conditions impacting the outsourcing decision might have changed in the interim. The performance of service providers should be reviewed annually rather than the decision to outsource. Once the decision to outsource has been taken, it should not be subject to continual review since this will create uncertainty, demotivate personnel and consume resources and cost that would be better spent elsewhere.

Offshoring

Outsourcing and offshoring of services are generally seen as ways of extracting cost savings from operations. In terms of facility management, outsourcing should require no further elaboration here. Offshoring, on the other hand, does need to be explained. The principal question is one of how far the practice of outsourcing can go. The golden rule is that you do not outsource your core competence or move it abroad, just your capacity to perform work necessary to support the core business. The trouble with this view is that it stems from a time when it was easy to think in terms of a clear split between core and non-core business, where the former was sacrosanct and the latter could be sacrificed to the outside. This simple view is no longer valid for many firms as they actively question their definition of core business. Furthermore, the pursuit of new business opportunities challenges traditional assumptions to the extent that support services have become inter-twined with business processes and activities. Attempting to differentiate between them might prove extremely difficult and possibly counterproductive.

Statutory and other regulatory considerations

On a cautionary note, it is essential that the organization recognizes that the engagement of service providers does not absolve it of certain obligations and requirements. Matters demanding careful consideration include those relating to health, safety, security, environment, employment rights and public procurement. If in doubt, the organization should seek specialist advice. Whilst the *law* is the *law*, attention should also be given to national and international standards, indus-try standards and manufacturers' recommendations when determining relevant attributes of service provision and options for service delivery.

Attributes of service provision

It is necessary to identify attributes of service provision that are important in each defined service area to establish a basis for evaluating the suitability of options for service delivery. These attributes are therefore the criteria by which the various options should be evaluated. Criteria based on attributes of service provision that matter most to the organization and end-users help to focus on the option(s) or arrangement most likely to offer a best value solution that satisfies needs. They should be determined before discussing options for service delivery; otherwise, there is the possibility that the choice of criteria is influenced by the extent to which a given option might satisfy those criteria. The correct sequence is to understand *what is required, how it might be delivered* and then *what is appropriate*.

The attributes of service provision that are considered uppermost in impor-tance for the organization and which form the criteria for evaluation purposes should start with the following:

1. end-user service;
2. uniqueness of service;
3. priority of service, flexibility and speed of response;
4. direct cost;
5. management and indirect cost; and
6. control.

There is no reason why other criteria could not be introduced as, indeed, does occur because of an organization's preferences. Whichever criteria are adopted, each criterion will help to pinpoint strengths and expose weaknesses in the options available. In cases where the nature of requirements is highly specialized, other criteria might have to be considered in addition to, or instead of, the above. Priority of service, flexibility and speed of response could, for instance, be split into three separate criteria if so desired. So long as a consistent basis is used to judge each option against the attributes that matter, then the outcome of the evaluation will point to one or more front-runners from which a recommendation can be made – see the later discussion.

There is the temptation when moving to outsourcing to regard the need for any in-house personnel as minimalist. Exercising an outsourcing option does not relieve the organization of the need to manage the relationship with the service provider (or contractor). The extent to which a management function with appropriate resources should be maintained has therefore to be considered. There are implications for resourcing in all cases, as well as the cost that goes with it, and these factors should be taken into account before making a final decision on which option(s) to recommend.

End-user service

The organization will need to establish the scope and standard of the services it requires (see Chapter 8). In addition to the many *hard* measures that are usually associated with them (e.g. responding correctly to a need) a number of *soft* measures must also be considered (e.g. the level of end-user service expected and provided). These become particularly important when dealing with external customers, although they are still important when dealing with internal customers. Soft measures might include, for example:

- A courteous and responsive helpdesk in preference to a logbook in which faults are simply noted.
- Call-back to the person lodging the request, to verify that the work has been carried out.
- Adoption of performance measures for courtesy, response, presentation and tidiness.

Uniqueness of service

When contemplating different ways of providing a service, the special demands of the service must also be considered. While most services and the tasks they comprise will not represent an undue challenge to providers within the facility management sector, the organization might, for example, possess specialist plant and equipment unfamiliar to maintenance operatives. This could restrict the potential choice of the provider of maintenance and the supplier of spare parts. In some cases, legislation will ensure that only qualified persons and firms are authorized to perform maintenance. The maintenance of lifts/elevators is an obvious example. General considerations include the:

- Number of external providers that can potentially offer the service.
- Location of the service provider and its distance from the facility in question.

- Cost of, or premium charged for, the service.
- Average delivery time – that is, waiting time and time for undertaking the service.
- Level of specification needed to place orders.

Priority, flexibility and responsiveness

The priority of services to be delivered must be expressed clearly, so that critical services can be highlighted and the required level of response taken into account. A risk assessment should be undertaken for high-priority services, so that the impact or consequence of failure is made clear and an appropriate level and speed of response can be planned. This can be undertaken as follows:

1. Identify all sources of risk that might affect delivery of a high-priority service.
2. Undertake a preliminary analysis to establish the probable risks for further investigation.
3. Examine these risks to assess the severity of their impact and probability of occurrence.
4. Analyse all risks to predict the most likely outcome.
5. Investigate alternative courses of action (i.e. risk treatment).
6. Choose the course of action, including allocating responsibilities, deemed necessary to hold, avoid, reduce, transfer or share risks.

High-priority services and their related risks must be identified and assessment made of the probability and impact of such risks should they materialize. Questionnaires and checklists can be used to identify risks, which could then be scored as shown in Table 7.1.

Risks attracting a total score of 5 or more (by combining the individual scores for chance of occurrence and impact) would be unacceptable and consideration would need to be given to how such risks might be treated. Thus, risks can be recognized and assessed so that appropriate action can be taken. In the process of doing so, risks impacting on service provision might be ranked to allow the organization to look objectively at how they can best be managed.

For example, the occurrence of a significant failure in the heating system during the winter months might be improbable (score 1), but the consequences could

Table 7.1 Risk scores.

Probability	Chance of occurrence (%)	Score	Consequences/impact	Score
Improbable	10	1	Insignificant	1
Unlikely	25	2	Marginal	2
As likely as not	50	3	Serious	3
Probable	75	4	Critical	4
Highly probable	90	5	Catastrophic	5

be serious (score 3). The full impact of this risk is rated as 4 and is something that the organization might be prepared to accept (hold). This can be contrasted with the *as likely as not* event that fuel will not be delivered on time (score 3). If this were so, the consequences for heating the facility could be serious (score 3). This gives a total score of 6. In other words, fuel deliveries are a high-priority service and, as such, must be made at the required time. The organization should take steps to reduce the chance of non-delivery on specified dates or to hold a reserve fuel supply, whichever is more appropriate in terms of cost and practicability.

The organization should also consider the level of flexibility required for each of the services provided. Variable demand for some services, such as porterage and transport, which might peak at certain times of the year, can be difficult to maintain at a constant resource level. In such instances, the ability to call off manpower from an agency or other source at short notice can help and is also likely to provide a cost-effective way of delivering those services.

The speed with which a service provider can respond to orders or requests is a factor for further consideration. For example, the response time of a service provider in the case of an emergency call-out might be longer than that of an in-house resource. In the case of a remote site, the response time for a maintenance service provider might be significant and a premium to reduce this time might prove prohibitive. Alternatively, if an emergency were to escalate, a large external provider might be preferred to the in-house alternative, because of ready access, out of hours, to necessary equipment and personnel.

Direct cost

Generally, direct cost is fairly easy to ascertain. In the case of an outsourced service, the contract sum or value of the purchase order will signify its likely cost. For insourcing, the direct cost calculation includes salaries and benefits, but there might not be the same certainty because of unknown productivity and performance. In any case, the more obvious costs should not be looked at in isolation from the associated indirect costs – see below.

Management implications and indirect cost

Total cost is frequently misreported when considering the options for service delivery. In evaluating the comparative cost between insourced or outsourced services, the organization should identify all costs, both direct and indirect. A common mistake is for direct costs only to be reported. Indirect costs include those incurred in the internal management of service contracts and the ongoing training, induction and development of in-house personnel. Furthermore, the full administration of services such as *permit-to-work* procedures and competent and approved person regimes, together with the technology to support them, all attract a cost that must be recorded.

The organization also needs to consider the cost of financial administration. For instance, a small number of *time and materials* contracts means that invoices can be processed more cost-effectively than in situations where invoices are many and frequent. Clearly, the approach to service delivery has an implication for the accounting function.

The decision whether or not to outsource services must take into account both the capability of service providers and the effort required to manage them. An organization that takes the decision to outsource can delegate the direct supervision of work and operatives to the service provider. The role of the facility manager then becomes the management of the output of the service provider, who should act as an informed client (see Chapter 1), managing performance against specifications and service level agreements (see Chapter 11). The organization needs to consider its approach to this management role carefully.

When contemplating a mix of services such as cleaning, security, building maintenance and building services engineering maintenance, it is easy to see the diversity of tasks involved. This can mean that a facility manager or supervisor who is trying to cope with a wide range of services might not be proficient in all. This could prove to be a problem for smaller organizations where, although the tasks are not extensive individually, their diversity is great, requiring the facility manager or supervisor to be multi-skilled. For larger organizations, specialist management and supervision might be cost-effective and efficient, because more of it is required.

A further consideration is that of the expertise available within the organization for the management of these services if insourced. Whilst space-related services such as general cleaning and porterage do not require high levels of expertise, statutory equipment testing and maintenance of major appliances do. For a facility manager whose remit includes the management of such services on a part-time basis, the initial learning and the continuing professional development/education (CPD/CPE) to keep abreast of legislation and industry best practice represent a significant investment in time and effort. Consequently, insourcing might not be the most cost-effective choice.

Control

Linked closely to the management variable is the extent of control desired or required. For many organizations considering outsourcing, a significant concern is perceived loss of control. The level of control that can be achieved is closely correlated with the nature of service delivery and the contractual relationship established between the organization and the service provider. A traditional contract might well mean that the level of control is limited. For greater control, a partnering arrangement might be appropriate (see Chapter 10).

Whatever arrangement is put in place, ICT has a part to play in the delivery of reliable management information. It is through accessible management information that most control issues can be resolved. Value can also be added if management information is delivered as a consequence of service provision and is, therefore, available without cost or, at least, for a nominal sum (see Chapter 15 on information management).

Options for service delivery

The organization should consider which option, or combination of options, for service delivery most closely matches its identified needs. It should take account of the extent to which the informed client function has been developed. In cases where it believes the function to be underdeveloped, it should consider an arrangement that supplements its current capability. The following options should provide a suitable basis so long as the organization has established that the market for services supports them – see the later section:

- *Separate company/business unit* – the reconstitution of the in-house team into an independent company, with the objective of expanding its business by gaining contracts from other organizations.
- *Managing agent* – the appointment of a specialist to act as the organization's primary professional advisor on facility management. This person (or organization) is then responsible for arranging the appointment of service providers – see below.
- *Managing contractor* – appointment of a single entity to manage individual service providers. The contractor is paid a fee for providing this service, usually as a percentage of the value of the expenditure managed – see below.
- *Managed budget* – a variation on the *managing contractor*, where a contractor takes responsibility for the payment of all suppliers and provides a consolidated invoice at the end of each month. The fee is related to the contractor's own resources as deployed – see below.
- *Total facility management* – responsibility for providing services and for generally managing the facility is placed in the hands of a single organization – see below.
- *Off the shelf/agency* – contracted employment of personnel through a manpower agency. Agencies provide variable standards of selection expertise, personnel support and training, as well as customer support.

In addition to the above, there is the default option of insourcing; that is, services delivered by the organization's personnel and operatives, namely an in-house team. Whilst obviously not outsourcing by any stretch of the imagination, its comparative performance in an evaluation of options still has to be established. In summary, the above options provide choice for the organization in its procurement of services and the different ways of treating risk. Each option presents downside and upside risks, of which service delivery in accordance with specified requirements is a concern on the downside. These issues, and others relating to the nature of the main options, are discussed below.

The managing agent

This arrangement is adopted when the organization has determined that it does not wish to hand control of its facility to service providers, yet does not have the skill or expertise with which to manage them efficiently and cost-effectively. By bringing in an external organization to manage its facility, the organization is essentially appointing a managing agent. This person – almost invariably the appointment will specify an individual – will act as if he or she were part of the permanent establishment of the organization. The managing agent will perform better and more reliably if performance criteria are laid down; in fact, as they would apply to an in-house facility manager. Under this arrangement, contracts with service providers will be with the organization acting as the employer.

There are distinct and, perhaps, obvious advantages in adopting this arrangement. Both the agent and the various service providers can be selected on the basis of competitive tendering. Moreover, the appointment (or reappointment) of the agent should not affect contracts with service providers and vice versa. Dissatisfaction with a given service provider would not place other contracts at risk; indeed, it could positively assist in those cases where poor performance has a potential knock-on effect and action has to be taken without delay.

The managing agent approach offers flexibility for the organization to find and then hold on to the combination of contracts that suits it best. There is no reason why services should not be part-insourced and part-outsourced. The managing agent role attracts particular significance, since the organization would be using the agent to contribute expertise and exercise judgement when deciding between insourced and outsourced service delivery. There are, however, potential disadvantages for the organization in adopting this approach. For example, it is possible that gaps might occur between the scopes of the various contracts, including that of the managing agent. Even so, managing agents can be made responsible for ensuring that the scope of service contracts is such that gaps do not occur.

From a risk perspective, the organization is moderately exposed. It might have to accept the possibility of introducing an uncertain combination of risk factors by its own selection of service providers (including the managing agent) on an individual or piecemeal basis. The reasoning here is that a number of service providers coming together for the first time will place extra demands on the managing agent. Sound relationships between different service providers are needed if services are to be provided efficiently and cost-effectively and the facility is to operate safely and correctly. These relationships might take some time to develop. A conscious effort will therefore be required on the part of the managing agent to integrate the work of different service providers in such a way that they become moulded into a single, efficient team.

Some words of caution are necessary. The organization might find that administration costs increase as the number of separate contracts rises. Allowance must be made for higher indirect costs when evaluating this option. Risks can be treated and administration reduced by appointing the managing agent first and requiring that he or she establishes the suitability of service providers. In deciding to adopt this option, the organization should allocate adequate resources to planning and start-up of service delivery where new service providers are involved (see Chapter 14 on transition).

The managing contractor

Under this arrangement, there is one contract between the organization and the appointed service provider (contractor). In most cases, there will be some component of service delivery for which the service provider does not employ its own personnel and so will subcontract the work. These subcontractors (or secondary service providers) will be under contract to the managing contractor and so will not have any contractual relationship with the organization. This means that the organization has a single point of contact with the contractor on all matters pertaining to service delivery. If a service falls below the required performance for work carried out by a subcontractor, the organization need only direct its complaint to the managing contractor. However, as the chain of command is longer, delays in receiving prompt action might occur. Although subcontractors are contracted to the managing contractor, the organization should protect its position by reserving the right to approve the selection of all subcontractors.

Since there is a single point of contact and responsibility, there should be a sizeable reduction in documentation, fewer payments and, therefore, lower transaction costs. Gaps in service provision should be eliminated because the managing contractor is required to ensure that they do not occur. By using a managing contractor to undertake some or all of the work, with the support of subcontractors, the organization is able to mitigate much financial risk. The managing contractor is generally paid a fee, usually expressed as a percentage of the value of the expenditure managed, and this can, of course, be related to performance. The organization is, despite the limitation of being in just one contract, largely able to see where its money is being spent because open-book accounting is usually adopted, allowing access to the contractor's premises, books and records, including invoices from subcontractors. However, it might be difficult for the organization to get a true account of expenditure where the contractor delivers services directly.

The right to access is necessary, as the managing contractor might insist on larger trade discounts than are acceptable or might demand some other preferential terms that are inconsistent with best practice. Established supply chain agreements can give rise to retrospective discounts; for example, in the catering sector. Open-book accounting also ensures that there are few misunderstandings as to the cost of services. Under this arrangement it will, however, be more difficult to make changes to a contract, once it is formalized, than would be the case under the managing agent arrangement, unless changes are anticipated in advance and provision made in the contract.

The managed budget

The managing agent option, whilst valid for many organizations, does not fit with the culture of some, notably those that have invested in enterprise-wide management (ICT) systems and that wish to reduce the number of transactions. The major objection is the requirement to establish purchase ledger accounts for service providers (suppliers), although a managing agent handles all but the payment process.

In order to overcome this objection, the managed budget option was developed, in which a managing contractor takes responsibility for the payment of all suppliers and provides a consolidated invoice at the end of each month. A management fee is agreed, which is larger than that found in the managing agent option, since turnover from specialist subcontractors goes through the managing contractor's accounts. The management fee is based on a combination of the resources as deployed and the value of budgeted expenditure – all subcontract invoices and contract-specific personnel costs are processed without any mark-up (for overheads and profit). Usually, the managing contractor places an element of the management fee at risk, subject to the attainment of pre-agreed service levels. For discretionary expenditure, such as stationery and couriers, a simple handling charge can be added to the invoice.

Contractually, the managed budget approach is similar to the managing contractor option. However, important differences lie in the apportionment of risk and in an improved relationship between the organization and managing contractor. Through the removal of supply chain mark-up and remuneration based upon a management fee, the friction that might otherwise build up between the two main parties is alleviated. There is also the further advantage of fewer transactions to be processed, thereby reducing administration for the organization.

Total facility management

Under this arrangement, the organization is able to pass the full responsibility for managing its facility to a single-service provider for a fixed price. This does mean that the organization has to provide the service provider with sufficient flexibility to be able to manage the various services efficiently and cost-effectively. Even so, there is no universal model for total facility management, just as no two organizations are likely to have exactly the same service requirements. Each service provider is likely to position itself differently in the marketplace to reflect its interest in particular services.

While total facility management might appear to offer an ideal solution, because it provides a single purchasing point for the organization, the reality can be that the service provider subcontracts all or most of the work. Since there is just one contract – that between the organization and the total facility management service provider – there is the chance that terms and conditions between the service provider and subcontractors do not mirror those of the main contract. Difficulties can arise because terms and conditions that are embodied in the contract between the organization and the service provider might allow for situations that are not subsequently recognized in the contract with the subcontractor or vice versa.

The total facility management service provider might be better able to offer a more complete and competitive solution to an organization's needs than in the case of the managing agent or managing contractor. Relationships built up over years with subcontractors can mean that efficient working relationships are established from the start. Total facility management can provide a sound solution, but only if the organization is prepared to spend time in identifying the right basis for such an arrangement and then in selecting the best service provider.

In practice, problems can arise as alluded to above. Causes include the service provider's relationship with its subcontractors. For example, as with the managing contractor arrangement, the total facility management service provider might insist on larger trade discounts than are acceptable or some other preferential terms that are inconsistent with best practice. Also, during the currency of a contract, the service provider might decide to change a subcontractor. These decisions are not always made to improve performance; they might arise because the service provider is seeking to increase margins through the employment of a less expensive subcontractor. As with any change, newly appointed subcontractors, for whatever reason they are employed, will undergo a learning process. In this case, the organization should ensure that the procedure for assigning or subcontracting is open to inspection and that it has the right, under the contract, to prior approval before subcontracting. Open-book accounting should also be in place and its basis properly defined.

In terms of risk, the organization is moderately exposed and can derive a good deal of comfort from knowing that there is a single point of responsibility and less administration. Value for money might be less than in the managing agent approach, although the additional (indirect) cost of organizing and managing many more individual contracts in that approach must be taken into account.

Over the years, the criteria by which organizations have evaluated the benefits from their total facility management contracts have changed. It is no longer enough to use the one service provider, one invoice approach as the basis of a strategic decision; nor is it *base cost*, as many organizations have subsequently found. The total facility management option has proved to be inflexible, lacking in visibility and requiring a high level of policing. In many cases, because the types of organization involved in this work originate from a particular service delivery background, they will seek to *self-deliver*, with the emphasis placed on the number of operatives on site to achieve their return. Consequently, the focus is on task management and not on the strategic management of the organization's portfolio or relationships. Typically, service providers have sought to make a return on the supply chain they lead, usually expressed as a percentage of the value of the subcontracted element. An argument supporting this view is justified where the service provider is carrying significant risk or adding something unique in service delivery. However, the desire to improve overall margins results in the addition of a traditionally accepted mark-up to this element, irrespective of risk or value added. Market pressures, as described earlier, have driven the questioning of such contractual arrangements and the conflicts of interest that arise through the application of a percentage-based mark-up. The organization should be looking to achieve a partnership-based relationship where returns are agreed in advance and both parties work together to innovate and raise levels of performance and end-user satisfaction, whilst reducing costs (see Chapter 10).

For some organizations, such as those experiencing rapid expansion, it might not be so much a matter of bringing service providers into their facilities, but a case of establishing their business in a fully serviced facility. The number of serviced office providers has increased in the marketplace and can provide greater levels of flexibility using a *menu of prices* geared to levels of service delivery. Obviously, the question of ownership of space and real estate has to be considered. A fully serviced facility does not, however, need to be provided externally. It can be created internally where there is a desire to change and so long as financial controls are put in place. For example, where a serviced office is priced appropriately and recharged, it can provide business units with real information that can enhance decision-making. Evidence suggests that the old habits of liberal space usage are quickly reformed when the true cost is revealed. Serviced space is a valuable and significant component of the cost equation and is where the greatest prospect for cost reduction often lies. Even so, the opportunity to tap this potentially rich seam is dependent upon the appetite of the organization for change, as well as having the resources for this purpose. Implementing a successful flexible working arrangement requires information which, under a typical total facility management relationship, is in the hands of the service provider, not the organization. Service providers can offer expertise in these areas, but the key to this lies in the level of management expertise deployed on the contract and in the congruence of its objectives with those of the organization. Traditional arrangements have inhibited this congruence, with commercial imperatives often driving the service provider in another direction.

Single versus multiple services

Some organizations will rightly consider that they have a well-developed, informed client function and the resources to manage service providers and their contracts directly. The prior appointment of a managing agent can help in this respect. In such cases, the organization can choose from amongst the following arrangements:

1. Single-service providers, with as many service providers as there are services.
2. Multiple-service providers, where two or more services are bundled and delivered by each of one or more service providers.
3. A combination of the above.

In most cases, the requirement is for a number of services rather than a single service. There are implications in choosing any of the arrangements; for example, the ability to attract competitive tenders, ongoing management of service providers and commercial risks to which the organization is exposed. Deciding which services might be bundled is an integral part of determining the most appropriate basis for outsourcing and the procurement that follows. A matrix of services against prospective service providers can be prepared to help determine the mix of single and multiple service contracts that might be appropriate ahead of any procurement activity. While clearly a subjective basis for determining how services might be combined, it does nonetheless provide some idea as well as transparency in decision-making.

Single-service providers and multiple-service providers are not mutually exclusive. A combination of single-service and multiple-service providers is fairly common for large organizations, because of the wide range of services typically involved. One other arrangement open to the organization is the total facility management service provider discussed earlier, where all services are delivered by a single point of responsibility. Last, agencies can on occasion be a useful source of manpower where there is a temporary requirement for the delivery of a specific service. They should not, therefore, be considered on a long-term basis or as a substitute for an established service provider.

The selection of the most appropriate arrangement or combination should, as noted above, take proper account of the resources and costs involved in managing the relationship with service providers. These indirect costs should be included within budgets.

Evaluating options

The option evaluation matrix

Once the criteria for evaluating options have been assembled, the next task is to perform the evaluation. Aside from the aim of identifying the most appropriate option, there is also the matter of objectivity and transparency. For some organizations, the route by which any recommendation is reached is as important as the outcome. In extreme cases, the outcome might have to be defended in the face of strong resistance to change, as might occur when moving away from a currently insourced arrangement. In any event, a stakeholder workshop should be considered so that the process by which the recommendation is made can be as rigorous and open as possible.

Table 7.2 shows seven options that an organization has identified and that it believes are capable of satisfying the attributes of *service A* to a greater or lesser extent. Each service should have a separate matrix, where the attributes are entered as rows in the matrix and the options are placed against them in columns. Experience and personal judgement is used to ascertain the scores and weights where one or more attribute is rated as more important than the others. In this case, weights of 2 might be sufficient to indicate that a particular attribute is significantly more important than the others. The danger in having larger weights – for example, 4 – is that it becomes difficult to explain what four times more important actually means in practice.

Table 7.2 Evaluating options for service delivery based on attributes of service provision.

Service A		Options						
		Insourced	Special company/ business unit	Managing agent	Managing contractor	Managed budget	Total FM	Agency
Attributes of service provision	Weight							
End-user service	1	1	1	2	1	2	1	0
Uniqueness of service	1	0	1	1	1	1	1	0
Priority, flexibility and responsiveness	2	2	1	2	2	2	1	2
Direct cost	1	1	0	0	0	1	0	0
Management and indirect cost	1	0	1	1	1	2	2	0
Control	1	2	2	2	1	2	0	1
Totals (unweighted)		6	6	8	6	10	5	3
Totals (weighted)		8	7	10	8	12	6	5

Key: '2' means that the attribute is most likely to be satisfied by the option, '1' means that the attribute might be satisfied and '0' means that the attribute is unlikely to be satisfied.

Scores are entered against each option, where a range of 0–2 is sufficient to spread the results. A larger range does not necessarily improve the results. The particular interpretation represented by this model is hypothetical. The total scores, unweighted or weighted, will point to the option or options more likely to satisfy the attributes of each service. Common sense needs to apply when interpreting the total scores. In our example in Table 7.2, we can see that the *managed budget* attracts the highest score and should be considered appropriate for service A. But what if other services point to different options? It would make no sense to recommend that service A be delivered under a managed budget, service B under, say, total facility management, service C under a managing contractor and so on. We need to look at those options attracting the next highest score and then reach a decision that is, on balance, capable of satisfying most attributes as well as being practicable. In cases where many services are involved, the outcome will probably be a compromise and might, for the sake of a hypothetical example, involve a managed budget covering a majority of services with the rest insourced.

Markets for facility-related services

Markets are dynamic and, therefore, subject to change. In the way that needs in relation to services are specific to an organization, the nature of a market is specific to a location or region. In some cases, the market might not support the demand created by the organization. Over time, both organization and market will change, with a peak in market demand followed by a peak in supply, albeit separated by a period of perhaps some years. Unregulated markets are cyclical in nature, rarely homogeneous and subject to the influence of economic cycles. Pragmatically, it is a matter of matching the current and likely future requirement for services with their availability in the market and keeping the situation under regular review. Needs will always drive decision-making and the specification of requirements; however, it might not be possible to satisfy them exactly because of imperfections in the market. Understanding where the market is presently in the cycle of business activity, together with an appreciation of likely trends in supply and demand, is essential to selecting the option that best matches needs in line with the organization's facility management strategy.

There will be physical limits to any market from which service providers will be drawn; for example, the extent to which the local market is able to offer the required services and the geographical limits that are acceptable when considering prospective service providers. There would be little point evaluating a particular option – for example, total facility management – if there were no service provider capable of offering this service. The organization should therefore investigate the current state of the market in terms of prospective service providers and the extent to which they cover the services required by the organization. Service providers should be contacted directly in order to understand the current state of supply and demand for services or, alternatively, the trade bodies that represent them. Other reasons for engaging with service providers at this time include gaining advice on specialist services and on matters affecting health, safety, security, environment, access, inclusion and equality. These preliminary contacts should not be confused with prequalification (see Chapter 8) and should take place before embarking on the procurement of any service.

The above investigation represents the first step in what is generally termed *market testing*, and should represent a genuine attempt to engage existing and prospective service providers in discussion about service provision and the options for service delivery. A subsequent step is likely to be to request indicative cost estimates to guide decision-making, although this should be limited to a few service providers and should acknowledge the likely effort to be expended in providing estimates. It would be unreasonable and inappropriate to ask prospective service providers to provide detailed costs at this time. Chapter 8 explains the procedure for prequalifying service providers and the information that is appropriate to request from them.

Conclusions

Various strengths and weaknesses are attached to the different options for outsourcing. The organization must decide upon the route that satisfies end-user requirements, whilst providing best value. This is achieved by taking full account of the implications, including the true cost of all viable options. Thorough preparation takes time and so contemplating the decision of whether or not to outsource means planning well ahead and building in adequate time. If followed prudently, the procedures that lead to recommending a particular outsourcing arrangement can provide a firm basis for the subsequent procurement of services. Indeed, the decision to outsource can be made rationally and objectively, based on attributes of service provision that are relevant and transparent. At any time, the organization can evaluate the suitability of the options open to it – see Table 7.2 – and determine if its arrangements are appropriate to its current and future service provision. The benefit in using a model of this kind is that specific options can be evaluated with sensitivity and the most appropriate decision for the organization at any time can be made. In fact, time is an important factor, because needs change and sometimes the most appropriate option is the one that can be adapted to suit new conditions as they arise. Limited and periodic market reviews are useful for information gathering, but habitual market testing is not considered best practice and can be counterproductive. In defining its approach to service delivery, where the recommended action is to outsource, the organization has, in effect, defined the basis of its procurement strategy. What remains are the detailed workings of a process that will lead to the selection and management of suitable service provider(s).

Checklist

This checklist is intended to assist with review and action planning.

	Yes	No	Action required
1. Has sufficient base information been gathered and synthesized prior to exploring the decision on whether or not to outsource?	☐	☐	☐

		Yes	No	Action required
2.	Have all stakeholders with an interest in the services to be provided been properly engaged and have their needs as end-users been defined?	☐	☐	☐
3.	Has the scope of services been sufficiently defined to support an evaluation of whether or not to outsource?	☐	☐	☐
4.	Have risks and opportunities surrounding the decision on whether or not to outsource been identified and has their impact been assessed?	☐	☐	☐
5.	Has account been taken of any existing sourcing policy within the organization?	☐	☐	☐
6	Is offshoring a relevant option for the delivery of any service?	☐	☐	☐
7.	Have the necessary attributes of service been defined and have their comparative importance been considered?	☐	☐	☐
8.	Have both hard and soft measures been considered?	☐	☐	☐
9.	Have the options for service delivery been determined and are the implications of each properly understood, including risk exposure for the organization?	☐	☐	☐
10.	Has an appropriate scoring basis been fixed to evaluate the extent to which each option satisfies each attribute of service?	☐	☐	☐
11.	Have both the direct and indirect costs of delivering services under each of the options been properly determined?	☐	☐	☐
12.	Have the management implications of delivering services under each of the options been considered?	☐	☐	☐
13.	Has a clear recommendation on the most practicable option or combination of options for service delivery been made?	☐	☐	☐
14.	Is market testing undertaken periodically irrespective of the route taken to service delivery?	☐	☐	☐

8 Procurement

Key issues

The following issues are covered in this chapter.

- There is a logical sequence to the procurement of services, which covers policy, prequalification of service providers, tender documentation, the request for proposals, tendering and financial close. If the most suitable service provider is to be selected, a realistic timescale must be allowed for the procurement process.

- Defining the scope of services is a crucial step in successful procurement, by providing the basis for inviting proposals or tenders and, subsequently, in managing the performance of service providers. A poorly defined scope will lead, almost inevitably, to problems in service delivery and a negative impact on end-users.

- Key stakeholders – typically the end-users of services – must be involved in procurement if their needs are to be adequately addressed and communicated. Success depends on commitment to the process from all who could contribute.

- The capability and capacity of service providers needs to be established before any are invited to submit proposals or tenders.

- Prequalification criteria – of which there can be many – should be searching, but fair, and take account of service providers' competence, skills and experience, which can be used to frame requirements.

- Service specifications and SLAs are tools for managing the quality/performance and value of services. They are the organization's expression of requirements in a way that will motivate service providers to deliver services that achieve end-user satisfaction and best value. They form the basis of any request for proposals or tender.

Total Facility Management, Fourth Edition. Brian Atkin and Adrian Brooks.
© 2015 John Wiley & Sons, Ltd. Published 2015 by John Wiley & Sons, Ltd.

- A service specification is a document that quantifies the minimum service that is acceptable if end-users' requirements are to be met. It provides a benchmark against which standards of service can be assessed.

- An SLA is a commitment by the service provider or the in-house team to end-users to deliver an agreed level of service. It should specify rewards and penalties, yet retain flexibility so that evolving end-user requirements can be taken into account.

- Tendering is the formal process of inviting proposals or tenders. Procedures for conducting a tender competition are generally highly prescribed, not least in the public sector.

- The evaluation of proposals or tenders involves defining criteria to differentiate prospective service providers. Once a suitable service provider has been selected, additional steps – pre-contract meeting and formalization of the contract – are involved in moving to financial close.

Introduction

In procuring services from external service providers, an organization has taken the decision to outsource. However, the procurement of such services extends beyond simple purchase and supply decisions to represent a major and integral part of an organization's facility management. It is for this reason that it is important to ensure that it is carried out in a way that is both consistent and thorough, taking into account all necessary factors that are most likely to result in the achievement of end-user satisfaction and best value. As a reminder, services cover, for example, cleaning, security, waste disposal, pest control, building maintenance, building services engineering maintenance, minor construction works, reprographics, helpdesk, catering, energy supplies and ICT. The range and extent of such services can be broad, reflecting the particular needs of the organization and the end-users' requirements. Once the decision to outsource has been reached, policy and the procedures that follow tend to be somewhat prescriptive, though they are certainly not mechanistic. This means that the facility manager can rely upon legislation, standards, guidelines and practice notes from a wide range of sources. There is benefit from this situation, but there can be disadvantages arising from adherence to procedures that might have been designed for a different purpose. Some interpretation is likely in order to take account of local conditions – for instance, custom and practice – and the current supply of and demand for services. Narrow interpretation of legislation in particular runs the risk of creating anomalies that can thwart the good intentions that lie behind the legislation in question. The approach taken here is one of highlighting current best practice, drawing on guidance from various sources and the authors' fieldwork. The chapter begins by examining the general approach to the procurement of services and supplies, referred to for convenience as services, in the context of an explicit process for procurement. Within it is recognition of the organization's facility management strategy and procurement policy. The procedures that devolve from the policy are considered in some detail. These also apply to situations where currently outsourced services are subject to transition (see Chapter 14). For clarity, the procedures are presented in chronological order as far as practicable – see the section on Procurement policy and procedures. Important guidance is available within standards. In particular, the provisions of BS 8572, which are reflected in this chapter, cover the procurement of services.

The procurement process

Procurement involves a number of distinct stages, steps and procedures that must be followed if the organization is to have a dependable basis for service delivery. The procurement process should be supported by a time-plan or, ideally, a schedule in which stages, (higher-level) activities, (lower-level) tasks and their resources, decision gates and milestones are shown. If a schedule is to be prepared, it should take the form of a Gantt chart and be network-based so that all tasks are linked. Resources should, wherever possible, be loaded on to the schedule by allocating them to individual tasks in order to test the feasibility of what is being proposed. Typically, these will include human resources, consumables, equipment (operated and non-operated), budgets and ICT. Milestones are intended to represent noteworthy events and should, therefore, signify commencement dates, completions and deadlines. Approvals and other key decisions are better considered as tasks having durations and not as milestones, since they are hardly ever instantaneous events; that is, milestones have no duration.

The organization's facility management strategy should have anticipated the need for a plan of the procurement process following the decision to outsource. It is important that the plan should complement existing business processes and procedures as far as practicable, including the requirements of corporate governance. Furthermore, the plan should incorporate a tendering process – see the later section. In overall terms, it should be capable of providing a roadmap with which to manage procurement through distinct stages from establishing a baseline for service provision (see Chapter 7) to a steady state of satisfactory service delivery (see Fig. 8.1).

The downside risks encountered in outsourcing and, by implication, procurement were discussed in Chapter 7. Appendix C provides a checklist of those risks, although it does not lay claim to being exhaustive. For this reason, it is essential that the organization considers risk assessment and risk treatment as serious matters and an integral part of the procurement process (see Chapter 7 on Risks and opportunities). Failure to recognize risks, or even the likely extent of their impact should they materialize, could prove to be the undoing of an otherwise well-conceived plan for procurement.

The timescale for procurement will vary according to the scope and scale of services being outsourced. However, many of the critical activities and the time they require – for instance, dealing with legislative aspects, tendering, financial close and mobilization – will remain more or less the same across a wide range of contract types and values. The timescale might reduce for activities such as

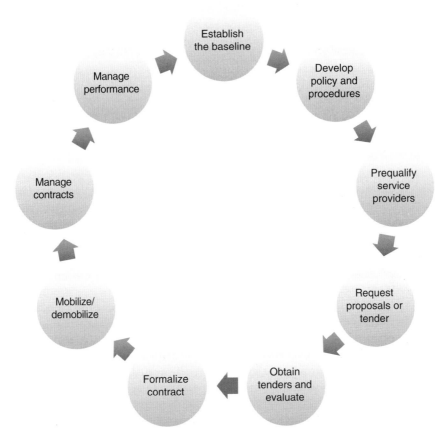

Fig. 8.1   The procurement process.

definition of services, proposal/tender evaluation and contract award, where the service to be outsourced is of minor economic importance and is relatively uncomplicated. Even so, it is important to ensure that the time to move from the decision to outsource to the delivery of the service is realistic. Too often, there is pressure from senior managers to compress the time-plan or schedule – all it needs, or so it is claimed, are a few changes here and there. The result is usually a schedule with a low probability of completion in the timescale demanded. Cutting a schedule is the same as arbitrarily cutting a budget and is bound to lead to missed deadlines and knock-on consequences. Figure 8.2 is a simplified timeline for procurement based on the allocation of a reasonable amount of time for reaching each milestone.

Centralized versus decentralized procurement

Usually, an organization has either centralized or decentralized procurement; in a minority of cases, both apply. The organization has to be clear about services that could be procured locally and those that can only be procured centrally.

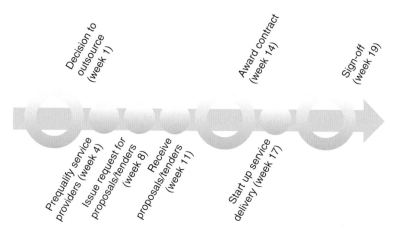

Fig. 8.2   The timeline for procurement (simplified).

A centralized procurement function might retain control over certain service contracts for reasons of uniqueness of service, security or economy of scale. Elsewhere, service contracts might be awarded and managed locally for reasons of flexibility, speed of response or, perhaps, corporate social responsibility. The demarcation between centralized and decentralized control has, therefore, to be made explicit. Any policy that covers prequalification for the purpose of inclusion in a list of preferred tenderers might also be treated in the same way. The financial authorities for awarding contracts, approval of payments and significant changes in the scope of services and/or the value of contracts are best defined in a manual of authorities, so that it is clear *who can approve what*, including the extent of their authority. In all cases, it is better to define the arrangements upfront rather than risk delay later.

Stakeholder engagement will also need to reflect any recognized split between centralized and decentralized procurement, so that resources and time are directed towards dealing with stakeholder interests that are applicable to the prevailing arrangement. Engaging with stakeholders centrally, where they have little influence over, or interest in, procurement decisions at the local level, or the reverse situation, would not be a good use of resources or time.

Procurement policy and procedures

The policy should reflect current best practice in a number of key areas. In keeping with the principle of scaling discussed in Chapter 3, it is important to consider the extent to which each applies; in any case, none should be simply omitted without good cause.

- *Compliance* – applicable legislation on HSSE, access, inclusion and equalities – see below.

- *Manual of authorities* – authorized personnel, budgetary limits, contract awards, payments and actions in the event of significant changes in the scope of contracts or their value.
- *Stakeholders* – the nature of engagement at each stage in the procurement process.
- *Corporate social responsibility* – principles and initiatives.
- *Bribery and anti-competitiveness* – means for preventing malpractice.
- *Conflicts of interest* – avoidance of situations where contracts are managed by personnel who were once part of the in-house team.
- *Dispute resolution* – procedure and notices.
- *Risks and opportunities* – identification, assessment and treatment.
- *Contract management* – service provider and supplier relationships.
- *ICT* – use of systems.
- *Performance measurement* – the basis for payment, incentives and penalties.
- *Intellectual property* – background and foreground rights.
- *Public procurement regulations* – legislation, where applicable.
- *Freedom of information* – legislation and access arrangements, where applicable.

Responsibilities for HSSE should be reviewed and a policy statement prepared and made available on request. Procedures for ensuring access, inclusion and equality for all occupants and other users should be included in the policy statement. These should extend to covering actions in the event of emergency evacuation.

Explicit procedures for the management of contracts should be followed where available. Account should be taken of the ICT systems, including both hardware and software, to be used in the management of contracts. A conscious decision should be taken as to whether or not service providers are required to use common software and where, in its absence, arrangements might have to be made to input service providers' information and data into the organization's ICT systems. These requirements have to be carefully considered because of cases where significant quantities of data have had to be manually entered because of incompatibility between the service providers' systems and those of the organization.

The above matters of policy also apply to situations where service delivery is subject to transition from one arrangement to another (see Chapter 14). In general, procedures follow in chronological order where the objective is to ensure that critical success factors are not compromised:

- The scope of the services and interfaces between them are defined so that there are no gaps or unnecessary overlaps.
- The service levels required by end-users are clearly specified.
- Service providers have the capabilities and capacity to deliver the services.
- Service delivery, in the case of multiple services, is achieved through a team approach where each provider is working towards a common goal.
- Service delivery is continually reviewed and action taken to improve performance.

Roles, responsibilities and accountabilities

Ordinarily, the organization would be expected to have a distinct function for the procurement of goods and services, although not expressly in relation to facility-related services. It is important to clarify this position before setting about procuring any services. Furthermore, the procurement of services should be regarded as a distinct function and, as such, something that is best covered by a designated role. Existing systems, processes and procedures will have to be examined in order to determine if arrangements covering facility-related services have been included and, if so, how these might be applied. There is obviously no point in duplicating anything existing.

It is important to identify all roles connected with the function of procuring services and to determine their nature and the relationship between them. Roles will need to be defined so that responsibilities and accountabilities are clear. A responsibility assignment matrix (RASCI chart) should be considered for this purpose. If necessary, the organization should designate additional personnel where the tasks to be performed fall outside existing roles. Expert advice from external sources could be used to supplement any lack of internal competence and skills. If the organization is unable to fulfil required roles, then the appointment of a managing agent or other consultant should be considered.

A developed informed client function will serve the organization's wider and long-term interests in the procurement of services (see Chapter 1). The informed client function should therefore be maintained to enable an appropriate level of communication and cooperation between the organization and service providers as part of a mutual commitment to continual improvement. An organization acting as an informed client is more likely to achieve end-user satisfaction and best value in its procurement of services than those without an understanding of best practice in this area. The informed client function applies irrespective of the size or type of organization procuring services. In the absence of an informed client function, the organization could easily fail to establish the most appropriate arrangement for services, as well as running the risk of under- or over-specifying requirements.

Prequalification of service providers

The facility management strategy, and the stages that lead up to it, deal with a wide range of matters including business objectives, stakeholders, risks and opportunities, end-user requirements, legislation, current and proposed sourcing arrangements, options for service delivery and types of service provider. Having created an all-important baseline, the next step is to define a process for selecting the most suitable service provider(s). This is normally achieved by obtaining competitive tenders. First, the organization has to consider the information it requires from prospective service providers before it can consider if they should be invited to submit a proposal or tender. The term that applies to this stage is *request for information* or, simply, RFI and forms a major part of the prequalification of service providers – see below.

The means by which the suitability of a service provider can be established thus involves a formal request. An RFI can take the form of a prequalification question-naire, where the aim is to capture information and data about prospective service providers so that only those qualified to undertake the work are invited to submit a proposal or tender. It is a form of *due diligence* that needs time for gathering and evaluating information from service providers. The time likely to be needed before an RFI can be issued has to be considered too. It can take weeks, turning into months, to reach this point. The arrangements for these stages, including the timescale, for both the organization and prospective service providers to prepare information – one to ask, the other to reply – have to be properly considered. Normally, a period of between two and three weeks is reasonable for service pro-viders to respond to an RFI.

Local versus national service providers

The nature of the market for services should have already been investigated by the organization (see Chapter 7). The information gathered should indicate if the market locally, regionally or nationally is likely to have the capacity to satisfy requirements. Since service providers' workload can change – sometimes very quickly – it is important that the information reflects the current situation as best it can. Other relevant considerations should include the specialization, number and size of service providers able to offer the services required. Prospective ser-vice providers might be prepared to say if they are in a position to undertake new work; however, caution should be exercised when making judgements about their capacity based on mere say-so.

Knowledge of the respective market is an ongoing process because of the dynamic nature of markets in general (see Chapter 7). An organization that is aware of the prevailing conditions and the balance between supply and demand is better able to anticipate a particular reaction or response on the part of service providers than one that is unaware. In some cases, the demand for a given service, or perhaps several services, exceeds the capacity of local service providers. It might therefore be necessary to look at the regional or national level. Some large service providers have a local presence with significant autonomy: others do not. In either case, they might be seeking opportunities to develop their presence. As with any market, the competitiveness of individual firms will be a major factor in their success or failure. From the organization's perspective, there is a potential down-side from encouraging a national service provider to enter a local market in the belief that a worthwhile new contract might be forthcoming. There is the prospect of the service provider buying the work; that is, submitting a tender where the price is at or below estimated cost or what appears to be an economically viable threshold. Of course, it is possible that competition amongst local service provid-ers for work might produce similar behaviour: such is the nature of markets.

Request for information (RFI)

When preparing a request for information, or prequalification questionnaire, it is important to capture information that will adequately inform the decision on whether or not prospective service providers have the necessary capability and capacity to succeed. Typically, the information that should be requested includes the:

- Legal form and ownership of the service provider.
- Areas of specialization, competences and technical skills.
- Intended approach to service delivery (i.e. method statement).
- Extent of sub-letting (i.e. subcontracting).
- Track record in successfully performing similar work.
- Financial capacity and dependency.
- HSSE policy and procedures.
- Awareness of legislation and practices in regard to access, inclusion and equality.
- Evidence of cultural fit.
- Corporate social responsibility policy and initiatives.
- Alignment with the organization's business process and systems, where these have been disclosed.
- Criteria for assessing suitability.

The RFI can be undertaken in two parts: first, a preliminary assessment to weed out service providers that are unsuitable and confirm those that appear to be suitable; and, second, a detailed evaluation aimed at objectively assessing the service provider's suitability. The preliminary assessment enables the organization to quickly establish suitability, enabling attention to be given to those providers best qualified to deliver the service. The number of service providers invited to submit an RFI should be between six and nine. It is important to bear in mind that, when considering services, the organization is not procuring a commodity where lowest price is likely to be the dominant consideration. Performance capability – that is, quality of service delivery – over the longer term is a more realistic consideration. Once RFIs have been returned and assessed, the organization needs to check that it has all the information it requires to move ahead. Checklists should be considered for this purpose based on the above.

Financial appraisal

It is vital for the organization to determine the financial capacity and dependency of prospective service providers. Larger organizations are likely to have a formal procedure in place for this purpose, whereas others might not. If they are being actively considered for appointment, service providers, both prospective and existing, should be equally subject to due diligence: there should be no exceptions. Due diligence should cover the inspection of the financial accounts for the past two years of trading. Where accounts are unaudited, other information that demonstrates the service provider's financial standing should be found. The service provider's capacity to deliver the service at the current estimated contract value should be estimated with sufficient allowance for a margin of error (and possible scope growth) before reaching a decision.

References obtained from third parties can be taken as evidence of capability, but they are unlikely to answer adequately the question of their capacity to deliver. Business failures are often the result of a lack of financial means rather than poor technical competence. The turnover of a service provider can be an indicator of its financial capacity and dependency, and thus its ability to take on a contract within a certain financial limit. Service providers that are successful, active and growing might not be able to demonstrate financial capacity in the same way as longer-established and larger service providers. Eliminating a prospective service provider on the basis of contract limit alone would be unfair unless the service provider was being overly ambitious and likely to become financially stretched.

Profit and loss accounts and balance sheets are historical records and do not provide a complete financial picture. A more detailed examination is likely to be necessary. Reports from credit reference agencies can be useful in establishing a service provider's current financial standing and can supplement the detailed examination of financial accounts. Most service providers need cash (i.e. liquidity) to undertake their work and so an assessment of their cash-flow position and cash-generating ability is strongly recommended.

HSSE

The organization's policy on HSSE should be brought to the attention of prospective service providers, as well as being displayed on the organization's public website, so that all are aware of the organization's position on these matters. Responsibility for HSSE extends beyond the organization's personnel to the extent that no activity should pose any risk to visitors, including service providers' personnel, or people outside the facility. In other words, the responsibility is to anyone who might be affected by the action of another in the context of the facility.

Information about substances, plant and equipment that could pose a potential hazard to anyone should be brought to the attention of prospective (and existing) service providers. Arrangements for keeping this information up to date will be necessary. Since the organization will need to require service providers to take responsibility for ensuring the competence of their own personnel in HSSE matters, it must include this requirement in the RFI. Later, during the evaluation of proposals/tenders, the organization should seek proof of satisfactory completion of training and certificates of competence in HSSE, as appropriate.

Specific requirements for access, inclusion and equality in regard to the services being procured have implications for HSSE and must be identified and included in the RFI.

Cultural fit

The organization will be judged by its actions, core values, honesty, integrity and respect for people. Altogether, these characterize the organization's culture. Cultural fit is an important criterion for many organizations to the extent that most will not work with those who do not share their own values. Service providers have to be able to recognize this characteristic and act appropriately; otherwise, they are likely to fall at the first hurdle. They are going to be, in effect, an extension of the organization. As such, they should be aware of the organization's general business principles, workplace charter and/or other statements expressing core values and business ethics. This information, or access to this information, should be provided to prospective and existing service providers by the organization. Those attributes of end-user service for which a specific response from service providers is required need to be highlighted. Since delivery of services occurs within occupied environments, it is necessary that end-users are treated with consideration and care. Where there are areas and operations that require particular standards of conduct, behaviour, apparel or other requirements, such as those relating to HSSE, these should be outlined in the RFI.

Corporate social responsibility (CSR)

CSR is a concept whereby the organization considers the interests of society by taking responsibility for the impact of its actions on stakeholders as well as environmental sustainability. It imposes duties that extend beyond legal requirements by committing the organization to measures that improve the quality of life for personnel and their families, the local community and society at large. Acting responsibly as a corporate citizen means that the organization engages in activities that are beneficial to society. This involves using technology responsibly, protecting and sustaining the environment, supporting local and regional communities and observing high ethical standards in business relationships. Chapter 13 discusses CSR in more depth as part of a wider treatment of sustainability.

A policy statement on CSR should be issued to all existing and prospective service providers and be displayed on the organization's public website. Details of any specific activities or initiatives in CSR should be included in the policy statement. All service providers should be asked to furnish evidence of their own commitment to CSR in terms of initiatives or other actions of a non-philanthropic nature.

Assessment criteria

The suitability of prospective service providers should be assessed on the basis of the best information available to the organization. Whilst obvious, it can sometimes be the case that opinion substitutes for fact. There will undoubtedly be, over the course of time, occasions where decisions have to be made on less than complete and accurate information. Even so, the aim should be to undertake an objective and transparent evaluation of the suitability of prospective and existing service providers based on the criteria of capability, capacity, compliance with legislation and alignment with policies. It is necessary that such criteria are made known to service providers when making initial inquiries and, therefore, in advance of issuing the RFI, because they have to be aware of the seriousness with which the organization is conducting its procurement. At the same time, the organization should not appear overbearing or intimidating, particularly if it has significant purchasing power. Guidelines on dealing with service providers at this stage in the procurement process can be found amongst the points covered in Appendix C.

Table 8.1   Assessing service providers (prequalification).

Assessment	Criteria	Score
Very poor	Unable to demonstrate capability, capacity, compliance and alignment with requirements	0
Poor	Limited evidence of capability, capacity, compliance and alignment with requirements	1–4
Satisfactory	Adequate evidence of capability, capacity, compliance and alignment with requirements	5–6
Good	Significant evidence of capability, capacity, compliance and alignment with requirements and, in some areas, reveals innovation that exceeds requirements	7–8
Excellent	Considerable evidence of capability, capacity, compliance and alignment in all areas and reveals innovation that exceeds requirements in most areas	9–10

Service providers should be scored against the agreed criteria and then ranked. The ranking indicates which prospective service providers are most suitable for consideration at the next stage – the request for proposals or tender. Table 8.1 shows typical assessment criteria and scoring.

Once the ranking is complete and verified, the organization should interview individually those service providers who have been judged to be suitable. The interview should be used to brief them on the facility and their understanding of requirements and to give them the chance to ask questions on matters that require clarification.

The organization can then finalize its shortlist of service providers as a basis for the request for proposals or tenders. The number of prospective service providers that are invited to submit a proposal or tender should be based on the concept of fair competition. In any case, it would be wasteful to invite more than five service providers to submit a proposal or tender – see the later section on Tender competitions.

Request for proposals or tender

In cases where service specifications are based on performance requirements (outputs), the organization is obviously leaving a certain amount of choice in terms of methods of working to the service provider. It would be inappropriate, therefore, to request a tender in the conventional sense of a price for a fully defined scope of service. Instead, it might be better to ask for suggestions as to the best way of achieving those performance requirements and, of course, the cost of doing so. For these reasons, it is more appropriate to think in terms of a request for proposals, as it provides some flexibility for service providers to apply their knowledge and experience in a way that might bring unexpected benefits for the organization. Alternatively, it might confirm that the organization already has a sufficiently developed understanding of requirements and has been able to communicate them effectively. It is also likely to mean that requirements based on a prescriptive specification, which might not make complete sense to a service provider, are mostly avoided. A simple example is cleaning, where a prescriptive specification would lay down requirements for *when* a particular space or room is to be cleaned and *how* it is to be cleaned. This could result in cleaning taking place when it is unnecessary, involving needless work simply to comply with the last letter of a requirement. Besides, the aim should be to maintain the space or room in a state of cleanliness in which there is no accumulation of dirt or debris. It leaves the service provider to plan and carry out cleaning in the most efficient and cost-effective manner – see the example in a later section.

When preparing a request for proposals/tenders, whether for single or multiple services, it is necessary to consider:

- An output-based service specification containing service-related requirements.
- Service levels stating acceptable levels of performance.
- Arrangements for performance measurement and reporting.
- The form of agreement and supporting terms and conditions or, where applicable, a standard form of contract including any amendments.
- Criteria to be used to assess proposals or tenders.
- The date and time by which proposals or tenders should be submitted, as well as the place and mode of submission.

The flexibility that a request for proposals confers can extend to alternative proposals for the delivery of a single service or multiple services. Whatever the preference, the format of the request should allow prospective service providers to submit their proposals or tenders for service delivery in a defined format for the purposes of consistency and comparability. It is worth noting that tendering procedures are, in general, highly prescribed and strictly enforced, not least in the public sector.

The point has already been made that a request for proposals is more than asking for a price, since it provides the opportunity for prospective service providers to submit their own suggestions. The aim of this stage is to allow comparisons to be made between competing service providers on the basis of a common scope definition and service levels (i.e. performance) to be delivered. The request therefore covers details of performance measurement, penalties and incentives, including the mechanism for adjusting payment in the event that performance falls below an acceptable level. A further function of the request is in helping to assess the impact of identified risks, additional risks that might have arisen during tendering and any treatment of those risks. A period of not less than four weeks should be set aside for service providers to respond to a request for proposals with a submission; however, this could be reduced to a minimum period of two weeks where the service is of minor economic importance and uncomplicated. Most importantly, the organization should avoid issuing supplementary information during the tendering period, as this can cause unnecessary and additional work for tenderers. It can also suggest that the organization is less than efficient and that a productive, working relationship might be difficult to develop.

Rationale for service specifications and SLAs

Service specifications and service level agreements (SLAs) are essential tools in facility management irrespective of whether services are outsourced or insourced. They provide the working guidelines for both the organization and service providers to focus on the services that should be provided, *where, when* and in *what* ways. Since they are intended to bridge the gap between end-user requirements and expectations on the one hand and the delivery of services on the other, they have a pivotal role in facility management in general and in the procurement process in particular. Moreover, they provide the organization with the means to monitor performance and a basis for rewarding excellent results, as well as penalizing service providers that fall short. Sometimes, they become the centre of attention when one party feels the other is failing to meet an obligation. In a positive light, they can provide clarity, certainty and motivation to succeed, something that is capable of improvement and, by implication, something that will change over time.

SLAs are often made by parties within an internal market – that is, between the departments or other operational units in the organization – and act as a type of contract. This type of contract is not necessarily accompanied by a charge for the service. SLAs are also highly applicable to situations where services are outsourced. Here, the SLA supplements the contractual arrangements and is the starting point for developing a partnership relationship (see Chapter 10). The preference to incorporate service specifications and SLAs as annexes to a contract is often encountered. Organizations will approach this matter differently depending on external factors and the specialist advice they receive on the whole question of contracts. What is important here is to emphasize the standing of service specifications and SLAs in binding together the parties' intentions.

In some organizations, SLAs are used for establishing service levels between the informed client function and the business, with OLAs (operating level agreements) used between the informed client function and service providers. OLAs tend to include a greater level of detail than SLAs, which are aligned more to principles.

Service specifications

For each service, a specification should be prepared in precise terms that make clear the outcomes required from the delivery of that service. The organization should, wherever practicable, avoid stating requirements in a way that restricts the service provider's ability to select the most efficient and effective approach, while having regard to the need to achieve end-user satisfaction and best value.

A service specification is a document that quantifies the minimum acceptable technical standard of service required by end-users and will generally form a part of the agreement or contract with the service provider. The production of the service specification is a prerequisite in the preparation of SLAs and should set out the following:

- *Internal guidelines and specifications* – relating to corporate or department policy, as well as those that have been adopted on previous contracts.

- *External guidelines and specifications* – covering conformance to statutory requirements, international and national standards, health and safety legislation, industry standards and manufacturers' recommendations.
- *Procedures* – required practices that the service provider must follow to achieve specified standards.
- *Quality and performance thresholds* – minimum technical standards that will be acceptable.

Service specifications should be drafted consistently throughout and be presented in a manner that is aligned with other documents such as the SLA. The organization should avoid assembling service specifications from disparate sources and, instead, approach drafting from the general to the particular, capturing best practices. Moreover, service specifications should be drafted in such a way that changes in operational requirements can be managed without invalidating the agreement or contract covering the service.

The adoption of a performance (or output-based) specification is preferable to one that prescribes how work is required to be undertaken; that is, an input specification. It is important to encourage service providers to look for better ways, at lower cost, for the delivery of services that meet the required specification and service levels. Nonetheless, there can be grounds for the organization detailing its requirements exactly, as might occur, for example, when work has to be undertaken in a specific manner or at certain times. For the avoidance of ambiguity, specific requirements that leave nothing open to interpretation might need to be stated. In the case of cleaning, for example, an output specification could describe the standard of cleanliness to be achieved in terms of the maximum amount of dust or debris permitted to remain following cleaning. In a contract for catering, the specification could state that a meal is to be two courses, nutritionally balanced and offering a daily choice including sauces and drinks. In these cases, there is clearly opportunity for the service provider to innovate (see the earlier section on Assessment criteria).

Over time, adjustment to the wording of specifications is likely to become necessary as a consequence of changes in legislation, technical standards, policy or procedures to improve performance, thereby enhancing end-user satisfaction whilst maintaining best value. The inclusion of spot inspections of permits, certificates, records and other documentation can help to provide evidence of the service provider's compliance.

Performance and quality targets

The extent of detail in the specification will depend on the importance and complexity of the service or asset. This is bound to be an area of concern. Quality, as we are aware, manifests in many ways. If a number of end-users were asked to write down what quality meant to them in the context of a facility, there might be as many different definitions as there were end-users. In order to avoid the potential for disagreement and dispute, facility managers need to spend time working closely with end-users to elicit their views of what quality means to them. In many instances, it will be possible to substitute the word *performance* for *quality*. This

Table 8.2   The contents of an example service specification.

Section	Contents
Part 1: Terminology	1.1 Definition of terms used
Part 2: Areas/items/services	2.1 Scope of areas/items/services covered by specification
Part 3: External standards	3.1 Statutory requirements 3.2 International/national standards 3.3 Manufacturers' recommendations 3.4 Industry-accepted best practice
Part 4: Internal standards	4.1 Corporate/department requirements 4.2 Previously accepted standards
Part 5: Categorization of areas/items/services	5.1 Detailed procedures for each category 5.2 Frequency of procedures for each category

is not meant to avoid the issue of defining quality; rather, it is a pragmatic and realistic way of focusing on what exactly end-users expect and, therefore, mean by quality. In the context of service delivery, quality is something that can be defined, detailed and determined as due performance. For example, the quality of cleaning of, say, offices can be stated in terms of either what end-users will accept as clean or how often cleaning must be performed. Ensuring that worktops are always free from dust is an example of a performance requirement and a target to be achieved. It also says something tangible about the quality of service being delivered. In the case of catering, there is the intrinsic quality of the food to consider, as well as the whole experience provided to end-users from the performance of the service. The examples are simple, but not trivial, and illustrative of how we are able to express quality and performance and translate them into practical actions.

What does a service specification contain?

When undertaken for the first time, the drafting of specifications can be a time-consuming task. Advice and information on how to write specifications are available from a number of sources and will generally follow accepted practice. Table 8.2 shows the typical format of an example service specification. For some services, trade associations provide guidance to their members and offer model forms of specification. Common sense dictates that any model will require some adaptation to suit the organization, facility or contract in hand.

The approach to specification writing can vary depending on whether or not a prescriptive view is taken or one that is performance-related – the former is based on inputs and the latter is based on outputs. Table 8.3 shows extracts from an example service specification for cleaning showing, first, prescriptive specifications and, second, performance requirements.

There are obvious differences between the two approaches. The prescriptive specification – because it dictates *what* shall be done – will ensure that the cleaning of the specified areas and items will take place on a daily and weekly basis come what may. For example, floors will be cleaned and work surfaces wiped over whether or not this work is absolutely necessary: there is really no discretion.

Table 8.3 A service specification – an example of cleaning open-plan offices.

Prescriptive specification: daily tasks

1. Empty rubbish containers and bins (clean as required). Collect all rubbish and waste material, place in receptacle provided by the contractor and remove to the nearest designated disposal point.
2. Sweep floors using appropriate antic-static mop sweeper, leaving floors clean and free from visible dirt, dust and smears.
3. Lift primary matting and vacuum beneath.
4. Vacuum all soft floors and carpeted areas (loose or fitted). This is to include all raised areas and stairways.
5. Spot clean hard floors.
6. Spot clean tables, desks and chairs.

Prescriptive specification: weekly tasks

1. Damp wipe furniture, fittings and horizontal surfaces.
2. Using high-speed vacuum floor-polishing machines, spray clean hard floor areas with an approved cleaning agent and maintainer, and then use an appropriate brush or pad until floor is cleaned and polished.

Performance-based specification (all tasks)

1. Ensure that bins and other containers for waste and rubbish are emptied regularly so that they are not allowed to remain full – deposit at the nearest designated disposal point.
2. Do not permit the contents of bins and other containers to pose a threat to health or allow them to detract from the normal enjoyment of space by users.
3. Ensure that all floors are maintained in a clean, enduring and non-slip state, free from debris and other deleterious materials.
4. Do not permit spillage, contaminants or other deleterious materials to remain on floors.
5. Ensure that all work surfaces, fittings and other furnishings remain free from accumulated dust and other debris, and are maintained in a condition that does not detract from the normal enjoyment of space by users.
6. Do not permit spillage, contaminants or other deleterious materials to remain on work surfaces, fittings and other furnishings.

If there were, then it could easily lead to conflict where one party disagrees with the other's definition or interpretation of what is necessary. In the performance-based approach, the service provider is able to schedule cleaning according to need, which arises from patterns of use, access hours, weather and so on. More likely than not, the performance-based specification will deliver the quality of service required at less cost than the prescriptive approach.

Apart from these differences, there is the issue of flexibility. Prescriptive specifications are, by definition, restrictive and difficult to change once the contract has been awarded. The performance-based approach, on the other hand, avoids this problem by setting targets that the service provider can use to determine the most appropriate operational response. Detractors of the performance-based approach would argue that the minimum effort will be put into the task and that, at least, with the prescriptive approach we can see the work being performed at specified intervals. This line of argument is, however, flawed. In the specific example of cleaning, the aim should be to ensure that the workplace is cleaned when necessary and without inconvenience to users. Moreover, as far as practicable, service delivery should for the most part be unobtrusive. When performed at the highest level, with all services being delivered as required, facility management can be regarded as an *invisible* service.

Service level agreements (SLAs)

SLAs are statements of intentions between the organization and service providers on behalf of the end-users of the service. They can apply to a number of services and facilities and are, therefore, written in general terms, or they might be facility- or service-specific. In all instances, they should embody or cross-reference relevant service specifications.

End-users normally have particular expectations about levels of service. These expectations have to be translated into formal requirements and targets that end-users (or the facility manager on their behalf) can use to judge the level of service received from the service provider. Discussion with prospective service providers can help to ensure that targets are both appropriate and practicable. An example target is one where the response to a problem – for example, a breakdown in an item of equipment – is required within a specified period that is both practicable for the service provider and tolerable for end-users. In these instances, it might be useful to specify the tolerance threshold for rectifying failure or malfunction.

The responsibility for preparing SLAs rests with the organization. In certain cases, the service provider produces the SLA and the organization has to accept the provisions or go elsewhere. This situation normally arises where commodities are involved, such as in ICT services (e.g. server hosting and cloud storage), utility supplies (i.e. water, electricity and gas) and some professional services (e.g. legal and accountancy services). The SLAs are generally found in the supplier's standard terms or conditions and are unlikely to change unless the organization has significant purchasing power. In all other cases, the organization should consider the following basis for drafting an SLA:

- names of the parties;
- roles and responsibilities of the parties;
- scope of services to be provided, limitations and exclusions;
- resources supplied by the organization;
- prioritization of requirements;
- quality- and performance-related targets;
- time-related targets;
- prices and rates (fixed and/or variable);
- open-book accounting;
- communication between end-users and service providers; and
- change control.

The organization has to decide whether it requires fixed prices and rates or if it will accept variable prices or rates for which additional costs will have to be met into the future. This decision would be better taken earlier, at the time of prequalification, to take account of current and forecast market inflation, as well as any other factor that might affect the balance of risk between the organization and service providers. Instead of providing a transparent basis for cooperation, *open-book accounting* can become a source of conflict if not clearly defined. On the one hand, it does not mean that the organization has complete freedom to inspect the service provider's accounts as and when it chooses. Then again, it does not mean that it has to make repeated requests for details of personnel and the cost of materials, where these are clearly stated as a requirement in the SLA.

Experience shows that, over time, some adjustment is necessary to working arrangements, including targets, remuneration, penalties and incentives to improve performance, achieve end-user satisfaction and best value. SLAs should therefore be drafted so that changes to these performance-related aspects can be managing without invalidating them or the overarching contract between the organization and its service providers. This is perhaps easier said than done, but it is necessary to ensure that there is room to manoeuvre. In any event, contracts should stipulate that payments will depend on the service provider achieving performance targets.

A key feature of facility management is that it is a continuous process into the future, and learning by all parties is bound to reveal the need for adjustment in the interest of improving performance to deliver enhanced end-user satisfaction and best value. Continual improvement is more than a concept; it is a fundamental component of facility management. Over time, the ability to accept changes will yield worthwhile savings in cost and greater rewards for both the organization and service providers.

Table 8.4 shows the top-level contents of an example SLA. The typical sections of an SLA can be found in Appendix E.

Table 8.4   The contents of an example SLA based on a total facility management service.

Section	Contents
Part 1: Agreement details	1.1 Names of parties to the agreement 1.2 Date agreement signed 1.3 Effective date of agreement 1.4 Period of agreement
Part 2: Scope of services – service specification	2.1 Management of maintenance of structures, fabric, plant and equipment, and external landscaping 2.2 Management of minor building works 2.3 Management of accommodation services 2.4 Management of utilities and telecommunications
Part 3: Delivery times, fees	3.1 Service priority categories and times 3.2 Fees and payment
Part 4: Performance	4.1 Submission of performance reports 4.2 Performance measures
Part 5: End-user/service provider interface	5.1 Communication 5.2 Incentives and penalties 5.3 End-user rating and feedback 5.4 Procedures for revising the SLA

Formal contract

Contracts should be awarded on a multi-year basis unless the service is of less than 12 months' duration. For most services, a contract term of three years is appropriate, with the organization retaining the option to extend for a further one or two years. Annual break clauses should be incorporated in all cases as far as practicable. Any perceived gains from more frequent re-tendering of service contracts than the recommended three years are likely to be outweighed by the additional time and cost incurred in tendering. There is also likely to be the prospect of reducing levels of performance towards the end of the contract as the service provider directs attention elsewhere.

A key assumption is that contracts for services are likely to be awarded following a tender competition; however, it is possible to procure services in other ways. For example, a contract could be negotiated with one or more service providers or a partnership could be formed between the organization and a service provider (see Chapter 10). For large and/or multinational organizations, a framework agreement might be used to cover an arrangement where a select number of service providers are retained on the basis that all work will be distributed amongst them over a defined period.

Performance measurement and reporting

The measurement of performance and its subsequent reporting should be included as part of the duties of a service provider, with the detailed requirements covered in the SLA. Service providers are better placed than the organization to measure performance and so there is little, if any, point in it taking on this task. Apart from the resources and cost involved, there is needless duplication of effort, as service providers generally measure performance for their own purposes. The responsibility for verifying work performed by service providers does, however, rest with the organization or someone acting on its behalf; for example, a managing agent. The organization should reserve the right to require evidence to be produced before considering an application for payment – something that ties in with the concept of open-book accounting.

The means for dealing with situations where performance falls below an acceptable level, including the imposition of penalties for poor performance, needs to be clearly defined. Equally, incentives for achieving higher levels of performance than those set as minimum levels should be considered, as should the sharing of cost savings or other gains that a service provider achieves. Incentivization must be handled with care. Sometimes an incentive scheme can create unwanted behaviour and achieve quite the opposite of what was intended. Extreme care needs to be exercise where incentives are linked to HSSE. An incentive scheme that based reward on maintaining a level of zero accidents might dissuade personnel from reporting accidents for fear of missing the incentive. In the worst case, an unreported accident could lead to severe consequences for the injured party, even death, because of the failure to receive urgent medical attention.

Tendering

Market testing

Going to the market should be an honest attempt at establishing the attraction or otherwise of outsourcing. This does not, however, imply frequent tendering exercises, where an in-house team competes for work alongside external service providers. It is preferable for clear-cut choices to be made between insourcing and outsourcing, wherever possible. This avoids the counterproductive effects that the anxiety caused by market testing, or the demoralization caused by an unsuccessful tender, might have on the in-house team and its subsequent dealings with its new, external employer as a result of a transfer of employment (see Chapter 4).

Appropriate use of the market would include regular comparisons of current prices and rates for services using published data, participation in a benchmarking club (see Chapter 11) or indicative quotations from prospective service providers. An awareness of the state of the market for services means that at any time a judgement can be made as to whether or not a particular decision is the most appropriate. Some of the requisite information might, however, be already contained within market audits carried out during the preparation of the facility management strategy (Chapter 3). Even so, it might need to be updated, since market conditions can be unpredictable and are subject to change.

The performance of the service provider should be reviewed on an annual basis, rather than the decision to insource or outsource. Once a decision to outsource has been taken, it should not be subject to continuous review. As noted earlier, it is important to avoid letting contracts on less than an annual basis. Longer-term contracts for three or more years can be let with break clauses. Annual reviews should, in any case, be incorporated into contracts running for two or more years. In some countries, legislation might force re-tendering on an annual basis for public-sector contracts. This can add to cost, as well as limiting the performance of the service provider. In such cases, it can only be hoped that the institutions concerned eventually recognize the short-sightedness of their approach and move to an arrangement that is capable of achieving best value. It is surely not beyond the ability of those institutions to draft contracts that incorporate annual reviews and break clauses to cover the eventuality of poor performance by the service provider. The mechanisms for reviewing performance are covered in Chapter 11.

Tender competitions

Ordinarily, it would be wise to invite proposals/tenders from three to five service providers. Increasing the number of invitations will not improve competitiveness and might well result in an otherwise competent and competitive service provider withdrawing. The cost incurred in preparing proposals or tenders is not insignificant. This cost adds to the overheads of service providers, which have then to be borne by those contracts where they are successful. The more service providers that are invited each time, the less chance there is to be successful. In the long run, the cost of service contracts increases and that is clearly not in anyone's best interest.

While little has changed in some aspects of tendering, the use of e-tendering and electronic auctions for services has increased significantly and has implications for many sectors in industry and commerce. E-tendering is an electronic tendering process involving the exchange of documentation in electronic format. Benefits can include:

- A reduced timescale for the tendering process.
- An improved workflow with inbuilt decision gates.
- A more consistent prequalification and evaluation.
- The automatic rejection of non-compliant tenders.
- A reduction in human resources for gathering and analysing information and tenders.
- An improved audit trail and management information.

Examples of e-tendering are to be found in both the public and private sectors and include contracts for facility-related services. However, public procurement is highly prescribed in many countries and might preclude certain practices.

Tender evaluation

The organization should define the criteria by which each tender, as represented by a completed request for proposals, is evaluated. These criteria should be consistent with the criteria used at the RFI stage – see the earlier section on Request for information. Lowest price should not be the sole factor in deciding which tender to accept, although some tenders seem to be accepted on the basis of price alone. If best value is to mean anything, quality should play an equal part in any evaluation. For some contracts, it might be difficult to determine the quality of service: rarely can performance (or quality) be considered in absolute terms. It is possible to take account of quality by judging it against benchmarks established in service specifications or through other objective measures. Normally, service providers should be asked to submit a fixed-price tender for the term of the contract, together with a breakdown of prices and rates, including the annual equivalent value of the contract. Alternatively, a fixed price per annum for a specified number of years might be sought, also with a breakdown of prices and rates.

There are other ways in which quality and cost might be judged. For example, one approach would be to operate a two-envelope tender system. Shortlisted service providers are sent model agreements and asked to submit a lump-sum tender, along with their time charges for extra work. The first tender describes the quality of service to be provided; the second gives the price. Two separate panels look at the tenders.

A quality panel of, say, four people is convened to consider the proposals/tenders according to the quality that they believe each tenderer represents. Table 8.5 can be used to guide the panel in these deliberations. This involves the panel scoring the quality of proposed services delivery for each service provider: it is better that panellists reach a consensus. Once the quality panel has finished its deliberations, the price panel opens the envelopes containing the price tenders. The decision is then taken to award the contract to the service provider offering the highest quality (as indicated by the scores), at the lowest price based on a simple calculation. The subsequent contract award can be founded on the most economically advantageous tender.

Table 8.5   Assessment of service providers (tender evaluation).

Assessment	Criteria	Score
Very poor	Unable to demonstrate acceptable quality/ performance, operational methods, delivery/ response time and likely end-user satisfaction	0
Poor	Limited evidence of acceptable quality/ performance, operational methods, delivery/ response time and likely end-user satisfaction	1–4
Satisfactory	Adequate evidence of acceptable quality/ performance, operational methods, delivery/ response time and likely end-user satisfaction	5–6
Good	Significant evidence of quality/performance, operational methods, delivery/response time and likely end-user satisfaction and, in some areas, reveals innovation that exceeds requirements	7–8
Excellent	Considerable evidence of quality/ performance, operational methods, delivery/ response time and likely end-user satisfaction in all areas and reveals innovation that exceeds requirements in most areas	9–10

Increasingly, least whole-life cost is considered as part of the evaluation of proposals or tenders for services involving maintenance and replacement of plant and equipment. From the organization's perspective, whole-life cost or total cost of ownership (TCO) is likely to be a key concern in its management of facility assets. TCO takes into account cost over the longer term (typically, the life of the asset), including initial capital cost, depreciation, annual servicing costs, repairs and replacement costs, inflation, taxation and opportunity costs. In the case of service contracts, it is a matter of determining the full cost that each tender represents, enabling comparison on a like-for-like basis. The concept would be covered in Table 8.5 under the criterion of *innovation that exceeds requirements*.

Financial close

Once proposals/tenders have been evaluated, the preferred service provider should be requested to submit details of the following as a prerequisite to reaching financial close and the formalization of the contract, otherwise termed *contract award*:

- Plan of work or schedule for mobilization and start-up of service delivery.
- Managerial and supervisory personnel (including CVs or résumés).
- Operational personnel (including certificates, where appropriate).
- Arrangements covering transfer of undertakings, where applicable.

- Subcontractors to be engaged.
- Contract prices and rates.
- Insurances and banking details.
- Information required from the organization to support mobilization and start-up.

Further information should be requested from prospective service providers if considered necessary to resolve any difference of interpretation or to eliminate potential conflict. It is vital that any outstanding matters are fully resolved before a proposal or tender is accepted and the contract is awarded. In the case of subcontracting, it is important not to deny the service provider the right to subcontract aspects of a service where justified. Nonetheless, assignment of the contract to another service provider should be ruled out by the conditions of contract. Failure to do so could leave the door open for abuse and resultant conflict.

Completed proposals/tenders place the organization in the position where alignment between its service requirements (established at the RFI stage) and what the market is prepared to offer come to the fore. Despite the relatively short period that will have elapsed, it is possible that assumptions or circumstances might have changed. Negotiation between the organization and a service provider would then be necessary to resolve any aspect of the tender that is deemed non-compliant. This stage is generally referred to as *tender negotiation*. It should not be taken as an indication of significant divergence from the request for proposal. Even so, minor issues have to be resolved before the tender can be accepted; otherwise, there is a risk that these issues could grow. Once resolved, financial close can be achieved, as signified by the award of the contract.

In the simplest example, a purchase order for the service can be raised, based on contract conditions that are common to other areas of the organization's business. In other cases, contract conditions might reflect the custom and practices of an industrial sector that is supported by a strong trade association. In any event, the contract conditions and any intended use of a standard form of contract are matters that prospective service providers will have had the opportunity to comment upon and challenge in the request for proposal stage or, perhaps, prior to that at the RFI stage.

It is not uncommon for service providers to subcontract part of their scope of work to other specialists. Some services involve highly specialized tasks, but for relatively short periods, that would render them uneconomical to manage other than through subcontracting. If subcontracting were disallowed, the organization would pay a hefty premium, and for what could amount to an inferior outcome. Subcontracting for reasons of maximizing profit or due to a lack of resources created by the service provider's commitments elsewhere are different matters and are clearly unacceptable.

Operational considerations

This stage can be one of the most worrying for the organization, because it has come a long way and, yet, is not in the position where the new service provider can commence or take over from the incumbent service provider (see Chapter 14 on Transition). In spite of previous work in carefully considering the suitability of the new service provider, the organization must satisfy itself as to the service provider's practical grasp of the conditions and demands concerning the service to be delivered. It is important to receive satisfactory answers to all questions; otherwise, the organization is embarking on a journey involving doubt and uncertainty. For this reason, it would be wise to keep the second-ranked service provider in reserve until such time as a sound basis for a contract with the preferred service provider is in force.

The preferred service provider needs to demonstrate the suitability of its operational approach by providing information on its management, supervision and personnel, and full details of any intended subcontractors. Where transfer of undertakings is involved, arrangements for a seamless transition between the existing arrangement and its replacement must be scrutinized (see Chapter 14). The preferred service provider should be interviewed to discuss its approach and to ensure that there is an acceptable state of readiness for service delivery to commence.

Pre-contract meeting

Once the preferred service provider has been selected, a pre-contract meeting should be called to address the following:

- The service provider's plan for mobilization and delivery of the service (see Chapter 14).
- Insurance cover with respect to statutory obligations and specific eventualities.
- Contract administration (e.g. payments, meetings and other key events).

The service provider should be given a sufficient mobilization period to organize all resources, thus ensuring a seamless continuation of service delivery for the benefit of end-users. Where the service(s) affected are to be outsourced for the first time, it is recommended that the service provider visits the organization to explain expectations to end-users of the service. During this period, it will be necessary to plan for the regular review of the service provider's performance. The frequency of reviews will depend on the duration and complexity of the contract. Normally, three-monthly reviews would be appropriate, although monthly or weekly reviews during the early stages might be advisable in order to deal with teething problems.

In cases where the organization's personnel have been transferred to a service provider, special arrangements will be required to deal with the transition – see Chapter 14 for a more detailed treatment of this subject.

Contract award

Once all matters relating to the recommendation of the preferred service provider, including operational considerations and the pre-contract meeting, have been satisfactorily concluded, the organization is ready to enter into a formal contract on such terms and conditions (or adoption of a standard form of contract) as have been previously agreed. The unsuccessful service providers should be informed of the contract award, including the name of the successful service provider. They should be given the opportunity to discuss their performance in the tender competition, since feedback can be helpful when preparing subsequent proposals/ tenders. Care should be exercised over the extent to which information can be disclosed, not least details of the successful tenderer.

Conclusions

Procurement is more than a purchasing decision. It can involve the organization in a plethora of considerations, decisions and actions in order to arrive at the point where it has sufficient confidence in a service provider to award a contract. There is a defined process for procurement that needs to be followed if the most suitable service provider is to be identified. Prospective service providers have to be qualified for the service or services in question. Those that do not have the capability (i.e. competence and skills) and capacity (i.e. financial means) to undertake the work have to be filtered out. Prequalification is a key determinant of successful procurement and must not be taken lightly. Various criteria have to be assembled to judge prospective service providers and these should be transparent and fair. Once the choice of qualified service providers has been confirmed, they can be requested to submit proposals or tenders, depending on the extent to which services have been specified. A firm basis for service contracts is essential and this can be assured by service specifications and service level agreements (SLAs) that collectively define the quality and performance required for a service and from a service provider. Time spent in preparing robust service specifications and SLAs that accurately capture end-user requirements and represent best value will be amply repaid, as contracts will be easier to manage and less prone to misinterpretation. The evaluation of tenders, in particular, will need to be undertaken on an objective basis against predefined criteria that weigh quality and performance against price, so that the best value outcome can be determined and the most suitable service provider can be selected. The organization should ensure that formalities are concluded before announcing the successful tenderer.

Checklist

This checklist is intended to assist with review and action planning.

	Yes	No	Action required
1. Does a process exist for the purpose of procuring facility-related services?	☐	☐	☐
2. Has a policy for procurement been prepared and is it supported by appropriate procedures?	☐	☐	☐
3. Where there is a split between centralized and decentralized procurement, does this affect facility-related services?	☐	☐	☐

	Yes	No	Action required
4. Have roles, responsibilities and accountabilities in procurement been adequately defined?	☐	☐	☐
5. Is the market for service providers understood at the local and regional level?	☐	☐	☐
6. Have prospective service providers been identified for each service or multiple services, as applicable?	☐	☐	☐
7. Has a request for information (RFI) been prepared and issued to prospective service providers?	☐	☐	☐
8. Has the suitability of prospective service providers been established in terms of their capability and capacity to deliver services?	☐	☐	☐
9. Have the scope of services, service specifications and service level agreements (SLAs) been prepared as part of a request for proposals or tenders?	☐	☐	☐
10. Has the organization determined if it will accept alternative proposals or tenders?	☐	☐	☐
11. Is the tendering process sufficiently rigorous to allow for proper competition?	☐	☐	☐
12. Does tender evaluation focus in objective terms on quality/ performance as well as price?	☐	☐	☐
13. Has a pre-contract meeting been arranged for each service provider prior to contract award?	☐	☐	☐
14. Are arrangements in place to ensure productive ongoing relationships between the service provider and the organization?	☐	☐	☐

9 Service Delivery

Key issues

The following issues are covered in this chapter.

- Facility management provides essential service support for the organization's core business. Any break or loss of service delivery could impact operations and threaten business continuity.

- The delivery of services, whether insourced or outsourced, should satisfy end-user requirements and achieve best value. End-users should observe no perceivable difference in the way services are delivered or in how they are treated.

- Services have to be started up and so a period for mobilization has to be planned and implemented; similarly, services might have to be phased out at some point as a new arrangement for service delivery is phased in.

- Mobilization and demobilization are key components in the transition from one service arrangement to another. If there is to be no loss of service delivery or disruption to operations, the transition must be adequately resourced and controlled.

- All service providers have to be managed – the nature of the relationship between the organization and service providers is where it varies.

- The organization has to develop its informed client function if it is to manage contracts and control finances – this applies irrespective of whether services are insourced or outsourced.

- Procedures should be transparent and follow accepted accounting standards.

- Actions must be performed according to the contract and at intervals stipulated to ensure compliance on the part of service providers and prompt payment for work completed satisfactorily.

Total Facility Management, Fourth Edition. Brian Atkin and Adrian Brooks.
© 2015 John Wiley & Sons, Ltd. Published 2015 by John Wiley & Sons, Ltd.

- Service providers should receive payment, including incentive money, or attract penalties appropriate to their performance against the service specification and SLA.

- An in-house team should be assessed against the same criteria as external service providers. Any changes that are required should be controlled in accordance with the agreement between the organization and its in-house team.

- Contract costs should be monitored against both the tender price and budget on a basis that is appropriate to the contract duration and size. Similar arrangements should apply to insourced services.

- Contracts should run for not less than three years. The period of contract review should be appropriate to the value and complexity of the contract. For most services, this period should be 12 months unless otherwise agreed. Similar arrangements should apply to insourced services.

Introduction

From the perspective of end-users, there should be no perceivable difference between services delivered by an in-house team and external service providers, or the way in which they are treated. In other words, end-user satisfaction should not be affected by the particular arrangements for service delivery. The primary reason for choosing one in preference to the other is the need to demonstrate best value. The performance expected is the same in both cases; its cost, however, is subject to market conditions, productivity, incentives and quality of management and supervision, amongst other factors. Over time, the cost of services will change, so that the decision on whether or not to continue with the existing arrangement will have to be revisited (see Chapter 7). Since facility management provides essential service support for the organization's core business, any break or loss of service delivery could impact operations and threaten business continuity. Where a service is newly introduced, it has to be started up and, possibly, ramped up until a steady state of service delivery is achieved. A period for mobilization has to be planned and implemented. In a similar vein, services will have to be phased out as the new arrangement is phased in. A crucial point is, therefore, the transition from one service arrangement to another – for a more detailed treatment of transition, see Chapter 14. Throughout, service providers have to be managed irrespective of the nature of the relationship between them and the organization. Managing service delivery is about managing service contracts and that applies equally to insourcing and outsourcing. The informed client function needs to be maintained, even enhanced, if the organization is to successfully manage contracts and control finances. Contracts – in the case of outsourcing – and agreements – in the case of insourcing – will embody specific requirements with which the parties must comply. These will regulate various aspects of service delivery – not least payment and matters concerning actions in the event that service delivery falls short of, or exceeds, targets. This chapter considers how the organization can achieve the best outcomes irrespective of the source of service delivery. Important guidance is available within standards. In particular, the provisions of BS 8572, some of which are reflected in this chapter, cover aspects of service delivery.

The internal customer as end-user

End-users must be recognized as customers and the relationship between them and the in-house team or external service providers must be taken seriously and managed professionally. For these reasons, performance management should be regarded as applying to insourced as well as outsourced services. A process of continual improvement will need to be implemented to ensure that productivity and standards of quality and performance are consistently raised.

For outsourced services, it is generally recognized that success is dependent upon the clear definition of the services, including their interfaces. In other words, there are *no cracks to fall down*. This view is also true in the case of insourcing, but for different reasons. Where services have been outsourced, definition is required to ensure that all necessary services are provided and that no gaps exist between the interfaces of each service. The in-house team also requires clear definition in order to manage its resources effectively. Without obvious delineation of roles and responsibilities, it can be difficult to measure the performance of the in-house team.

If the customer – taken to be a department or operating unit within the organization – is unsure as to the nature and extent of service delivery, it is hard for those delivering the service both to achieve and to demonstrate best value. This is also important in the context of avoiding conflicts of interest, because of unclear splits between the procurement function and the in-house team at the time of preparing tender documentation and during the subsequent tendering period.

Since stakeholders are critical to the success of service delivery of any kind, those directly affected by the delivery of services must be clearly identified. It is important for the in-house team to understand the relative influence of respective stakeholders, as the team could be serving many end-users simultaneously. At the same time, it would be wise to avoid embarking upon any path that could conceivably prove divisive and create conflict with the organization's business objectives, thereby potentially impacting upon business continuity – see the later section.

The in-house team perhaps has the benefit of many years of experience of the organization, which must not be lost by failing to be responsive to the needs of the customer. Internal departments must be regarded as customers and their needs served accordingly. There should be no difference in the in-house team's attitude towards internal and external customers where the latter could be, for instance, members of the public who make use of the facility. A professional and business-like approach must be adopted and maintained towards all customers as end-users of services. Organizations that grasp this point are likely to be providing services that are responsive and appreciated by all.

Insourcing

Sourcing from within the organization might be seen as less demanding, even of lower importance from a management perspective, than outsourcing. In a sector that has grown large on the back of a tide of outsourcing, it is not difficult to see insourcing as having a perceived lower economic worth. However, this is far from the reality. In most countries, a significant proportion of facilities are competently managed by in-house teams, who consistently deliver end-user satisfaction and best value. They have achieved this position by being highly professional and as demanding of their own personnel as others are of external service providers. Some organizations have brought in-house services that were previously outsourced. The purpose here is not to argue for either insourcing or outsourcing, since that is a consequence of earlier steps in formulating a strategy, policies and operational plans to deliver best value. The intention is to underline the importance of managing insourcing to the highest standard. A policy and supporting procedures will therefore have to be adopted where services are insourced.

The in-house team

The in-house team must be able to adapt to meet changes in requirements in order to support the core business effectively, achieve end-user satisfaction and provide best value. The ease with which this might be possible will depend upon the competence and skills of personnel and their willingness to continue in training and personal development. If necessary, in-house teams might have to recruit new personnel with the necessary skills. Chapter 5 outlined examples of how existing personnel can be motivated and challenged. Retaining and investing in personnel should be seen as preferable to – and probably less costly and time-consuming than – recruitment.

In technical areas such as maintenance of building services engineering installations, many external service providers invest heavily in training to ensure that their personnel are competent and qualified. This is especially so where new legislation and standards come into force and where it is necessary to retain membership of an industry body or association. For a small, in-house team, this might represent a significant time and cost overhead. If the in-house team is to satisfy requirements, the investment has to be made.

It is essential that members of the in-house team recognize that they should operate in the same way as would an external service provider and that they will be judged on a similar basis. Given that the organization's senior managers might be looking periodically at the market for service providers, it makes sense for the in-house team to operate in a business-like way so that it can compete fairly if the need arises. Most organizations manage to do this, but the weakness is in maintaining consistency over time. One of the biggest threats to the in-house team's success is from complacency, which is easily noticed by end-users.

The in-house team should be considered in terms of its efficiency and cost-effectiveness. The constituent personnel must operate as a team if they are to deliver a value-adding service. The starting point for engendering team spirit is through sharing common goals and key objectives. Customer charters have become increasingly popular. These set out the type and level of services that can be expected in a number of service areas. Many private-sector organizations do so. This kind of SLA has the added benefit of articulating the objectives to be achieved by the team. By sharing common goals and key objectives, and working as a team, additional benefits can result. These will help the in-house team measure up to the organization's expectations, as well as its own. Care must be exercised, however, in ensuring that charters are not seen as some kind of management fad or, worse, as a collection of imperatives written up as superlatives. If they do, they might well attract disparaging comment.

The in-house team must be proactive in looking for areas where value can be added. It should not regard service levels as permanent, but as providing the basis for improvement. Its expertise can help to assess whether or not the perceived service levels are, in fact, the most appropriate. This is particularly relevant in the case of response times when ordering work. If informed discussion can take place as to real needs as opposed to perceived needs, the service, with its corresponding resource levels, can be designed to meet those needs. This value-adding activity can enable the in-house team to differentiate itself from external service providers with intimate knowledge of the organization used to good effect. Even so, such knowledge is no substitute for a service that does not satisfy end-user requirements and consistently so.

Many support service processes are manpower-intensive and consist of a high volume of low-value activities. ICT could therefore be of help to the in-house team by improving communication and producing appropriate management information. Through the use of low-cost ICT tools, the in-house team can measure the performance of service delivery against the service level agreed with each identified end-user group – see the later section. Thereafter, by means of continual improvement, increases in performance can be compared and reported against benchmarks (see Chapter 11). This activity should extend to a comparison with external service providers, both to assess the relative competitiveness of insourcing and to gain new insights into achieving best practice.

Many of the stages and issues that an in-house team should consider are comparable to those that apply to outsourced services. The difference lies in the clarity of roles and responsibilities, which are usually made more obvious in the latter by following an explicit procurement process that involves a degree of formality (see Chapter 8). The in-house team should try to achieve the same position both for the benefit of its end-users and for its own management needs. This, in turn, will support ready measurement of performance. The retention of insourcing is bound to be the primary goal of the in-house team. It is only likely to reach that goal if it delivers end-user satisfaction and best value and can demonstrate both.

External service providers

The opening assumption is that the organization will have determined which services to outsource and will have done so by taking account of the market for services (see Chapter 7). Earlier actions will have established whether or not the market is able to deliver what is required. An important consideration should have been the bundling of individual services in a way that will achieve end-user satisfaction and provide best value. There are two aspects to consider. First, the organization will have worked out how best to arrange its outsourcing to ensure that best value is likely to be achieved. Second, service providers will take a commercial view on what is profitable for them. Bundling of services can be attractive for service providers; likewise, carving up the totality of services into very small contracts might not be. It is also useful to recognize that arrangements involving a lot of subcontracting – and, possibly, sub-subcontracting – can be financially disadvantageous because a transaction cost is added at each point in the supply chain without necessarily adding value.

The facility manager should be informed of the financial standing of each service provider before contract award. Credit references should be sought in addition to performance references from other employers of the service provider. Failure of a service provider, large or small, would be detrimental for the organization. Whilst it is never possible to eliminate the likelihood of this happening, its occurrence can be minimized by taking up references with reliable sources.

Mobilization

Once a new service provider has been appointed – or, for example, the in-house team has been awarded a previously outsourced service – there has to be a period of mobilization in order that the service can be correctly started up. Control has to be exercised over start-up and in any phasing in and ramping up of delivery. As noted earlier, there should be no disruption to normal operations from any change in the arrangements for service delivery unless, of course, there is a deliberate decision to limit or, in some other way, adjust operations at this point. Operations that are critical to the organization's core business are less likely to be capable of adjustment to accommodate transition from one service arrangement to another. Steps should therefore be taken to maintain levels of service for end-users during transition in general and throughout mobilization in particular.

Even in the most straightforward of cases, the service provider or in-house team will need information immediately following contract award and prior to the start-up of the service to prepare for its delivery. Typical of this information are the following:

- Scope of service, including limits, access, working hours and use of in-house resources.
- Representatives of the parties, with contact details, including out-of-hours contact.
- Procedures in the event of an emergency.
- HSSE compliance.
- Human resources requirements.
- Supply chain requirements.
- Operational processes and procedures.
- Management information and reporting.

- Performance management.
- Valuations and payments.
- Dispute resolution procedure.

Lines of communication with service providers should be defined and a single point of contact for managing contracts established by the organization. Similarly, each service provider should provide a main point of contact to cover delivery of the service in the facility and contact at its main place of business. Details of the service provider's health and safety person should be made available. For an in-house team, there is a requirement to ensure that personnel know how to obtain help or assistance, or report an incident or event. A central helpdesk might be necessary, if none exists, to coordinate communication between end-users and service providers and/or the in-house team. Where changes to the arrangements for service delivery are significant, the likelihood is of increased levels of uncertainty on the part of end-users. Having a helpdesk makes sense and can often result in suggestions for end-users on how to alleviate a problem pending its resolution.

The period during which the service provider makes arrangements to start up delivery of the service can last from a few days to a few weeks, or even longer. From the organization's perspective, checking the proposed working arrangements of a number of service providers, if undertaken in parallel, could represent a significant task for which sufficient time and resources have to be set aside. Allowing for this work is a prerequisite of successful service delivery.

The mobilization plan

Service providers need to provide details of their planned working arrangements for starting up service delivery. A plan should be prepared for each service based on the tasks involved, their timing and key resource requirements (see Chapter 14). It is better if the plan takes the form of a schedule that can be used by both parties to track and report on progress, since a plan loses its effectiveness if not updated regularly with progress. Some service providers might find it difficult to comply with such a requirement because they lack the necessary in-house skill to prepare schedules, typically those in the form of a network-based Gantt chart. A workaround is to give each service provider a template that suits its needs in tracking progress. In addition, weekly meetings should be used to exchange information until both parties have agreed that mobilization is complete and confirmed by end-users of the service. The scale and complexity of service delivery will determine the extent to which meetings and progress reporting are necessary. Similar requirements should apply to the in-house team, so it is clear that there has been enough preparation to start up service delivery. If start-up is not carefully controlled, the in-house team could make unrealistic assumptions about the availability of resources or other aspects.

When replacing an incumbent service provider, it will be necessary to check that arrangements for transition are sufficient to ensure that end-users experience no break in service delivery (see Chapter 14). Events could occur to threaten successful mobilization. It is sensible, therefore, to include some form of contingency to cover the possible impact of such events. Time spent in a risk assessment will be amply repaid because it helps to identify previously unknown events and the most appropriate way to deal with them should they materialize. Whilst certain eventualities might be unlikely to occur, having a contingency plan would help to mitigate the impact of a risk event if it did materialize. For those events where there is a more likely than not chance of occurrence, some allowance should be built into the plan before it is implemented. Contingency is over and above allowances.

Supply-side considerations

Service providers should not be permitted to subcontract any part of the service without written prior permission. Whilst the matter of subcontracting will have been discussed at the pre-contract meeting, it is worth having intentions confirmed. In the course of a contract, it is possible that a service provider might encounter difficulty in obtaining sufficient resources with the required competence and skills. There can be a number of reasons and so it is necessary to understand what they are so that the situation can be rectified without delay. Up-to-date and reliable information on performance and progress helps to highlight such an eventuality. As a rule, at each review meeting, service providers should be required to report on any matter affecting or likely to affect their ability to fulfil their obligations under the contract for reasons of shortage or non-availability of resources. Moreover, they should be required to say how they intend to overcome any such shortcomings. Depending on the circumstances, it might be possible for the organization to act to minimize the impact on operations.

Business continuity and transition

Business continuity is concerned with managing the recovery or continuation of the primary processes and activities of the organization should a disruption occur that affects normal operations and, hence, the running of the business. The purpose of business continuity management is to safeguard the interests of key stakeholders, value creation and reputation. Any change in the delivery of services has the potential to threaten business continuity. Risks and opportunities should therefore be identified and assessed. Where there is a concern about business continuity, thought should be given to strengthening organizational resilience as a way of countering the effects of any disruption arising from start-up (or winding down) of service delivery, including transition from one arrangement to another. Simply, it might not be possible to mitigate identified risks sufficiently; besides, resilience is likely to demand continual monitoring and review. During the phasing in of a new arrangement, any departing service provider must not hinder the incoming service provider or leave any part of the facility in an unsafe or insecure state that could potentially impact people or processes.

The organization needs to assess the potential impact of changes in the delivery of services upon its ability to maintain operations at a level that is acceptable, bearing in mind the motivation for transition. Processes and activities that are essential to sustaining normal operations should be categorized according to their priority for recovery. Those processes and activities the loss of which would have the greatest impact in the shortest time and that have to be recovered rapidly should be regarded as *critical*. Depending on the processes or activities, the maximum period for resuming normal operations could vary between minutes and weeks. Those that are time-critical might have to be specified with a high degree of precision, in minutes or hours. Armed with this information, the organization is in a better position to manage transition (see Chapter 14).

Operational processes and procedures

Service providers should be required to produce plans of their operations, including the category, level and number of operatives. These plans should be accompanied by details of the managerial and supervisory personnel necessary to achieve safe, efficient and cost-effective service delivery. The time horizon for planning should be typically three months, although a longer period might be advisable where changes in the work environment are under consideration.

Changes to operational processes and procedures should form the subject of discussion at performance review meetings – see the later section on Performance reviews. Other than for reasons of safety or inoperability, changes should not be approved until or unless they have been properly considered in a review meeting. As a general rule, the organization should monitor the performance of all service contracts to identify any deviation from agreed plans, processes and procedures. Service providers should be made responsible for bringing any matter that is likely to impact on service delivery to the attention of the organization. In many cases, this will mean raising questions about performance and progress so that there is active consideration of the matter with opportunity for discussion.

The organization should avoid commenting on, or interfering in, operational processes other than for reasons of HSSE. Service providers must be allowed to concentrate on operational matters, with the organization in an overseeing role. Matters such as human resources management, whilst highly important, might not be time-critical. Any concern should be recorded by the organization and relevant information should be requested from the service provider so that the matter can be considered at the next performance review meeting.

Management information and reporting

The successful management of service contracts depends to a large extent on the quality of information provided by the service provider in a form such that the organization knows almost in an instant how well or not service delivery is going. If it is necessary to puzzle over information in reports before it can be comprehended, then it has failed as a means of communication. Information must be communicated to the right person, at the right time and in the right format (see Chapter 15).

Contract management

If earlier procedures have been adhered to carefully, the management of contracts should – in the sense of their administration – be relatively straightforward. Sufficient precedents exist for contract administration, largely in the context of monitoring, control and, where necessary, corrective action. Contract management and financial control, which is closely linked to it, are facets of facility management that can represent a significant resource issue for the organization, not least because they are ongoing commitments. As such, they will always involve a minimum level of resource whether services are insourced or outsourced. In these respects, the role of the informed client function (see Chapter 1) is one that should develop over time as working knowledge accrues about how service providers perform. Contract management covers contract conditions and terms, payments, cost monitoring, performance monitoring, change control, contract administration and review. Together, they offer a sufficiently broad range of controls to enable service contracts and/or the in-house team to be managed. Even so, there might be additional controls – most likely linked to accounting provisions – that will necessitate further development of certain functions.

Contract conditions and terms

In general, contracts tend to address the obligations and duties of the parties and the remedies for a failure by either party to fulfil their side of the *bargain*. Contract conditions will touch on many aspects of the performance of a contract for services. A key principle is that, in all cases, payment must be dependent upon the performance of the service provider in delivering the specified service. Contracts should define, therefore, how payments are to be adjusted when performance deviates from acceptable limits. Given that facility management is about the delivery of services, rather than tangible products, it is important to see reimbursement as something that should vary according to the performance of the service provider. This will mean that the organization (as employer under the contract) has to define the level of poor service delivery at which reduced payments are no longer sufficient recompense, so that the contract can be terminated. Contracts might need to contain a clause stating that if the organization does terminate the contract, the service provider can seek arbitration or some other less expensive and speedier alternative dispute resolution procedure. Appendix D outlines how contracts should be approached and the terms that should apply.

In the case of an in-house team, a written agreement outlining terms and conditions should be prepared. There will, however, be some important differences compared with external service providers; for instance, payment for services in the conventional sense of settling invoices will not occur. Termination by either party will be excluded. Other terms and conditions will apply to greater or lesser extents as part of a need to provide the in-house team with clarity over its obligations and duties. The agreement cannot be onerous; otherwise, it would be self-defeating. Nonetheless, the organization should adopt a business-like stance, since the in-house team has, in all likelihood, competed with external service providers for the work and has undertaken to deliver services that will achieve best value. For these reasons, it will be necessary to establish performance measures – that is, KPIs – so that the in-house team is able to demonstrate that it can deliver against its various promises.

WESTEN SCIENCE PARK	Month: 7

Service contract:
Mechanical and electrical maintenance

Service provider:
Emeny Installations

Covering period: 1 July to 31 July

Payment # 7

Annual contract sum: 334 000.00

Gross values to date:

01	Planned contract services	176 320.00
02	Changes to planned services	19 080.00
03	Unplanned/reactive services	15 346.00

Sub-total   210 746.00

Less previous   181 020.00

Payment due (excl. tax):   **29 726.00**

Prepared by:	**Date:**
Authorized by:	**Date:**

Fig. 9.1   A payment form.

Payment

The organization will need to be aware of the implications of cash flow both for itself and for service providers. Whilst the organization might be expected to have up-to-date financial information and so be informed of its cash-flow position, service providers might not be so well aware. It is likely to prove beneficial, therefore, for service providers to submit a cash-flow forecast for service delivery before the contract comes into force and to keep this up to date. This tends to be less of an issue in general facility management contracts; however, forecasts or allowances for reactive works and discretionary expenditure items can be useful. Taking these issues into account will mean that both the organization and service providers will know what their likely pattern of payments will be. This will also help in measuring actual performance against forecast performance. Regular payments to service providers are essential to ensure that they do not fail financially. It is dangerous to assume that a large service provider will always have funds flowing in from other contracts. Occasionally, too many organizations think the same, resulting in the failure of the service provider.

The structure and format of the payment form should be clear and simple: an example is shown in Fig. 9.1. The advantage of this format is that as the gross value of services is recalculated each month, any overpayment in a previous month will

WESTEN SCIENCE PARK					Month: 7
Item	Service or service element	(A) Annual contract sum	(B) Approved changes	(C) Anticipated final cost at end of contract (A+B)	(D) Gross value to date	Comments
01	Planned preventive maintenance	334 000.00	27 280.00	361 280.00	176 320.00	PPM behind schedule
03	Unplanned/reactive maintenance		18 450.00	18 450.00	18 450.00	Large number of repairs
	Totals	334 000.00	45 730.00	379 730.00	194 770.00	
Prepared by:		Date:				
Verified by:		Date:				

Fig. 9.2   A cost control form.

be automatically taken into account without the need for credit notes. In addition, the value of planned contract services and any changes in them are clearly identified.

Cost control

All contract costs should be monitored and controlled systematically. An example format is shown in Fig. 9.2. This should incorporate all monthly payments to service providers, as referred to above, as well as the anticipated final cost under the contract. The use of the organization's accounting system – or, failing that, spreadsheets or a database management system – can easily improve the efficiency of this process and is highly recommended.

The complexity and value of the particular service contract should determine the frequency and detail of the report. For some contracts, a one-line item might suffice; whereas, for example, expenditure under a building services engineering maintenance contract might be broken down into the following elements:

1. planned preventive maintenance;
2. unplanned/reactive maintenance;
3. special equipment maintenance; and
4. performance-related payments.

Where contract values are above a certain threshold, it might be advisable to separate them from minor contracts so that there can be closer scrutiny of expenditure against budgets. Chapter 12 examines maintenance management in detail, including the above categories of maintenance.

Performance appraisal

A formal system of performance appraisal should be implemented, if it has not been already, to cover personnel engaged in managing service contracts, with similar arrangements for incentivizing service providers. Targets or goals should be aligned between the organization's personnel and service providers and there should be no conflict of interest in the arrangement. Care should always be exercised when contemplating the introduction of any incentive scheme.

In the case of an in-house team, it would be reasonable to expect that performance appraisal has already been undertaken. If not, it is highly advised. It is important to ensure alignment between, for example, senior managers, including the facility manager, and operational personnel. Appraisals are normally linked to the organization's business objectives. Remuneration and rewards for personnel stem from performance appraisal and the overall success of the organization. Developing skills and expertise can be achieved by providing opportunities for personnel – for example, training and personal development – identified from performance appraisals. These principles are essential to enhancing the informed client function (see Chapter 1). Similarly, there is a role, as far as it is practicable, in encouraging service providers to develop their competence and skills. It might therefore be beneficial for the organization to consider offering incentives to service providers to ensure their commitment to continual improvement. In this case, the incentive could be attending training and personal development courses and the like.

Incentivizing service providers is a fairly common practice; but again, care needs to be exercised when contemplating the introduction of any incentive scheme. Fortunately, the flexibility that is built into SLAs and contracts to accommodate change allows incentive schemes to be modified in light of actual performance. In addition, the long-term nature of some service contracts tends to encourage a more obliging attitude to incentives and the adjustments in performance that are tied to them. This situation can be contrasted with that of contracts of a limited duration, in which the parties might attempt to maximize their own gains, each at the expense of the other.

Performance reviews

Formal meetings between the representatives of the parties should be held to review performance and to resolve outstanding difficulties and disagreements. Performance review meetings should provide the forum for considering changes that might be necessary, for example, to raise performance, realize targets and agree incentives. Monthly meetings are likely to be appropriate for most situations, although fortnightly or weekly meetings might be advisable in the early stages of a new arrangement, or where the scale or complexity of operations demands more frequent review.

A typical agenda for a performance review meeting would cover:

- end-user review;
- operational review;
- financial review and payments;
- human resources review;
- statutory/regulatory compliance review; and
- action for the coming period.

Performance measurement is normally based on *work done* and *work outstanding*. It focuses on what has been achieved or not (i.e. outputs) and provides an indication of performance. Trends in performance emerge over successive reporting periods – improving, declining or remaining the same. A minor disadvantage of this approach is that performance indicators follow events, with action focused on correcting a deviant trend. It might be more useful to measure or require service providers to measure inputs too; for example, human resources deployed and consumable materials ordered. Whilst not the most meaningful basis for performance measurement, quantified inputs can alert the organization to instances of under-resourcing. If it becomes clear that insufficient resources are being committed upfront, there is no need to wait to see the hard evidence of missed targets.

Actions arising during performance reviews should be determined by the following:

- Comparison of tendered cost versus actual cost.
- Effectiveness of performance measurement in highlighting trends.
- Current performance rating and targets for the coming periods (see Chapter 11).
- Changes proposed versus those approved.
- Ideas for increasing end-user satisfaction and best value.
- Discussion of any contentious issues to avoid escalation and dispute.

Change control

If the facility is to be properly managed, it must be possible to control changes in the scope of services. As a matter of principle, changes to the scope, service specification or service levels should be avoided unless the implications are fully understood and agreed beforehand amongst the parties, including key stakeholders. Where a change is necessary and significant, its effect on performance and cost should be evaluated before approval. Where cost/price data are unavailable, it should be made clear to the service provider that additional works will be valued at current market rates. The evaluation of changes should be consistent with the conditions of contract. Similar provisions should apply to the in-house team, where the procedure for approving a change is covered by its agreement with the organization. In general, it is necessary to:

- Approve changes before they are implemented.
- Prior to approval and for significant changes, undertake a risk assessment to determine the acceptability of the change in terms of its impact on safety, quality or other aspects of performance, likely end-user acceptance, cost and time.
- If approved, request the service provider to implement the change.
- Sign off the change once it has been implemented and performed satisfactorily.

In any event, changes should be avoided unless the consequences are agreed beforehand. Where they are necessary, their cost should be based on tendered prices and rates. Where this is not possible, it should be made clear that the contract manager, contract administrator or facility manager will value the additional works at market rates. The evaluation of changes must be consistent with the conditions of the contract.

Contract administration

If there is to be continual improvement in the management of the facility, diligent contract administration is essential. Successful contract administration includes the following key features:

- Roles and responsibilities that are clearly defined and allocated, with responsibility for the supervision of service delivery vested in the informed client function (see Chapter 1).
- A contract manager, or contract administrator, for every contract and therefore for each service provider.
- A helpdesk or central coordination point to manage the interface between end-users and service providers, regardless of whether service providers are in-house or external.
- An open-book agreement, where the organization has the right to inspect the service provider's accounts for the contract.
- In the early days of the contract, frequent meetings with service providers to discuss performance and to deal with teething problems; as the contract progresses, the need for such meetings should diminish.

Contract review

In the case of outsourced service delivery, contract review is necessary in order to establish whether the decision to outsource is still valid in terms of the facility management strategy, the prevailing market conditions and the performance of the service provider. The necessity for reviews will have been built into the SLA and formalized in the contract, although here the concern is primarily with an internal review. The frequency of contract reviews will depend on the size and complexity of the contract – as reflected by the nature and scope of service delivery – with more frequent reviews likely during the initial period of delivery.

Operational review

The relationship between the service provider and the organization is crucial to ensuring that the service is provided as expected. Moreover, performance improvement will be expected over time, so sound working relationships are important. Problems that could sour the relationship should be prevented at the outset rather than resolved later. For example, the organization's representative – typically, the facility manager – might also be the person who prepared the unsuccessful in-house tender. The organization should therefore be prepared to make changes, if necessary, to ensure that poor working relationships do not arise as a consequence of earlier decisions – regarding the acquisition of new competences and skills, and the redefinition of roles and responsibilities, see also Chapter 4.

Conclusions

Once contracts have been awarded, purchase orders placed or internal requisitions issued, service delivery can begin. Service delivery should, however, be seen through the eyes of end-users; in short, there should be no perceivable difference in quality or performance between services delivered by external service providers and those delivered by an in-house team. Where outsourcing provides the basis for service delivery, the requirements, roles and relationships might seem obvious. In the case of an in-house team, there is the hidden danger of a blurred distinction between the department or operating unit responsible for service delivery and other internal departments as customers and end-users. Starting up a new service or phasing in and replacing an existing service provider are activities that have to be carefully managed. Resources have to be mobilized and the plans for doing so must have regard for business continuity. Failure to take account of the inherent risks in moving from one arrangement to another could easily compromise normal operations: transition has to be properly managed (see Chapter 14 on Transition). Service delivery must have regard to the clear separation of responsibilities between the organization and its service providers, irrespective of source. This requirement applies equally to contracts with external service providers and to agreements (SLAs) with an in-house team. The principles and procedures must be appropriate to the contracts and agreements being managed and provide a realistic level of flexibility, not least where change is necessary and has to be controlled (see Chapter 14 on Managing change). Performance measurement is an essential tool for providing an accurate understanding of how service delivery is matching end-user requirements. Whichever approach is adopted, resources will be consumed in managing the relationship and in overseeing service delivery.

Checklist

This checklist is intended to assist with review and action planning.

	Yes	No	Action required
1. Does the organization understand that, from the perspective of end-users, there should be no perceivable difference in service delivery between insourcing and outsourcing?	☐	☐	☐
2. Where both insourcing and outsourcing apply, is the demarcation between services clear and are roles and responsibilities correctly assigned?	☐	☐	☐

		Yes	No	Action required
3.	Have final checks been made on the financial standing of service providers, where appointed?	☐	☐	☐
4.	Have service providers, where appointed, provided details of their plans for start-up including key resources?	☐	☐	☐
5.	Has a mobilization plan been prepared for start-up or phasing in of services?	☐	☐	☐
6.	Have risks to business continuity been assessed and has due allowance been made for transition from one arrangement for service delivery to another?	☐	☐	☐
7.	Are service providers compliant with HSSE regulations?	☐	☐	☐
8.	Has the organization considered the cash-flow implications for itself and for service providers?	☐	☐	☐
9.	Are service providers aware that their payments will be adjusted in the event of under-performance?	☐	☐	☐
10.	Are arrangements in place to enable continuing assessment of the performance of service providers against service specifications and SLAs?	☐	☐	☐
11.	Are adequate controls in place to deal with changes to the service specification and SLAs?	☐	☐	☐
12.	Are appropriate cost monitoring and control arrangements in place?	☐	☐	☐
13.	Is the organization satisfied with its contract administration?	☐	☐	☐
14.	Do contracts run for not less than three years, with annual reviews and break clauses to enable poor performers to be removed?	☐	☐	☐

10 Specialist Services and Partnership

Key issues

The following issues are covered in this chapter.

- The idea that some services are beyond the usual range of facility-related services means that we can justifiably refer to them as specialist.

- Information and communication technology (ICT) services represent an area that has evolved rapidly. To ensure continuity of business, the organization might need to consider specialist ICT service provision, not least to ensure security of data.

- Health-care services can be an emotive subject in the context of outsourcing – the reaction usually results from confusion over the distinction between clinical and non-clinical services. A majority of services are related to ancillary equipment and information systems and are, therefore, non-clinical.

- Security and protection services are closely aligned with the concept of building intelligence and can involve a mix of on-site and off-site support. Providing a safe and secure facility has become a concern in high-profile industrial sectors and in sensitive locations.

- The need to have robust service level agreements (SLAs) is paramount, not least when dealing with a service that might be complex and unfamiliar in terms of its performance.

- Procuring a service without concern for the ensuing relationship might be to ignore a useful source of skill and expertise – competent service providers and suppliers have much to offer if the conditions are conducive to their ability to offer expertise.

- Cooperative relationships with service providers can provide greater certainty of provision without being non-competitive or compromising on quality or performance.

Total Facility Management, Fourth Edition. Brian Atkin and Adrian Brooks.
© 2015 John Wiley & Sons, Ltd. Published 2015 by John Wiley & Sons, Ltd.

- Partnering is the most common form of cooperative relationship for managing service providers, but it is not an answer for all needs and situations. In the public sector, partnering can be an entirely acceptable alternative to competitive tendering provided that it has a competitive element.

- Continual improvement is a necessary part of the culture of cooperative relationships and one that must include measurable targets in all arrangements.

- A public–private partnership (PPP) is an arrangement that brings together a public-sector need with the expertise of private-sector organizations to deliver a solution.

- PPPs enable the public sector to procure services or the facilities to provide those services, whilst leaving the risks of facility asset and infrastructure ownership, operation and maintenance with the private sector.

- Facility management is an essential part of any major PPP project proposal and a key to its successful outcome – this can also apply to smaller schemes.

Introduction

Not all services required to support a business are the same – some will demand special consideration. As the scope of facility management increases, so must our understanding of how to handle additional or unfamiliar services. Our intention is not to suggest that the definition of facility management should cover all the services discussed in this chapter or to advance arguments for outsourcing, but to provide an understanding of the particular challenges that arise from the organization taking an interest in specialist services. The question of whether or not these services are to be classed as part of facility management is not one for the authors to answer, but for the organization to determine, just as it must differentiate between its core and non-core business. What will be core to one organization will be non-core to another, and for good reason. Likewise, what one might regard as part of the usual scope of service provision, another might see as novel and highly specialized and thus deserving of particular treatment. What matters is that the service to be received by end-users is precisely what is agreed. Increasing specialization can bring with it the need for the organization to work more closely with service providers to find better solutions at lower cost – another way of expressing best value – whilst maintaining, even enhancing, end-user satisfaction. The concept of partnering should be familiar to most and can provide the basis for building a relationship that can thrive well into the future. There is no single model for partnering, although most are founded on the common understanding of sharing risk and reward. This latter aspect is particularly emphasized in the case of public–private partnerships (PPPs), where consortia of firms bring their collective expertise to bear on providing services for public benefit on the back of a facility or other constructed asset financed by the private sector and managed on a concessionary basis for a fixed term. As in the general case of partnering, there is no single model for a PPP, but a range of options from which a successful arrangement can be forged between the parties. The PPP provides an interesting basis for discussion, because it aligns the capabilities of a team of diverse, but complementary, experts with the capacity to conceive, design, construct, operate and finance a facility or other asset over a period of perhaps 25–30 years. Above all, it means thinking through the needs of the operational phase during early design – a fundamental issue that was discussed in Chapter 2 in relation to design briefing and design for operability.

ICT services

Information and communication technology (ICT) spans a wide spectrum of needs and services; for example, the provision of desktop computers, training, accounts and payroll functions. At one extreme, webspace might be rented on a service provider's server; at the other extreme, just about every aspect of ICT support might be in the hands of a service provider, whose services might be based far away from the facility. Server centres and helpdesks are more likely to be located off-site. Most will be located with services for other clients of the service provider – an issue that must be considered, as there could be a potential conflict of interest or risk of breach in security. A later section discusses these and related issues.

ICT services can be considered in terms of:

- infrastructure (data centres, networks and customer services);
- applications packages; and
- performance and security.

When considering, for instance, the possible outsourcing of services that are presently insourced, the tendency might be to focus on the first and second aspects. As financially expedient as that inclination might seem, the last – performance and security – ought to be the primary concern: the other two are means to an end. No good is served if there is a failure in mission-critical systems and the services they support. Even a few hours of downtime for a system could spell disaster. At this point, it is too late to look at the fine print in an SLA that promised 99% uptime. Another issue could be malicious attacks for which the service provider is not adequately protected, or where the organization is responsible for appropriate preventive measures. The latter is known to be a common area of misunderstanding that has led to some organizations failing to appreciate that they are responsible for updating code and applying patches.

SLAs for ICT – in particular, web-based services – are generally stacked in favour of service providers. The matter of consequential losses, or rather compensation for them, is specifically excluded. From the organization's perspective, this might seem entirely unreasonable; however, for a service provider the consequential losses faced by just one customer could ruin its entire business. The advice is to choose service providers with great care and seek proof of service delivery through performance data and references from its existing customers. Arrangements for backing up data and, as importantly, for restoring data after a failure, are crucial matters. If the time taken to restore data runs into days, backups alone do not help in recovering from a failure.

A further issue relating to quality of service delivery is that sometimes it is difficult to pinpoint where the fault lies in a system (here, we are using *system* in its widest context). A server can be unresponsive, yet the problem could be caused by the local network. As data systems and networks expand, management of them can become more complex. Nonetheless, capacity and function tend to run ahead of demand for services. As a rule of thumb, the larger the service provider, the more comprehensive are the services on offer; the smaller the provider, the fewer are the services and, therefore, the more the organization has to work to integrate the different systems involved. The downside is that larger service providers might offer less flexibility, requiring the organization to adapt its approach or systems and accept particular brands of hardware or software. Smaller providers can be very flexible, yet might lack knowledge of what is required.

ICT infrastructure

With changes in technology sometimes outpacing the ability of users to keep up, the idea of another party taking responsibility for providing and maintaining infrastructure can be attractive. The benefits from outsourcing ICT include:

- Economies of scale from larger equipment purchases.
- Multi-vendor capability for a range of platforms.
- Personnel with knowledge of different platforms and operating environments.
- Up-to-date support tools and technology.
- The ability to implement solutions on demand to suit requirements.
- Integration of helpdesk services.
- Lower total cost of ownership (over product life cycles) when compared with insourcing.

Against these benefits, the organization needs to consider some possible disadvantages:

- More restricted choice of product and brand.
- Vendor/provider lock-in.
- Erosion of core competences.
- Over-dependence on an outsourced partner.
- Remoteness of support personnel.
- Steadily increasing costs year-on-year.

Taken together, the perceived benefits and disadvantages can be evaluated to arrive at a decision, indicating the option that satisfies end-user requirements and achieves best value.

ICT applications

Understanding how to get the most out of applications is a perennial issue for organizations of almost every kind. Service providers and vendors can be expected to be more familiar with the workings of specialist applications than an in-house team, unless the latter has been involved in joint development or testing – perhaps as an alpha or beta test site. Since packaged applications are intended to support or extend the capabilities of personnel, any loss of productivity or performance can prove costly. Savings in support can prove to be a false economy, so it is essential to be clear about what support is really necessary and included in monthly or annual payments, and what is optional – for which hourly charging is more appropriate.

The benefits of outsourcing packaged applications can be seen in terms of:

- End-user support, including queries.
- Solutions to application-related problems.
- Enhancements, customization, upgrades and associated user training.

Factors such as scale, volume and criticality of operations, number and complexity of applications and skill levels will need to be taken into account when evaluating options: these are, in effect, some of the attributes of specialist services.

ICT performance and security

One of the more specialist services within the ICT area is performance and security testing. Despite its importance, relatively few organizations seem aware of the dangers they might be facing and the cost and time involved in recovery following an incident. Apart from the risk of malicious acts, personnel can compromise system integrity without realizing they are doing anything untoward. Unfortunately, discovery might occur only after an incident. Typical services include:

- ISO/IEC 27001 compliance audit;
- network and system resilience (load and stress, scalability and volume, endurance and soak tests);
- server penetration;
- forensic services;
- migration assurance;
- business continuity testing;
- risk assessment;
- disaster recovery testing; and
- development of security policies and procedures.

Problems might never surface under normal operating conditions and the organization can be blissfully unaware of the danger lurking once a basic condition changes. The aim of tests for load, stress, scalability, volume and endurance is to be sure that systems can cope with changes in operational parameters. Predicting how and when a system might fail sets an upper limit on end-user demands and performance delivery.

Most organizations rely on client–server architectures for their ICT infrastructure. The vulnerability of servers is something that must be assessed through periodic testing, not least after any upgrading beyond minor patching of the operating environment. Servers that support work groups internally might suffer fewer threats. Those that create a firewall between internal systems and the outside world are in the front line and are likely to be under continual attack from malicious agents. Web servers are similarly vulnerable and will become a target for hackers and organized crime if there is any possibility that the databases running on them hold financial or personal data. Low-level data can be targeted nevertheless and so there is no escape from attack.

Most attacks are caused by automated and persistent agents, not by a lone hacker, with many going undetected. As discussed above, recovery following a failure or other serious incident can take time and prove expensive in resources. This is undoubtedly an area where prevention is better than cure. Once the full extent of risk exposure is known, it is necessary to act quickly to involve specialist service providers. Moving mission-critical systems into a secure facility is the first step; bringing in expert personnel to advise on data security follows a close second.

Health-care services

Of all the specialist services that might be suitable for outsourcing, health care is often the one that evokes the most impassioned reactions. Our primary concern here is not with clinical services, but support for them. Even so, we know of cases where clinical services are outsourced, although not in the conventional sense. A shortage of certain skills (e.g. radiologists) in some countries can be alleviated by using practitioners in different time zones and might even succeed in speeding up a diagnosis. There is a fine line between engaging personnel through an agency on a contract basis and outsourcing a service – a situation that can apply in many fields. Generally, health-care services cover the provision of:

- clinical systems;
- patient transport services;
- information systems;
- administrative systems; and
- practice management systems.

The first of these warrants particular attention. In some countries and health-care regimes, the maintenance of clinical systems can be included within facility management. This means that the service provider is responsible for ensuring the correct functioning of equipment within limits set by the manufacturer, and will handle sterilization, recalibration and testing of equipment and appliances. Whilst the idea of engaging such a specialist under a facility management contract can be worrisome, there is nothing irrational about it. If a health-care facility is to be available when needed, each contributory service must be managed correctly. Coordination and control over what happens must fall to someone; so why should this not be within facility management? There is a difference between performing work oneself and coordinating the efforts of specialists.

Telemedicine or telecare is becoming increasingly common and with it comes the need to provide adequate facilities (especially infrastructure) for medical practitioners and patients. There is a role here for the facility manager to ensure that the conditions provided at the centre and those available in the home are compatible. ICT will play a part, perhaps one that is significant (see Chapter 13 on Telecare).

Security and protection services

The protection of people and property is a major concern for individuals, organizations and governments alike. Security and personal safety are high on the agenda and are likely to remain so. Most facilities were designed and built during times when the real threat of an illegal or terrorist act was remote. Today, people's awareness is heightened and so organizations must take very seriously the potential threats in a rapidly changing and increasingly uncertain world.

It is essential to design a secure environment, but all too often a facility is created that is not. Specifically, measures have to be put into place to:

- Detect, deny and impede intrusion.
- Initiate an appropriate response.
- Provide accurate information and data for analysis.
- Provide evidence to support criminal prosecutions and civil actions.

These services might demand specialist service providers and reliance on remote surveillance, bringing in another specialist alongside those who might already be responsible for security. ICT figures highly in these arrangements. In this sense, there might come a point at which the in-house team can no longer cope realistically with potential threats from innumerable sources and the level of technology that must be deployed.

Whilst it is easy to dwell on the negative aspects, a greater concern for security and protection should translate into a feeling of safety and comfort for end-users. The best organizations are generally those that have assured the security and protection of their facilities and personnel without being intrusive. Most people recognize the necessity, even if they are reluctant to welcome it. In preparing service specifications and SLAs, it is important to engage all stakeholders and so be more confident of mitigating any additional measures that greater security and protection bring (see Chapter 13 on Building intelligence).

Custodial services

Few organizations have need of custodial services, although an increasing number are affected by the requirement to contain persons who pose a threat or who might have already committed an unlawful act. Public facilities are typical of locations under threat from those on the fringe of law-abiding society. Transportation hubs – railway stations, airports and ferry terminals – are examples where the movement of people has to be managed. If national borders are involved, the demands on the organization multiply. Stadiums and other facilities where the public gather in significant numbers also fall under this umbrella. The law can be complex and specialist advice needs to be sought on obligations and duties to protect the public, personnel and property.

Where custodial services are required, the most likely response will be for the organization to contract with a specialist service provider rather than attempt to develop its competence in-house. Typical of the services offered are:

- reception duties;
- post-charge administration (e.g. fingerprinting, photographs and DNA swabs);
- drug testing;
- detainee care and catering;
- forensic medical services;
- interpreter services; and
- ID parade support.

Care needs to be exercised in drafting SLAs and in the related areas of risk, performance measurement and financial control for anything in the area of custodial services. Again, specialist advice should be sought, including discussion with appropriate authorities.

Professional services

The scope for professional services is wide, and what might be regarded as specialist will have much to do with the organization's business objectives and internal competences. Typical in the range of outsourced professional services are:

- accountancy;
- law;
- architectural and engineering design;
- landscape design (internal and external);
- recruitment;
- vehicle fleet management;
- insurance; and
- travel.

The extent to which these might be managed as part of an overall facility management remit will vary considerably, often depending on the likely scale of the service or size of contract, as well as the facility management strategy and policies. For illustrative purposes, we can consider recruitment since, on the surface, it might not appear to be so specialist. A large facility management operation might share some responsibility for recruitment of its personnel with the human resources department because of requirements from the *soft* side of facility management. Outsourcing recruitment services:

- Allows human resources managers to concentrate on managing internal processes.
- Avoids the conflicts of interest that can arise over internal applicants.

- Enables screening and testing of applicants, using diagnostic tools that might not be available in the organization.
- Brings knowledge of the marketplace, talent availability and current remuneration packages.
- Assists in objectively selecting applicants for appointment based on merit.

Performance and SLAs

As with any service – insourced or outsourced – performance is paramount. In many cases, the outsourced service takes place on the service provider's premises and might not be accessible to the organization or its facility manager for reasons of security, or simply because it is in a remote location – possibly on another continent. The location where the service is performed can become a stumbling block in decision-making; in other cases it will be immaterial. Nonetheless, it is important to be objective and not allow irrational arguments to influence decision-making. For instance, the desire to gain access to the facility where the service is performed might be impractical and so it is important to be realistic about the benefits from pursuing such an approach. A situation could occur, for example, where servers are hosted in a secure facility. Being able to point to one's servers might feel reassuring, but hardly constitutes a proper assessment of the service to be provided. A more meaningful approach would be, for example, to undertake a penetration test to determine if the server is secure and stable – see the earlier section on ICT performance and security.

A more serious concern is how SLAs are drafted. For some specialist services, it might be that the provider enjoys a favourable position in the market because, for example, it has few competitors and can be more selective about the businesses it is prepared to consider. In these cases, it might be that the contract has to be signed on terms that are slanted in favour of the service provider. Terms that appear onerous will need careful examination as part of a risk assessment of the service and the provider. As discussed earlier in this chapter, failure to perform could put the organization in a vulnerable position.

Risk, insurance and indemnities

The most obvious risk for the organization is in the outsourcing of a service that is not fully understood or defined, with the result that the service is not provided as expected. Given the nature of the services described in this chapter, it should be obvious that a risk assessment must be carried out before embarking on any path that might lead to the engagement of specialist service providers. Moreover, mission-critical services should not be outsourced until all risks have been identified, assessed and treated. Other considerations, and thus risks, are in the relationships between the specialist provider's personnel and those of end-users and, perhaps, an in-house team. There are many interfaces – organizational, physical, technological and contractual – and these must be identified and managed correctly.

There is a tendency for some people to adopt the mindset of *out of sight, out of mind* over specialist services, especially where a significant part (or, perhaps, all) of the service is executed off-site. In such cases, over-reliance on a service provider could prove damaging and, in certain cases, the organization might be held jointly liable or culpable. Obtaining an indemnity from the service provider is one way of reducing risk and, thus, financial exposure. It might also be possible to take out insurance to cover consequential losses arising from the failure of the service provider.

There is also the possibility that, despite best efforts, SLAs might prove unworkable and some compromise or understanding might have to be reached between the organization and the service provider. All of this effort will take time and money, and even then it might not produce a satisfactory outcome. Errors and negligent acts (e.g. data loss, financial loss, reputation loss and medical negligence) can have wide repercussions and it might not be possible to indemnify or insure sufficiently in all cases. Close scrutiny of the specialist provider's financial and social standing, current assets and liabilities, ownership structure and business models are amongst the factors that have to be considered when contemplating outsourcing.

Supplier management

There is an obvious distinction between the provider of a service – taken to include the supply of manpower and equipment, as well as materials – and the supply of goods or materials alone. Often, the term *supplier* is used to cover service providers too. The term is all-embracing and is in keeping with current practice that recognizes supplier management as a critical success factor for organizations of most kinds.

Suppliers have traditionally been regarded as someone or somebody paid to provide. Where a supplier is responsible for a service that can be provided easily by many others – for example, cleaning – there might seem little need to bother about a relationship beyond that of a simple commercial arrangement. However, this ignores the possibility that the supplier's knowledge about products and processes could be used to reduce waste and raise productivity. Clearly, where the supplier is of economic significance to the organization, it makes sense to explore ways in which unnecessary cost might be eliminated. Having a close working relationship with the supplier can achieve this goal, yet does not necessarily risk being non-competitive.

The term *supplier* therefore needs to be broadened to embody any person or body external to the organization who can contribute to its success. A contract cleaning company is a clear example, but so is an architectural practice working on a refurbishment scheme. Each has a relationship with the organization and this has to be managed to ensure the success of the contract.

When considering the nature of the relationship with suppliers, it is important not to focus on contractual arrangements until a sensible basis for working with a supplier has been found. Contractual arrangements should not override how a given service (or product) should be delivered. Relationships with suppliers can be improved by incorporating incentives for levels of performance that exceed agreed targets and by making use of the expertise that many suppliers undoubt-edly have. Successful relationships will come from treating suppliers as partners, even where there is a contract based on traditional price competition in which different terminology prevails and for which the evaluation criteria might not be so straightforward.

Collaborative relationships

There are a number of options beyond simply entering into a price competi-tion each time a new service is required or a contract is renewed. For instance, collaboration with other organizations can often enable more favourable terms to be leveraged from suppliers, especially for commodities, because negotiation and procurement powers are improved. In fact, there is a wide range of possible relationships from which to choose the one that best suits the requirements.

At one end of the scale, both organization and supplier might be concerned primarily with optimizing their immediate interests, without making long-term commitments. Such relationships are typical of many commodity markets. At the other end, both parties might look for a long-term, cooperative partnership. The type of relationship that will produce the greatest benefits will depend upon cir-cumstances such as the nature of the market and the demands of the service to be provided. Choosing the right relationship with suppliers and managing it well requires experience, skill and judgement.

The best contribution that can be made to the raising of supplier competitive-ness is to manage procurement intelligently. An important element of this will be to combine competition and cooperation to optimal effect. Mutually satisfactory relationships between buyers and sellers are fundamental to successful procure-ment activity. Yet, whatever the chosen relationship with suppliers, an adversarial or unaccommodating approach should be avoided. Relationships should be as open and supportive as possible – given the need to maintain competition and to treat suppliers even-handedly – and should be based on mutual respect. The organization should recognize that it is in its interests to help suppliers develop in ways that make them better able to provide what is required, and to do so to the desired quality level and at a competitive price. The relationship should be one that encourages continual improvement.

Few services or supplies are of exactly the same degree of importance. Failure in certain of them could prove disastrous – for instance, a failure to test electrical appliances – whilst other types of failure might be tolerated, or at least a means found to minimize their impact. It is therefore important to recognize where the kinds of suppliers with whom the organization is dealing lie within the matrix in Fig. 10.1. Locating suppliers in the correct position within the matrix focuses attention on the kind of relationship that has to be managed (Gadde, 1996). Procedures will then need to reflect the different emphases that are required of the relationship. In this way, it should be possible to achieve higher levels of service from suppliers.

Understanding the kinds of relationship that are possible is only the beginning. The organization will need to adopt appropriate controls and incentives, which

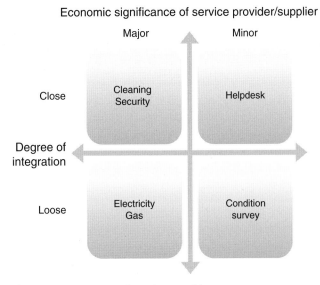

Economic significance of service provider/supplier

Fig. 10.1   The integration and significance of service providers.

might well differ between sets of relationships. It should be possible for it to devise relationships with individual suppliers that are more closely aligned with the needs of both parties. For example, the relationship demanded of a cleaning contract might embody incentives for ensuring that areas are cleaned in ways and at times that provide maximum flexibility for end-users. The extent of the requirements might be so complicated that without a close working relationship – perhaps founded as a partnering arrangement – the quality of service expected might be unattainable. Extensive dialogue and discussion might be needed before a deep understanding can be reached.

In another example – that of the helpdesk – a well-managed service for responding to requests and complaints could yield worthwhile savings. For instance, helpdesk personnel who are well versed in technical procedures and competent in some aspects of problem-solving could obviate the need for further action by providing timely advice on how to deal with problems concerning heating, ventilation or other aspects of engineering services. Savings from the avoidance of calling out service operatives could amply repay the cost of providing the helpdesk. However, helpdesk personnel would need to be specially trained to perform in this way; consequently, the organization might then have to pay more for their services. Establishing a close working relationship with the service provider – or assessing the capabilities of pro-spective providers – would seem sensible. In terms of controls, the service provider could be rewarded for reductions in the cost of calling out service engineers and, if the situation arose, penalized for failing to deal promptly and sensibly with requests (for further comment on providing incentives, see Chapter 11).

In other areas – for example, the supply of a utility such as electricity – there might be little point in attempting to bring about a closer working relationship other than in arranging a consortium purchase. Generally, the greater the involve-ment or interaction with the supplier, the more indirect costs there will be.

Partnering

Sourcing services based on partnering or partnership has become a popular (even established) basis for relationships with suppliers. Partnering is a particular arrangement for procuring services that offers the chance to develop a strong relationship with a service provider who can ensure that best value is achieved whilst risks are better managed at the same time. Organizations and their service providers decide to collaborate closely in order to deliver requirements such as cost reduction, improved quality or innovative solutions, rather than to conduct their business at arm's length. Essentially, partnering is acceptable in terms of accountability – which is particularly important in the public sector – if the following apply:

- There is competition at the outset in the choice of partners and periodic re-competition.
- The partnering arrangement is established on the basis of clearly defined needs and objectives over a specified period.
- There are specific and measurable milestones for improved performance as part of the contract in order to demonstrate, through the use of benchmarking (see Chapter 11), that best value is being achieved.

Partnering is likely to bring greater benefits than other approaches under certain circumstances; for example, where there is a poorly developed or highly specialized market, or where the requirements of the purchaser are complex and continuously developing. The organization should consider carefully whether or not a partnering arrangement best suits its needs in each particular case.

Some see partnering, erroneously, as the means by which competitive tendering of a service can be avoided. The correct use of partnering is to help build a business relationship that is founded on trust. It is not a way of working around financial constraints. Partnering aligns the objectives of the organization and service provider in an attempt to maximize the benefits to both. There can be savings from not having to tender repeatedly; for the supplier, it can mean regular work from an organization the requirements of which are better understood than they would be otherwise. Business arranged in this way can bring about significant savings over the medium to long term. A comparison of partnering with a traditional arrangement is given in Table 10.1.

Table 10.1   **Partnering compared with a traditional arrangement.**

Partnering	Traditional arrangement
Innovative, not so well-developed	Established, well-developed
Ability to negotiate on price	Difficult to negotiate on price
Close interaction between parties	Arm's-length relationship
Quality improvement possible	Quality likely to be minimum specified
Proactive service provider response	Reactive service provider response
Disputes less likely	Disputes common
Long-term benefits	Short-term gains

The essence of partnering is that the organization decides to work with a select number of firms or individuals who will share the work in a prescribed area. This is easy to achieve for a large owner of new facilities. In other situations, the opportunities to partner are more limited, although they do exist in the sense of sharing with someone or somebody who can provide a real gain for the organization.

Partnering could exist in transportation services and vehicle maintenance, or where there is the chance to purchase utility supplies in bulk by forming a procurement consortium. Such arrangements create an economy of scale that can provide smaller organizations with better value for money than under an arrangement where they attempt to negotiate on their own. An additional benefit from this kind of collaboration is that expertise and risks are also shared – see the section on Risk, reward and opportunity below.

Contracts and agreements generally serve two main purposes: they identify the service to be provided in terms of scope, quality or performance, cost and timing, and they apportion risk. Partnering arrangements are, however, concerned mainly with the way in which the work will be carried out. In this way, partnering should theoretically be achievable with any method of procurement. However, while no procurement path can compensate for an adversarial approach, some approaches might be more readily adapted to certain aspects of partnering such as gain-sharing – see the later section on Gain-sharing.

From the organization's perspective, the early involvement of partners, selected for their long-term perspective and willingness to use collaborative working arrangements, can help to overcome cultural and organizational barriers such as those associated with a more traditional outlook. The implementation of partnering is, however, likely to require the use of procurement procedures that are quite different from those more commonly used. Hence, the organization will need to reassess its procurement process and tailor it to this different context (Eriksson *et al.*, 2009).

Certain kinds of partnering relationship have no contract at all and it has been claimed that a formally binding contract can inhibit the partnering process. In most cases, a standard form of contract is used, even when partners declare business objectives that appear contrary to the principles of partnering. This view is to be expected, as partnering remains somewhat new to many organizations and a contract is seen as a safety net.

While contracts can embrace some aspects of a partnering approach, such as gain-sharing, others, such as ideas of cooperation and goodwill, might be less easily expressed within them. Other issues concern the management of long-term partnering arrangements under workable contract terms. For instance, contracts to undertake future work might be rendered void because of uncertainty, since it is not possible to predetermine the value of future work and many factors can come into play even over a short period. However, this does not preclude non-binding framework agreements – those covering a number of contracts over a specified period – that stipulate terms on which the parties intend to contract and the type and extent of the services and/or work envisioned.

Partnering charters can be used to outline the organization's philosophy, its commitments and the goals of the arrangement. For some, partnering charters are regarded as vital support for its contracts. Charters can also be used to indicate ways of overcoming problems, establish roles and responsibilities, and define clear lines of communication. Even so, the relationship between a partnering charter and the contract might appear unclear. Put simply, the contract defines the obligations and duties of the parties and to some extent covers the process implicit in delivering the specified service. However, a partnering charter does not sit on top of the contract but is complementary to it, and vice versa. Typical of the commitments embodied in a charter are to:

- Respect confidentiality and the intellectual property rights of the parties.
- Encourage open-mindedness and receptiveness to change.
- Establish clear objectives, milestones and benefits.
- Redesign processes and procedures to increase performance in service delivery.
- Eliminate non–value-adding activities unless they directly support value-adding work.
- Integrate systems and people by sharing information and knowledge.
- Maintain intrapersonal communication through discussion.
- Achieve continual improvement through the above.

The adoption of a means for measuring the performance of a partnering arrangement is critical to ensuring that its objectives are met. This generally involves the organization and service provider outlining the improvements over traditional arrangements that the parties intend to pursue, together with the measures of success in achieving their objectives. In the case of longer-term partnering relationships, targets for performance improvement can be incorporated into the partnering arrangements. With appropriate monitoring and feedback, continual improvement – considered to be central to the whole idea of partnering – can be achieved. Some features of continual improvement are easy to identify and address, but others might require more of a change in organizational culture.

Risk, reward and opportunity

The familiar adage *where there is risk there is reward* is often said without necessarily appreciating its practical implications. In an arrangement to deliver a typical range of services, identified risks should have been recorded, assessed, treated and monitored, and then reflected in cost estimates and price structures. The likelihood of getting anything terribly wrong should be relatively small. The reward for the service provider is payment that matches performance. For the organization, the reward is that the service represents best value, whilst achieving end-user satisfaction. A more apposite coupling is of risk and opportunity – the downside and upside risks referred to in Chapter 1 – where the chance to innovate or, simply, to capitalize on a new situation or a change can repay handsomely. It seems more appropriate, therefore, to keep with the risk and opportunity view as if they were the two sides of a coin. Working on solving a common problem automatically aligns the parties and incentivizes them to seek solutions that favour both, even though the gains do not necessarily accrue at the same time.

Gain-sharing

Some partnering arrangements include gain-sharing. This is where cost savings arising from performance improvements are shared between the parties. This can provide an effective incentive for performance that exceeds a given level (see Chapter 11). In practice, gain-sharing arrangements can be straightforward, with the organization and service providers dividing any savings above a target price on an equal basis, with the providers liable for 100% of any loss. They can also be more sophisticated, with partners exposed to levels of risk and reward according to their degree of influence on service delivery. Whatever means is devised, a commitment to open-book accounting is necessary if efficiency gains are to be encouraged. There must be no incentive or opportunity for the parties to achieve a higher return through adversarial behaviour or by hiding behind the contract.

Public–private partnerships (PPPs)

PPPs are not a recent phenomenon. They first appeared hundreds of years ago and many governments around the world have long established the practice of sharing the risks of major projects for public benefit with the private sector. This section considers how organizations can ensure that opportunities for private investment and partnership can be fully and effectively considered in plans to develop or improve the quality of their facilities. There is a clear linkage between facility management and private investment and partnership, specifically within the context of new capital schemes. Private finance arrangements offer a chance to challenge traditional practice, yet also have the potential for problems that must be recognized and properly addressed. When first introduced, the greatest interest in this kind of project was found amongst consultant architects, consultant engineers and construction companies, each seeing an opportunity to create work when workloads were depressed. A more developed understanding recognizes the pivotal role that facility management and, therefore, service providers play. Ensuring that the design of the proposed facility – the creation of the asset upon which the proposed function and services will be performed – will not cause financial problems requires expertise of the kind that, possibly, service providers are best able to provide. Even so, caution is advised, as PPP projects stretch into the future and much can change in the fortunes of service providers and other key stakeholders. Furthermore, 30 years can be a long time over which to suffer a loss instead of a profit.

Interest in PPPs has risen steadily in many countries, to the extent that it has become a sector in its own right, supported by a market in secondary financing. This market provides the opportunity to refinance a project once the asset is in use, enabling the equity partners to trade their shareholding and exit cleanly. This is especially important for construction companies, the business planning horizons of which would not normally extend beyond a few years. PPPs are concerned with the delivery of services, which in most cases happens over a long period, perhaps 20–30 years. The characteristics and extent of services are dependent upon the authority of the public-sector body involved and how a given service fits into its business plan; that is, core or non-core activities. Regardless of the object of the PPP, the public-sector body is withdrawing from activities that formerly have been carried out within its own organization. It has, therefore, a strong interest in ensuring satisfactory quality and performance in the outcome. The risks and responsibility for delivering and managing the asset during operations are, to a large extent, transferred from the (client) organization to a private-sector body. Thus, attention is turned from the perceived needs of the organization to the provision of end-user services. This creates a different situation for firms in the architecture, engineering and construction (AEC) sector to those traditionally experienced where, in the main, they have been largely content with short-term commitments, investments and returns.

The definition of a PPP – as broad as it is – together with the wide perception of partnerships has given rise to a large number of arrangements that could be legitimately termed PPPs. To make matters more confusing, the term PPP is also used in a narrower sense in attempts to describe the characteristics of specific projects. Thus, in order to provide a description of how PPP applies to the AEC sector, it is necessary to break down the term into more manageable categories.

A PPP is essentially a method for procuring capital projects, to enable enhanced service delivery, but where capital expenditure in the present is converted to an expenditure commitment in the future. An external company will usually design, build and operate the facility, by sponsoring a project and holding an equity stake in it. The financial interest that the sponsor holds in the project helps to ensure efficiency. In this sense, in particular, it is easy to see how the principles of a PPP are transferable to other types of organization.

Several broad types of partnership can be differentiated. They are, however, general and there will be projects/arrangements that can overlap two or more categories. These categories of partnership are briefly presented below:

- Public-sector assets are sold to the private sector in the belief that private-sector finance and management can increase the value of the asset and thereby provide the taxpayer with better value for money.
- Shares in state-owned businesses are sold to the private sector, with the state retaining either a minority or majority stake of the business. This could be done with or without the use of legislation or regulations in order for the public sector to retain control of the business. The main objective of this kind of PPP is to improve the overall achievement of the business by bringing in private-sector finance, managerial and marketing skills.
- The public sector uses private finance, managerial and marketing skills so as to exploit the potential of public assets, both physical and intellectual, that cannot easily be sold or in which the state wishes to retain ownership.
- Arrangements where the public sector contributes to the funding of private-sector projects/establishments that are considered to be of public benefit, but which are not capable of fully funding themselves on the capital markets.

- Arrangements where the public and private sectors under joint management combine their assets, finance and expertise in order to pursue common long-term goals and shared profit.
- The public sector contracts services, with defined outputs, from the private sector, including the construction and maintenance of the required facility and/or infrastructure.

The procurement and contractual approach

In order to describe the particular project's contractual arrangement, terms other than PPP are used. Generally, the various kinds of contract are given three- or four-letter abbreviations or acronyms, most of which are not so easily differentiated. Indeed, some of them are confusingly alike. It is more important, therefore, to understand the main characteristics of projects than it is to be able to match a specific project directly to a contract abbreviation or acronym. Nonetheless, most of them are presented below:

- BOOT – build, own, operate and transfer;
- BOR – build, operate and renewal of concession;
- BOT – build, operate and transfer;
- BRT – build, rent and transfer;
- BTO – build, transfer and operate;
- DBFO – design, build, finance and operate;
- DCMF – design, construct, manage and finance;
- MOT – modernize, operate and transfer;
- MOOT – modernize, own, operate and transfer; and
- ROT – rehabilitate, own and transfer.

Short descriptions are given below for the two most common – BOT and DBFO:

- *BOT* – build, operate and transfer – is by far the most widespread and it is not uncommon for literature to use the term to represent all types of PPP project. BOT and BOOT are often used interchangeably, although there is a marked difference between them. These types of project are characterized by the major part of the payment for the private sector coming directly from external customers in the form of user fees of one kind or another.
- *DBFO* – design, build, finance and operate – and to a certain extent DCMF, are the most common for projects where private-sector revenues come exclusively, or to a large extent, from a public-sector body.

The benefits of private investment and partnership to facility management within the public sector can be summarized as follows:

- All types of organization have the potential to simplify their procurement of capital schemes and subsequent operations.

- Organizations acting as clients/sponsors can transfer responsibility and risk to a single provider and concentrate on their core business.
- Consideration of the operation of the new facility can be built-in at the design stage – the input of reliable life-cycle cost data into the design is at the heart of successful arrangements.
- A long-term focus can be built into the project, thus avoiding the dangers and costs of short-term, reactive facility management; that is, applying the concept of design for operability.

Since the operational period will far exceed the design and construction periods combined, facility management receives higher priority as its importance to the efficient and successful operation of the core business is recognized. The focus on the overall package can ensure integration between design, construction, finance and operation, avoiding the pitfalls of other, more fragmented approaches to the procurement and operation of new capital schemes.

Partners need to work towards common goals within a long-term relationship of openness, trust and compatibility. Private investment and partnership can add real value to the organization's core business if the service provider:

- Is focused on the long-term needs of end-users of the service(s) provided by the facility.
- Can translate those needs into an efficient design for the facility with maximum flexibility for future change.
- Specifies a solution that optimizes the whole-life costs of both the facility and support services, thereby minimizing cost.
- Works in partnership with end-users to deliver services aligned to (changing) needs.
- Enables the (client) organization to maximize its efficiency, thereby adding real value rather than simply cutting costs.
- Offers a solution as part of a transaction that covers risks at minimum cost and is financed at the least rate of interest, to provide both best value and a more affordable outcome.

The generic PPP set-up

A PPP brings together a large number of stakeholders, each with its own agenda, priorities and goals. This plethora of overlapping – and potentially conflicting – interests ensures that any PPP will abound with contracts and agreements. The exact nature of these and their interrelationships are, of course, specific to the project in hand, but there are some common features. A generic project set-up is presented in Fig. 10.2. The rest of this section deals with the main parties (often referred to as actors) and their roles in a generic PPP project as presented by Leiringer (2003).

The public-sector client

It is a government's responsibility to provide essential services for society. To help in this task, the government typically sets up a wide range of institutions. The

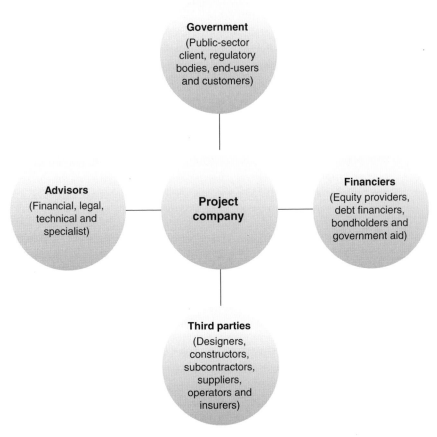

Fig. 10.2   A generic PPP set-up (after Leiringer, 2003).

exact division and legislative empowerment of these public-sector bodies vary from country to country. The following could, however, be considered generic:

- governmental departments;
- governmental agencies;
- municipalities;
- local authorities; and
- single-purpose agencies.

One of the above will become the public-sector client organization in the project. It is this body that contracts with the private sector for the delivery of a service over a specified period and it is not uncommon that the public-sector body creates a client's representative organization the primary task of which is to monitor the project.

Regulatory bodies

Depending on the nature of the service that is contracted, the project will – apart from the particular sponsoring public-sector client – also come under the jurisdiction of one or several other public-sector bodies. These could be anything from governmental departments or agencies to local authorities or single-purpose agencies. The size and statutory powers of the public-sector bodies involved that claim regulatory jurisdiction vary widely. Each has its own standards and regulations and, in certain cases, the relationships between the bodies are quite complex.

Customers and end-users

There would be no need for – and, in fact, no interest in – a project if there were no demand for the service that it could provide. Of importance here is the relationship between use of, and payment for, the service. A distinction is made between *paying customers* and *indirectly paying end-users*. If users pay for the service they are called customers. If the service is paid for by other means, such as through taxes, the users are deemed end-users of the service.

The project company

The company – known as the concessionaire – is the legal entity that tenders for, develops and supplies the required service(s). The precise form of this entity will depend on the circumstances at hand, taking into account fiscal, accounting and legal issues as well as the physical nature of the required facility and service. In some cases, the project company could be an existing body that takes on the project by itself – on the balance sheet – or a subsidiary of a larger company established to undertake PPP projects. However, it is far more usual that it takes the form of a special-purpose vehicle (SPV), established either in the form of a consortium or as a joint venture for undertaking the project. Arrangements exist to make it possible for companies of different sizes, financial strength and objectives to participate in the SPV. Participation is grounded in the added value of the skills that a company brings to the consortium/joint venture. Projects that involve more than a modest amount of construction will most commonly have a construction company as a shareholder, with the same being true for the operational phase and for the operators.

Equity providers

The equity providers in a project own that project. Equity is the lowest-ranking form of capital in the project and the claims of the equity investors are therefore subordinate to those of the project's debt financiers – see the next section. Hence, the equity providers bear the greatest risk of loss if the project is unsuccessful. This risk is balanced by a greater return than that of the debt lenders: they stand to gain the most if the project performs better than expected. The principal equity investors are the members of the project company, although several other parties might contribute. Equity providers can be divided into three groups:

1. *Long-term providers* – the entities responsible for construction and operation, major suppliers of technology and some specialist investment funds and banks.

2. *Retail or institutional providers* – these tend to be institutions such as superannuation funds, life insurance companies and fund managers without controlling interests in the business.
3. *Quasi-equity providers* – these are mainly risk capital funds and institutional investors that do not have a controlling stake in the project company.

Debt financiers

Debt finance is, as mentioned above, senior to equity. It also distinguishes itself from equity in the sense that it is secured against the assets of the project. Accordingly, the return expected by the debt financiers is lower than that of the equity providers. The debt financiers have no controlling stake in the project company, but they have considerable leverage in issues concerning project execution. A project usually has a mixture of short- and long-term loans. Once the project is operating, a syndicate of commercial banks generally provides the long-term debt. The short-term loans – they are sometimes referred to as bridging loans – are used to finance the construction phase. Several different kinds of financial institution are capable of providing short-term finance.

Bondholders

There is also the possibility of obtaining finance by raising bonds. Bondholders generally do not have any interaction with the project company after the bond has been issued and do not exercise any control over the execution of the project.

Government aid

Government aid is by no means normal in PPP projects and it can take a wide variety of forms. Usually, though, it consists of the provision of equity or additional debt financing and various forms of guarantees. In addition to host governments, institutions such as the World Bank, the European Investment Bank (EIB), the European Bank for Reconstruction and Development (EBRD), the African Development Bank (AfDB) and various development finance institutions provide aid.

Design and construction contractors

The construction contractor will normally be signed to design and build the asset. Depending on the size and scope of the project, it could either be a single construction company that takes on the work by itself – with or without the additional hiring of designers – or a consortium of design and construction companies. Either way, it is usual that responsibilities are passed on to a variety of subcontractors. It is common that the main contractor has a stake in the project company.

Operators

If the contracted service includes the operation of the asset, then this would normally be outsourced to a specialist operator. In these cases, it is usual that the operator would be part of the project company. Operation is normally divided into *soft* and *hard* services, and it is not unusual that the operator has one or more subcontractors. In the case that the service provided is of a maintenance character, it would be likely that the construction contractor, or else a major, dedicated service provider, would take on the role of the operator.

Suppliers

The role of supplier is very much dependent on the required service and the characteristics of the built asset. Strategic suppliers and suppliers of major components and/or large technology owners usually take a part in the project company.

Insurers

Insurance is sought to cover as many commercial risks as possible. It is often the case that all or a significant part of the insurance cover is reinsured with other insurers. These can be either local/domestic or international, and a mix of them is usually preferred.

Legal advisors

Due to the complex nature of the projects and the large number of agreements that have to be created and later interpreted, the need for legal advice is crucial. Both public- and private-sector parties use legal advisors.

Financial advisors

Financial advisors are retained by the public-sector client as well as by the project company and will have expertise in risk management.

Technical advisors

Technical advisors are used by the public-sector client as well as by the project company, irrespective of whether or not the construction contractor has a stake in the company. The financiers in the project might also retain technical advisors in order to oversee the design and any changes during the project life.

Specialist advisors

The competences of specialist advisors vary from project to project and could include, for example, transportation engineers, behavioural scientists and clinicians as appropriate to the nature of the project.

Assets and services

In PPP projects, one of the most significant problems will be caused by the different interfaces between the public and private sectors. These interfaces will vary according to the authority vested in the public-sector body and this will, in turn, influence the nature of the contracted service. Four broad groups of PPP projects can be identified, each with rather distinct operating characteristics, where the operator provides:

- A facility for a single client, most probably a public-sector body.
- Services directly to end-users (public or private).
- Several different, but interrelated, services to a single client/sponsor.
- Several different, interrelated services to a variety of end-users.

Payment mechanisms

The choice of payment mechanism is a key factor that will inevitably affect the project set-up. There are three typical approaches in which the private sector collects revenues depending on the service that is provided and those who are considered to be the end-users. Whichever form is used, its influence on the management of the project is highly significant. The typical approaches are where:

1. Revenue streams are collected from customers – for example, users of a toll road or sports centre.
2. Revenues are collected from the client organization – for example, a road with shadow tolls.
3. Revenue is provided by a combination of the above.

There is a marked difference between a toll road, where all revenue is collected from the end-users, and a prison, where the revenue could be collected according to the availability of cells and the quality of service provided.

Facility management and private-sector participation

In terms of new capital schemes, a PPP project offers public-sector bodies the opportunity to procure the design, construction, finance and operation of a facility from one provider and to transfer the attendant risks. This enables the (client) organization to concentrate on its core activities. The facility is, therefore, designed with proper consideration for its management by a party with a vested interest in the long-term success of the project.

In any new capital scheme proposal, especially those involving private-sector investment or partnership, due consideration must be given at the feasibility stage, or earlier, to the extent of potential facility management provision. Facility management will need to be provided on a best-value basis and the means for demonstrating this has to be included in any study.

In all cases, it will be necessary to assess whether or not facility management is appropriate for inclusion and, if so, in what ways. This can cover those situations in which the bundling of services for other facilities might make the proposal more attractive because of economy of scale. Equally, it might be that facility management is not suitable for inclusion and so should be omitted, perhaps because of implications for the organization's overall facility management provision. Additionally, the organization might consider other variations to service delivery, such as partial facility management involving selected services only. Whatever is decided, the organization will need to demonstrate that it has considered the relevance of facility management to a proposed new capital scheme and the options available for its delivery. A sound articulation of the case for and against, as appropriate, should be provided.

The mode by which facility management should be supplied needs careful consideration. This refers to the choice between insourcing and outsourcing. The same assessment criteria as apply routinely to determining which of these paths to follow also apply to assessing capital scheme proposals for private-sector investment and partnership. In this regard, it is essential to assess risk transfer, including the risks of insourcing and outsourcing as appropriate.

Output specifications

Chapter 8 proposed an approach to specifying service requirements. In any capital scheme proposal likely to include private-sector investors or developers, it is essential to advance consideration of facility management to the point at which all of the issues and likely actions have been examined. The thoroughness that should apply to specifying service requirements without direct private-sector participation should apply to the same extent to those schemes with it. The (client) organization might find this easiest to achieve when contemplating an entirely new scheme, unencumbered by past arrangements.

Risk and private investment

The crucial criteria for assessing direct private-sector involvement in capital scheme proposals are best value and risk transfer. The opportunity to transfer all risks inherent in the design, construction and operation of a new facility might be very tempting. A balance has, however, to be struck between the two so that the (client) organization should not be seeking the maximum risk transfer, but the most appropriate for securing best value. Risk transfer will always attract a cost. The principle of optimal risk transfer has an impact on value assessment, as any change in risk apportionment will have an impact on the total cost of the project and therefore on value achieved. In this instance, of course, best value is to be looked for in the full duration of private-sector involvement, which, as we have seen, could be up to 30 years. Value in the context of facility management services is therefore linked with the wider concern for best value in the total project. However, as the period of operation will far exceed that of design or construction, facility management becomes the focus for best value and risk issues.

The contractual documentation required for a PPP will deter or rule out those contractors who do not have a balance sheet able to cope with the contractual liabilities involved in creating the asset and operating a service on the back of it. While this is useful in the selection of suitable partners, the chosen contractor will look for profit margins that are commensurate with the risk. In turn, the risk issues that must be addressed in advance increase the complexity of the tendering process.

Issues with private investment and partnership

The potential benefits of private investment arrangements inevitably bring associated issues, including the following:

- The arrangements for private investment can be complex and therefore difficult to comprehend fully, as well as expensive to implement.
- The accounting complexities might need to be resolved into a simpler set of principles – it is vital to make well-advised judgements concerning which party carries the asset in each case, as wrong decisions can prove costly and damaging.
- Few contractors are substantial enough or financially prepared to accept the risks; consequently, there might not be sufficient choice of contractors to ensure true competition and interested companies might enjoy premium pricing.
- Some contractors have limited their long-term risk exposure to notional liability for future defects – the focus must therefore be centred on the long-term service issues rather than on the short-term construction project.
- The attractions of risk transfer might discourage its careful consideration on the twin bases of affordability and best value.

Conclusions

A fundamental question arises when considering specialist services: in whose opinion are they specialist? Since there can be no universal agreement on what is specialist and what is not – it depends on how the organization sees it – applying a blanket treatment could well prove counterproductive. There are few hard and fast rules for dealing with outsourcing of specialist services, since each service must be evaluated individually and not classed as if it were just like any other. The organization needs, first and foremost, to be very clear about those attributes of service provision that are uppermost in importance. Understanding the intrinsic nature of the service required and sound knowledge of the market will help to point the way forward. The next step is to undertake a risk assessment to see where the organization stands – financially, legally and physically – if it enters into a contract with the specialist provider. Specialist services are obtained from external sources – there might be no other way – and in many cases the service or parts of it will be performed remotely. Insisting on overseeing what a specialist service provider does could be regarded as irrational, since a thorough risk analysis would probably reveal other factors that are more deserving of attention. Particular concerns, such as those over *vendor/ provider lock-in* and *competence-stripping*, are real and represent potential risks. The relationship with a supplier does not end once the contract has been placed. That is just the beginning and it will take hard work to manage the relationship successfully into the future. Ways can always be found to add incentives for both sides to ensure the satisfactory performance of a service or supply. Setting targets as part of a process of continual improvement is possible. These can be based on gain-sharing to provide an added incentive. In any event, engaging the competence and skills of the service provider in the process – as opposed to traditional arrangements that actively exclude it – can lead to better ways of delivering end-user satisfaction at lower cost.

Partnering or other forms of cooperative relationship can be entirely appropriate in the search for best value. Partnering is not, however, a panacea and its selection must be based on a well-founded case. Nonetheless, it can be a perfectly acceptable arrangement even in the public sector, where there is rightful concern about the probity of contractual arrangements. Partnering can succeed so long as there is a competitive element to it – the latter does not invalidate the approach; rather, it improves the prospects for delivering best value. The concept of partnership can extend to the long term. PPPs have become commonplace in many countries. Private-sector participation in one form or another is likely to remain important for the provision, financing and management of capital scheme proposals within public-sector bodies. Facility management is a key element in all proposals and (client) organizations are free to consider many options. They must, however, demonstrate rigour, especially in the areas of best value and risk transfer. It will also be important to ensure that appropriate priority is assigned between capital procurement, financing and facility management aspects of project proposals. Ensuring that services can be maintained over the long term requires much early thinking and planning.

Checklist

This checklist is intended to assist with review and action planning.

	Yes	No	Action required
1. Does the organization possess in-house all the service-related competences that it requires?	☐	☐	☐
2. Have needs in regard to services that fall outside the normal range of provision been identified?	☐	☐	☐
3. Does the organization have the competence to prepare service specifications and SLAs for any service identified as specialist?	☐	☐	☐
4. Does the organization have knowledge of the market for specialist services and is it aware of trends?	☐	☐	☐
5. Has a risk assessment with respect to the engagement of specialist service providers been undertaken?	☐	☐	☐

	Yes	No	Action required
6. Is the organization able to obtain indemnities and/or insurance as part of any risk mitigation?	☐	☐	☐
7. Is the economic significance of each of service provider and supplier understood?	☐	☐	☐
8. Is the organization benefiting from consortium arrangements for the supply of utilities or has it at least examined the economic case for them?	☐	☐	☐
9. Are appropriate strategies in place for managing relationships with service providers and suppliers?	☐	☐	☐
10. Has partnering been considered as an alternative to traditional, competitive tendering?	☐	☐	☐
11. Is the organization aware of the relevance and benefits of public–private partnerships, irrespective of whether it is a public- or private-sector body?	☐	☐	☐
12. Where relevant, is the organization aware of the nature of PPP projects in terms of project set-up, bodies involved and mechanisms for handling risk and finance?	☐	☐	☐
13. Where relevant, is the organization aware of the options for pricing the service created by the asset and how this will generate a return on the investment?	☐	☐	☐
14. Where relevant, are the facility management requirements properly reflected in the output specifications for partnership schemes?	☐	☐	☐
15. Where relevant, is the organization aware of the balance between best value and risk transfer in assessing partnership proposals, including facility management?	☐	☐	☐

11 Performance Management

Key issues

The following key issues are covered in this chapter.

- Performance management involves reconciling the levels of service delivered to end-users against agreed standards and targets set out in service specifications and service level agreements (SLAs).

- A distinction between quality and performance might need to be drawn for some services – for example, catering and maintenance – where they include tangible products as distinct from the physical performance of tasks alone.

- Performance should be reviewed from a number of perspectives, including end-users, operations, finance, human resources and regulatory compliance. Performance review meetings should be held on a regular basis, usually not less than monthly.

- The correction of discrepancies and the updating of service specifications and SLAs require the joint participation of the organization and those delivering the services.

- The organization should describe its performance requirements in terms of critical success factors for service delivery. Performance indicators can then be defined and used to measure actual achievement, as well as any deviation from specifications and SLAs. The most significant are referred to as key performance indicators (KPIs).

- Performance reporting needs ICT to handle the wealth of information and data that are now routinely gathered and analysed. This has led to the emergence of the facility management *dashboard*, where performance in key areas can be immediately grasped from the simple, but compelling, use of graphics.

Total Facility Management, Fourth Edition. Brian Atkin and Adrian Brooks.
© 2015 John Wiley & Sons, Ltd. Published 2015 by John Wiley & Sons, Ltd.

- In the case of a new or refurbished facility, a post-implementation review will be necessary to determine if performance in use *measures up* to requirements agreed during design briefing and design development, especially those relating to the safe and correct operation of the facility.

- A post-occupancy evaluation (POE) undertaken from the perspective of end-users should complement the post-implementation review. It should measure the extent to which requirements are being satisfied by the services currently being delivered.

- Benchmarking is one tool of a number that can assist facility managers in pursuing improvement. It offers an external focus on internal activities and supports the drive towards best practice through objective comparisons and insights gained as a result of studying the best organizations.

- Benchmarking can work well between organizations that might otherwise regard themselves as competitors. The gains from benchmarking with others can far outweigh the disadvantages.

Introduction

Performance management involves monitoring, measuring, analysing, controlling, reporting and improving the efficiency and effectiveness of facility management, and applies to both insourced and outsourced services. Various models, methods and tools are available to assist in measuring performance and in indicating where improvement is required; examples include value management, balanced scorecards, *Six Sigma* and benchmarking. Performance management can be used as a means to foster efficient and effective working relationships between the organization and service providers and/or the in-house team in order to drive continual improvement in service delivery. It is not intended to be used as the basis for penalizing service providers and/or the in-house team, but instead to encourage better performance. Requirements in regard to performance management should have been formulated as part of the facility management strategy and policy, and then communicated to all affected stakeholders. Periodic review will indicate if performance targets continue to be appropriate or if some adjustment is necessary. In this regard, the need for a performance management system, based upon SLAs, should be considered. The system will need to incorporate the means for measuring performance over time to indicate progress towards meeting defined objectives. It will be necessary to capture and report on current and past performance, to highlight where improvement has been achieved and where it has not. Performance indicators should be defined for the purpose of measuring and reporting achievement and those performance indicators that are regarded as significant amongst them should be defined as KPIs. A process for reviewing and, where appropriate, updating performance indicators will have to be established as part of the commitment to continual improvement. Objective comparison of the performance achieved against an understanding of best practice should form an active part of performance measurement and reporting. Benchmarking provides such a basis and can help to gain insights into different and better ways of delivering services. Where a quality system is in place, the relationship between it and the performance management system needs to be clearly defined to avoid duplication of information, data and effort. Information and data should be entered once into either system and should be accessible from both (see Chapter 15).

Quality or performance

Often, the terms *quality* and *performance* are, in a facility management context, used interchangeably without any chance of miscommunication or misunderstanding. Sometimes it is necessary, however, to differentiate between the two. The intrinsic qualities in a service that involves a tangible product – for example, food in the case of catering – and, less tangible but no less important, the end-user's experience of the way in which the service was performed, are easy to differentiate. In the maintenance of plant and equipment, components and parts have to be replaced. The workmanship and care that goes into replacing old with new might be seen more in terms of quality than simply performing the task of replacing one part for another. Even the example of cleaning has a clear quality dimension, where the results can be expressed in terms of the resulting cleanliness of space and surfaces. When considering performance measurement, it might therefore be necessary to consider if aspects of quality need to be defined, as part of the delivery of the service, or if performance of the service will be enough. The decision should turn on whether or not products (or goods) are involved. In any event, the organization should be clear about its intentions when, initially, agreeing service levels and, later, in measuring performance against them.

The post-implementation review

For a new or refurbished facility, a post-implementation review, which is sometimes referred to as a post-construction review, should be undertaken within the first few months of operations. The purpose is to determine how everything *measures up* to requirements agreed during design briefing and design development, especially those relating to the safe and correct operation of the facility. It can be a substantial undertaking in some cases, because of the scale of the facility involved and the need for a thorough debriefing of the design and construction team. Where facility management briefing has been undertaken as part of design briefing, the organization should find it relatively easy to determine if functional requirements have been fulfilled and whether or not the facility is operating as planned. More likely than not, there will be some issues that have to be resolved and these might include, for example, making good defects and optimizing the performance of building services engineering installations. Feedback from stakeholders, especially end-users, will have to be organized so that sufficient information and data are to hand in order to inform the review process. The post-implementation review should be informed by any post-occupancy evaluation based on the recent experiences of end-users rather than repeating the exercise, unless significant issues and actions have arisen in the meantime.

Post-occupancy evaluation (POE)

A POE is intended to determine how well the new facility matches end-user requirements. Whilst it can be as far-reaching as the organization wishes, it should not duplicate the scope of a post-implementation review; rather, it should complement it. A POE assists in:

- Obtaining structured feedback to help in fine-tuning the facility in general and optimizing the performance of building services engineering installations in particular.
- Resolving persistent or recurrent problems in a facility that might otherwise go unchallenged.
- Providing information and data for facility planners and designers to support them in the planning and/or design of future facilities.

Garnering the opinions of end-users can be expected to provide an objective basis for evaluating the extent to which the facility is providing what was intended, so long as the method is rigorous. The normal method of undertaking such an evaluation is to conduct a survey of end-users using a questionnaire and might also involve interviews as a follow-up activity. Questionnaires are the most common tool for eliciting opinions and care needs to be exercised when drafting one. To do the job properly requires more than a few hours of work. There are two golden rules: first, the more time spent on designing the questionnaire, the greater will be its usefulness; and, second, no questionnaire should ever be distributed unless it has been piloted and found to be fit for purpose.

A POE differs from many conventional surveys because it seeks the opinions of those directly affected. The worth of any evaluation will depend on how well it has been designed and conducted, not least the extent to which it aligns with the facility management strategy, the design brief and functional requirements, since each of these help to establish a baseline against which actual performance of the facility can be measured. Interviewing end-users is one way of eliciting those opinions and any questionnaire used for this purpose will have to be properly structured if the data collected are to be analysed in a meaningful way. In the course of a survey or interviews, it is possible that some end-users will be reluctant to discuss issues.

In large organizations, a representative sample of end-users should be considered rather than attempting to involve everyone. Claims to representativeness should then be verified statistically to avoid misunderstanding over inferences that might be drawn on behalf of all would-be respondents; in this case, all end-users. In many cases, the population of end-users from which a sample is drawn will be known, perhaps exactly. However, different groups of end-users might have to be considered, where each can be considered as a population in its own right. The point is that over- or under-representation in any sample and in subsequent responses has to be avoided.

When preparing questions, it is better to adopt an approach where respondents (i.e. end-users) can indicate the extent to which they agree or disagree with a statement about their situation, or the extent to which they are satisfied or dissatisfied with aspects of the facility. Questions that require a simple *yes* or *no* might not provide anything very meaningful and can also leave respondents feeling frustrated that their opinions have not been properly canvassed. The best advice is to allow respondents to express their feelings about those matters they believe are important and about which there is concern. It is not wrong to ask standard questions through which to establish some basic facts, but others should be asked to help understand what end-users truly experience. The use of a five- or six-point *Likert scale* can be useful in eliciting opinions and measuring experiences, with additional *open* questions used to capture free-form responses. There is, however, some criticism over the use of self-evaluations based on Likert scales, which is concerned with error (Purdey, 2013). Care needs to be exercised when analysing responses and, wherever possible, *measures of association* involving correlation should be considered for the purpose of statistical analysis in preference to simpler, numerical scoring. In most cases, it is as important to understand the extent to which respondents in a sample are in agreement on the various issues before them as it is to know which are ranked highly and which are not.

Evaluations can also help to draw out suggestions from personnel about how to improve their well-being and that of the organization. Means for reducing waste, pollution and energy can be found when personnel are motivated to make suggestions in the belief that they and their feedback will be taken seriously. Finally, it is important to stress that a POE should not be seen as a one-off exercise. For it to be of benefit, it has to be repeated. In between times, personnel must be provided with the results and details of how the organization intends to deal with any issues that have arisen.

The service review

The end-user review

A distinction needs to be drawn between end-user opinions on a new or refurbished facility that are concerned mostly with the physical assets, on the one hand, and the performance of services delivered to them on the other. Feedback on the performance of the in-house team and/or service providers should be garnered from end-users periodically – see Post-occupancy evaluation above. Whilst a structured approach to feedback is preferable, it should not preclude less formal means; in fact, informal feedback is likely to complement formal feedback to the extent that a more developed feel for end-user experience can be gained. Even so, a balance needs to be struck between regular surveys and informal or occasional enquiries. In the case of formal means of feedback, end-users should be provided with a summary of their responses; otherwise, they will fail to take future surveys seriously – see the previous section. Validated responses should be made available to service providers and used in performance review meetings.

The operational review

The most frequent reviews tend to be those that are concerned with the regular delivery of services, as would occur with many domestic services; for example, security, cleaning and waste disposal. Repeated cycles of operations generally lend themselves to measurement and, hence, comparison with targets. Data capture can be automatic, as in the case of security, where physical presence at a given location is easily logged using some form of ICT. A similar arrangement can apply to the cleaning of defined areas and spaces, where the completion of the task can be recorded, often electronically. Collecting and analysing data are only part of the picture. For the in-house team or service provider's personnel, the purpose is to:

- Compare actual versus planned performance for each unit of measurement.
- Identify criteria met and exceeded.
- Determine overall performance.
- Highlight matters requiring attention.

Unit of measurement refers to each separately identified output or outcome defined in the relevant SLA for which a target or goal has been defined and agreed.

The financial review

Where services are outsourced, an up-to-date account needs to be maintained of the organization's financial position covering service contracts and the financial exposure it faces in the event that a contract is terminated. Exposure will change over time and so it will be necessary to reassess this figure periodically. It is advisable to report monthly on commitments and expenditure against budgets, in the following manner, where a *commitment* represents an order placed or contract awarded and, therefore, future expenditure:

1. original budget;
2. approved changes;
3. current approved budget;
4. total commitments;
5. estimated uncommitted work;
6. estimated net expenditure $(4+5)$;
7. cost contingency;
8. estimated total expenditure $(6+7)$; and
9. forecast over or under-expenditure $(8-3)$.

Cost contingency is necessary to cover conditions or events the occurrence or effect of which is uncertain and where experience shows that additional cost would likely be incurred. One of the benefits is in providing room to manoeuvre with respect to purchase orders and contract sums. If contingency were not included, then any increase in expenditure beyond the current approved budget, no matter how small, would break financial accounting rules: it is not possible to enter into a commitment and then spend money for which there is no budget. It is a prudent way of managing service contracts whilst complying with accounting rules.

A similar arrangement to cover insourced services, where these apply, should be maintained in accordance with financial accounting rules. In this regard, budgets tend to be set for the duration of a contract where it is of less than 12 months; otherwise, budgets are normally set for the financial accounting year. The use of an enterprise resource planning (ERP) system will probably dictate the format of financial control and reporting. The facility manager will need to consider how useful this form of control and reporting might be from a facility management perspective and, if necessary, to supplement what can be utilized from the ERP system with additional financial analysis and reporting. However, it is important to avoid needless departure from the use of the ERP system in favour of stand-alone applications, such as spreadsheets, to which one person or very few people have access (see Chapter 15).

For outsourced services, costs and budgets should be updated as and when new information is to hand. The actual costs incurred against budgets should form part of monthly financial reporting and be tabled at performance review meetings with service providers and/or the in-house team. Where increased costs incurred by service providers are reimbursable, the details should be included under actual costs.

The financial capacity of service providers to continue to deliver services should form part of the review process, because the financial health of any business changes over time (positively or negatively). The organization needs to be kept abreast of any issue that might impact negatively on the service provider's ability to deliver the service. This matter needs careful handling, since it could imply that there are doubts about the service provider's capacity which, after discussion, prove to be totally unfounded. In building a working relationship with service providers, it helps if there can be an open discussion on matters relating to business development without it appearing to be a form of interrogation. Moreover, it could open up new opportunities for doing business.

The human resources review

The primary interest of both the organization and service providers in regard to human resources should be HSSE performance. Reporting on health, safety and security in particular should include details of all accidents and incidents logged in the period, a diagnosis of their cause and immediate actions taken to prevent recurrence. The performance review meeting should consider the lessons to be learned from actual events or reports of any incident that might have had the potential to compromise health, safety and security.

The extent to which service providers have fulfilled their obligations in terms of quality and performance and timeliness of service delivery depends in large part upon the deployment of appropriate resources, especially human resources. This refers primarily to the quantity, type and productivity of human resources. Shortcomings in any of these three areas are bound to impact on performance and the achievement of targets. Accidents and near-accidents are often an indicator of poor performance and, in the latter case, a portent of accidents to come. Where evident, a review of safety culture, training, induction in the workplace, supervision and management style should be instigated without delay.

The regulatory compliance review

It is necessary to stress that wherever a facility is located, it and the personnel using it will be subject to legislation and regulations. The latter must be complied with regardless – *the law is the law*. There is therefore little to be gained here in discussing regulations that are defined by statues and byelaws, and that vary from country to country and from time to time. Nonetheless, a reasonable line to take is that legislation and regulations generally define minimum requirements. An organization intent on continual improvement would be expected to exceed minimum requirements in most cases. In the event that a breach of legal obligations or duties has occurred, details should be reported and the matter examined at the next performance review meeting. A full account of any breach or non-compliance should be provided together with the actions taken, or required to be taken, to remedy the breach.

Updating service specifications and SLAs

Service specifications should not be regarded as fixed statements of service requirements, but as a basis for continual improvement as circumstances and end-user requirements change. Experience will reveal how better results, greater end-user satisfaction and improved value for money can be achieved by a change in specification. Service providers and/or the in-house team should be involved in the process of updating service specifications and SLAs in order to draw upon their experience of providing the service. If necessary, visits to other facilities might be necessary to provide insights into how improvements are possible. These actions will ensure that the organization is able to determine if the specified service was obtained and so draw lessons for the future. It is essential that the ability to adjust service specifications and SLAs is incorporated into contracts with service providers and/or the agreement with the in-house team.

Performance measurement

Critical success factors (CSFs) and key performance indicators (KPIs)

CSFs are those actions that must be performed well in order that the organization's business objectives and goals set for facility management are achieved. Within each CSF will be one or more KPIs. The purpose of a KPI is to help in measuring, understanding and controlling progress in a CSF. For example, the goal of *providing end-users with the highest-quality service that achieves best value* might have been set. A CSF in achieving that goal would be *agreed SLAs*. One KPI would be *published service level agreements*, to show clearly what has to be achieved and then, subsequently, to note that it has been achieved. This example is fairly simple and does no more than recognize that something has been done once or perhaps repeated. If most KPIs took this form, the organization would not be in a position to know what performance was being achieved across all of its services. In most cases, actual performance has to be measured at intervals and compared over time. The task is therefore repeated so that any deviation in performance can be easily highlighted and corrective action taken as necessary.

In another example – an internal perspective on productivity – KPIs might highlight abortive work, a backlog and an ability (or inability) to perform tasks concurrently:

- Percentage of total work completed at a given time.
- Percentage of activities planned against unplanned.
- Percentage of total hours for the above by asset.
- Breakdowns against planned preventive maintenance hours.

Where end-user satisfaction is concerned, a CSF could be quality, for which one of the KPIs would be complaints (or the lack of them). This KPI could then be used to measure the number of complaints over time or, alternatively, to produce a satisfaction rating or index.

CSFs are not exclusive to the organization. CSFs can be used to establish the suitability of service providers during the prequalification stage of the procurement process. Tan *et al.* (2014) have identified client satisfaction, certification of the company, reliability of service, quality of service and company reputation amongst a number of CSFs that could be used to prequalify maintenance service providers. From a service provider's perspective, these could provide useful insights to help improve service delivery, as well as increasing the chances of inclusion in a tender competition.

When establishing CSFs and KPIs, it is vital that they correspond to goals that, in the case of the organization, are aligned with its business objectives. Without this alignment, successful attainment of service levels might contribute nothing to the success of the core business. This is not just about doing things right, but about doing the right things. KPIs are seen as a valuable tool in this regard and have penetrated all areas of business. In practice, there will be many CSFs and KPIs that interact and combine to create the basis for continual improvement. Performing at the top end of these measures is an indication of having met best practice and, with that, best value in service delivery.

As a rule, performance indicators, including KPIs, should be reported in simple and direct terms that allow progress towards achieving goals, and against targets, to be readily understood. Performance indicators regarded as key to understanding performance overall should be identified, including any trends that might reveal improving or declining outputs. KPIs should represent the significant few measures that allow the organization and service providers and/or the in-house team to act quickly and decisively upon any deviation in performance. Not all performance indicators are significant; for instance, it is implausible to talk about 120 KPIs. Perhaps no more than 20 will be significant and, therefore, KPIs. All the rest will be performance indicators – no more, but no less. Measuring a large number of performance indicators and labelling all as *key* is therefore best avoided. Apart from obscuring the view of what is important to note and act upon and what is not, this can waste valuable resources. In the worst case, it can create a false sense of well-being for senior managers. Taking KPIs from another organization might be tempting. They are, however, likely to have been determined by that organization's CSFs and business objectives. Their KPIs might have a purpose in revealing an aspect of performance that is not adequately quantified at present, but they make sense only where there is a clear link to defined CSFs. KPIs that are not linked to success criteria (and in turn to business objectives) can amount to misinformation, with senior managers tracking performance and trends that might serve little or no useful purpose. Since performance indicators naturally follow events, there is bound to be a delay in detecting any deviation in performance. For this reason, it is sensible to minimize the time between an output or outcome and its measurement and reporting.

Misunderstanding the distinction between a KPI and a target is fairly common. KPIs indicate a level of achievement that can be compared over time to determine if performance is getting better, worse or staying the same: *what is the trend?* We can take an example from everyday life, such as driving. Take fuel consumption at, say, 45 miles per gallon (6.3 litres per 100 km). If we had a budget that demanded greater economy – say, 50 miles per gallon (5.6 litres per 100 km) – that would be a target. If actual consumption was then recorded on a weekly basis, we could see if it was better, worse or the same. KPIs are those measures of consumption; they are not targets. Miles per gallon (or litres per 100 km) is the KPI, because it is an indicator of actual performance achieved.

Performance monitoring

Details of what to measure should be included in service contracts as a task for the service provider to undertake on a regular basis. The organization's role is largely one of overseeing as opposed to direct involvement. Similar arrangements should apply to the in-house team, as it needs to show that it is achieving, or not, the agreed levels of performance. The essential steps involved in performance management are:

- Comparing actual performance with expected performance stated in SLAs.
- Monitoring end-user satisfaction.
- Informing senior managers of any deviation in expected performance.

In order to help ensure the continued performance of the service provider against the service specification and SLA, a performance scoresheet should be completed regularly by the organization, so as to arrive at an agreed performance rating. An example format for a performance scoresheet is provided in Fig. 11.1.

The performance rating can be applied to a performance-related payment table that would reward the service provider for exceeding the specification – if it had previously been agreed that enhanced performance is to be pursued – and penalize the service provider for not meeting the specification's minimum requirements. The level of detail in the table must be commensurate with the size and complexity of the service provided. However, the golden rule is to concentrate on KPIs – those that can be determined and analysed cost-effectively.

WESTEN SCIENCE PARK			**Month:** 7
Item Service criteria	**Priority weighting**	**Monthly rating**	**Score (weighting x monthly rating)**
01 Planned preventive maintenance	5	2	10
02 Response times to breakdowns	5	0	0
Total score			10
Performance rating (Actual total/maximum x 100)			50%
Prepared by:	**Date:**		
Verified by:	**Date:**		

In this simple example, the scoring is based upon the following:

0 = service does not meet specification

1 = service meets specification

2 = service exceeds specification

A more sophisticated scoring system can, however, be employed where a specific measurement basis has been agreed.

Fig. 11.1   The performance scoresheet.

The importance of maintaining continuity of service is one aspect of performance that might require special attention, particularly in the case of building services engineering installations. Persistent non-functioning of such installations could have serious consequences in terms of health and safety. Financial penalties to cover the losses that might be faced by a serious failure in an installation or service have to be carefully considered. It is, however, necessary to set these in the context of the value of contracts. For instance, it would be unreasonable to expect a service provider to accept a level of penalty so onerous that any failure on its part would outweigh all payment.

An end-user's view of the quality of a service or product is based on tangible and intangible factors, both of which are important. Tangible factors are those that can be objectively measured, such as the time taken to deliver an item, the charge made and the level of performance achieved. Intangible factors include those that are more subjective in nature and, therefore, more difficult to measure: for example, the utility of the item to the end-user, its adaptability and advantages over other types, or merely the courtesy of the service provider's personnel. The difficulty of quantifying some factors should not preclude measurement, as they can be as important as those that are easily measured. The organization should, however, be cautious about imposing too many or overly demanding performance measurements and excessive monitoring on service providers and/or the in-house team, as this can become counterproductive. A sensible approach is to concentrate on KPIs. Table 11.1 suggests some performance indicators and Table 11.2 shows a possible scoring scheme. The organization will need to determine which of the

Table 11.1   Example performance indicators for planned and unplanned maintenance.

Element	Service	Output/measure	Perspective
1	Planned maintenance performance	Tasks planned in period Tasks completed in period Time taken per task Mean time taken per task Resource attendance in period Number of tasks reworked Percentage of tasks reworked of total tasks in period Service delivery resource utilized	By end-user group By facility/location By facility/space type By service provider By asset type By asset
2	Unplanned maintenance performance	Number of breakdowns/faults in period Percentage response times met Number of breakdowns/faults completed in period Number of breakdowns/faults outstanding in period Time taken per breakdown Mean time taken per breakdown Number of tasks reworked Percentage tasks reworked of total tasks in period	By end-user group By facility/location By facility/space type By service provider By asset type By asset
		Asset availability in period Downtime in period Unplanned stoppages in period Service delivery resource utilized	By end-user group By facility/location By facility/space type By service provider By asset type

performance indicators should be regarded as KPIs and, therefore, summarized in reporting.

In practice, the overall performance of a service provider and/or in-house team can be determined by monitoring adherence to the following:

- Compliance with regulations and any relevant standards or guidelines.
- Quality or performance-related targets.
- Expenditure limits.
- Time-related targets.
- Relationships with end-users.

Performance data can be collected in a number of ways. For example, the service provider might complete worksheets and job reports, or feedback from end-users might be sought actively in the form of comments on worksheets, complaints and end-user surveys. Once the organization has collected these data, they should be used to complete a scoresheet, similar to that presented in Table 11.2, at regular intervals. This should be undertaken for a sample of the services delivered by each service provider and/or the in-house team based on KPIs, unless there are relatively few. These will be shown in the SLA or contract and will provide a basis for measuring performance in a way that involves both the service provider and end-users. Table 11.2, column 4 (actual level of service delivered) contains the service

Table 11.2 An example of an unplanned maintenance scoring scheme – a report on faulty lighting.

(1) Service criteria	(2) Agreed target level of service (targets in SLA or specification)	(3) Value[a]	(4) Actual level of service delivered	(5) Value	(6) End-user satisfaction	(7) Value
Regulations/ standards	Work carried out according to health and safety regulations using certified products	10	Work carried out according to health and safety regulations, using certified products	10	Satisfied	10
Performance/ quality	Fault to be rectified so that it is prevented from reoccurring Minimize level of disruption to users	20	Fault diagnosed and problem rectified Minor disruption to end-users	18	Concern over disruption to work	12
Delivery time	*Minor lighting fault* Maximum response time = 2 hours Maximum service time = 4 hours (Total delivery time = 6 hours)	10	Response time = 3 hours Service time = 2 hours (Total delivery time = 5 hours)	8	Concern over delay in response	5
Delivery expenditure	*Minor lighting fault* Total cost = 120.00– 250.00 (range)	10	Total cost = 200.00	10	Satisfied	10
End-user– service provider interaction	Keep end-users informed of status of work and likely completion time	20	End-users informed that fault had been rectified following completion of work	16	No contact between report of fault and completion	14
Overall service delivery	Work to be carried out according to the targets given above	70	Work carried out satisfactorily, within agreed cost; however, not within agreed response time	62	Work and cost satisfactory, delivery time and contact unsatisfactory	51

[a]Each activity is assigned a weighted target level of service value. The actual level of service delivered and end-user satisfaction values are determined relative to this base value.

provider's measurement of the service, based on data and information held by the organization. These measures will relate to response times to fault reports, end-user surveys, charges made for services and measures of quality levels. End-user satisfaction (column 6) relates to the end-user's view of the level of service delivered, based on records held by the organization. Reasons for any discrepancies between the three values in Table 11.2 then need to be established and corrective action taken as necessary. This will entail the active engagement of the organization and the service provider or the in-house team.

The service provider's level of service delivery could be, to a greater or lesser extent, affected by the quality system that the organization has in place. The satisfactory performance of the service provider will be more assured if the quality system is geared to the levels of service performance established in the SLAs. In other words, the ways in which quality and service performance are measured, in accordance with the SLAs, should reflect those incorporated in the quality system.

Performance reporting

Performance reports should be completed by the in-house team or service provider each month as close to the last working day as possible, since this helps to fit in with routine accounting and business reporting cycles. Whilst it will be the service provider's duty to complete the reports, the organization will need to furnish the service provider with a master service performance record sheet.

For the organization looking across all of its services, a consolidated performance report will be necessary and might, as an example, collectively record the following:

- Maintenance details – the incidence of maintenance-induced failures, and adherence to agreed planned preventive maintenance schedules (see Chapter 12).
- Job cards – responses and actions within service levels for each service.
- Security – compliance with security procedures, and the absence of misuses or losses.
- Cleaning – completion of all specified work.
- Safety – completion of all recorded action items.
- Space and facility planning – space database kept up to date, and users informed of progress.
- Reception – the procedure for dealing with visitors has been followed.
- Reprographics – photocopiers serviced within four hours.
- Stationery and printing – all orders fulfilled on a timely basis.

Operations and service assessment

Operations and service assessment should be undertaken adopting the same procedure as for service performance records. This assessment might, as an example, record the following items:

- Effective communication – timely reporting and prompt response to requests.
- Documentation – complete, sufficient, on time and maintained.
- Additional work – positive attitude, flexibility and proactiveness.
- Image – satisfactory general housekeeping and appearance of personnel.
- Management and coordination – efficient use of resources and protection of the organization's interests.
- Process and methods of work – proposed innovations and effective solutions.
- Service provider/supplier relationships – control of performance and quality of service delivery.
- Feedback – space utilization opportunities, with advice on locations.

Other performance measures

The following performance measures could be applied to monthly service performance records:

- Criteria met or exceeded – *yes* (score 1) or *no* (score 0) for each item.
- Total service performance must be not less than 6 at each monthly assessment.

The following performance measures could be applied to operations and services assessment:

- Criteria exceeded, met or failed – *exceed* (score 2), *meet* (score 1) or *fail* (score 0) for each item.
- Total service performance must be not less than 9 at each monthly assessment.

The above are typical of those measures used to determine the overall performance of a service provider.

The facility management dashboard

In the past, the facility manager spent days at the end of each month, and sometimes into the beginning of the next month, compiling the information required to report upwards in the organization. Today, ICT greatly assists in this work (see Chapter 15 on Computer-aided facility management). As the breadth and complexities of reporting have increased, so has the demand for obtaining regular updates on progress, with the aim of controlling and reporting in real time. ICT applications have developed significantly and solutions exist for pulling together disparate performance data, but the challenge of turning data into relevant and timely information remains.

Corporate intranets and the technology supporting them have provided the key to unlocking the potential of this information in real time. In the past, delivering management reports using data from across the organization was only possible with the support of ERP systems. The development of web-based, front-end reporting has allowed timely, comprehensive reporting to become a cost-effective reality and has been marked by the arrival of the facility management *dashboard*.

The dashboard is seen as a vital performance management tool. Whilst simple in its underlying principle, the tool can be likened to the instruments in an aircraft cockpit. For the pilot, the instruments provide multiple views of the operation of the aircraft and progress towards its destination. A pilot would not be satisfied with merely knowing about the aircraft's altitude, direction and speed. The pilot needs a wide range of data to fly the aircraft safely to its destination. The dashboard aims to provide information in a simple manner that aids understanding and insight at a glance.

The dashboard adopts the same approach as a scorecard, based on a cascading or drill-down technique as a means for measuring the performance of operations. The images in Fig. 11.2 show the dashboard, with comparisons of actual performance over time.

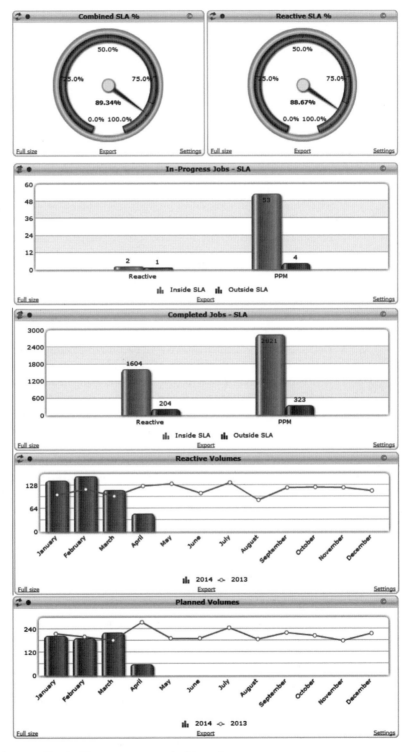

Fig. 11.2   The facility management *dashboard*.

Facility managers who have experience of reporting in this dashboard style appreciate the benefit of responsive real-time information and the benefits this provides in reporting status upwards in the organization.

Benchmarking

The basic approach

Benchmarking is about establishing the norms for performance in terms of financial management, organizational management, innovation and change management and, importantly, end-user service. People tend to have notions of what things might cost, how long they might take and what they should expect. Benchmarking is chiefly concerned with formalizing these notions to provide a baseline against which performance can be compared, and often with out-of-sector bodies. In making organizations look out from themselves into another sector, benchmarking also directs energy towards serving the organization's business interests and away from internal conflict that could arise where there are mixed opinions on the best way forward.

One of the barriers to successful benchmarking is that it is often seen as a one-off exercise. Another is an inability to accept the idea of out-of-sector comparisons. Detractors tend to claim that an out-of-sector comparison is hardly a case of equating *apples with apples*; indeed, it is not. The whole purpose is to introduce new thinking to help break from the belief that there is nothing better than the current way of working since it is the result of years of fine-tuning. Over time, any imperfections will have become accepted because of familiarity, thereby reinforcing the belief that there is, indeed, nothing better. The trouble is that it can prove impossible to contemplate any alternative because it falls outside of what is known as an individual's bounded rationality – you cannot understand something for which there is no information and where it falls outside your cognitive limits. Breakthroughs occur in many fields of endeavour where individuals step outside their present experience and explore other possibilities, leading to significant shifts in thinking. Facility management is hardly rocket science and is capable of advancing through ideas borrowed from other fields. The message is that if you want to learn how to do something better, by all means see what your competitors are up to; but take a look at what others are doing with fundamentally the same problem in another field.

The origins of formalized benchmarking are well documented (Leibfried & McNair, 1994): it is *an external focus on internal activities, functions or operations in order to achieve continuous improvement*. The main purpose is to measure quality of service, and the processes that support it, against internal goals and targets and the best-performing bodies in other sectors. In these cases, it is likely that the best performer is better, because what it does is different. The selection of an acceptable best performer for comparison is one of the most difficult aspects of benchmarking and those conducting the benchmarking exercise should look as widely as possible to find valid comparisons.

A benchmarking study begins with an analysis of existing activities and practices within the organization. These processes have to be properly understood and measurable before comparison can take place with another – if you cannot measure it, you cannot improve it. Usually, benchmarking is a one-on-one activity; that is, it is used by one organization to help identify improvements in its own processes by exchanging information with another. The activity is normally a collaboration of mutual benefit – however strange it might seem to look so closely at a competitor and vice versa. Alternatively, benchmarking can involve a group of competitors, the benchmarking data of which are exchanged, but where anonymity is preserved. Competitors provide not only the challenge, but also the insights into how performance can be improved and costs reduced.

Benchmarking also provides management with a tool for making decisions about policies and procedures in regard to how services should be procured; that is, whether they should be insourced or outsourced (see Chapter 7). It is neither complicated nor expensive to apply, and might be a relatively easy route for establishing and then recording KPIs. Since some organizations lack basic information on their own services, benchmarking can provide the necessary focus to enable such information to be gathered objectively and relatively painlessly.

In partnering arrangements – especially where the workload is shared amongst a few select service providers or suppliers – the need for benchmarking becomes all the more apparent. Continual improvement is an integral part of any partnering relationship, without which there can be no purpose served – see below. By comparing one partner's performance with that of other service providers, it is possible to provide stimulus for improvement. This can effectively replace the stimulus provided by the competitive tendering of each new contract. Concerns that a partner might have about feeling exposed are unlikely to arise, since all partners are aware from the outset about the arrangements to be adopted and have signified their acceptance of them by entering into a partnering agreement.

Openness in relationships between the organization and service providers, whether as part of a formal partnering arrangement or not, is essential to the successful operation of facility management. The role of ICT in enabling the efficient transfer of information cannot be underestimated in this respect. Information management has an essential role to play (see Chapter 15). As such, it is a major tool for the strategic management of a facility.

Best practice

So far, the term *best practice* has been used to convey the sense of a level of performance or standard of achievement that is about as good as we are likely to find at a given time. For this reason, best practice is not fixed, but nor is it arbitrary. Sometimes it is prefaced by *current* to make clear that it is temporal in nature. When we find something of a higher level or standard, that will then become *current best practice*. Raising the bar to achieve higher performance can mean doing things differently. Step changes in performance often come from radical changes to the way in which work is organized and undertaken. As noted earlier, we might fail to see any way in which something can be improved or performed differently because of our experience and lack of information on what might be possible. All it takes is for others to show what they have done to achieve higher performance – and then it seems so obvious that we wonder why we had failed to see it ourselves.

Those who cling to the belief that what they are doing is the best and that there cannot be anything superior fail to appreciate one essential lesson. If it were the best, then how would that explain all of those past occasions when people believed that something was, at the time, the best that could be achieved? Put another way, how is it possible that we have made such progress over many decades, right up to the present, and yet from now on things are simply not going to get any better?

Continual improvement

Benchmarking is a tool for supporting a process of continual improvement. Its purpose is to identify current performance in relation to best practice in areas of interest. In this context, it is about measuring performance in the underlying processes of facility management. This means, for example, establishing what is being paid for services and supplies. Typical in these respects are domestic services such as security and cleaning, and the costs of energy – electricity and gas – and other utilities (e.g. electricity, water and telecommunications). In these cases, cost or price and quality or performance of service should become the main targets for study if best value is to be achieved, and there is to be a basis for pursuing continual improvement.

Benchmarking should not be used simply to compare the costs of services but, where appropriate, to measure the effectiveness of the process that leads to those costs and a given quality or performance. As was shown in Chapter 3, the facility management strategy will outline a basis for measuring whether or not business objectives have been met and best value achieved. If the optimal cost level is to be reached relative to a defined level of performance, it must be possible to compare the costs of different methods of delivering the required performance. Benchmarking can therefore be used to measure the effectiveness of in-house practices against external practices in out-of-sector bodies and against an organization identified as achieving best practice in the area under scrutiny.

An organization that has raised the profile of facility management, perhaps as the outcome of restructuring its business processes, and been given the clear mandate of it having to add value, needs to know whether or not this goal is being achieved. Benchmarking can supply the answers not once, but at intervals as part of the pursuit of continual improvement. Comparisons with other bodies recognized as achieving best practice allow the organization to see then close the gap between its own performance and that of the best.

The benchmarking process

Performance measurement is at the centre of efficient and effective facility management. Benchmarking begins by identifying perceived critical success factors (CSFs), typically the strategies, roles and processes existing within the organization. Preliminary questions are:

- Who is involved in delivering the service?
- Why are they involved?
- What are they doing?

- Why are they doing it?
- Is what they are doing adding value?

The last question recognizes the need to add value to the services provided to end-users.

In offering an approach to benchmarking, there is bound to be the danger of appearing too prescriptive. The approach outlined below should take account of any practical issue that might be an obstacle. Authors differ on their prescription for benchmarking. Here, we identify eight steps in a typical benchmarking exercise.

1. Identify the subject of the exercise.
2. Decide what to measure.
3. Identify who to benchmark within the sector and outside.
4. Collect information and data.
5. Analyse the findings and determine the gap.
6. Set goals for improvement.
7. Implement the new order.
8. Monitor the process for improvement.

Step 1 – Identify the subject of the exercise

- Agree on the objective(s) of the exercise.
- Decide on whom to involve internally.
- Define the process.
- Identify the scope.
- Set the limits for the exercise.
- Agree on the process.
- Produce a map or model of the process.

Step 2 – Decide what to measure

- Examine the elements of the process.
- Establish measures of performance.
- Verify that measures match objective(s).

Step 3 – Identify who to benchmark within sector and outside

- Identify the main competitors and *rising stars*.
- Agree on those to benchmark.
- Identify out-of-sector comparisons.
- Identify the best-in-class outside your own sector.

Step 4 – Collect information and data

- Draft a checklist or questionnaire.
- Pilot the questionnaire.
- Conduct interviews.

Step 5 – Analyse the findings and determine the gap

- Score answers/responses and weight them, as necessary.
- Analyse any qualitative responses.
- Summarize the findings.
- Measure the gap between your own performance and that of others.

Step 6 – Set goals for improvement

- Identify goals for performance improvement.
- Establish criteria for judging performance.
- Draft an action plan with milestones for improvement.

Step 7 – Implement the new order

- Draft new procedures.
- Communicate procedures to all stakeholders.
- Train those affected by the new order.
- Implement the new process.

Step 8 – Monitor the process for improvement

- Conduct regular review meetings.
- Observe the progress of the best-in-class comparison.
- Determine if corrective actions are required.
- Document changes and communicate to all stakeholders.

Benchmarking facility management

Many organizations now routinely collect data and engage in their own bench-marking of the costs of energy, water, maintenance, cleaning, security and so on. Some also participate in benchmarking clubs and in arrangements with very different kinds of organization. Commercial enterprises have been set up to bring together those seeking to benchmark, and some universities have become involved in benchmarking. The organization should look closely at the costs of getting involved against the likely benefits, as not all benchmarking arrangements deliver on their promises.

Facility management, as a recognized discipline, is not only relatively new, but also has great potential for reducing cost and increasing service levels over the long term. Mechanisms for benchmarking should be built into newly defined facility management operations, whether services are insourced or outsourced. One example of benchmarking the overall approach to facility management is described below. It is based on a validated model of best practice facility management and has been tested with a large number of organizations across different sectors over many years.

The Micro-Scan*fm* diagnostic tool enables the organization to review, discuss and modify its facility management in the light of responses to a detailed questionnaire, which is held and analysed by computer. Micro-Scan*fm* provides an opportunity to understand and assess the scope for business improvement and to highlight the potential gain. It does this against four separate perspectives:

1. *End-users* – how do end-users see us?
2. *Financial* – how is the function managed to achieve best value?
3. *Operational* – how efficient and effective is the delivery of services?
4. *Innovation* – how does facility management continue to improve and assist the core business in creating value?

The overall approach is consistent with that of the perspectives adopted in *The Balanced Scorecard* (Kaplan & Norton, 1996). Areas of potential improvement are easily identified and can be monitored over time to gauge the extent of improvement achieved. *The Balanced Scorecard* relies upon the minimum amount of information that is necessary in order to obtain a balanced view of the organization's performance. Micro-Scan*fm* adopts the same approach through 80 questions, the answers to which can then be compared across respondents and their organizations. Thus, it is possible to compare understanding, attitude and actions within a single organization as well as across many.

The baseline (or benchmark) against which scores are calibrated is that of best practice. This is established from industry sources and is reviewed periodically so that recalibration of the tool can be undertaken as required. In this connection, it is important to appreciate that understanding develops over time and so today's best practice will not necessarily be tomorrow's best practice. The diagrammatic presentation of the scores resulting from an individual analysis is shown in Fig. 11.3. This reveals at a glance where a respondent (or organization) needs to direct attention. Likewise, it can confirm that current initiatives are measuring up to best practice.

The four perspectives have shown themselves to be purposeful and aligned to both the facility management strategy and, implicitly, business objectives. The idea that one can have strong financial controls and yet be less concerned about, say,

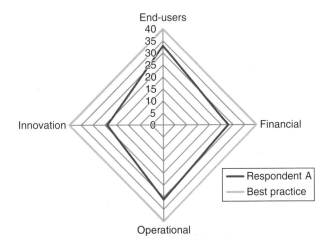

Fig. 11.3   A radar graph showing an individual set of scores.

Table 11.3 An example dialogue taken from Micro-Scan*fm*.

1. We allocate our budgets based on a priority of needs.
2. We measure improvement by achieving lower costs this year than last.
3. We conduct tendering competitions for all services and supplies over a specified minimum contract value.
4. We require our insourcing costs to be compared against the costs of buying in the same services.
5. Our service contracts are procured on an annual basis.
6. We form cooperative relationships with our major suppliers and service providers.
7. We seek the advice of external consultants in areas where we do not have the expertise ourselves.
8. We manage our services effectively by leaving them with the same provider.
9. We insource as many of our services as possible.
10. We assess the cost-effectiveness of all services whether insourced or outsourced.
11. We are more concerned about value for money than cost or quality alone.
12. We have indicators for measuring the cost-effectiveness of all services and supplies.
13. We compare the costs of our services and supplies with those of organizations similar to ourselves.
14. We compare the costs of our services and supplies with those of the best organization irrespective of its business sector.
15. We undertake skills audits to determine our management needs in regard to the facility and services.
16. We have explicit procedures for buying in services and supplies.
17. We produce service level agreements for services and supplies.
18. We measure the performance of our service providers whether insourced or outsourced.
19. We have up-to-date specifications for our services whether insourced or outsourced.
20. Our data on the costs and performance of services are held centrally and are readily accessible ...
    and so on.

Against each of these questions, respondents are required to indicate the extent of their actions according to the following scale: always, frequently, occasionally, seldom or never.

end-users, is easily highlighted. Balance across all four perspectives, as shown by best practice, should be the only sensible path to follow. In this respect, it is not a matter of having the right answers, but more a case of knowing where improvement lies and how this might enable the gap with best practice to be closed. Examples of the many issues that stand behind the four perspectives are information technology, human resources management, education and training, and end-user satisfaction. Typical questions used in dialogue with respondents are given in Table 11.3.

Micro-Scan*fm* has been constructed so that each element in its dialogue with a respondent – typically a facility manager when benchmarking across multiple organizations – relates to a CSF. Quantitative analysis of a more detailed series of questions could be added to enable actual performance to be measured against best practice. However, the aim is not to provide measures of performance, but to guide facility managers and their organizations to understand better how they are thinking and behaving now. Developing that understanding is the cornerstone of Micro-Scan*fm*.

Beyond benchmarking

Other methods of providing objective comparison of performance have been devised and are widely implemented. Their supporters claim considerable success, and this is not in question. What is important is that processes are understood precisely – in this context, facility management – and that it is possible to apply tools that lead to answers consistent with business objectives. For some, benchmarking is able to provide a simple and direct solution, but for others more developed tools and techniques are deployed; for example, *Six Sigma* (Pande *et al.*, 2000). *Six Sigma* is used to help companies improve end-user satisfaction, profitability and competitiveness through a focus on end-users by the disciplined use of facts, data and statistical analysis – the term itself refers to a statistically derived performance target. The whole approach is more demanding and more rigorous than that of the benchmarking methodology outlined above. In the right hands, *Six Sigma* can deliver benefits.

The quality system

If a satisfactory level of service is to be achieved, not only should there be a quality system in place, the same must be required of service providers. In fact, service providers' quality systems should form an integral part of their service delivery. To add value, service providers have to apply the principles of quality assurance in order to enhance service delivery through a reduction in errors and reworking, and as an effective means for handling end-user complaints (non-conformance), action and feedback. A quality-assured approach can save money. The existence of a quality system on the part of a service provider should therefore be one of the criteria used in the assessment of tenders. However, there is a difference between having a quality system and using it as a key means to support the pursuit of continual improvement.

A common misconception is that a quality system is administratively burdensome, costly and, therefore, unnecessary. If a quality system were to be seen as simply generating paper or adding a layer of administration, then it would have been misunderstood or misapplied. Formal recognition through accreditation under ISO 9000 (quality management) is important in underscoring commitment to achieving total end-user satisfaction and that the organization is prepared to open its system to external scrutiny. By means of a third-party audit – in addition to periodic internal audits – the organization is more likely to meet this commitment and, furthermore, be able to demonstrate it visibly.

The approach advocated here should be sufficient to provide a basis for a quality system, embracing the facility management function. A quality system normally consists of a policy statement and a quality manual with procedures. The policy statement is an explicit commitment to quality-assured processes and activities. The quality manual provides a detailed interpretation of the way in which each of the quality standards is to be met within the context of operations. The procedures, not surprisingly, explain the detailed steps that must be followed in order to comply with the quality system. For a system to be effective, it needs to be applied as work is being done. Thus, for example, logs and reviews should not be completed retrospectively. Maintenance should ideally be inspected while it is being undertaken and immediately after completion to ensure that it complies with requirements. Records and accounts rendered for maintenance work should be checked for completeness and accuracy.

Conclusions

Performance of service delivery has to be measured and used as a basis for understanding if agreed service levels, based on goals and targets set down in SLAs, are being achieved. An objective means for relating actual performance in facility management, particularly in service delivery, to the business objectives needs to be implemented and this is where CSFs have to be defined. Progress towards achieving them is indicated by comparing actual performance achieved over time. Performance indicators will be many, but relatively few will be significant (i.e. KPIs). It is essential to measure those aspects that matter and that provide a ready and accurate picture of progress in all areas critical to the business. The aim is to raise performance and therefore improve service delivery. In addition, there has to be a clear understanding of what is being achieved and what is not. Service reviews, as part of formal performance management reviews, bring focus to areas such as end-user satisfaction, operations, finances, human resources and regulatory compliance. There are various tools at the disposal of facility managers and organizations committed to continual improvement. Each will have its proponents and detractors. Benchmarking is not a new discovery and so has the benefit of being tried, tested and refined. It is a relatively simple tool to apply so long as there is a clear understanding of the process that is to be measured. There is no one form that benchmarking can take and it is neither exclusively quantitative nor qualitative; it can be both. Moreover, it can provide a simple, but effective, means for measuring performance and cost, leading to a better understanding of best value. It can be applied easily and can produce immediate benefits as soon as the results are available. The organization's quality system should support its facility management and vice versa. This will ensure, as an absolute minimum, that a consistent set of standards and supporting arrangements is applied as a basis for pursuing continual improvement.

Checklist

This checklist is intended to assist with review and action planning.

	Yes	No	Action required
1. Where the facility is new or has been refurbished, is there a commitment to undertaking a post-implementation review?	☐	☐	☐
2. Where the facility is new or has been refurbished, is there a commitment to undertaking a post-occupancy evaluation (POE)?	☐	☐	☐

		Yes	**No**	**Action required**
3.	Is the performance of service providers and/or the in-house team reviewed periodically; for example, monthly?	☐	☐	☐
4.	Are reviews of service delivery carried out in advance of performance review meetings?	☐	☐	☐
5.	Do service reviews cover end-users, operations, finances, human resources and regulatory compliance as a minimum?	☐	☐	☐
6.	Have CSFs for facility management in supporting the core business been defined and in sufficient number?	☐	☐	☐
7.	Do the CSFs link to the organization's business objectives and any targets set for the coming period?	☐	☐	☐
8.	Have performance indicators been defined in sufficient number to measure actual performance achieved in all service areas?	☐	☐	☐
9.	Do the performance indicators support the CSFs and, in turn, do they help in understanding progress towards achieving business objectives?	☐	☐	☐
10.	Have performance indicators that might be regarded as significant amongst the many been identified as key performance indicators (KPIs)?	☐	☐	☐
11.	Is there a commitment to continual improvement in service delivery and, if so, is it clear what it means in practice?	☐	☐	☐
12.	Have arrangements been made for the benchmarking of facility management in terms of the performance of services delivered?	☐	☐	☐

	Yes	No	Action required
13. Is the organization actively seeking out best practices and implementing them where they can improve performance in service delivery?	☐	☐	☐
14. If requested, can best practice facility management be articulated in relation to end-users, operations, finance and innovation?	☐	☐	☐
15. Is the organization's quality system used to support performance management of facility management?	☐	☐	☐

12 Maintenance Management

Key issues

The following key issues are covered in this chapter.

- Facility management has a long-standing association with building maintenance management, including building services engineering, for the simple reason that in many countries the discipline has emerged from such a background.

- Once the organization has taken delivery of a new or refurbished facility, it needs to protect and enhance its capital investment, which will be expected to support the functions for which it was designed well into the future.

- The operation and management of a facility requires appropriate planned maintenance and procedures for responding to unplanned maintenance to keep it in a safe, efficient and cost-effective state. It is necessary that facility assets continue to perform as intended, retaining their value at minimal cost.

- A process approach to maintenance management should be adopted at the strategic and tactical (i.e. policy) levels, with links to operational activities. There has to be a close coupling between the organization's business objectives, its facility management strategy and its maintenance strategy.

- Regular and planned maintenance should be regarded as a value-adding activity and not as simply a cost to the organization. A whole-life perspective needs to be adopted so that decision-making is adequately informed when having to choose between different options or methods.

- If the organization is to be compliant with legislation and to continue to provide a safe and efficient environment, it will be essential to document the maintenance that will be carried out in or on the facility. A building

Total Facility Management, Fourth Edition. Brian Atkin and Adrian Brooks.
© 2015 John Wiley & Sons, Ltd. Published 2015 by John Wiley & Sons, Ltd.

logbook or its equivalent might be a requirement and its use should be investigated.

- Success in maintenance management can be attributed to many factors, amongst which having reliable and accurate *as-built* and *as subsequently altered* information to hand is essential. It is better if this is in digital form from the outset. A full history of maintenance applied to facility assets, including details of spare parts, is necessary.

- In most cases, changes to the facility will be required at some point during its operational life, to anticipate or respond to new demands on the organization. It might therefore be economically desirable to carry out maintenance at the same time as improvements, additions or alterations.

Introduction

The maintenance of a facility in general and building services engineering installations in particular are long-standing interests within facility management. Indeed, facility management emerged in large part from building maintenance management in many countries and still occupies a high position on the agenda of senior managers in that regard. One of the functions of maintenance management is to determine which option, or combination of options, for the delivery of maintenance-related services best aligns with the organization's business objectives and primary processes. In this regard, it is important to understand the extent of maintenance requirements and the capability and capacity required to deliver appropriate services to end-users. Planning is a key factor in the success of the maintenance strategy, which will be used to define maintenance policy and operational responses. Whilst it is not be possible to anticipate or pre-empt events and incidents leading to failure of facility assets, a well-rehearsed procedure for dealing with such eventualities is possible and makes sense. In addition, the organization should consider the factors that might take it down one particular path or another. Specifically, it has to identify the most appropriate maintenance method or combination of methods, having regard to its business objectives and the expected use and the serviceable life of its facility assets. Permits, inspections and other matters of compliance should not be taken lightly: these are aspects that have implications for the health, safety and security of both maintenance operatives and end-users. The requirements for HSSE in general, in and around a facility, together with the need to discharge the responsibilities of ownership, imply a proactive approach to maintenance management. The extent of building services engineering installations in a modern facility means that close attention will have to be paid to how these installations perform and, particularly, to the maintenance that will be necessary to ensure safe, correct, efficient and cost-effective operation of facility assets. Important guidance is available within standards. In particular, the provisions of BS 8210, which are reflected in this chapter, cover maintenance management.

The maintenance strategy

A well-defined maintenance strategy will support the organization's business objectives; whereas a poorly defined strategy, or none at all, could have significant adverse safety, legal and commercial consequences. The ability to fulfil sustainability, environmental and corporate social responsibility commitments and targets is also dependent upon a clear maintenance strategy. Targets are normally subject to revision and are progressive; therefore, a static maintenance plan is unlikely to support evolving needs and business objectives. A review process is particularly important, as changes in legislation in regard to HSSE, for example, can influence the way in which maintenance has to be undertaken.

A maintenance strategy should be prepared that meets current and likely future needs, as well as taking account of the facility's capacity to deliver the services demanded of it. The strategy should be reviewed at least annually to ensure that it aligns with business objectives. The needs of stakeholders and the impact of those needs from the perspective of maintenance have to be assessed and taken into account when preparing the strategy. A communication plan to disseminate the strategy to stakeholders, as well as policy and operational actions that devolve from it, will also need to be prepared. Details of any reviews or audits that are relevant to the strategy should be included, with confirmation that actions arising from it are aligned with business objectives. Where a new or refurbished facility is to be procured, the requisite operational requirements, including those covering maintenance, will have to be taken into account during design briefing (see Chapter 2). In this connection, whole-life cost or total cost of ownership (TCO) will need to be ascertained for key facility assets.

A maintenance strategy can be suggestive of different methods of maintenance; for example, corrective, preventive, condition-based or a combination of these and other methods – see the later section on Maintenance methods. Each method should be assessed in terms of the extent to which it satisfies (or not) the criteria defined as part of the strategy; for example, financial objectives and goals for efficiency improvement. The strategy should therefore make clear the criteria by which an appropriate method or combination of methods can be assessed. A combination of methods is bound to be evident in many cases, because a planned approach that takes little account of unforeseen circumstances might prove unworkable. In addition, a view has to be taken on the criticality of facility assets; put simply, not all assets are of equal importance. Crucially, the maintenance strategy should form an integral part of the facility management strategy.

The maintenance policy

A facility has to be maintained to ensure that it fulfils its intended purpose and continues to function correctly throughout its planned life. It is also important that the value of the investment is protected or, possibly, enhanced. Disregarding maintenance risks failure of components and systems and invites needless additional cost, as well as impacting upon normal operations and threatening business continuity. These consequences are in addition to HSSE risks. A reluctance to maintain a facility can arise from a belief that it is an enduring asset that deteriorates slowly and that enough has been spent on it to assure long life. Unfortunately, failure to maintain the structure and fabric can affect its function and compromise safety, as well as reducing its value as an asset. The maintenance requirements of a facility are to a large extent a consequence of its original design and construction. Inefficient design, inappropriate specifications and poor-quality workmanship can result in faults that are subsequently difficult and expensive to diagnose and remedy. Inappropriate maintenance and repairs amount to unnecessary cost and inconvenience, which can be compounded by further attempts to remedy faults.

A policy should be developed to support the preparation of operational plans in line with the maintenance strategy. The policy should outline the scope and actions to be taken to meet business objectives and how those relate to goals defined in the facility management strategy with respect to maintenance. Appropriate expertise needs to be available for both maintenance *and* its management. Where this expertise is not available, external resources should be employed, perhaps through the appointment of a managing agent. Those responsible for managing maintenance, including building services engineering installations, should possess appropriate management competence and technical skills.

The policy should reflect the concept of best value to protect both the asset value and resource value of the facility. It should cover anticipated future requirements for the facility, including the organization's sustainable space provision, and take into account performance and functional suitability, for example:

- Use of the facility, including likely upgrades and the effect on the life cycles of materials, components and building services engineering installations.
- Change of use for the facility and the impact of any alterations or conversion work on the life cycles of existing materials, components and building services engineering installations.
- Timing of alterations, conversion or refurbishment work.

Cycles of maintenance and the methods to be employed, together with the holding of spare parts to replace those that are beyond repair, outside their useful life or technically obsolete, need to be considered. There should be a policy on which spare parts to hold in, or close to, the facility, so that any disruption arising from failure of a component or part is minimized.

Maintenance planning

Maintenance plans should be driven by and support the intended outcomes in the maintenance strategy, as well as being fully aligned with the business objectives. In addition, plans should be prepared in consultation with stakeholders and take account of:

- Requirements for operational demands and constraints.
- Financial circumstances and/or corporate taxation position.
- Feedback on prior maintenance outcomes, including expenditure incurred.

Annual maintenance is likely to be preferable to any *ad hoc* arrangement, not least because it takes a more holistic account of climate, seasonal changes and conditions, physical environment, business continuity and end-user requirements. If at all possible, multi-year maintenance plans should be put in place as part of long-term planning and finance. They will, however, have to be reviewed annually to assess performance and progress, as well as the introduction of updated requirements arising from condition surveys and inspections.

When formulating maintenance plans, different maintenance methods should be evaluated. The links between maintenance methods, maintenance performance, facility asset performance and service delivery should be established through key performance indicators (KPIs), based on a practical and effective maintenance process. In other words, the optimal approach to maintenance needs to be determined and defined so that there is clarity over what is expected and then measurement of what has been actually achieved. The correct KPIs will alert the organization to any deviation from plan so that corrective actions can be taken as appropriate.

The extent to which external environmental factors could influence the condition of the structure, fabric, building services engineering installations, fixtures and external finishes need to be assessed. Likewise, the extent to which internal environmental factors, as well as the performance of maintenance actually undertaken, influence the condition of the structure, fabric, building services engineering installations, fixtures and internal finishes should also be assessed. Factors that can have a damaging effect on physical condition – for example, moisture, infestation and static electricity – as well as potential risks to maintenance operatives and end-users, should be included in these assessments.

The rationale for maintenance planning

Investment in facility assets requires actions to be taken to protect and maintain standards of performance in support of the primary processes and activities of the organization. There is a very simple rationale for maintenance and its efficient and effective planning, which can be summarized as follows:

- Supporting the business objectives, including business continuity.
- Protecting the value of facility assets.
- The availability and reliability of the facility at optimal cost.
- Satisfying key stakeholder interests and end-user requirements.
- Providing performance data for drafting SLAs and, later, for benchmarking.
- Demonstrating a practical commitment to sustainability.

Materials and components

Facility assets are composed of materials and components of myriad types, each with its own properties, not least durability and service life. Maintenance plans should be prepared to ensure that service life matches or, where desirable, exceeds design life. When drawing up maintenance plans, including inspection schedules, the likely maintenance cycle of each element/sub-element (in accordance with known properties of the materials and components and manufacturers' recommendations, where available) should be incorporated. In addition, account should be taken of materials, components and forms of construction that might pose a threat to HSSE, especially the following:

- Hazardous materials and components such as those containing lead, asbestos and materials that are highly combustible or that release large quantities of smoke and fumes when involved in an established fire.
- Forms of construction that, under certain conditions, might become dangerous (e.g. water penetration into a roof construction that could precipitate a collapse).

The cleaning of a facility could be argued to fall within the scope of maintenance. Cleaning before, during and after maintenance are important for attaining satisfactory performance. Poor cleaning or the use of inappropriate cleaning methods or materials can have a significant, adverse effect on the life of materials and components. It is advisable that those responsible for maintenance should coordinate their work with those responsible for cleaning.

Facility assets and maintenance resources

A facility, and the individual assets that it comprises, should be maintained to deliver the most effective outcomes in terms of best value at minimal risk. Facility assets should be classified into risk categories – for example, small, medium, severe and critical – according to their potential impact on normal operations in the event of a failure in performance. The condition of facility assets should be determined and a decision made as to the most effective maintenance option. Throughout, details should be kept up to date in an asset register – see the later section.

A resource plan should be prepared for facility assets operating under normal conditions. Operational requirements will need, therefore, to be integrated into the maintenance plan. The plan might, however, have to be modified to accommodate operating conditions that fall outside specified requirements or tolerances, as might occur when production (or other activity) has to be raised to meet an unusually high demand. A condition assessment of facility assets should be undertaken before preparing the resource plan; otherwise, any maintenance plan might not be reflective of the condition or performance of facility assets. The cost of implementing the maintenance plan should be estimated and provision made within budgets, noting any subdivision into annual forecasts of expenditure. It will help if a time-plan or schedule is prepared so that the feasibility and practicability of the maintenance plan can be assessed. Once implemented, the plan should be monitored for its effectiveness, with performance measured and then compared with targets.

There will also have to be alignment between service needs, including service dependency, utilization, location, capacity and functionality, and maintenance planning at a defined level of asset performance. In the case of a new or refurbished facility, adequate provision must be made during design and construction to incorporate these requirements. Detailed appraisals are likely to be necessary as part of the feasibility study of a new or refurbished facility (see Chapter 2).

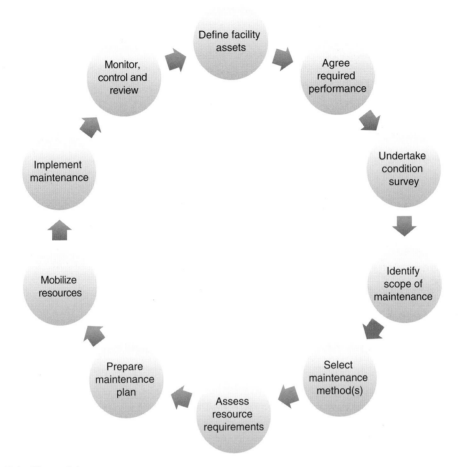

Fig. 12.1   The maintenance process.

Maintenance should be planned to take account of the usual maintenance cycle of each element/sub-element. Inspections will be necessary at regular intervals as determined by the properties of each element/sub-element and its anticipated service life. Annual maintenance should take into account subsequent years' plans, so that additional costs or abortive works are minimized. In this regard, decisions to replace or repair components should be taken after due consideration of whole-life costs (or TCO), unless the affected components are of such low cost that the expense of undertaking whole-life costing exceeds any possible gain.

The maintenance process

A number of steps are involved in maintenance and these cover the following (see Fig. 12.1).

1. *Define* the facility assets required to support the business objectives and delivery of services.

2. *Agree* the required level of facility asset performance, including KPIs.
3. *Undertake* a condition survey of facility assets to determine their fitness for purpose.
4. *Identify* the required scope of maintenance.
5. *Select* the appropriate maintenance method or methods.
6. *Assess* the resources required for the selected maintenance method(s).
7. *Prepare* the maintenance plan and budgets to cover the scope over the short, medium and long term.
8. *Mobilize* appropriate resources to undertake maintenance.
9. *Implement* the maintenance.
10. *Monitor*, control and review performance.

The maintenance process should be repeated at a time or frequency to be determined having regard to the extent and condition of facility assets and the organization's business objectives.

Maintenance costs and finance

Financial control is a key aspect of maintenance management. It ensures that proposals for maintenance justify the funds requested and that best value is achieved. Unnecessary maintenance wastes money, and maintenance performed on facility assets that should be replaced does likewise. If costs are not estimated correctly and expenditure is not controlled, budgets can become seriously depleted.

All maintenance plans should be accompanied by estimates of the cost of known work and provision for work that might be required, but where its extent is unknown. In other words, an allowance or cost contingency needs to be added. Cost estimates should be used as the basis for preparing budgets for maintenance, in line with financial planning and management accounting rules. Budgets should reflect repair/replace decisions, planned preventive maintenance, condition surveys and inspection costs. Cost estimates for budgetary purposes should set out, as far as possible, the:

- Impact on the capital value of affected facility assets.
- Costs and benefits that will accrue from maintenance.
- Risks and associated costs of deferring maintenance.
- Costs and benefits of repair against refurbishment and/or replacement.

Cost estimates need to take account of optimal response times and the preferred method of delivering maintenance; that is, insourced, outsourced or co-sourced. Account should also be taken of planned portfolio decisions such as relocations, mergers and disposals that might fit a particular planning horizon. Budgetary control is therefore needed for each financial year over which maintenance extends. In the case of outsourced contracts, the contract sums and the costs associated with the management of the contracts will have to be estimated. Whilst this needs to be reviewed in each financial year, it is important that it forms part of the longer-term planning horizon, in order to optimize expenditure over the lifetime of a lease or of the economic life of the facility assets in question. The total cost of ownership of facility assets is therefore a key factor in decision-making.

An annual audit will reveal the extent to which best value has been achieved from expenditure in the previous year on maintenance and will help to determine if any changes are needed to improve value for money. The extent to which maintenance has provided any operational benefits should also be determined. This information should be used to inform decisions on budgets for maintenance plans in subsequent years.

Maintenance methods

Maintenance methods can be grouped into three broad categories: planned, which includes planned preventive maintenance and shutdown maintenance; preventive, which includes condition-based maintenance, reliability-centred maintenance (RCM) and total productive maintenance (TPM); and unplanned, which includes corrective maintenance, breakdown maintenance and emergency maintenance. Some might be unsuitable, although they could serve as the basis for exploring alternative approaches. For many organizations, the best approach might not be to adopt a single method, but a combination of them.

Planned maintenance

Planned preventive maintenance (PPM)

PPM allows maintenance to be organized and carried out with forethought and control, based on a predefined plan informed by the results of condition surveys and inspections. The method aims to avoid or to mitigate the *consequences of failure* and to minimize maintenance-induced failures and their consequential costs. It is based on the *criticality of failure* and is also referred to as scheduled maintenance.

PPM is a plan of actions aimed at avoiding breakdowns and failures. The objective is to avert failure of facility assets and to improve their reliability by replacing worn components and parts. Tasks include inspections, equipment checks, diagnostics, adjustments and overhauls at specified intervals. Service personnel can record wear and other deterioration so that they know when to repair or replace worn components and parts to avoid failure. PPM is not, however, confined to building services engineering installations and extends to cover the structure, fabric, finishes and furnishings. Periodic painting to protect components, parts and finishes is a common task within PPM; in certain cases, it can be a continuous operation.

Maintenance can be scheduled in a number of ways. On the lowest level, it can be by means of a diary or calendar entry. For more complex maintenance, a planning and scheduling tool should be considered, with a supporting database if possible. Some tools are purpose-built to deal comprehensively with PPM and can support data exchange with other applications. The decision on which tool (or system) to adopt should be made as part of a broader evaluation of information systems within facility management (see Chapter 15 on Computer-aided facility management). There will be differences in the functionality of proprietary systems and the extent to which data can be exchanged between them. Chapter 10 noted issues in relation to *vendor/provider lock-in* and other constraints, from which it should be clear that a decision taken in isolation might result in *islands of automation*.

PPM should be implemented from the start-up of facility operations. Information and data for this purpose should be provided by the designer in a form agreed with the organization (see Chapter 15 on Building information models). PPM is necessary for the early and correct diagnosis of under-performance or failure of systems, as well as the integrity and performance of the structure and fabric of the facility, and any actions that have to be taken to rectify any failure or other shortcoming. PPM helps in promoting energy efficiency and carbon reduction, as well as lowering expenditure on replacement components and parts.

Shutdown maintenance

This is normally used where there is continuous production and where a detailed plan needs to be prepared for all facility assets so that work can be carried out during a total shutdown. These are often termed *turnaround* projects and have to be planned meticulously if the facility is to be taken *offline* and then be ready for start-up on a precise day and time. Often, huge penalties are attached to contracts for turnaround projects because of the potential losses faced from any delay in resuming production. Another method, *opportunity maintenance*, takes the form of a *window of opportunity* that appears as a result of a breakdown, enabling maintenance to be performed on facility assets that would otherwise require a partial shutdown.

Preventive maintenance

Condition-based maintenance

This utilizes the results of condition monitoring of building services engineering installations, but can extend to the structure, fabric, finishes and furnishings. It is aimed at avoiding loss of function or failure by selecting and monitoring a factor that indicates efficiency or other aspect of performance. For example, fuel efficiency or the lack of it could indicate that consumable parts might need to be replaced, or that some adjustment is needed to the set-up of the plant. Data are collected and analysed and any required maintenance is determined from the results. This work can be carried out periodically or in real time, and is often used for monitoring the condition of facility assets in remote locations.

Reliability centred maintenance (RCM)

RCM is a systems-based method used to determine maintenance required to ensure that a facility asset continues to function safely and correctly to fulfil its purpose, as designed, in its current operating context. It enables a complete maintenance regime to be defined: monitoring, assessing, predicting and understanding the operation of facility assets. RCM therefore includes facility asset condition monitoring, based on the provision of an asset register. Specific criteria are used to determine if a method can be termed RCM, because of the reliance that is placed upon achieving a safe minimum level of maintenance.

Total productive maintenance (TPM)

TPM is a systematic approach to improving maintenance effectiveness that operates at a higher level than methods such as RCM. It normally builds on methods such as RCM and involves the implementation of facility asset condition monitoring, based on the provision of an asset register.

Unplanned maintenance

Corrective maintenance

This is normally introduced as the response to an observed or measured condition in building services engineering installations and other elements, before or after a functional failure. It is used to resolve the problem and ensure a return to correct functional performance. This maintenance could also be planned.

Breakdown maintenance

This relates to the task of restoring facility assets so that they can fulfil their original function after failure has occurred. This method can result in high replacement costs over the life of facility assets, although it has a low initial maintenance resource requirement. It is sometimes used for simple facilities that have few operatives and no critical environments to support.

Emergency maintenance

This results from a sudden, unforeseen occurrence requiring immediate corrective action to restore a facility asset to its function as quickly as possible and avoid potentially serious consequences.

Case study – Aerospace corporation

The challenges confronting senior managers when faced with a substantial and age-ing portfolio are illustrated in this case study. The organization is a major corporation in the aerospace industry, with a portfolio of more than 150 buildings, amounting to approximately 500 acres (roughly 202 hectares) of space. Increasing reactive mainte-nance and rising operational expenditure led senior managers to take action to halt the decline and to deliver fit-for-purpose maintenance.

The level of reactive maintenance and the risk of major plant and equipment failure represented a serious concern. The increasing workload of the in-house main-tenance team added to the organization's concerns. A short-term solution to the workload problem would have been to expand the maintenance team. However, the Head of Facility Management recognized that such an action would increase fixed costs and longer-term employment liabilities for the business. Furthermore, long-established working practices, which included a low level of flexibility from subdividing tasks, would probably make matters worse. In the event, it was decided that an independent review of maintenance was needed – one that should include benchmarking against other organizations. The expectation was that a review would identify areas of industry good practice that could be implemented by the maintenance team. A consultant was duly appointed to carry out the review.

The review focused on maintenance operations and sought to determine if they were meeting the needs of the organization in regard to its facility assets. In order to assess this position adequately, the consultant applied an audit methodology, which involved a comprehensive, in-depth examination of maintenance performance using qualitative and quantitative indicators. The methodology provided an objective framework for auditing from the adoption of a consistent approach across all categories of activity within the review process. In the first instance, the scope of the review was limited to maintenance management.

The review established that work routines were based upon activities that had not been updated for many years and, moreover, modern methods of maintenance planning were not being utilized. Manual systems were still evident and where computerized maintenance management systems (CMMS) had been introduced, their usability was limited. Working routines that provided historical labour allowances for each task were acting as a barrier to improved levels of productivity. Since modern maintenance operations rely upon multi-skilled personnel undertaking the work, task management based upon historical divisions of labour would have simply exacerbated the lack of flexibility. Levels of end-user satisfaction were also identified as an area where there was significant scope for improvement. Central to this issue was a communication breakdown that arose from the absence of a feedback loop to keep end-users informed, particularly where delays occurred in gaining access to plant or when parts had to be ordered. In the absence of any progress updates, end-users assumed that nothing was being done. The audit concluded that a significant change programme was required to deliver a fit-for-purpose function that would reduce the risks associated with maintenance in general and plant failure in particular. It would, however, necessitate investment in people, processes and support for ICT.

Senior managers considered the options available to them, mindful of the pressure to remain competitive in order to avoid the offshoring of production to lower-cost economies. They concluded that the change was best achieved by partnering with another organization the expertise of which was in this area and that had a track record of bringing about transformational change within maintenance management.

The consultant was retained to manage a procurement process aimed at finding a suitable partner that would transfer the existing personnel and develop them with the assistance of the partner's mature processes and modern working methods. A long list of potential partners was produced and a request for information (RFI) was prepared. Subsequently, five organizations were shortlisted and were asked to respond to a more detailed request for a proposal. A rigorous evaluation was followed by interviews and a partner was chosen.

The consultant continued to work with both the organization and its partner to mobilize the new contract. Once the mobilization phase was completed, an audit was carried out by the consultant to ensure that the obligations of both parties had been covered and to establish a baseline against which any improvement could be measured. The contract set out a process for the partner to self-certify the work undertaken, subject to external audits at six-monthly intervals. These audits followed a similar format to the post-mobilization assessment, but with a focus on contract compliance coupled with the encouragement to adopt a regime of continual improvement. The first six months proved to be a challenging period, with the change taking longer and the partner supporting the contract with a greater level of management than had been originally envisaged. Nonetheless, significant progress was made.

The first major audit covered 11 key areas: statutory compliance, financial management, quality, HSSE, service delivery, supplier organization, resources, end-user satisfaction, best value, innovation and continual improvement. Scores were determined for each area, resulting in the achievement of an overall score of 65%. Whilst this was lower than the contract target, it was a reflection of the change achieved in this initial period. The audit was followed by a workshop attended by representatives of the organization and its partner. The areas were discussed and a plan for the next six months was formulated. The consultant acted as an impartial third party, whose objective assessment was encouraged and accepted by both parties.

At the end of the first year of the contract, a second audit achieved a score of 75%, representing a marked improvement over the first audit. In addition, a cost saving of 18% had been realized. The key improvements can be summarized as follows:

- transparency of function and role;
- documented specifications;
- defined service standards;
- supply chain efficiencies;
- operational flexibility;
- improved management information;
- introduction of up-to-date ICT;
- performance-related remuneration;
- reduced headcount;
- cost savings; and
- an emphasis on continual improvement.

The project was considered by the senior managers to be a success – achieving its objectives and providing the organization with maintenance that was fit for purpose. Moreover, it embraced a culture of continual improvement, which is vital within a manufacturing environment.

Building logbooks

A logbook is a reference source of information and data required to operate a facility and to enable those with the responsibility for it to understand their obligations and duties (CIBSE, 2006). It summarizes design assumptions, describes building services engineering installations, including their operational and maintenance requirements to ensure the safe and correct use of the facility, and does so in terms that non-specialists can follow. Notwithstanding its basic purpose, the intention is that the logbook can be a dynamic document, recording the performance of the facility over time. In this connection, it covers energy performance as well as maintenance. In some countries, the logbook, or its equivalent, is a legal requirement.

For maximum benefit, the logbook should be incorporated into the facility handbook, which is a broader document (or file) covering legal, commercial, financial, technical and managerial information and data. If no logbook is available, information and data on the operation and maintenance of the facility, including measures to conserve energy and other scarce resources, should be incorporated into the facility handbook. Other documents, such as a building manual and user guide (BSRIA, 2011), should be prepared to ensure the widest possible support to stakeholders. Taken together, the manual and user guide exceed the scope of the logbook. Similarly, the facility handbook extends the scope of a building manual by considering a broader base of information and data required to manage a facility (see Chapter 15).

Permits and approvals

The extent to which permits and approvals apply to maintenance work needs to be established. For some processes and activities, a *permit-to-work* will be necessary to indicate the work to be done and when, as well as those parts of it that are safe. The permit-to-work forms a basis for communication between managers, supervisors and maintenance operatives. Amongst other things, it helps in coordinating different work activities, to avoid conflicts. In this respect, safety should be checked at each stage of any maintenance. A risk assessment will normally determine the need for a permit-to-work.

Inspections

Facility assets have to be inspected to determine the quality of the internal environment and the condition and performance of building services engineering installations, as well as the structure, fabric, finishes and furnishings. Inspection intervals should take into account the properties and anticipated service life of the elements/sub-elements concerned. For instance, inspections might involve many types of operations and maintenance covered by legislation. Where maintenance is outsourced, the performance of the service provider will be subject to audit and will, therefore, include inspections.

The organization normally has a duty to identify a responsible person for inspection purposes, which should be carried out as follows:

- *Routine* – consultation with end-users to determine the existence of any maintenance matters that might require action and, where such work has been undertaken, measurement of end-user satisfaction with the outcomes.

- *General* – visual inspections of the main elements carried out on an annual basis that inform the budgets required for maintenance.
- *Detailed* – full inspection at an interval of not more than five years.

Inspections can be based on checklists made up of facility elements/sub-elements and arranged in a way that supports safe working. The obvious benefit of a checklist is that it provides a consistent approach to inspection across facility assets; however, it can blind personnel to other conditions that might materially affect maintenance as well as HSSE issues. Inspections should always be carried out with care, because unrecorded dangers can exist. If any area or task is suspected of being hazardous, suitable precautions should be taken and communicated to whoever might be affected or at potential risk.

A maintenance report should be prepared following an inspection, with information presented in one of two groups: first, the degree of urgency associated with repairs; and, second, a comparison of maintenance plans, based on the most appropriate method(s) of maintenance. In the event that there is a need to postpone seemingly non-urgent work, it is important to look carefully at the circumstances, so that it does not precipitate a major defect or failure over the longer term. The anticipated life of the facility, and of the affected elements within it, will need to be properly considered. Evidence of anticipated failures and defects expected to lead to failure should be arranged in three categories: (1) items requiring immediate attention; (2) those that can be placed into a maintenance plan; and (3) others that can be postponed but that should be monitored and reviewed. It is important that the report addresses all maintenance requirements not covered by any PPM over a period of five to ten years. Information in the report should be arranged as follows:

- Location.
- Name of element (e.g. external wall).
- Name of sub-element (e.g. cladding).
- Existing condition (e.g. excellent, satisfactory, adequate, poor or unsafe).
- Prioritization of the element, (e.g. redecoration of an office would have a higher ranking than similar work in a storage room).
- Anticipated phasing of maintenance.
- Cost of maintenance.

Building services engineering installations

For some facilities, two thirds of the capital cost can be attributable to building services engineering installations: HVAC, plumbing, lighting, power, transportation, fire, security and communication systems. For other facilities, it will still be a significant proportion of capital cost. Control over these installations is vital if the facility is to perform optimally and not exceed targets for energy consumption or impact negatively on end-users. Information about building services engineering installations can be extensive; it has to be, not least because of compliance with HSSE and the needs of end-users. The maintenance of facility assets requires accurate information and data if HSSE requirements are not to be compromised.

The following subsections review the typical range of information that is required for maintenance and compliance purposes. For ease of presentation, building services engineering installations are grouped into mechanical installations, electrical installations and fire protection. These three groups are not meant to be exhaustive, although they do capture most of what has to be considered.

Mechanical installations

Records, digital or paper-based, should be kept of the following details of the installations which relate mostly to the location and layout of:

- External connections for gas and mains water supply, together with the points of origin and termination, size and materials used for pipes, and line pressure.
- Piped services, showing sizes and pipe material, together with valves for regulation, isolation and other purposes, as well as the results of all balancing, testing and commissioning.
- Plant, machinery, apparatus and control equipment served by, or associated with, each piped service, together with copies of any test certificates.
- Air ducts, showing dampers and other equipment, acoustic silencers, grilles, diffusers or other terminal components.
- Each room or space housing plant, machinery, apparatus and control equipment.

Drawings, or digital models, should cover the following aspects of the installations:

- Detailed general arrangements of boiler houses, plant rooms, tank rooms and similar rooms or spaces housing plant, machinery or apparatus.
- Isometric or diagrammatic views of boiler houses, plant rooms, tank rooms and similar rooms or spaces housing plant, machinery or apparatus.
- Diagrams that show pneumatic or other control piping.

All records and drawings, including those used during construction work, should be verified against the *as-built* facility. Where any discrepancy is found, full details should be recorded and the affected record(s) and/or drawing(s) should be labelled *as subsequently altered*. Failure to detect discrepancies can contravene legislation as well as posing unnecessary risks to personnel and property.

Electrical installations

Records, digital or paper-based, should be kept of the following details of the installations:

- Single- and three-phase power conduits and final sub-circuit cables;
- Main and sub-main cables.
- Lighting conduits and final sub-circuit cables.
- Locations of lighting fittings, distribution boards, switches, draw-in boxes and point boxes.
- Locations of emergency light fittings and circuitry.

- Secondary power sources for any *safe system of work*.
- Lightning conductor air terminals, conductors, earth electrodes and test clamps.
- Locations of earth tapes, earth electrodes and test points.
- Other miscellaneous equipment, conduits and cables.

Drawings, or digital models, should cover the following aspects of the installations:

- Incoming supply details.
- Main switchgear details.
- Transformer, capacitor and power plant details.
- Distribution diagrams or schedules.
- Schedule of lighting fittings.
- Schedule of escape and emergency lighting fittings.
- Battery systems.
- Smoke detectors, sprinklers and fire precautions.
- Security systems.
- Completion certificate.

As in the case of mechanical installations, all records and drawings, including those used during construction work, should be verified against the *as-built* facility. Where any discrepancy is found, full details should be recorded and the affected record(s) and/or drawing(s) should be labelled *as subsequently altered*. Again, failure to detect discrepancies can contravene legislation, as well as posing unnecessary risks to personnel and property.

Fire protection

Records, digital or paper-based, should be kept of the following aspects of the installation:

- A description of the fire detection and fire alarm system.
- Details of any fire suppression systems.
- Locations of fire alarm and call points.
- Locations of risers, hose reels, extinguishers and other fire-fighting equipment.
- Locations of fire compartment walls, doors, floors and screens.
- Locations of areas of exceptional fire hazard.
- Fire escape routes.
- Details of the application of any fire protection treatment.
- The location of any installation for smoke control or protection of escape routes.
- Details of any master key system.
- Names and contact details of key holders.

All records, including those used during construction work, should be verified against the *as-built* facility. Where a discrepancy is found, full details should be recorded and, wherever practicable, the affected records(s) should be labelled *as subsequently altered*. Failure to detect discrepancies can contravene legislation as well as posing unnecessary risks to personnel and property.

Building management system (BMS)

A BMS can help to reduce energy consumption and, therefore, carbon emissions, improve occupant comfort, operate building services engineering installations more efficiently and transfer data to other systems, such as those for maintenance management (Pennycook, 2001). A BMS typically maintains the indoor climate within a specified range (e.g. a set point of 21 °C (± 2 °C), as well as managing other energy-saving measures, such as controlling lighting based on occupancy of rooms and other spaces (Carbon Trust, 2007). In addition, the system would be expected to monitor plant and equipment and overall system behaviour for signs of failure or deterioration in performance. Where the BMS is used to monitor and control building services engineering installations, it is important that its maintenance requirements are fully incorporated into the maintenance plans. In the event of an actuator failure or other fault, corrective actions should be initiated with the minimal of delay.

The use of a BMS automatically implies a computer-based system that oversees and controls facility operations, energy and safety management. Whilst it is possible to integrate all functions into a single system, practical and economic considerations make such a development particularly challenging, despite claims from vendors. Software developers and control engineers face difficulties in producing sufficiently robust systems to satisfy facility managers. Nonetheless, an integrated approach is desirable. For most purposes, a user interface with access to separate systems – HVAC, power, lighting, fire and security – is the more likely scenario. Such arrangements are reliant upon high-speed communications and, of necessity, require significant wiring-up of the facility based on standards such as ASHRAE's *BACnet* or the proprietary *LonTalk*. The introduction of wireless-based systems means that the cost and disruption of wiring-up an existing facility is substantially reduced. There is a close connection between building management systems and the concept of the intelligent building (see Chapter 13).

Manuals, registers and inventories

Procedures for undertaking maintenance should be contained in a maintenance manual or manuals. The manual might form part of wider documentation covering technical aspects of the facility; in this case, all documentation should be incorporated in the facility handbook (see Chapter 15). In the event of a change in ownership or facility manager, an up-to-date manual and/or the facility handbook would ensure continuity of maintenance. Copies of maintenance manuals should be held by the organization and be provided to maintenance operatives or service providers, as appropriate, on a controlled basis. In the case of multiple facilities, the preparation of a manual for each facility can prove beneficial, because it allows facility-specific requirements to be defined and managed.

Maintenance manuals

The maintenance manual should be prepared for the facility in two parts: the first should cover matters that are better considered by the organization; the second should be addressed to those responsible for inspection and reporting.

First section (example content)

- Recommended intervals for, and details of, routine, general and detailed inspections, maintenance and other periodic work.
- Provisions for means of escape in the event of fire or other emergency.
- Critical environments, including special arrangements for gaining access for the purpose of inspections or when undertaking maintenance.
- Proprietary maintenance materials.
- Names and contact details of service providers responsible for inspections, maintenance and emergency repair work.

Second section (example content)

- Information taken from the facility handbook and needed during inspections, arranged in the sequence in which inspection is likely to take place.
- Schedules of materials and components that experience shows to be prone to failure or likely to need attention.

The maintenance manual should be reviewed annually and updated as appropriate to reflect changes in legislation, especially HSSE, and arrangements with respect to the facility's operation and management. When changes occur, or where new information becomes available, all controlled copies of the maintenance manual should be revised accordingly.

Asset register

The following information regarding facility assets should be held in a register that can be easily kept up to date:

- Description of asset.
- Identification number or other unique reference.
- Make and model.
- Manufacturer.
- Vendor, if different from manufacturer.
- Date of manufacture.
- Date of acquisition, installation or construction.
- Location of asset.
- Details of any access equipment that might be required.
- Details of any *permit-to-work* requirement.
- Initial capital cost.
- Predicted lifetime.
- Specification.
- Replacement cycle.
- Servicing requirements, including type and frequency of service.
- Other maintenance required.
- Maintenance costs.
- Accumulated depreciation.

- Written-down value.
- Source(s) of components and spare parts, where applicable – see the next section.
- Energy consumption and, where applicable, energy-efficiency rating.
- Details of hazards or other risks to people or property.

This register should be embodied in the facility handbook (see Chapter 15).

Warranties and spare parts

Details of warranties relating to plant, equipment, components and systems should be held and cross-referenced to the relevant operational and maintenance requirements. An inventory of spare parts should be kept up to date and a decision taken on which parts to hold in, or close to, the facility – see the earlier section. Details typically include the following:

- Description of part.
- Identification number or unique reference for the part.
- Original manufacturer of part.
- Contact details of current manufacturer and/or distributor.
- Availability and minimum delivery period.
- Minimum number of parts to be held in stock.
- Precise location of parts within or close to the facility.
- Predicted lifetime of part.
- Operational parameters affecting lifetime of part.
- Where applicable, repairs undertaken to the part.
- Where permissible, details of any alternative part and its source.
- Warranty period.
- Current cost of part.
- Transportation and logistical considerations.
- Details of other parts potentially affected by failure and/or replacement.
- Specialist equipment or tools required.
- Specific competence/certification required.
- Details of special conditions or arrangements when installing.

If kept up to date, the above would minimize disruption and/or loss of business continuity in the event of a breakdown or failure.

Maintenance management system

Dedicated computerized maintenance management systems (CMMS) are available and should be used to support maintenance management where there are clear benefits. The use of a CMMS (or CAFM system) should be based on its interoperability with other systems, notably the organization's ERP system. In this connection, it is important to avoid creating islands of automation from the propagation of stand-alone systems. The typical features of a CMMS include the following:

- Financial control (e.g. budgets, commitments and payments).
- Cost accounting.
- Asset register.
- Condition-based monitoring.
- Early warning of problems.
- Fault reporting, linked to asset history.
- Operational plans, including activities to be performed.
- Risk and hazard assessment.
- *Safe system of working* and *permits to work*.
- Personal protective equipment (PPE) issued and returned.
- Planned maintenance.
- Reactive maintenance.
- Emergency maintenance.
- Change management.
- Job orders and other requisitions for goods and services.
- Job logging, prioritization and tracking, including backlogs.
- Energy use and carbon (dioxide) equivalent (CO_2-eq).
- Resource consumption and productivity measures.
- Key performance indicators (KPIs) for service delivery.
- End-user experiences of services delivered.
- Space planning and space utilization.
- Workstation location and furniture management.
- Audit trail of system transactions.
- Exception reporting for senior managers.

Conclusions

Maintenance management is a significant undertaking for many organizations, not least because of the scale and complexity of modern facilities. Since a facility represents a major capital investment, there needs to be a strategy, and a policy and procedures, for managing maintenance. If the facility is to support operations as intended, the maintenance strategy should be aligned with business objectives at all times. An increasing focus in the area of asset management means that facility managers have to be continually aware of the serviceability and condition of facility assets and the various liabilities associated with them. Various maintenance methods or regimes are available and the organization needs to understand which of them, or which combination, is likely to best satisfy needs. Documentation – or, rather, information and data – about facility assets of all kinds is essential to understanding their current and expected performance in use. Efficient oversight of facility assets, based on the most reliable and accurate information and data, should ensure that there are few, if any, surprises. This means capturing *as-built* and *as subsequently altered* information. It is, however, accepted that failure in a component or part will occur and that a response will be needed that minimizes any threat to normal operations and business continuity. Legislation ensures that, up to a point, the facility will be maintained in a safe state. The difficulty arises when there is insufficient or unreliable information to hand to inform decision-making. A proactive approach to maintenance, in the sense of being adequately informed of how facility assets are performing, will reduce the exposure to penalties and prosecution. Maintenance regimes such as RCM can provide a workable approach, although they do not provide a complete answer. There are tools and guidance for ensuring that the most appropriate maintenance response for a given facility, and the individual assets it comprises, is adopted. The organization must ensure that adequate resources are provided for this purpose, so that its investment is protected and the value of facility assets might be enhanced.

Checklist

This checklist is intended to assist with review and action planning.

		Yes	No	Action required
1.	Is there a strategy for maintenance management and is it aligned with business objectives?	☐	☐	☐
2.	Has a policy for maintenance management been defined in terms of maintenance plans for the facility?	☐	☐	☐
3.	Is the organization aware of the serviceability and condition of facility assets?	☐	☐	☐
4.	Has the most appropriate maintenance method or combination of methods been determined for the facility?	☐	☐	☐
5.	Has a whole-life approach to determining the costs of maintenance been applied?	☐	☐	☐
6.	Are procedures in place for dealing with unplanned maintenance, so that there is minimum disruption to normal operations?	☐	☐	☐
7.	Is a building logbook or equivalent document available and is it up to date?	☐	☐	☐
8.	Is the organization aware of its responsibilities and accountabilities with respect to permits and inspections?	☐	☐	☐

		Yes	No	Action required
9.	Is documentation about the facility, including *as-built* and *as subsequently altered* information, readily available and is it up to date?	☐	☐	☐
10.	Are operating manuals available for all facility assets that require them?	☐	☐	☐
11.	Is an asset register held and is it up to date?	☐	☐	☐
12.	Is an inventory of spare and replacement parts held and is it up to date?	☐	☐	☐
13.	Is a computerized maintenance management system (CMMS) or its equivalent used?	☐	☐	☐
14.	Is a complete history of maintenance on the facility readily available?	☐	☐	☐

13 Sustainable Facilities

Key issues

The following issues are covered in this chapter.

- Sustainability is often quoted, but less frequently defined in practical terms. In the case of facilities, it covers, amongst others, operations that do not impact negatively on the environment and the provision of space that is affordable into the future.

- Sustainable development, environmental management and corporate social responsibility are closely aligned, since they draw together the principles of sustainability, environmental impact and obligations to the rest of society.

- Environmental management systems should be adopted by all organizations, irrespective of size. They can produce cost savings and reduce corporate and individual environmental liability, and are increasingly regarded as a responsible way of doing business.

- Zero carbon is an achievable goal for all facilities in the future. For the present, facilities need to be designed, constructed and managed in ways that minimize their contribution to carbon emissions in each key phase of their life cycle.

- Energy efficiency is a target for legislators and so organizations need to act to ensure that the energy performance of their facilities falls within acceptable limits. Building energy management systems (BEMS) support the drive for greater energy efficiency by monitoring, controlling and optimizing building services engineering installations.

- Water is a scarce resource and one that can be needlessly wasted. Effective arrangements for managing water resources as efficiently as possible are not difficult to design and implement, and should be in place for all facilities, wherever practicable.

Total Facility Management, Fourth Edition. Brian Atkin and Adrian Brooks.
© 2015 John Wiley & Sons, Ltd. Published 2015 by John Wiley & Sons, Ltd.

- Managing waste generated in the processes and activities of operating a facility involves planning for sorting, storage and removal. These requirements are in addition to any waste management with respect to industrial/production processes.

- The extent and complexity of building services engineering installations in a facility – responsible for the health, safety, security and comfort of end-users – require a control regime that can respond rapidly to changing conditions and demands.

- Building automation is the broad term used to cover the smart control of building services engineering installations: it does not, in itself, constitute an intelligent building. Nonetheless, a working concept of the intelligent building has been defined and demonstrated to embody *responsiveness to change*.

- Knowing how a facility is behaving in terms of the conditions existing within it and immediately outside it is vital to successful facility management. Sensors can provide reliable data and detect changes in operating conditions rapidly, not least where fire, smoke or intrusion are involved.

Introduction

Sustainability is a balancing act between nature and the demand for improved lifestyles. Competition for scarce resources has created new global pressures, with the addition of evidence on climate change increasingly concentrating minds on reducing human impacts. Greater energy efficiency has long been recognized as an imperative and is now accompanied by a wider concern for the environment. A whole-life perspective on facilities has become routine practice and has been largely achieved through the enforcement of legislation. Organizations and their facility managers face these and further challenges as they ensure their facilities are compliant as well as efficient and cost-effective. It is now expected that facility managers will provide answers on energy consumption/saving, as well as other aspects of sustainability. Principal amongst other current concerns are a reduction in carbon emissions and environmental management, including water conservation and waste recycling. Facilities must now take less from the environment and are increasingly required to put something back into it. All of these pressures point towards a serious rethinking of how facilities are designed, constructed and managed. Some of this thinking surfaced in Chapter 2 with respect to briefing, where decisions have to be made today to anticipate a future shaped by the drive towards sustainability.

Innovative thinking and solutions are called for in a move towards more sustainable facilities that can anticipate and support changes in functionality and end-user requirements. Flexible corporate real estate, integration of facilities serving different but complementary needs and housing that can support health care are all part of this move. The changes brought about by an increasing focus on sustainability also create opportunities and rewards for those who can deliver appropriate solutions and services. A sustainable facility is also intelligent by design. Indeed, the concept of the intelligent building has been debated for about 30 years and has produced facilities that are able to respond to – and even anticipate – the needs of end-users. They are equipped with technology that allows decisions to be taken without manual intervention. Smart sensors and controllers are routinely incorporated into building services engineering installations, allowing energy use to be managed more efficiently. A degree of autonomous control can be used to create and maintain an internal environment for the safety and comfort of users, and to monitor and secure the immediate surroundings. Significant in this innovation are smart devices that are small enough to be attached to components and parts, or embedded in structures and fabric. As we strive for more technology in our facilities do we, in fact, move in the opposite direction to the principle of sustainable development? Facilities that are required to be energy-efficient also consume materials and products that might deplete natural and scarce resources. The technology required to control our facilities has to be manufactured, at some cost to the environment. There needs to be, therefore, a whole-life view of facilities to be sure that there is a net gain to the environment. Ultimately, responsibility for sustainable facilities will come from a combination of actions involving all stakeholders.

Sustainable development

Organizations are under increasing pressure to think through the longer-term implications of what they do; in other words, they need to plan for operations that are sustainable into the future. Sustainable development is a core concept that embraces the three broad themes of social, environmental and economic accountability, referred to as the *triple bottom line*. It is development that meets the needs of the present without compromising the ability of future generations to meet their own needs. The essential challenge of sustainable development is to find ways of enhancing wealth for everyone while consuming common natural resources wisely, so that renewable resources can be conserved and non-renewable resources consumed at a rates that take account of the needs of future generations. In this regard, it is necessary to consider if there is a risk of irreversible environmental effects and, if so, how significant they might be.

In practical terms, sustainable development involves integrating the decision-making process across the organization, so that every decision is made with an eye to the greatest long-term benefits. In particular, it means eliminating waste altogether and thinking cradle-to-cradle rather than cradle-to-grave; building on natural processes and energy flows and cycles, whilst at the same time recognizing the interrelationship of our actions with the natural world. Sustainable development is not a ready-made formula or prescription to be applied to whole nations on one level, or to organizations, public or private, on another; nor is it something for which there is a clear-cut, correct answer.

Whilst it is tempting, and wrong, to regard sustainable development as aspirational, it does help to envision a future that could be very different. There is something compelling about a facility producing more energy than it uses – water cleaner when it leaves the facility than when it arrived, natural light and air, and healthier and more productive work environments. These notions might seem fanciful, but it is possible to generate more energy from a facility than it uses and to create workplaces that are a pleasure to experience. The trouble is that they are isolated examples – a few eco-efficient facilities do not constitute an entire development. Large-scale communities need to be planned and based on a holistic design and assessment of their eco-efficiency – see the later section on Sustainable communities.

Like any journey, this process of change has to start somewhere and many organizations have taken active steps towards making their facilities more sustainable. Typical of the measures adopted include procuring green products and services, using materials with recycled content and managing waste. Implementing waste prevention strategies – including reuse of waste – is another step forward. This does, however, mean educating end-users to think in terms of sustainability and how they can play their part. Sustainable development is more than reducing harm to the environment. Slowing the rates of contamination and depletion of nature is important, but it does not stop degeneration. For example, recycling can reduce the quality of a material over time (referred to as *down-cycling*), making reuse and disposal more difficult. In order to be sustainable, there needs to be *up-cycling* involving regenerative instead of depletive processes and activities.

Environmental management

The environment is something for which all organizations, especially businesses, must now have a clear policy and commitment. The bigger the business, the more susceptible it will be to both the reality of the environmental impact of its operations and the concerns of neighbours and other interest groups – see the section on Corporate social responsibility. No business or other corporate body is immune from either the legal responsibilities or the ethics of protecting the environment for the benefit of future generations. The aim is not to argue for sustainability or environmental correctness to the extent that legitimate businesses would fail, but to seek out a workable balance. A structured and systematic approach is needed to ensure that each gain builds on the last and is not eroded by other actions that disregard the environment. Environmental management systems (EMS) need to become as commonplace as quality systems or even surpass them.

The environmental management system (EMS)

An EMS can assist the organization in meeting its increasing burden of responsibility for the future condition of the environment. In many cases, the introduction of an EMS can also help to generate cost savings and reduce corporate and individual environmental liability, and is increasingly been seen as a responsible way of doing business. Waste of resources and the creation of pollution are normally indications of matters in need of significant improvement. All of the EMS standards stress the need for continual, never-ending, improvement in striving to protect the environment, not only for the present but for the future.

Advice on EMS is widely available, including standards around which to model an EMS. At the international level, there is ISO 14001. This standard forms part of the ISO 14000 series, providing a specification, with guidance on a wide range of environmental issues, including auditing, labelling and life-cycle assessment. The standard seems to have become the common currency of environmentally conscious organizations. Achievement of registration under an accredited environmental management scheme should demonstrate that there is a serious commitment to protecting the environment. Some organizations might fear that in the drive to improve environmental performance, registration will (rightly) involve casting a critical eye on their environmental achievements. It is in this way that the need for environmental management is spread and will continue into the future, in much the same way as ISO 9000 (quality management), although for slightly different reasons.

An EMS is a continual cycle of planning, implementing, reviewing and improving the processes and actions undertaken to meet business objectives and environmental goals simultaneously. An EMS can be built on the plan–do–check–act model found in quality management. This model leads to continual improvement based upon:

- *Planning* – identifying environmental aspects and establishing goals (plan).
- *Implementing* – applying operational controls and training personnel (do).
- *Checking* – monitoring, measurement and corrective action (check).
- *Reviewing* – reviewing progress and making changes to the EMS (act).

Successful implementation of EMS should result in both business and environmental benefits. These can be considered from three perspectives: leadership, value creation and outcomes.

Leadership

The organization and its senior managers can show leadership by acting in the following ways:

- Demonstrating an open commitment to the principle of sustainability.
- Establishing objectives for long-term improvement across the organization.
- Embedding environmental aspects and the impact of operations and services in the facility management strategy.
- Measuring the effectiveness of EMS through KPIs that track operations daily.
- Procuring sustainable products.
- Training personnel in environmental ethics and practices.

Value creation

The EMS can contribute to value creation in the following ways:

- Creating flexible workplaces that respond to changing work practices and culture.
- Reducing operational costs.

- Enhancing well-being and raising productivity.
- Reducing liability for potentially hazardous materials and practices in the workplace.

For more discussion on value creation, see the later section on Smart tagging, sensing and control.

Outcomes

Through the implementation of EMS, the organization stands to gain from the following outcomes:

- Reduced consumption and waste of natural resources and increased conservation.
- Increased efficiency of equipment, systems and resources.
- Increased quality of indoor air, light, temperature and humidity.
- Reduced impacts on the environment and elimination or reduction in use of hazardous substances.
- Creation of liveable environments.
- Reduced negative transportation impacts.
- Enhancement of the community's quality of life (see the later section on Sustainable communities).

These are some of the considerations and arguments for implementing EMS, which will be seen as an outward statement of a formal commitment to environment management in particular and sustainability in general.

Corporate social responsibility (CSR)

CSR has been discussed, albeit briefly, in Chapter 8 as part of the prequalification of service providers. Here, a more developed treatment of the subject is presented. CSR is a concept whereby the organization considers the interests of society by taking responsibility for the impact of its actions on stakeholders of all kinds – shareholders, personnel, customers, suppliers and communities – as well as on the environment. The concept imposes obligations that extend beyond statutory legislation by effectively mandating the organization to take steps to improve the quality of life for its personnel and their families, and the local community and society at large.

CSR is subject to debate and criticism, with proponents typically arguing that there is a strong business case. Conversely, critics argue that CSR is a distraction from the fundamental role of business – and some even regard it as cheap publicity. In another sense, it can be seen as a voluntary code that avoids governments having to step in and impose legislation.

CSR means understanding the consequences of decisions, not measured merely in short-term profit and loss, but in the impact they have in the wider community and on the environment. More astute organizations will have decided to be proactive and, therefore, will have defined their responsibilities, strategy and policies for achieving CSR objectives. Transparency and willingness to contribute to local communities sets them apart from those looking to ease their corporate conscience with one-off, philanthropic contributions. The key, as with many aspects of the *green agenda*, is sustainability.

Facility managers should be at the heart of organizations' CSR strategy and policies, because they are expected to act as the custodians of many CSR objectives. Their task is to balance the demands of their facility with the need to deliver sustainability initiatives that they might well have helped to shape in the initial design concept. Since information is vital for demonstrating that proposed initiatives are progressing towards their objectives, the facility manager has a pivotal role to play, because services are the source of much of this information. The facility manager should be an active member of the CSR team in establishing a pathway between the CSR strategy and the physical delivery of CSR objectives.

Zero carbon

Carbon is increasingly becoming the new currency with which to decide on what is built and what can be sustained into the future, and it has begun to drive yields for developers and investors. In effect, carbon is replacing long-held views of what it takes to make a scheme feasible. Carbon is driving design and so impacts directly on construction and, most of all, on operations. The primary driver for the design of new or refurbished real estate is, therefore, low carbon or, more correctly, zero carbon. This shift brings with it the need to re-engineer design, delivery and operational processes. Rethinking of processes is essential, not least for developing new methods and tools to guide facility owners and designers towards solutions that satisfy important criteria – energy efficiency being just one of them.

Whole-life carbon

A challenge in many countries is upgrading existing facilities, because there are simply so many that fail to measure up to modern standards. When considering an upgrade, it is worth bearing in mind that refurbishment can also lead to increases in energy use and, hence, carbon emissions. The refurbishment of an existing facility can impose higher demands on its support infrastructure – for example, utilities and transportation – as well as in servicing an increased number of occupants and other end-users. A holistic assessment is necessary in each case to avoid sub-optimal schemes going forward.

Demolition is generally the last resort for facilities that have outlived their useful purpose. The terms *reuse* and *recycle* are sometimes adopted euphemistically to soften the blow. Attempts at remodelling and refurbishing can go only so far before the cost of upgrading becomes prohibitive and the demolition ball swings into action. Such destruction and waste rarely goes without opposition, with the public as well as preservationists quick to lobby for official intervention. If it can be saved, then it should – or so the reasoning goes.

Many practically obsolete facilities have been retained because people have got used to them and prefer not to see change. Yet, those very facilities can represent a serious threat to meeting carbon reduction targets. Faced with a multitude of facilities that leak energy like sieves, authorities and owners – small and large – will have to face some tough decisions. With new-build schemes, it is far easier to predict energy consumption and, hence, its carbon equivalent than for refurbishment schemes, where uncertainty exists in terms of performance and original construction. Proof of these points is found daily by designers and builders who have made entirely reasonable assumptions about an existing facility only to find – once work has begun – that the reality is different.

A further concern is finance. The need to upgrade so many facilities would draw on funds that are hardly plentiful. Even so, energy-inefficient facilities either have to be upgraded to meet targets and limits or they will have to go. Protests from the community will be fierce under the latter scenario, but hard decisions have to be faced. In some countries, this predicament is due in large part to the legacy of too many rehabilitated and patched-up facilities. This situation is particularly marked in the housing sector, where taxpayers' money has been wasted on improvement schemes that were more decorative than transformational.

The struggle to have whole-life cost recognized as a key tool in design took decades. For too long, capital cost and internal rate of return (IRR) determined the feasibility of schemes. If someone had the bright idea of saving long-term operational costs, it was quickly scotched. No one could justify spending more upfront to save money later. Whole-life cost brings balance to the equation, but it is clearly not enough. No sooner than whole-life cost became routine, the carbon agenda – dominated by energy consumption and saving – emerged as a potential showstopper. Whilst cost remains a key driver, it is not the sum total of decision-making in design. Carbon has succeeded in drawing us away from narrow interpretations of what might be needed to make a scheme feasible: in effect, carbon is now driving design.

This shift brings with it the need to re-engineer design, construction and operational processes. Considerable rethinking of these processes away from conventional means is required, not least in finding robust models and tools to guide owners and designers towards solutions that also satisfy numerous other criteria. Existing methods need to be supplemented by more and better tools to aid design and construction. Cosmetic change will not succeed in achieving the substantial reductions in carbon emissions mandated by governments.

Whether or not governments are currently championing change is largely irrelevant. Common sense should suggest a stronger focus on carbon reduction to ensure that it will be possible to create, upgrade and sustain facilities across the board. This is a tall order, but it is the only logical way. The response has to be interdisciplinary, because no single discipline has all the skills and knowledge with which to solve complex problems of the kind now being faced. Further issues need attention, including wider stakeholder engagement and managing uncertainty (covering opportunities as well as risks), alongside the established concerns of environmental impact and energy saving.

Environmental performance and energy efficiency

Once, the organizations that were considered to be environmentally responsible were those that encouraged their personnel to reduce energy consumption through good housekeeping. Today, efficient energy management is considered a hygiene factor for a new or refurbished facility. Today's targets are the achievement of excellence in sustainability based on a complete package of measures – sustainable design and materials, with a supply chain that has environmental goals aligned to those of the organization.

Specifically, the energy performance of a facility is subject to legislation in many countries. In Europe, a comparative energy performance measurement for buildings over a specified floor area has been mandated. The legislation requires the latest energy performance rating to be prominently displayed in the publicly accessible space – typically the entrance lobby. Ultimately, it seems likely that all facilities will be required at some point to display a rating certificate, enabling closer awareness of energy consumption. None of this should be surprising, since facilities in general are believed to account for approximately 40% of a developed nation's energy consumption. Wasted energy accounts for a similar range. Whilst statistics can be challenged, the scope for energy saving is clearly enormous. Given a straight choice between two otherwise identical facilities, it is reasonable to expect that the one with the better energy performance rating would be preferred.

Assessing the energy performance of a design is amongst a range of measures routinely applied to a new facility. Awarding ratings for environmental performance is firmly established in design decision-making and owners, as well as designers, are generally intent on achieving the highest rating. The BRE Environmental Assessment Method (BREEAM) in the UK, Leadership in Energy and Environmental Design (LEED) in the United States and Green Star in Australia are the dominant methods and have become accepted in many other countries as the basis for measuring the environmental performance of a proposed design. A derivative method is BREEAM *In-Use*, which – as the name suggests – is applied during the operational phase to help reduce operating costs and improve environmental performance. These methods have, however, to be supported by tools so that the design process is informed by reliable information and data based on the performance of the facility in use.

In a study of existing office buildings, Aaltonen *et al.* (2013) found that relatively minor changes to the processes supporting service delivery could have a marked, positive influence on environmental performance. By exploiting the expertise of an experienced service provider, it was possible to generate significant environmental benefits based on objectives adopted from a commonly used *green* assessment method. The expertise of service providers should not, therefore, be underestimated. Indeed, service providers' attitude and performance could be decisive in securing improvement in environmental outcomes, not least those in relation to energy efficiency.

The *Green Deal* is a UK scheme for improving the energy performance of existing buildings, whether commercial or domestic, by retrofitting energy-efficient products or systems. Under the scheme, instead of paying for the cost of the installation, owners pay for the improvement through their energy bills over the lifetime of the products or systems. Importantly, the liability for the debt stays with the building, not the owner. Funding is provided through the *Green Deal Bank*.

The building energy management system

In the context of a facility, an energy management system is used to monitor, control and optimize building services engineering installations covering heating, ventilation, air-conditioning and lighting. The aim is to reduce power demand which, in turn, leads to reduced energy consumption (electricity and/or gas), energy costs and carbon emissions. It should not be confused with what is, arguably, the more widely accepted definition of an energy management system, namely a computer-based system for monitoring, controlling and optimizing the performance of an electricity generation and/or transmission system (i.e. a utility grid). To avoid confusion, it is better to use the term building energy management system (BEMS). A BEMS controls the distribution and management of levels of lighting, heating and ventilating in response to changes in use within different areas or zones within a facility throughout the day and night. Office equipment, as both a user of power and a source of heat output, can also be taken into account when planning and operating a BEMS. Normally, a BEMS would be incorporated within a new or refurbished facility as a matter of course. Older facilities can suffer from significant energy inefficiency and might also benefit from a BEMS if they are to satisfy tightening energy performance regulations. The conventional approach would be to install a wired system, which is both disruptive and expensive. A wireless BEMS largely overcomes these shortcomings and can be installed in a fraction of the time that it takes for a wired system.

A BEMS can be extended to cover other systems within a facility, such as personnel access control, other security systems (e.g. CCTV and motion detection) and fire detection. Integration of these systems can improve the response time in the event of an incident (i.e. a fire) by shutting off ventilation systems to prevent the spread of smoke and sending lifts/elevators to the ground floor, where they are parked to prevent use. Under these circumstances, it would be more appropriate to use the term building management system (BMS) – see Chapter 12 and the later section on Intelligent buildings.

Managing water resources

Water is a scarce resource and needs to be regarded as such. In countries where there appears to be an abundance of water – potable and non-potable – there is still a strong argument for safeguarding sources and supplies. The cost of treating water supply and, later, waste water is hardly insignificant. Consequently, the organization should take steps to minimize water consumption and harvest rainwater wherever possible. In this regard, end-user behaviour will be a significant factor in determining the extent to which consumption can be kept in check. It will be important, therefore, to make end-users aware of the ways in which they can prevent waste. Campaigns to highlight actions that can be taken to avoid waste will prove beneficial, but their impact will diminish once they come to an end. Active measures should be considered for managing water consumption so that fluctuations or restrictions in water supply do not threaten normal operations. Site design is an important factor to consider where rainwater harvesting is concerned. It helps if landscaping is designed to make use of rainwater run-off. On-site treatment, storage and use of rainwater and wastewater should be considered if space permits.

In general, conservation measures for water management cover the provision of:

- rainwater harvesting (grey water);
- dual-flush toilets using grey water;
- appliances with low water use; and
- education of occupants and other end-users.

Managing waste

Effective testing, commissioning and start-up of a facility are essential to ensure proper and efficient functioning of systems and, hence, operations. The latter, in particular, benefit from the monitoring of indoor air quality and energy, and from policies for water conservation, waste reduction and environmentally sensitive maintenance. Waste and inefficiency can be reduced during minor building work by recycling demolition and surplus construction materials, reuse of on-site materials and monitoring of material use and packaging. During operations, the possibilities for waste reduction are likely to be much less, because the design should have taken account of the need to minimize waste. Even so, some waste is inevitable, if only from the activities taking place in the facility. Cardboard waste has increased in most sectors, as more supplies are shipped in small quantities to meet immediate demands. Since purchasers no longer face a hefty premium for small loads (at least not to the extent that they used to), more deliveries are made and each of these comes with its own packaging – some of it in excess of what might be regarded as sufficient. Fortunately, most is recyclable, but first it has to be sorted and compacted for removal.

Most organizations will have clear policies for waste management, especially recycling. Whilst fairly easy to implement in terms of separate bins and other containers for different types of waste, recycling requires space for segregation and storage (see Chapter 2 on Design briefing). From a design perspective, this means creating areas to which waste can be brought – and sorted if necessary – then stored until it is time to remove it from the facility. Most organizations do not have the means for, or interest in, recycling on the premises. The management of waste containers can become problematic where access to them cannot be controlled. *Drive-by contamination* – that is, waste placed in a container by a third party – can represent as much as 30% of the total volume removed, so it matters where they are placed.

Where any refurbishment or minor building work is involved, there will be many types of waste. By weight or volume, wood, drywall and cardboard is reckoned to make up 60–80% of job site waste. The largest proportion of waste that could be considered hazardous is generated from painting, sealing, staining and caulking, with one notable exception. Asbestos is often encountered during the refurbishment of facilities from the 1950s to the mid-1980s, when it was a commonly used building material. Left undisturbed and sealed, asbestos is unlikely to pose a threat to health. Even so, the organization would be well advised to seek specialist advice in the event that asbestos is encountered or believed to be present. Registered firms should be employed for the purpose of removal, containment, transportation and disposal. Steps will need to be taken to ensure that there is no threat from asbestos to people inside or outside the facility. Penalties and litigation costs in most countries can be substantial, and for good reason.

Some forms of waste – notably food and chemical waste – are likely to require the services of specialists for their containment, transport and disposal. Regulations are strict in regard to how transportation and disposal are carried out and so the organization needs to be sure that it is employing *bona fide* specialists only.

Management and end-user responsibilities

The extent to which the organization empowers senior managers, not least the facility manager, to intervene in the behaviour of those using the facility will be a deciding factor in achieving successful energy and environmental management, amongst other initiatives. The extent of success will depend on the split between end-users (temporary and permanent personnel and visitors, including customers) and the control or encouragement required for them to behave in a particular way. Controls and procedures can go only so far in minimizing the environmental impact of a facility. End-users must play their part too by modifying their behaviour. Switching off lights when no longer required, turning off taps and segregating waste at source are simple measures that everyone should be able to implement. The effective and efficient use of a facility is therefore not a matter for the facility manager alone. End-users have a responsibility for ensuring that energy and other scarce resources are not wasted. When they adopt a more thoughtful attitude towards the use of energy and other resources, the extent of waste can be significantly reduced.

Technology-enhanced facilities

Intelligent buildings

Smart buildings and *technology-enhanced real estate* are other terms for the intelligent building and exemplify the association of technology with intelligence. The provision of a high level of connectivity for users within a facility and the means by which they can communicate readily with the outside world can be vital for organizations. Even so, a wired-up facility is no more intelligent than one that is without such enhancements. Moreover, a facility that is designed to use natural means of ventilation and cooling cannot be dubbed unintelligent. Passive systems are no less worthy of our attention than active or mechanically-assisted systems. Many new facilities do, in fact, combine both passive and active systems, utilizing nature's forces when conditions allow and intervening with mechanical systems when required.

A facility can use technology to improve the internal environment and support functions for users. Security, safety, health, comfort and accessibility are capable of improving productivity and providing a satisfactory end-user experience. Particular benefits include (CABA, 2002):

- Increased individual environmental control, leading to a higher-value facility, with improved leasing and rental potential.
- Managed energy consumption through zone control on a time-of-day schedule.
- Upgrading and modifications to control systems from standardized systems wiring.
- Monitoring and control of systems after hours via PC, tablet/pad or smartphone.
- System for tracking occupants after-hours.
- Tracking of service/replacement history of individual zone.
- Controlling the assignment of physical access rights, telephones, wireless devices and parking spaces, and the updating of the occupant directory from a single user interface.

In the context of office buildings and similar facilities, we can differentiate between three broad categories of system:

1. building management;
2. office automation; and
3. communications.

All three are concerned with technology, and the second and third can be combined under the heading of workplace automation. In particular, office automation systems are focused on the productivity of personnel and include:

- computer workstations (PCs);
- digital storage and archiving;
- office productivity software;
- technical and specialist software; and
- scanning and printing equipment.

Communication systems can be seen in terms of:

- private telephone exchanges;
- voice over internet protocol (VoIP), teleconferencing and videoconferencing;
- satellite communications;
- virtual private networks; and
- instant messaging, email, intranets and extranets.

The dependence on technology is understandable; however, we need to add a further dimension that stems from our concern about intelligent design. *Responsiveness to change* is a fundamental requirement for any intelligent building and this characteristic could just as easily be applied to other types of facility. No facility is going to support an organization adequately if change is not possible or cannot be achieved without significant disruption and threat to business continuity. Predicting the future is impossible, but anticipating change and having the means to accommodate it is a sign of intelligent design. Too many facilities – even some under construction today – have a fixed purpose and adaptation will prove difficult. Evidence is all around us in the form of too many modern developments that remain unoccupied for the reason that there are no potential owners or tenants willing to take them.

Smart tagging, sensing and control

Progress is often made by very small steps. One technology that has begun to affect industry generally is that of smart tagging – a process in which tiny devices or tags holding unique information are attached to a component or part. The tags are encoded with data that can be read by a scanner in close proximity. Their size and reducing cost means that they can be easily fixed to individual components and parts during manufacture and then used to monitor their journey through the life cycle of the facility into which they have been incorporated. In concept, it is possible to uniquely identify every component or part in a facility and to use that information to monitor performance in use – and even to predict failure. Figure 13.1 illustrates the basic concept, where individual components are tagged and their details recorded in a hierarchy of facility assets as would be found in a computer-based asset register (see Chapters 12 and 15).

Inventory management and equipment monitoring are amongst current applications for these smart devices, also known as radio frequency identification (RFID) tags. Applications include guided control of equipment and tags that can communicate fatigue or excessive stress in structural members, as well as important information for safety management purposes.

Maintenance applications probably hold the key to accelerating the use of RFID in facility management. RFID tags can be used in the management of a completed facility, thereby justifying expenditure on the RFID system and, importantly, adding value to the facility by automating, or at least simplifying, the facility management process. Unfortunately, the cost of implementing RFID solutions remains

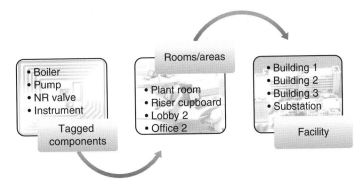

Fig. 13.1   Tagging components.

relatively high and there has been fairly slow take-up. Some manufacturers of products, components and systems have, however, begun to use RFID tags for tracking within their production processes; the tag-fixed components are not normally removed and remain available for use in the construction and operational phases. Take-up of the technology in other industries is likely to help bring down costs to a level at which the attachment of tags to systems, components and products becomes routine.

Value creation

The drive towards more efficient design, construction and facility management can be illustrated by considering the value chain, which follows the life cycle of a facility from raw materials through to operations. Construction projects less frequently follow the conventional (i.e. linear) model, where a completed facility is handed over to the owner through a snagging process, after which the constructor can simply walk away. Today, it is not uncommon for the constructor to retain a measure of control, either as part-owner or as the operator of the asset or facility, as would occur under integrated procurement routes. In this way, the cost-efficiency of the completed facility becomes the constructor's responsibility and so it is important to manage the operational phase as well as the construction phase – perhaps more so, because of the long-term nature of the former.

RFID is well placed to provide solutions for inventory control and location that conform to recognized data exchange standards and that provide efficient links across multiple platforms. Even so, open-source software is more likely to trigger adoption than proprietary software, where licensing costs are bound to uphold artificially high end-user prices.

Two important factors have, therefore, revealed themselves for the successful application of RFID in facility management.

- The cost of the technology will be better justified when its use is spread across more than a single process. It is the final stage in the supply chain, operations, where significant benefits can be produced by ICT, including RFID.
- RFID technology must conform to standards across industry so that multiple suppliers, especially small and medium-sized enterprises (SMEs), can participate.

Technical issues

Read-only tags are generally used for simple identification purposes and derive their power from radio frequency energy received (induced) from the reader; they can store only a limited amount of information, which cannot be altered. These passive tags are the simplest form of RFID, but nevertheless have far greater capacity for storing information than barcode labels. RFID tags can typically accommodate up to 96 bits of data. Since barcode labels are only capable of identifying that the item is, for example, a particular specification of window, door, pump, control or item of furniture, RFID tags could identify exactly which one in the batch it was, together with its production history. Furthermore, the unique product identifier can be hyperlinked to unlimited additional information, such as manufacturing batch and production history, product handling instructions, storage or delivery instructions, expiration dates and other details. Read/write tags, on the other hand, generally require battery power (i.e. they are active tags), which limits their operational life; but they can support larger memory arrays that can be changed/updated to accumulate the history of a product as it moves from manufacture into service.

Sensor-coupled tags are a more recent development, allowing a sensor-measured value to be transmitted to the reader in place of the tag's stored memory contents. Temperature sensors, for example, can be buried in freshly poured concrete to capture *in situ* temperatures, thus allowing concrete maturity to be tracked. A handheld reader allows reliable records of the curing process to be logged without the need for cables.

One of the most important differentiators between barcoding and RFID tagging is the ruggedness and environmental performance of tags. RFID tags can operate effectively in temperatures ranging from −40 to +200 °C and can perform under rugged conditions and even when dirty. Although radio frequency devices do not require line-of-sight and can transmit through almost any material, metals can cause signal attenuation. As metal is a common material in facilities, such signal degradation could indicate a limitation. The RFID tag's orientation and fixture methods might have to be altered so that the tag can be clearly identified. Newer RFID technology aligns the tag's antenna and a non-insulated metal material in such a way that the metal actually amplifies the signal of the RFID tag. Second-generation RFID devices based on ultra-high frequency (UHF) offer up to 4 m proximity scanning, allowing readers to be fixed on ceilings or within ceiling voids for tracking objects in a zone, or fixed to desks for tracking objects inside boxes (without the need to open and verify the contents).

The manufacturing process for RFID devices has been developed further to produce tags as flexible printed circuits, increasing their ruggedness and reliability for many applications. The flexible circuits can be produced on reels as *smart labels*, complete with adhesive backing.

Cyber-agents and intelligent systems

As noted above, technology is recognized as an increasingly integral component of value creation. As an example, electronic data interchange (EDI), which uses the internet as a communication medium, has reduced administration costs and increased flow performance. It permits workflow tracking of progress and response to reactive repair or complaints and maintenance tracking using plant and equipment identifiers.

As RFID becomes widely implemented in products, the extended use of tags in facility management can be envisioned – from inventory control, security and maintenance of building services engineering installations through to cleaning. Just as with the EDI example above, RFID will find application in many areas of the value chain. A number of examples are given below of applications that can use RFID (and related technical concepts) for effective and automated management of processes.

Applications of smart systems technology

A facility that requires control of access can use RFID tags attached to personnel ID badges. The method is already in use in many facilities to permit/control access of personnel to specific areas. Active tags are used, transmitting two short-burst signals every second. The tags, which are recyclable, can be mass-produced at low cost. Airports, where control over the movement of people is an important part of operations, are one such type of facility that can benefit from these devices.

Delivery logistics and materials tracking

Materials tracking management systems can provide owners with the ability to determine work progress and materials delivered by simply walking around a facility where all materials have been identified and tagged using an RFID system. This can guarantee more accurate estimates of the number and quantity of delivered goods and enable reliable monitoring of the *percentage of work complete*.

An early example of materials tracking was developed as a logistics delivery agent system. The project demonstrated the use of cyber-agents in combination with e-tags performing as an automated information management system. Cyber-agents supported information gathering of the material delivery process and were able to make decisions for planning and control of processes. The use of such a system points the way to several improvements in logistics:

- Reduced costs from less waste of materials, theft and waiting times.
- Enhanced communications to provide information in real time about deliveries, placement of products and components and their subsequent use.
- Efficient document management, since all data are digital, with instructions to delivery drivers, inspectors and operatives.

Document tracking

RFID technology can be used for rapid document tracking, which is essential for identifying the latest version; for example, *as-built* and *as subsequently altered* information. Each document is tagged with an adhesive smart label (RFID printed circuit) that contains a unique ID together with human-readable information. The file description is entered into a database along with its tracking number and can be assigned certain parameters, such as expiration date, permitted movement and personnel authorized to see it. Over time, the database could build up an audit trail of the handling and workflow history of each document.

Product life-cycle tracking

Manufactured products and components already utilize RFID tags for tracking progress through production and delivery. The same tags are suitable for continued use during the subsequent life-cycle phases, primarily operations. Where equipment requires regular servicing, functionality checking, safety inspection and so on, the tags can provide an accurate log for maintenance operatives. The safety application is significant, as automated digital record-keeping can provide regular, unbiased records that are virtually tamper-proof. Tags containing safety information, including regular test records, can be attached to safety equipment such as slings, safety harnesses and belts, scaffolding and hard hats. Similarly, containers of hazardous materials can carry their own handling instructions and usage records in an attached read/write tag.

The location of buried services

Buried pipes and cables can be located using attached RFID tags, so long as the read-range is not exceeded. For plastic pipes, a more suitable technology (nanotechnology) uses magnetic nanoparticles during production of the pipe. It is possible to introduce conductivity into plastics by simply mixing in conductive nanoparticles in the production process. Thus, magnetic nanoparticles can be used to introduce a unique magnetic signature to plastic items, which can then be scanned like a barcode. Doing so allows simple and accurate location and identification of underground services such as gas and water pipes and telecommunication cables. If the magnetic signatures are repeated at regular intervals along the entire length of the pipes and cables, they can be tracked throughout the facility.

Sensor and network combinations

RFID active tags can be interfaced to networked sensing systems, to add further capability to the basic read or read/write tag data function. Wireless networks in a health-care facility, for example, can allow real-time location of vital mobile assets. This provides an ability to find equipment immediately and also improves asset utilization, as well as reducing theft. Tags with integrated sensors provide not just simply electronic barcode data, but also measurements of physical parameters such as temperature, shock (acceleration) and even GPS-enabled tracking. The sensors can be applied to structures and fabric to warn of fatigue or impending failure. Sensors will eventually be embedded within structures, supplying data when scanned for shear, strain, pressure and other forces that can affect them. Wireless networks return the scanned results to a data centre, thereby saving the expense of sending out safety inspectors and engineers to observe the structures.

Building energy management and climate control

An efficient building energy management system (BEMS) is one that provides lowest-cost energy, by avoiding wasted energy and delivering optimal comfort conditions to end-users – see the earlier section. By monitoring space within the facility and taking measurements of conditions outside, information from different sources can be integrated in a centralized control function. Advances in sensor miniaturization, wireless communication and micro-system technology enable networks of tiny autonomous sensors to be formed that can make accurate measurements of environmental parameters such as temperature, humidity, light, acceleration and so on without the need to lay cables. The use of wireless communication, as noted earlier, brings control over the internal climate within the reach of most organizations, where retrofitting with a wired system would be otherwise costly and disruptive to normal operations.

Sensor networks, RFID included, can involve the handling of large quantities of data. The limited processing capability of sensor devices requires a back-end infrastructure for processing and storage of results. This could be provided by connection to a virtual private network or cloud storage and post-processing. Agent technology can be used to minimize data movement, and to provide local control functions where required. With a BEMS, these functions could provide security alarm functions and information on energy use on a room-by-room basis.

The future of these devices – given advances in miniaturization and cost – should be seen as a key contributor to a reduction in energy costs. Once distributed around a facility, the sensors can form a network, relaying data about each room's temperature, light, humidity, occupancy and so on to a central point to regulate energy use in the facility, optimizing energy delivery to each room or space, and using passive heating and ventilation control methods wherever possible.

Innovative workplaces and housing

Flexible corporate real estate

Many businesses demand highly serviced workspaces and as much flexibility as possible. In response, industrialized building systems have been developed to provide the levels of building services engineering installations and ICT that are needed in most facilities. Flexibility is generally claimed, but is often limited to changes in office layouts and workplace settings. Sometimes flexibility can amount to little more than demountable internal partitioning and system furniture. Building systems that can offer reconfigurable, serviced space, without adverse effects on the structure or services installations, would represent a breakthrough in space provision, reduce waste, raise profitability and avoid premature obsolescence. This implies designing building systems to provide a choice of multi-configurable end-products to create not only the spaces needed now, but also the spaces required in the future.

The manufacture of customized end-products from modular components – the concept of mass customization – is a common approach in many industries in order to create variants of end-products that satisfy different end-user requirements. To be competitive and remain so, especially in international markets, the real estate sector faces the challenge, amongst others, of creating design concepts that take advantage of advanced manufacturing methods. As part of a platform technology approach, this helps to identify how product variance, component life cycles, maintenance and replacement costs and intervals can be used to create concepts for modularized building systems that are adaptable to a variety of real estate needs. A more realistic account could therefore be taken of the design life for different concepts and preferences in regard to reuse and recovery.

Obsolescence is a characteristic that can occur for many reasons, including technical limitations, premature failure and shifts in fashion. In their day, many facilities represented the then state of the art, but as time passed and the demands placed on them changed, so did their usefulness and attraction. There is no guarantee that a facility constructed today will not suffer a similar fate, unless it is deliberately designed with change in mind. But even that might not be enough. The increasing focus on whole-life costs – primarily the concern for energy use and zero carbon – brings into question some long-standing and basic assumptions. A design life of 50 or 60 years is rarely questioned, yet a facility designed 20 years ago might have already reached technical or another form of obsolescence.

Present needs are not capable of extrapolation over decades. A plausible approach would be, therefore, to develop design concepts and real estate products that have deliberately defined lives more in step with the growth patterns of the businesses they are intended to support. This is likely to mean products that are easy to refurbish, reconfigure and relocate. This kind of flexibility most probably requires a redefinition of what it means to be an owner, at least in the context outlined here. It will be possible to take advantage of total service packages that include all manner of support for the knowledge workers that are housed in those spaces.

Effort needs to be aimed primarily at creating manufactured modular products that provide a rapid response to the need for highly serviced, flexible space. The specific objectives would be as follows:

- Define innovative service concepts that support business growth, whilst minimizing risk exposure for businesses, especially SMEs.
- Develop novel concepts for scalable real estate solutions, based on high levels of service provision and reconfigurable space.
- Develop know-how to support the rapid deployment (and redeployment) of robust, state-of-the-art ICT infrastructures anywhere.
- Devise workplace strategies that support end-users in their work, making them more efficient and comfortable with their conditions.

Effort should be directed towards defining service concepts that adapt to, or better still anticipate, shifts in the marketplace. The concept of networks of knowledge-based enterprises could be used to create access to human resources for selected industrial sectors – in terms of specialist skills and knowledge – so that both physical and virtual proximity are taken into consideration. The approach should adopt an *inside-out* strategy for defining end-products, relying heavily on the preferences of end-users to guide design decision-making. The nature of workplaces, as spaces that are conducive to productive knowledge-intensive activities, requires an indoor environment to match. Moreover, this must be capable of satisfying the various needs of all facility occupants. The kind of real estate that is likely to satisfy these needs is highly ICT-serviced, reconfigurable and relocatable, matching the pattern of growth for knowledge businesses. The feasibility of these concepts will need to be fully explored including modularization, methods of assembly, fixing and disassembly. The focus should be on how to produce real estate solutions in terms of designs that can be adapted according to product variance requirements. Additionally, they must allow for maintenance, replacement and upgrading to be done economically over the life cycle. ICT infrastructures will need to be designed and tested for their efficacy in supporting the mobility of personnel.

A substantial proportion of new facilities will never experience the full service life for which they were designed. Delivering business support is grounded on the use of many resources, of which real estate is both obvious and primary. As such, real estate must provide an effective platform for businesses to develop and grow, so that flexibility – in the sense of adaptability – is achievable in practical terms. The scale of the problem of creating flexible real estate products is significant and has to be tackled by a major push on the part of producers of industrialized building systems, real estate developers, owners, operators and tenants. Overturning opinions in the real estate sector that are fixated on permanent structures, albeit with scope for adaptation, and that are built to last several lifetimes will not be easy. The task can, however, be made easier by demonstrable action on the part of major players in the sector, particularly forward-looking real estate developers and owners, as well as producers of industrialized building systems. The areas of competence required to meet these challenges include, but are not limited to:

- workplace design;
- virtual design environments;
- building information modelling;
- modular building system concepts;
- modular building components;
- large-scale production of industrialized buildings;
- field-factory automation systems;
- sensor and control systems; and
- mobile technology.

Sustainable communities

The underpinnings of sustainable communities are sustainability, economy, environment and equality. This concept is not new and, in some countries, forms a basis for legislation to promote sustainable living. Achievements on a significant scale are, however, relatively few, with some questionable practices included in them. Advances in greener sources of energy, higher standards of construction leading to substantially reduced energy consumption, and a perceivable shift in the attitude of people towards the environment bode well for a major push aimed at establishing workable sustainability concepts. Significant changes in demand and in the use of energy cannot, however, continue without further action or incentive. Demonstration of how entire communities can work successfully must be actively considered. It is not enough to show how novel concepts can work in a selection of specially commissioned show-homes. Zero-carbon schemes designed for large settlements must be implemented and must be clearly seen to work economically and socially, as well as technically. Physical demonstration seems to be one of the few ways in which it is possible to change people's attitudes to energy use and other activities that impact negatively on the environment.

Facilities of all kinds are responsible for a significant proportion of the energy consumption in any nation and are an obvious and legitimate target for action. How they are designed and constructed is an important subject, and one that cannot escape a root-and-branch review based on workable sustainability concepts.

The realization of targets for carbon reduction and decreased energy consumption is only likely to be achieved by a concerted effort to implement new standards in design, construction, heating, power and waste management. Furthermore, such effort has to bring together a package of measures that can be tested, proven and released to the wider community. A coordinated action is necessary to avoid sub-optimal solutions emerging, where gains in one area are negated by losses in another. Balancing community interests will require that many trade-offs have to be considered and adjustments made to ensure an overall optimal solution. In this way, it will be possible to demonstrate a holistic approach to sustainability that could be then replicated across a wider geographical area.

The challenge of designing and developing entire communities includes a proactive approach to managing the environment in the widest sense. In most cases, this is likely to be targeted at the regeneration of existing communities; typically, those areas where communities are living in poorly maintained conditions. Although action is needed across a broad front, the main focus is operational energy efficiency and, in particular, the use of materials that have a low energy input requirement. The need is to reduce energy consumption to such a low level that, by the addition of green sources of energy, it is possible to provide a net gain to the wider community from these zero-carbon communities. This requires new design philosophies, driven by the need to consider combinations of design concepts that minimize initial environmental impact and the longer-term consumption of resources.

The approach emphasizes the ecological and economic dimensions of sustainability and also takes into consideration social and cultural questions. The emphasis has to be upon communities and, as such, a holistic account has to be taken of the planning and realization of mixed-use settlements, where housing is just one part, albeit an important one. The current and narrower definition that focuses on sustainable living therefore needs to be broadened. In the case of urban regeneration, the intention must be to revitalize decaying areas, by offering decent, affordable housing incorporating space for work, health care, community services and shopping. Benefits from such regeneration are likely to include lower crime, improved health and a better economic base for the area. At the other end of the scale, recreational interests can be shaped to provide novel solutions to the need for new and greener sources of energy. The entire ecosystem for settlements of up to 1000 people has to be considered. On this scale, it might be possible to balance resource demands with renewable supplies of energy and to prove the viability of the concept of sustainable communities in which life is as normal and unrestricted as possible.

The primary aims are to bring about achievable actions in reducing the impact of real estate and construction on the environment and to create a net contribution of energy to the wider community. The specific objectives are to:

- Identify concepts for environmentally friendly design and construction that are achievable in practice, without detriment to owner and end-user requirements.
- Define and develop knowledge management systems to support an intelligent search for and analysis of appropriate know-how and technology in regard to sustainability.

- Develop tools and techniques for generating, evaluating and synthesizing design solutions based on whole-life costs and minimal environmental impact.
- Demonstrate the workability of the above concepts through full-scale facilities and infrastructure that minimize environmental impact and that make a net contribution to society's energy needs.

Legislative changes are pending in many countries and these should be examined to determine the timetable for conversion to practices that are consistent with the goal of zero carbon. Concepts for environmental design that minimize impact on the environment and the consumption of scarce resources in the construction of new facilities – as well as in the refurbishment of those existing – need to be investigated. This requires tools and techniques for selecting the most appropriate materials and components in terms of whole-life cost and zero carbon. These will require further support from knowledge bases used to select components that carry official labelling, certifying their compliance with environmental codes, and offering advice on relevant financial or other incentives; for example, tax breaks or rebates for exceeding minimum code requirements.

Attention also needs to be directed towards successful examples of combined heat and power and district heating, concepts that have, for instance, stood the test of time across Scandinavia and other regions. A further dimension that affects existing communities will be to devise strategies that strive to keep people in their homes until such time as they can be moved directly into new accommodation adjacent to their existing location. This approach will avoid the mistakes of the past, where communities were broken up and dispersed.

Measures to advance sustainability concepts and to introduce them into the community cannot be expected to succeed on the back of piecemeal initiatives that address parts of a wider problem. The idea that sustainable communities can be realized through a succession of minor measures that provide incentives to individual homeowners and tenants is unrealistic. Wholesale change is required and, therefore, this can only be done on a scale that has the ability to influence entire communities. Another aspect is that of involving all the necessary expertise and other ingredients that are needed to turn a working concept into a real community. This can only be done on the scale of major projects, in which demonstration on an equally large scale can be performed. Whilst there is little doubt that specific examples of novel technology and approaches are scalable, there is both a credibility and integration gap to fill. Projects should aim for a full-scale community in order to demonstrate working concepts so that replication can take place. True breakthroughs in establishing lasting actions are only likely to occur if the scale is real and convincing for ordinary people, as much as it is for other stakeholders.

The areas of competence required to meet these challenges include, but are not limited to:

- design for zero carbon;
- engineering infrastructure;
- timber platform technology;
- modular building system concepts;

- heat pump technology;
- photovoltaic technology;
- energy sources and their management; and
- building energy management systems.

Healthy living

Housing is the fundamental right of all people, yet gross distortions in housing conditions and in the balance between supply and demand exist across the world. This situation is not peculiar to poor regions. Affluent countries fail to provide decent and affordable housing for all, and this is an impediment to the advancement of modern and equitable societies. There are many excuses for this failure, but fewer for effecting workable solutions. A central theme is that housing must not impair the health of its occupants, yet there is evidence of ill health from recurrent problems such as moisture penetration, emission of harmful chemicals and, inexcusably, lack of basic amenities. In the future, houses must do more than provide shelter and protection – they must contribute to a minimum standard of living for everyone and eliminate conditions that give rise to building-related illnesses. Furthermore, housing must not be used to define strata in society. All households must have access to modern services, including ICT; otherwise, the digital divide will become reality for many people.

Maintaining control over the condition and functioning of homes and alerting occupants – and others with a legitimate interest – to the hidden dangers is fundamental to this thinking. Providing the means for monitoring and controlling the condition of facilities, especially housing, over the life cycle would represent a major breakthrough in preventive maintenance and servicing of the built environment. Technology is already capable of providing many solutions; for example, the introduction of embedded technology into factory-produced components. However, the application outlined above needs careful examination, development and testing of prototypes and feedback from full-scale demonstrators. In this regard, the workability of any new approach and products is unlikely to be assured by scale models – people's health is too important an issue for this kind of treatment. The scope of this challenge therefore includes mechanisms for monitoring and control throughout the life cycle by the use of embedded technology. Access to information on the condition of one's home should be readily available and should be provided to authorized third parties. The use of embedded technology is not, however, confined to the operational phase. Tracking of components from manufacture through transportation and incorporation into the facility can provide valuable histories for use in diagnostics and preventive measures – see the earlier section on Smart tagging, sensing and control. A term that could have been adopted here is that of *smart homes*; however, this would not necessarily convey the importance of healthy homes and living.

Households change over time: they grow and contract and their tastes and requirements alter. Generally, homes stay much the same, apart from minor alteration and periodic redecoration. The life cycles of households and homes could not be more out of step. Housing might be regarded as having to serve future generations, but when it fails to serve the present, something has to be fundamentally wrong. Adaptation for new services and upgrading of the fabric, building services engineering installations and interior fittings is necessary in many cases. Retrofitting is an option. However, where decay and obsolescence are too far advanced, replacement might be the only option. Clearly, the mistakes that have led to this situation must be avoided in new construction. For this reason, an implicit assumption is that the manufacture of customized products from modular components – the concept of mass customization – will provide the platforms for modularized house-building on a sufficient scale. This is necessary if people are to have affordable, decent-quality homes that are equipped for twenty-first century living. Moreover, homes must be capable of adaptation in a controlled and relatively easy way, to provide different configurations of space to suit households at different stages in their development. Often, people have to move to other accommodation if the present does not satisfy their needs. For many people, however, this might not be an option, either because they are unable to afford such a step or simply because they wish to remain within their community. In other words, housing provision must be driven by end-user needs.

The implications of this closer alignment of needs with the provision of housing amount to a radical departure from traditional house-building concepts, in which largely conventional methods of construction can build in obsolescence. Furthermore, the speed with which new or replacement housing can be built is unlikely to be satisfied by a traditional construction response. Factory-based production is necessary. In addition, building information modelling (BIM) can be used to manage flexibility in design and product customization, making the capabilities of platform technology more transparent (Wikberg *et al.*, 2014). The overall approach has already been demonstrated on low-to-medium rise housing projects.

The primary aim should be to produce sustainable, healthy homes that protect, support and stimulate occupants in their formal and informal activities. An implicit aim is to ensure that past mistakes in mass housing are not repeated. The specific objectives are as follows:

- Assess the needs of developers, owner-occupiers and tenants as a basis for developing housing concepts and support systems.
- Develop housing solutions based on high levels of service delivery, low energy consumption and reconfigurable, extendable space.
- Develop natural or passive methods for heating, cooling and ventilating that can be used alongside active systems and all necessary control regimes.
- Develop a methodology for selecting the correct materials, products, components and systems, including the detection of harmful materials and potential emissions.
- Develop systems using state-of-the-art sensing and navigational technology to support the tracking and interrogation of products and components.

In spite of an improved understanding of how to eliminate problems, especially in relation to multi-storey housing, failures occur and persist. Much of the blame can be laid at the door of design teams, in omitting to consider the broader implications of their work and in the lack of systematic feedback from projects past and present. Effort should, therefore, be directed towards adjusting the process of design and production to include tools for the systematic gathering of performance data and for detecting potential failures. For example, the quality of the indoor environment can be assured through a variety of measures – including, for example, methods for selecting the most appropriate components and for warning of the potential of harmful emissions.

The use of natural or passive methods for the heating, cooling and ventilation of internal spaces should be further explored so that the relationship between air quality and the energy used by more active methods can be better balanced. The efficient coexistence of these two approaches has to be determined so that effective monitoring and control strategies can be developed, thus ensuring that optimal comfort conditions are provided. The incorporation of embedded technology should be examined in the context of providing knowledge of how passive and active systems function together. The interconnectivity between different ICT infrastructures, standards and protocols for communication – for example, *Ethernet*, *Wi-Fi*, *BACnet*, *LonTalk* and *Bluetooth* – is central to this approach and questions in regard to their deployment will need to be carefully examined. This has to operate in parallel with the ongoing development of industry standards for product information to provide data for embedded technology. The use of internet-based cyber-agents – *search and do* agents – to assist in the coordination and control of design, construction and facility management needs to be investigated further. The aim should be to provide real-time support to occupants and other stakeholders such as maintenance teams.

The quality of housing in most countries is highly variable, with a significant proportion of dwellings lacking one or more basic amenities. If a serious impact is to be made, a radical overhaul of the housing supply market is required. Traditional methods of house-building have to be complemented by large-scale manufactured housing, through which affordable, decent-quality homes that reflect owners' and occupants' preferences are produced on a wide-area basis. Mobilizing the supply chain to support such an ambitious, but vitally important, initiative will necessitate the inclusion of major industrial companies and the collaboration of large municipalities. Inevitably, this means that major players are needed, at least for the manufacture, delivery, installation and commissioning of these products.

The areas of competence required to meet these challenges include, but are not limited to:

- stakeholder needs;
- home automation;
- building automation;
- embedded technology;
- building information modelling;
- modular building system concepts;
- modular building components;

- sensor and control systems; and
- logistics and supply chain management.

Telecare

People are affected by their surroundings and, especially, by the condition of their homes. When people are healthy, a less than ideal setting might amount to little more than irritation; but when people are elderly and/or in poor health, conditions in the home can have a significant impact. Poor housing conditions lead to poor health; conversely, good conditions can promote good health. The starting point for telecare is a healthy home into which can be introduced medical and ancillary equipment to allow people to be treated and cared for where they live. There are sound economic as well as medical arguments for treating people in their own homes. However, this cannot take place without serious investment in both housing to suit and technology to enable medical care to be correctly received. Inevitably, this will mean that new housing will have to be produced with such features and then maintained properly.

Retrofitting of the existing stock is also possible, but success is more likely when homes have been designed to take these features into account. Since one individual's needs are likely to be different to those of another, a strategy for delivering technologically enhanced real estate is needed. The adaptation of homes to accept a range of support functions and care regimes calls for a rethink of how dwellings can be equipped or re-equipped to deal effectively with these challenges. One concern, amongst others, is to minimize the impact upon occupants arising from changes to the original layout, functionality and appearance of the home. Furthermore, if it is subsequently shown that an alternative arrangement is better suited, changes will need to be reversible.

The design of an all-inclusive facility is a developing field, as opposed to an exact science in which all parameters are known. In addition to the provision of medical support, there is likely to be the need for homes that are responsive and that, as underscored above, do not adversely affect health. Many of the arguments and recommended solutions advanced for affordable, healthy homes would apply here, particularly in the context of enabling technology against the background of mass-customized end-products that are economical, of a decent quality and defect-free.

Homes equipped with ICT and medical apparatus could provide care, monitoring and education to patients who would otherwise have to be admitted to hospitals or other health-care facilities. Medical practitioners would be able to maintain continual contact with their patients, enabling them to be treated in their own homes and reducing the trauma and expense of hospitalization. The problem is one of designing and delivering both a home and a care environment – through the provision of modern, highly serviced, ICT-enabled housing – that can accommodate the equipment required for home telemedicine. Given the right kind of setting and conditions, there is no reason why medical equipment that was previously found in health-care centres and hospitals could not be adequately installed, protected and maintained in a person's home.

The development of mobile technology provides an important element in the provision of telecare services, especially since mobility in the home is likely to be a key issue and one where occupants might have restricted movement. Another aspect of concern is coping with an ageing population and one where the proportion of older people will become increasingly significant in the coming years. The approach advocated offers a realistic alternative to moving people from their homes to local health centres or hospitals and then back again, and repeating the cycle many times over. The economic and social arguments are powerful, and there is sufficient technology to ensure that this can be achieved. However, the latter has to be placed within a process that is designed for telecare purposes. It is not enough to graft it on to existing arrangements for procuring housing for the elderly and people in poor health.

The primary aim is to develop a range of innovative housing products that can provide a secure and safe environment into which telecare services can be introduced. The specific objectives are as follows:

- Assess the needs of different stakeholders (i.e. developers, owner-occupiers, tenants and medical practitioners) as a basis for developing inclusive environments and support systems.
- Develop housing solutions, based on high levels of service provision, low energy consumption and reconfigurable, adaptable space.
- Specify the characteristics of the indoor environment in terms of function, amenities, climate and support for medical and ancillary equipment.
- Create products that are acceptable to national health departments and the medical professions and demonstrate this to all stakeholders, not least the elderly and infirm.

Thorough investigation of the means for delivering medical care in the home is necessary. It is not enough to scale down the services of a professional health-care facility or simply to modify existing housing products. A detailed investigation of how elderly or infirm persons can be properly supported in their homes has to be undertaken. If housing solutions are to be real solutions to the needs of a growing proportion of the population, questions of mobility and dependency will need to be addressed. The interaction between occupants and their surroundings needs careful examination, so that workable solutions arise. It ought to go without saying that people should not be prisoners in their own home. The technical feasibility of the overall concept has to be fully explored and this will extend to modularization, methods of assembly, fixing and disassembly. Special attention will need to be paid to the added complexity arising from the incorporation of medical and ancillary equipment.

The growing proportion of the population and, hence, the housing market that serves (or should serve) the elderly or infirm is in need of radical overhaul. Attempts to provide health-care regimes for people in their own homes are, in many countries, generally limited to the affluent, with little commercial interest in extending this to the social and mass-housing sector. A concerted effort that would bring together the many interests, bodies and disciplines in this area is necessary.

The success of telecare in the long run will depend largely upon how effective housing solutions are at catering for the needs of their occupants. This will require that the results are adequately demonstrated so that practical solutions, as well as the concepts, can be replicated. It is also important that proprietary rights are not allowed to prevent the maximum penetration of telecare housing products into the marketplace.

The areas of competence required to meet these challenges include, but are not limited to:

- design of inclusive environments;
- telecare concepts;
- modular building system concepts;
- modular building components;
- sensor and control systems;
- telemedicine – equipment and communications; and
- mobile technology.

Conclusions

Sustainability is concerned with how we meet our environmental and social responsibilities, whilst at the same time avoiding economic collapse and other events that would undermine these responsibilities. The principle of sustainability is based on social progress that recognizes the needs of everyone, whilst protecting and, if possible, enhancing the environment and using natural resources prudently. Environmental management is a concept that affects organizations of all kinds. There are practical gains from implementing environmental management systems. Energy efficiency and the need to reduce carbon emissions require that the impact of a new and refurbished facility is determined ahead of making what could turn out to be an expensive mistake. Energy-efficient design and construction is a step in the right direction towards sustainable development. There is sufficient knowledge of how to design, construct and manage energy-efficient facilities such that there can be few excuses for not doing so. Other scarce resources – such as water, for example – also need to be managed. The means for ensuring that waste is minimized and that sufficient space is provided to handle it can be easily incorporated into the design of a new facility. Building management systems provide the means for monitoring and controlling the performance of building services engineering installations and take us some way towards the concept of the intelligent building – an energy-efficient, responsive facility – that can provide a secure, safe, comfortable, efficient and productive environment. Designing intelligently also has to be given a higher profile. The advent of low-cost, smart devices (e.g. RFID tags) provides both opportunity and reward with relatively few risks. Innovative workplaces and housing that combine the above measures are well within the reach of governments, developers, investors, owners and operators; in other words, stakeholders with a duty to act sustainably.

Checklist

This checklist is intended to assist with review and action planning.

	Yes	No	Action required
1. Is there a practical grasp of the meaning of sustainability as it affects the facility now and into the future?	☐	☐	☐
2. Does the organization recognize and understand the need for sustainable development and how it can be reflected in its facility management?	☐	☐	☐
3. Does the organization know how environmental management can help achieve business objectives?	☐	☐	☐
4. Is enough being done to promote environmental consciousness across the organization?	☐	☐	☐
5. Is there acceptance of the need to minimize carbon emissions through a reduction in energy consumption?	☐	☐	☐
6. Has energy use been properly investigated – are thinking and actions ahead of legislation?	☐	☐	☐
7. Have measures been adopted to conserve water and harvest rainwater where practicable?	☐	☐	☐
8. Is there a clear procedure for managing waste and one that is adhered to by end-users?	☐	☐	☐
9. Have steps been taken to encourage appropriate behaviour in regard to energy saving, water conservation and waste minimization?	☐	☐	☐
10. Is a secure, safe, healthy and comfortable environment being provided for users?	☐	☐	☐
11. Has the extent of responsiveness to change in the facility been assessed?	☐	☐	☐
12. Is the organization aware of the extent to which technology can help to increase the quality of the internal environment?	☐	☐	☐

	Yes	No	Action required
13. Do automatic sensing, monitoring and control of building services engineering installations take place?	☐	☐	☐
14. Has the potential for smart tagging been investigated?	☐	☐	☐
15. Have innovative concepts for the workplace and housing been investigated?	☐	☐	☐

14 Change Management

Key issues

The following issues are covered in this chapter.

- Change is a constant feature of facility management and the extent to which it can be effectively controlled will be a key factor in the latter's success.

- Transition is a typical example of change in the context of facility management and is closely connected with procurement. It covers change in the mode of service delivery from insourcing to outsourcing and the reverse situation.

- The scale of transition can be enormous – from a multinational corporation with a global presence wanting to outsource all of its services, to the owner of a single facility where one service provider is to be replaced by another. The principles that apply are the same, but the scale and complexity are very different.

- Transition has to be managed according to a defined plan, because it can involve simultaneously winding down and phasing in/ramping up services, with the potential to disrupt operations and threaten business continuity.

- The most appropriate model for managing transition is to create a project and to prepare a resourced plan for its implementation. Project management tools and techniques should be applied by those with appropriate competence and skill.

- The time, resources and costs involved in transition, including the services involved, have to be estimated as accurately as possible, with sufficient contingency to cover uncertain events or conditions.

Total Facility Management, Fourth Edition. Brian Atkin and Adrian Brooks.
© 2015 John Wiley & Sons, Ltd. Published 2015 by John Wiley & Sons, Ltd.

- Change is normal, but its consequences can be abnormal for personnel affected by it. A recognized methodology exists for guiding the organization towards implementing a managed change process that is sensitive to the needs of personnel.

- Change management is rarely, if ever, a linear process; instead, it is likely to involve some degree of iteration and/or reworking. Consultation with all stakeholders is essential; otherwise, just one disaffected group could ruin the chance of success.

- Planning is key to success and, in many respects, there cannot be too much of it. The time required for the thorough planning of a management of change project should not be underestimated.

- Innovation is not the same as management of change, but has a close relationship with it, with each supporting the other to a certain extent.

Introduction

Sourcing is rarely, if ever, a fixed arrangement that survives into the future without cause for change. In line with earlier chapters on outsourcing (see Chapter 7) and procurement (see Chapter 8), insourcing, outsourcing or co-sourcing should be regarded as the outcome of decision-making that strives for end-user satisfaction and best value. By definition, the outcome will be good for a given time or over a period, perhaps three to five years at most. Changes in the market for facility-related services mean that no one option will be good for all time. The decision on whether or not to outsource will have to be revisited from time to time. When it becomes evident that there will be a change to the sourcing model, the organization should develop a plan for transition from the existing arrangement to the new arrangement. From an end-user's perspective, there should be no perceivable difference in the service received from either a new service provider or the in-house team (and the reverse). Managing the transition so that there is no disruption to normal operations – or, worse, a break in business continuity – necessitates careful planning and preparation. During this period, the organization is likely to be significantly exposed to risks of one kind or another in a generally less than certain state. A plan for transition should cover the time, resources and costs of transition – that is, the direct costs – as well as those costs associated with managing this change process; that is, the indirect costs. Implementing transition follows once a state of readiness has been achieved and must be supported by further plans; in this case, a plan for mobilization/demobilization and the phasing in of the new arrangement. There are many individual steps and considerations to observe that make a carefully constructed and realistic plan essential. This latter aspect is no more critical in the case of time, where optimism tends to cloud judgement to the extent that overly ambitious and, frankly, unrealistic timescales are often agreed. If carefully observed, the procedures associated with transition will ensure that there is no impact on either operations or business continuity. To succeed does, however, require an ability to accept that, especially in the case of large and complex transitions, competence and skills in project management will be essential. Important guidance is available within standards in this regard. In particular, the provisions of BS 8892, which are reflected in this chapter, cover aspects of transition.

In moving away from the operational level to one that is more strategic, we should recognize that there are bound to be pressures to change more of the organizational structure to cope with a rapidly changing landscape. From a world in which stability was the norm, we entered an era where normality itself is a state of change. Of course, change has always been present: it is simply that the rate of change nowadays is so great as to be visible to all. Management of change can be defined as a set of techniques to aid the evolution, composition and policy of the design and implementation of an object or system. However, this starkly abstract view overlooks the human dimension that is a fundamental part of facility management. Another view is that it is an organized, systematic application of the knowledge, tools and resources of change that provides the organization with a key process to achieve its business objectives. The focus on business objectives helps to contextualize the definition, but in order to humanize it we must go further. By incorporating the *people side* of business and coupling it to the workplace, we can offer the following definition: *the process, tools and techniques to manage the people side of business change to achieve a required outcome and to realize that change effectively within the social infrastructure of the workplace.* In many respects, it is taking the organization away from its comfort zone to one where novelty, uncertainty and opportunity are the watchwords and, hopefully, the forerunners of success.

Transition

The transition process

Transition is a process that involves change in the mode by which services are delivered. Whilst facility management is expected to deal with routine change, transition often demands more from the organization. In order that change can be controlled effectively, a project-based approach to transition is generally advisable, because the tasks involved, together with their resources, time and cost, are subject to uncertainty and exposure to risks. Disruption from an uncontrolled transition could impact negatively on operations and so steps have to be taken to ensure that transition is properly controlled.

At the outset, a business case or equivalent statement of the need for transition should be prepared and used as the basis for planning transition, which should be overseen by the facility manager or other senior manager. The resultant transition plan should complement any existing policies and procedures and cover the following.

- Goals, including the expected impact on the business, primary processes and activities supported, service(s) affected, end-user requirements and criteria for measuring success.

- Governance, including the possible need of an overseeing body, clear roles, responsibilities and accountabilities, internal approvals, impact on organizational structure and financial controls to be applied.
- External permissions and notices required.
- Stakeholders, including arrangements for assessing their interest and likely impact, engagement and communication.
- Risks, including identification and assessment of risks and opportunities, and the response to risk events and controls to be applied.
- The procurement strategy, policy and procedures, where outsourcing is involved.
- Existing arrangements in regard to agreements, contracts and employment of personnel affected.
- A time-plan and deadlines, including critical tasks, milestones and controls to be applied.
- Costs and budgets, including controls to be applied.
- Resources, including personnel, equipment, materials, temporary facilities and controls to be applied.
- Contingency for both time and cost.

Contingency is not optional and will be required as part of the provisions for transition. The extent of contingency might not, however, be easy to assess and so a qualitative risk assessment might be needed or, in the case of large and/or complex transitions, a quantitative risk analysis might be more advisable – see the later section on Uncertainty management.

Transition control

An integrated approach to the control of transition will mean that the agreed scope of the project is tied to a realistic time-plan, resource plan and cost/budget. Ensuring that these elements are aligned will be a large factor in the success of any transition. Where any alteration is made to the scope, its impact on the time-plan, resource plan or budget can and should be assessed before proceeding; otherwise, there will not be a consistent reflection of the proposed transition across these elements.

Disruption and continuity management

Transition has the potential to disrupt normal operations that could, in turn, impact business continuity. It will be important, therefore, to determine the potential extent and impact of disruption to operations. For each primary process affected, the maximum tolerable period of disruption should be assessed. This period should cover the maximum time after the start of a disruption within which the process (or its activities) needs to be recovered, the minimum level at which the process has to be performed upon resumption and the time within which normal operations must be resumed. It is, in effect, a form of risk assessment that helps in understanding what could go wrong so that organizational resilience can be built in if necessary to safeguard operations. Indeed, risks have to be assessed and provision for unknown eventualities (i.e. contingency) has to be incorporated into the transition plan. Planning and scheduling the tasks necessary to achieve the defined goals and the resources for determining the feasibility of plans and schedules are essential for planning transition. They also create the basis for a controllable project, the proper management of which will attract a high probability of success. Importantly, measuring performance and progress against an agreed plan means that any deviation should be easily and, hopefully, quickly detected so that corrective action can be taken.

It will be necessary to take steps to counter the adverse effects of any failure in service delivery, especially if it is something that might reasonably have been anticipated, at least with some probability of occurrence. When creating a transition plan, thought should be given to plausible scenarios; for example, the financial failure of a key service provider part way through a contract or a deteriorating level of service in another that shows no sign of improvement. Each scenario can help *flesh out* actions that might minimize disruption to operations should such an event occur. In any case, it is quite possible that scenario analysis will provide some unexpected insights into current operations that would benefit from attention quite apart from the threat of disruption. Whatever action is taken in regard to scenario building and analysis, it should not be confused with predicting the future: that is not its purpose. From a practical standpoint, some form of contingency will have to be built into any transition plan with respect to both time and cost. Failure to include contingency would be almost begging for something to go wrong. The question is really one of how much should be added to cover the uncertainty – see the later section on Uncertainty management.

Types of transition

Transition often involves transferring the delivery of service from within the organization to an external service provider (i.e. outsourcing) or, if the service is already outsourced, from the incumbent service provider to another. In other cases, it can mean bringing services in-house (i.e. insourcing) following a period of outsourcing. It is important to classify the nature of a proposed transition so that an appropriate response can be framed:

- moving to outsourcing;
- changing the outsourcing model;
- reverting to insourcing; or
- insourcing for the first time.

Each of the above types has implications, to a greater or lesser extent, for the organization's structure, including personnel and their required competence and skills. It will be necessary, therefore, to describe the scope of the transition. For example, changing an existing outsourcing model can cover anything from the substitution of one minor service provider to a complete restructuring of all service provision involving new service providers. The former is a minor change, whilst the latter is a major and potentially complex transition, especially if it involves multiple facilities over a wide area or region and a large number of service providers.

Scope definition

The scope of transition is best described in a statement of requirements, which can be used for preparing the transition plan. The reasons for the transition will be a material factor in framing the project, as will any constraints or other factors that might shape the approach to be taken. It is important to differentiate between the *scope of transition*, being the work required to manage the desired change – that is, the project – and the *scope of service* that is the object of the change and reason for transition.

Criteria for measuring success

The successful transition of services will be greatly assisted by the clarity with which required performance and outcomes can be expressed. It will be necessary, therefore, to determine the criteria by which successful transition can be measured. The following can provide a suitable basis:

- no break in service delivery;
- no impact on operations;
- progress and completion as planned;
- resource consumption as planned; and
- expenditure within the approved budget.

Stakeholders

Successful transition also depends on other factors, of which the management of stakeholder interests is prominent. Where transition is large and/or complex, it would be sensible to prepare a plan for stakeholder engagement (see Chapter 2). In the case of a minor transition, stakeholder interests might be dealt with in a less formal way. However, this does not mean that stakeholder engagement should be played down. Simply, the facility manager needs to discuss and then document stakeholder interests in the proposed transition, including any direct involvement that affected stakeholders might have in transition and the new arrangement. Principal amongst those interests will be end-user requirements and questions in relation to the time required for transition. The creation of a project for transition will greatly assist in quantifying the answers to these questions.

Risk and opportunity management

As we have established, change involves uncertainty, which means risks of one kind or another. Understanding the nature, likelihood and potential impact of risks is the foundation of successful transition, particularly in the case of large and/or complex transitions. Recognizing opportunities that might prove beneficial to the organization is important. For these reasons, a process covering downside risks and upside risks (i.e. opportunities) should be regarded as an integral part of transition. An assessment should be undertaken, as part of the preparation of the transition plan, to identify any event or factor that could have an impact on transition.

A risk and opportunity register should be created, which must be kept up to date if it is to serve its intended purpose. The events and factors recorded in the risk and opportunity register can then be assessed in terms of their likely occurrence and potential impact on transition. The most appropriate response to each will need to be determined, taking into account the practicability and affordability of any recommended actions (i.e. risk treatment or opportunity realization). However, since transition is taking place in a live environment, events and factors are liable to change, and so it is important to monitor proactively the risks recorded in the risk and opportunity register and the results of any risk treatment or opportunity realization. Additionally, it will be necessary to scan the environment for new events and factors that might pose risks. Clearly, the scale of transition and the exposure of the organization to uncertainty and risks will need to be a deciding factor on the extent to which formal risk and opportunity management takes place.

Transition actions

Whilst the transition plan is intended to cover a broad base of interests and requirements, it is important to focus on the critical elements of transition to enable rapid exchange of key information and data. Doing so will avoid transition becoming a long, drawn-out process, especially where minor transitions are involved. Areas where action is likely to be required include:

- governance, including roles, responsibilities and accountabilities, internal approvals and organizational structure;
- external permissions and notices;
- agreements and contracts in force;
- procurement of services, where outsourcing is involved;
- the time-plan, milestones and deadlines;
- the resources required;
- the budget required;
- quantified risks and opportunities; and
- time and cost contingency.

Governance

Clarity of roles, responsibilities and accountability, amongst other factors, is essential if transition is to progress smoothly, with personnel fully aware of their own and their co-workers' positions. A framework for governance should be developed to cover each of the functions in terms of named personnel and their level of authority within an explicit structure for transition. This might usefully, and simply, take the form of a responsibility assignment matrix (i.e. a RASCI chart). In the case of outsourcing, the organization should consider the extent to which an incoming service provider might be able to fulfil certain roles and the level of authority it will need to discharge its responsibilities. The engagement of a change manager or human resources manager should be considered to ensure that restructuring is handled correctly and with sensitivity, especially in regard to any residual in-house team.

There is the possibility of the organization having to acquire knowledge about people, processes and technology in order to manage a transition involving insourcing. Conversely, it might be necessary to transfer knowledge to external service providers. In either case, the information and data required for transition should be identified and used to prepare an information deliverables plan as part of a broader interest in facility information management (see Chapter 15). This plan should show the source of information and data and the point at which it is required during transition. An information deliverables plan could be useful for highlighting the information and data to be exchanged during transition. A lack of key information or data could stall transition and lead to unnecessary delay. Cross-referencing information requirements against the facility handbook will reduce the likelihood of oversight (see Chapter 15 on the Facility handbook). For minor transitions, the information deliverables plan will be, likewise, a minor item but no less important. Where a large and/or complex transition is involved – perhaps across a number of countries – the criticality of efficient information management should be immediately apparent.

Contracts and agreements

The nature and extent of contracts and agreements in force will be a material factor in planning transition. The implications arising from the termination of any contract or agreement will have to be fully examined and legal advice sought before finally committing to transition. In a case where it is considered necessary to terminate the contract of a service provider, the organization should at least try to retrieve something; at the very least, it should try to prevent a deteriorating situation from worsening if at all possible. In extreme cases, a failing service provider might have to be removed immediately, quite literally, and barred from returning to the facility.

There is no single solution for a situation where a service provider is consistently underperforming. Each situation has to be considered in the light of the circumstances prevailing at the time and the urgency with which transition needs to be pursued. The extent to which a service provider is underperforming will have a bearing on the speed with which the situation might have to be rectified. Where performance is poor, but not detrimental to operations, it might be enough to take steps to replace the service provider at the end of the current contract or at a contract break point. In more serious cases, underperformance on the part of a service provider could risk exposure to hazards of one kind or another; hence the concern expressed above regarding immediate removal from the facility. If an impact analysis has been undertaken as part of the organization's business continuity management (see Chapter 9), it will be possible to identify potential weaknesses and pre-empt the consequences – or, at least, lessen their possible impact. Any contingency plan prepared as part of business continuity management should be activated as soon as it becomes reasonably apparent that a service provider is failing to the extent that its actions, or the lack of them, pose a threat to normal operations.

In the particular case where transfer of employment from the organization to one or more service providers is anticipated under a proposed move to outsourcing, the tasks involved and their most likely timescale should be incorporated in the transition plan. Transfer of employment is a complex area and legal advice should be sought.

Timescales, deadlines and phasing in

Transition will always be framed by a timescale with deadlines, some or all of which might have been imposed. External commitments and promises can add to the challenge of accomplishing transition within a tight timescale. Whilst it would be better to fix dates to suit everyone involved, this is unlikely to happen. More likely than not, deadlines will have been imposed, leaving little freedom to change them. The best outcome might be a compromise. Early involvement of key stakeholders might help in securing agreement to a timescale that is appropriate for the transition, with some flexibility over deadlines.

A time-plan showing the key phases, tasks, deadlines and milestones involved in transition should be regarded as a minimum requirement for its successful management. A more developed approach might be necessary for large and/or complex transitions; in which case a schedule should be prepared in accordance with a recognized convention (e.g. a Gantt chart) and methodology (e.g. the critical path method). The Gantt chart, in which the critical path of tasks is depicted, is a common tool in project management. It should show the key phases, tasks, deadlines and milestones, reflecting the order in which the tasks are to be performed and the dependencies between them. Transition schedules normally combine tasks covering the execution of work and the coordination of communication and information. Schedules should therefore depict not only *physical work* but also *supporting actions*, including the management of information. It is necessary to strike the correct balance between these two kinds of task and the level of detail with which they are portrayed in the schedule (see Fig. 14.1).

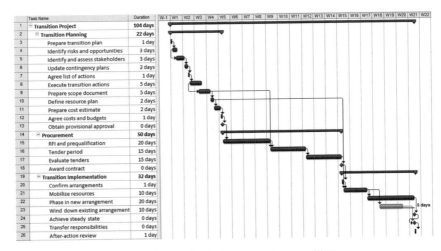

Fig. 14.1 Transition of a major service between service providers.

Thought should be given to phasing in the new arrangement either as a pilot project or in steps, where ramping up service delivery follows from evidence of satisfactory performance. Equal consideration should be given to the practicality of running down the existing arrangement as the new arrangement is phased in (see the later section on Phasing in new provisions).

Occasionally, the temptation for a senior manager might be to insist that a shorter timescale for transition is necessary and that the time-plan or schedule should be adjusted accordingly. Any such action must be resisted. It is the equivalent of saying that the cost estimate is too much and that it must therefore be cut. In the case of time, it is remarkable that some managers regard it as a flexible commodity that can be shaped to fit almost any timescale: all it requires is to re-schedule the same work to take less time.

Costs and budgets

Where the outcomes are likely to be broadly similar, the cost of alternative options for transition should be explored. This could apply, for example, to the rate at which one service provider is phased out and the new service provider is phased in. The relationship between time and cost should always be considered when evaluating options. For instance, one option might cost a little more than another, but the saving in time that might be gained could have a real value to the organization. Time–cost trade-offs are common considerations when managing projects, especially where each day saved or lost can attract a reward or penalty, respectively.

An important principle, when comparing costs or budgets for different options, is to ensure a *like-for-like* comparison and to make assumptions explicit. Transparency in preparing and reporting on costs is necessary if cost estimating is to be considered reliable. The best decisions can be made on the most reliable information and data available at a given time. The thoroughness with which costs are estimated and assumptions are made explicit will improve reliability, as well as confidence in outcomes.

The cost of transition should be estimated and should include the direct cost of service providers and, where applicable, in-house personnel. The cost of materials, equipment and any other items required in the delivery of services should be included in the cost estimate. The indirect cost of managing transition must also be included, since it is necessary to reflect the true extent of costs associated with transition. Decision-making must be correctly informed prior to transition and on future occasions when it might be contemplated. It is necessary to recognize that the simplest transition – replacing one service provider with another without any change in the scope of the service or any other condition – is unlikely to result in a *zero-sum* for the organization. There might well be direct costs associated with phasing in/starting up on the part of the new service provider and there will be indirect costs associated with transition.

Under-reporting of the extent of costs incurred in transition is therefore possible, especially the indirect costs associated with its planning and implementing. Direct costs, such as those covering service contracts and supplies, are easy to establish, since the actual cost should, initially at least, equate to either the contract sum or the value of the purchase order. Indirect costs, such as those covering management and supervision of whichever type of transition is followed, might be harder to isolate. Even so, these costs should be estimated as precisely as possible.

Allowance for the cost of work or for other expenditure likely to be incurred during transition, the full extent of which is unknown, should be estimated. The extent of some work might be unknown, but what is known for certain is that it will be required. Making appropriate allowances for unknown quantities, for instance, helps improve the reliability of cost estimates. All allowances and their associated assumptions should be made explicit.

Budget approval

Sufficient budgets have to be earmarked to meet the cost of the new arrangement following transition as well as the cost incurred in planning and implementing transition. Depending on accounting practices and financial controls, it might be necessary to seek separate approval for funds to cover the direct and indirect costs incurred in transition. In organizations where financial authorities are centralized, the facility manager should ensure that there will be no delay in obtaining necessary approvals. Normally, financial commitments – that is, purchase orders and contract awards – cannot be made unless a sufficient budget is in place. Where the organization is a publicly quoted corporation, there can be penalties for financial malpractice in this regard.

Uncertainty management

Any project contains elements of uncertainty. Managing uncertainty is, to some extent, covered by the organization's risk and opportunity management process. Nonetheless, further consideration of a project's exposure to uncertainty and risks is necessary. The importance of incorporating contingency in transition plans cannot be understated. Attempting transition within a budget that takes no account of events or factors that might impact negatively, or where there is simply a belief that nothing much can go wrong, is pure folly. Where change is involved, there will always be an element of uncertainty (apart from identified risks) and so it would be foolish to adopt an optimistic stance. Contingency must be added to the time-plan or schedule and to the cost estimate or budget. There can be a temptation to see contingency purely in terms of cost. Any thought of this should be banished – *time is money*.

Schedule contingency

The contingency to be added to the schedule should be assessed so that there is an even chance of the scheduled date for completion of transition being achieved. Where there is concern about a negative impact on operations from a delay to completion, further contingency should be added to improve the chance of completion. Additional time might be added at the end of the schedule or allocated to parts of the schedule where there is concern about maintaining regular progress. Such a situation would occur where two or more tasks must all be completed before the next in sequence can start. Since a delay in any one of the predecessor tasks would delay the start of the successor task, a dummy task could be incorporated to reduce the probability of delay occurring.

The schedule's duration, as defined by its critical path, has a reasonable chance of being achieved, but no more than that. This duration must not be taken as the time that transition will take to complete. Committing to it would be unrealistic and certainly unnecessarily optimistic, since it takes no account of the possibility of unknown factors and events that could materialize and impact negatively on the project. In most cases, and with the benefit of some experience, it is possible to make an assessment of the contingency to be added to the schedule. Less than 10% might represent too optimistic an assessment; whereas a contingency in excess of, say, 30% would bring into question whether or not planning had taken place, and the reliability of the information and data used.

For most transitions, a qualitative risk assessment would suffice so long as it is based on realistic estimates of task durations (for the schedule), resources and costs. Unrealistic scheduling assumptions and a bias towards optimistic outcomes pose needless challenges for personnel responsible for managing transition. Simply, they can find themselves unable to achieve the performance expected of them.

Cost contingency

The contingency to be added to the cost estimate should be assessed, so that there is an even chance of the cost not being exceeded. Additional cost should be added to the current estimate as a lump sum rather than allocating it to parts. Where there is uncertainty about costs in a particular area or item, allowances should be made – see the earlier section on Costs and budgets. In most cases, and with the benefit of some experience, it is possible to make an assessment of the contingency to be added to the cost estimate. Less than 5% might represent too optimistic an assessment; whereas a contingency in excess of, say, 20% would bring into question, as with schedule contingency, whether or not planning had taken place, and the reliability of the information and data used.

Readiness for transition

Implementing transitional arrangements, including clearly defined roles and responsibilities of the different stakeholders affected, is key to a successful outcome. Where these involve the transfer of responsibilities, the potential for failure rises substantially. Mobilization of resources, which is synonymous with start-up (and ramp-up) of operations, is a key feature in transition and is closely tied to the phasing in of the new arrangement.

Once planning for transition has been completed, it will be necessary to ensure that everything is in a state of readiness for implementation to begin. This mostly involves collating all the information required to support implementation. In this connection, an information pack should be provided to the service provider and/or the in-house team, as appropriate to the type of transition, in sufficient time prior to the start-up of service delivery to give time for mobilization to take place.

Stakeholder and end-user engagement

The process of engaging with stakeholders is continuous and should extend beyond the period covered by the transition. For the purpose of entering a state of readiness, it is important that key stakeholders are adequately informed of the steps involved in transition and their role, if any, in implementation. Arrangements should be made to induct personnel, where appropriate. Personnel who are to be engaged in service delivery, whether directly employed or employed by a service provider, must be adequately informed about roles, responsibilities and accountabilities. Responsibilities extend to all who are directly involved in the day-to-day operation of a facility, including – for example, in the case of insourcing – procurement and administrative personnel and the facility manager. Care should be taken to allocate responsibility in line with authority, with resources to cover the procedures for dealing with accidents and other events.

Arrangements for granting access to the facility will have to be made for new personnel. In the case of service providers, any prior vetting or clearance of personnel for reasons of security or any other matter requiring investigation takes time. Provision for such conditions has to be allowed in the time-plan or schedule. Common sense should suggest that it would be unwise to assume that vetting or clearance might be a formality or that it will take no time at all.

Personnel and/or service providers should be briefed on HSSE, including actions in the event of an emergency – for example, fire, flood, power cuts and bomb alerts – or any other incident that might compromise individual safety. This briefing should include instructions to end-users regarding action to be taken in the event of any situation in which they perceive a threat to the health, safety or security of personnel or personal property. Briefings should also cover known hazards or operations that pose a potential risk to personnel and the means for evacuating the facility in an emergency.

Permits and certification

The extent to which permits and approvals apply to the delivery of services should have been ascertained as part of the transition plan. A risk assessment might well be necessary to determine if a *safe system of work* or a *permit-to-work* applies, especially where hazardous work is involved (see Chapter 12). The entire matter of permits and certification should be approached with caution – and where there are any doubts, specialist advice should be sought.

Insurances and indemnities

In the case of outsourcing, the validity of insurance cover for each service provider, with respect to statutory obligations and specific eventualities, must be verified before service delivery can commence. In the event of a serious incident arising from the failure of a service provider to adhere to relevant legislation and codes of practice, those with responsibilities in purchasing, finance and accounting, including senior managers, might find that they are liable. Some insurance might be invalidated if there has been a lack of compliance or a failure to take all reasonable steps to avoid accidents, loss or expense. Lack of clarity over obligations and duties could lead to serious consequences, including injury or loss of life. It is essential, therefore, to address conditions and arrangements for HSSE so that there is complete alignment between the organization and service providers, where these have been appointed. It is probably advisable to seek specialist advice to be sure that there is no omission or gap in insurance cover.

Mobilization and demobilization

A mobilization plan should be prepared by the service provider and/or in-house team, as appropriate to the type of transition, based on a detailed list of tasks, their duration, start/end dates and key milestones. This plan should preferably take the form of a schedule that can be used to track and report on progress. Where an existing service provider is being replaced by another, details of the transitional arrangements should be requested from the incoming service provider, in consultation with the incumbent service provider, to ensure that end-users experience no break in service delivery. Transitional arrangements should always include contingency planning, no matter how modest, to take account of events that could threaten successful mobilization and the achievement of milestones or deadlines, or that might impact on operations. Arrangements for demobilization, including removal of property belonging to the incumbent service provider and the return of equipment, keys, identity passes and any other property belonging to the organization, should be incorporated in the mobilization plan as appropriate.

In the case of outsourcing, a meeting should be convened with the service provider for each service to discuss mobilization and any other matter that is beneficial to the safe and correct start-up and phasing in of service delivery. The following matters should be discussed:

- the service provider's plan for mobilization and delivery of the service;
- insurance cover with respect to statutory obligations and specific eventualities; and
- contract administration (e.g. payments and performance reviews).

In the case of a transition involving insourcing, a meeting should be convened with the in-house team (or the facility manager on its behalf) to discuss mobilization and any other matter that is beneficial to the safe and correct start-up and phasing in of service delivery. The following matters should be discussed:

- the in-house team's plan for mobilization and delivery of the service; and
- administration (e.g. training and performance reviews).

Personnel, supervision and management

A plan of the resources required for the new arrangement should be confirmed and should include, as a minimum, details of individuals and their job titles and functions, certificates held, expertise, and health and safety training completed. Supervisory and managerial personnel should be separately identified, together with their responsibilities and accountabilities. In particular, the resources plan should:

- assign personnel to their respective tasks and responsibilities;
- differentiate between working time and non-working time, drawing attention to the need for any overtime or shift working;
- define the procedure for dealing with queries and seeking clarifications;
- incorporate arrangements for on-the-job training and related tests and certification; and
- ensure that the timing of, and responsibility for, giving notice and other matters of compliance are defined.

Temporary facilities

The need for any temporary facilities, works or other arrangements identified when planning transition should be reassessed. The cost of such arrangements can be significant and can easily escalate if not controlled. It is not uncommon for these to be overlooked as attention focuses on the primary tasks involved in transition and a push to meet deadlines. In the case of temporary measures, consideration should also be given to the health, safety and security of personnel and their personal property.

Standby arrangements

Where identified as part of contingency planning, the resources (e.g. personnel, materials, plant and equipment) required to be present on standby should be clearly designated for this purpose. Arrangements should be made to ensure they do not interfere with implementation and, in the event that they are required to assist in some way, that they are deployed in a controlled and safe manner. A transition might require personnel in excess of normal requirements to be available on standby to make good a shortfall, or to assist in some other action to maintain or achieve the required level of service. This kind of situation can arise where, for example, a new arrangement necessitates additional support due to a lack of familiarity with the work. In other words, *learning curves* will be a feature. Starting up a service for the first time is unlikely to produce the same level of performance as one that has fully *bedded in*.

Controlling transition

The scope, schedule, resources and cost of transition have to be controlled to the extent that the facility manager should know at prescribed intervals the progress that is being made towards meeting goals, as revealed by measuring performance against targets. Those intervals have to be agreed before implementation and should take account of the overall duration and complexity of the work involved. At one extreme, progress might have to be reported in intervals of minutes, whereas a weekly review meeting would suffice in other cases. A busy outpatients department in a large hospital, where multiple services are being phased in, might require reporting at hourly intervals. At the other extreme, landscaping and grounds maintenance at the same hospital might warrant no more than weekly reporting.

The tasks to be performed in transition, together with the dependencies between them, should have been captured in a time-plan or schedule – see the earlier section on Time-scales, deadlines and phasing in. Any variation to this planned work should be investigated immediately and corrective action taken, as necessary, to ensure that transition proceeds as planned.

Performance and progress reporting

The extent and intervals of performance and progress reporting required for services during phasing in or start-up should be fixed before implementation. Intervals should have regard to the ease and speed with which corrective action can be taken in the event of a loss of performance or progress. Additionally, the resources required for measurement, analysis and reporting should be appropriate for the value derived from the information and data gathered. The correct balance has to be struck between the cost of reporting and its value to senior managers. It is important to measure what can be controlled and to monitor uncontrollable elements for their possible impact on operations. Expending resources on uncontrollable elements – for example, events, decisions and actions that are beyond control – diverts resources away from where they are needed most. Nonetheless, it is necessary to keep a watchful eye on elements that could have a bearing on outcomes in case conditions change.

Change control

Strict control must be maintained over transition, so that its scope, as well as the service(s) involved, is implemented as planned and agreed with stakeholders. It is recognized that it might be necessary to adjust plans in order to increase certainty in outcomes in the face of events or conditions that were not apparent when the plans were prepared or agreed. A scope change process should be followed to ensure that the implications of any proposed adjustment to plans are adequately assessed before approving them. It is important to differentiate between changes that are necessary by reason of compliance with legislation and those that seek to improve outcomes or safeguard value creation and reputation.

Controlling change in a project can be regarded as one of its most challenging aspects. A sensible balance has to be struck between assessing each change irrespective of its size, on the one hand, and allowing a free hand to make changes in the interest of expediency on the other. Defining the scope of transition as precisely as possible during planning helps reduce the incidence of changes arising during implementation. An approved change to the scope of transition and any associated work should be supported by an appropriate budget or approval to expend cost contingency.

Phasing in new provisions

It can be beneficial to pilot a new arrangement or to limit the extent of service delivery until sufficient evidence of its satisfactory performance has been obtained. The option of piloting a new arrangement must, however, take into consideration the ease (or difficulty) with which performance can be ramped up to the agreed level without detrimental impact on the quality of service delivery and end-user satisfaction. In some cases, it might not be practicable to introduce a service at a low level and then to step up delivery once feedback has confirmed satisfaction with the new arrangement. A full-scale approach might be necessary. Careful planning would be expected to have taken account of this requirement and so it should not come as a surprise.

The transfer of day-to-day responsibility to the service provider can occur immediately following review by key stakeholders – typically, end-users of the service – in light of performance data and, where necessary, formal sign-off to indicate satisfaction with the new arrangement. Measurement of performance should continue and be used to control delivery of the service against agreed SLAs. Action in the event of performance falling short of agreed service levels will need to be determined – see the later section on Post-implementation review.

During phasing in, it will be necessary to ensure that departing service providers do not leave any aspect of the facility in an unsafe or insecure state – see the earlier section on Mobilization and demobilization. This phase ends once delivery of the service has reached a steady state and end-users have confirmed their satisfaction.

Delivery of services

In the early days of a new arrangement, it is important to keep a watchful eye on performance and progress to head off any misunderstandings or errant ways. Typical considerations at this time include the following.

- Service delivery in accordance with agreed service definitions, service specifications and service levels.
- Efficient allocation of resources to meet day-to-day service demands in accordance with agreed service levels.
- Deployment of appropriately skilled and competent personnel.
- Active monitoring of plant, equipment and machinery within the scope of service to ensure that maintenance is planned and implemented, where appropriate.
- Logging lessons learned (see the later section on Lessons learned) as part of a process of continual improvement.
- Monitoring the impact of service delivery upon operations to highlight any situation where business continuity might be threatened.
- Guidance and, where appropriate, training to help end-users obtain the full benefits from service delivery.
- Obtaining and analysing end-user feedback on service delivery.

Ramping up and running down

Any service that is ramping up or running down should be monitored to ensure that it continues to support operations and presents no threat to business continuity. Action should be taken to adjust plans in the event that either situation arises. All reasonable steps should be taken to ensure that operations are supported by an appropriate level of service delivery. Where temporary facilities and standby arrangements have been provisioned, the continuing need for them should be reviewed so that resources can be released where no longer required. Maintaining temporary facilities and personnel on standby can add significantly to costs. It will, however, be necessary to ensure that resources are reduced in line with a lowering of risk exposure and an increase in certainty of outcomes.

Sign-off

Once a steady state of service delivery has been achieved, formal sign-off of phasing in should normally take place. Depending on the scale and complexity of service delivery, information exchange meetings should be convened until both parties have agreed that, indeed, a steady state has been confirmed by the consistent achievement of agreed service levels. In this regard, it is important to be realistic about the degree of consistency expected. Nothing would be gained by refusing to sign off simply because the service provider is unable to match exactly the agreed service levels each time they have been measured. Some tolerance has to be accepted. Moreover, inability to achieve the agreed service levels could indicate that they have been set at an impractical level. Early review of the SLA in question would be advisable. Meetings might be required on a daily basis or, possibly, more frequently; however, in most cases the interval is likely to be weekly, to cover differences in daily routines.

Transfer of responsibilities

As the balance of control over day-to-day service delivery shifts from one arrangement to another, so the roles and responsibilities associated with supervision and management will change accordingly. Changes in roles and responsibilities must be recorded and communicated to key stakeholders, together with new contact details. These details should be recorded in the facility handbook, together with other information and data reflecting the new arrangements for facility management, including any subsequent alteration that has been found necessary (see Chapter 15). This also requires:

- confirmation that procedures have been followed, including completion of induction and training;
- assessment and certification of personnel, where applicable;
- completion of knowledge transfer to assure safe, efficient and cost-effective service delivery;
- revisions to permissions, access levels and other rights, as well as restrictions, in the workplace; and
- updating of the contingency plan.

The facility's building information model will need to be updated, where applicable.

Information handover

The management of information and data used in transition provides a valuable history. It is important that such information and data are not lost and that the lessons learned from transition are captured in a form that can be accessible into the future. The information deliverables plan (see the earlier section on Governance) should be revisited to confirm that all necessary information and data have indeed been handed over. Where this proves to be otherwise, steps should be taken to ensure that it is captured in the facility handbook as far as practicable.

After-action reviews

In adopting the philosophy of continual improvement, the organization must undertake a systematic review of transition to understand the extent to which goals have been met and where adjustments to the transition process might be necessary to improve outcomes next time. An after-action review should be arranged for this purpose and used to update the transition process and the organization's business continuity management. The review should include further actions, end-user experience and the lessons learned resulting from transition.

Post-implementation review

It is possible that, as a consequence of transition, work might have to be undertaken that could not be foreseen during planning or implementation, and that now requires attention. For example, there could be an issue with the scope of a particular service, where experience of service delivery suggests that certain tasks might be better included in the scope of another service. This would require careful handling and negotiation between the respective service providers, so that end-users experience no break in service delivery. Details of any subsequent changes will need to be recorded in the facility handbook and building information model, where appropriate.

Post-occupancy evaluation

End-users of services affected by transition should be consulted to help establish the extent to which service delivery was maintained (or not) at agreed levels and the need for any corrective action. Other key stakeholders might be involved in this action. A formal evaluation should be prepared and communicated with all affected stakeholders and senior managers. Corrective actions that might be necessary should be implemented as soon as possible to assure the satisfaction of end-users.

Lessons learned

Learning from experience is a powerful concept, but is meaningless if lessons are not captured and utilized. A log should be maintained of lessons learned during transition. These should be summarized and a decision taken on the steps required for embedding them in the transition process.

Managing change

As we have seen from earlier chapters, facility management is about, amongst other things, helping the organization to manage change. Bringing about change in a controlled way will draw on many skills, not least social skills in dealing with the people affected by adjustments in some aspect of their work. The potential for failure, or a less than satisfactory outcome, looms large and demands attention to be directed to those factors that might threaten success. The need for early involvement of all stakeholders cannot be over-emphasized. These are the people upon whom the success of the outcome rests.

Routine change

Facility management is mainly concerned with routine change – the kind of everyday adjustments that have to be made to fine-tune the organization as it responds to the challenges of a rapidly changing world. Moving workplace sets and scenery is part of this routine, as well as dealing with minor alterations such as space subdivision and remodelling. For change beyond fine-tuning and corrective actions, the organization would be wise to consider a change project.

Disruptive change

Some actions can be translated into projects, enabling them to be subject to an established discipline with a proven methodology, techniques, tools and metrics. Where the size and/or complexity of a proposed change is such that it would be expected to channel resources and management attention away from day-to-day operations, consideration should be given to establishing a project with a clear set of objectives. The attraction is in the control that can be exercised over delivery to quality/performance, time and cost objectives. This thinking does, however, fall short of advocating a project-managed approach to facility management and it is important to avoid mixing concepts. Even so, there is the possibility of gaining benefit from looking at different approaches from which, hopefully, one can find better ways of achieving objectives. Any new insights that might be provided would justify the time expended.

Organizational change

Facility management moves an organization from where it is today to where it needs to be tomorrow to meet business objectives. In practice, this might mean the requirement for more, different or better space or pressure to adapt what exists. Such are the features of a rapidly changing business world. The organization can be sure of one thing – the nature of work and business will be different tomorrow. The difficulty is in predicting how and in what ways it will be different. For some organizations, the need to change might be one of extreme urgency and a consequence of events past or in anticipation of those to come. Organizational change can thus be the result of the need to:

- *refocus* – reduce diversification of activities;
- *downsize* – concentrate on core business;
- *de-layer* – remove redundant levels of management; and/or
- *re-engineer* – redesign business processes.

Other pressures for change might be faced and these can stem from a variety of sources:

- organizational structure/relationships;
- ICT;
- productivity demands;
- human resources and skills;
- time pressures; and
- HSSE.

Change can therefore occur in various ways and at various levels, and is often influenced by decisions and behaviour that are people-oriented. Change management is also about where an organization aims to be, how it will get there and how it will involve people.

Change as a process

Management of change should be seen in terms of a process – something that is eminently capable of being defined, detailed and determined. Figure 14.2 shows the essential form of the management of change process.

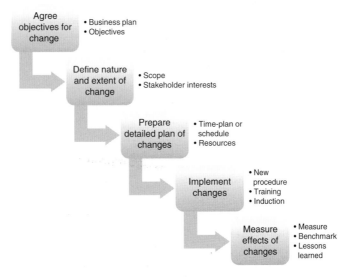

Fig. 14.2   Management of the change process.

By using the device of an explicit, shared model of the process, it is possible to obtain feedback and, importantly, *buy-in* from stakeholders. Used as the starting point for the redesign or re-engineering of an organization's business processes, the model avoids drawing people into descriptions where reading between the lines is one of many drawbacks. A process model, as an abstraction of the real world, can be used to focus attention on the sequence and logical relationship between activities that must be performed to deliver change. Moreover, the standard conventions adopted in the model can be used as a checklist of *who shall be involved*, *where* and with *what information and/or control*. The protocol thus helps to define the process.

Since the modelling approach is implicitly top-down, it is possible to break down (decompose) higher-level activities into their constituent tasks. In this way, the authors of the model – typically, change managers – have control over the level of detail that is required to portray the process (or any part of it) adequately. The golden rule is to decompose the model to a level that is consistent with the requirements of the job in hand. The level of detail is, therefore, as much as is necessary and sufficient and no more, since more would mean waste. Building such a model is an exercise in creating a single, integrated view of the process. When supported by appropriate ICT tools, it is possible to check the integrity of the model. Put another way, it is possible to see if the process is *all joined up*. Measuring the process – that is, determining its performance and outcome – completes the exercise.

Change management is rarely, if ever, a linear process; instead, it is likely to involve some degree of iteration or reworking. A further benefit of a process model is that it allows sequence and logic to be scrutinized – most of which can be accomplished from simple visual inspection – and adjustments made to improve, even optimize, the outcome. Like other techniques, such as project planning and scheduling, it is not so much the benefit of creating the plan (or model) in the first place, but the ability to be able to test different scenarios and to identify a superior plan. Without such techniques, one risks striving for the exact attainment of an inferior plan. This outcome is likely when processes are described in words and not shown as measurable actions.

Change management, and the approach advocated above, have much in common with the principles of action research, where scenarios are generated, tested and fed back into the organization so that their effects are observed. These results are then used to modify the approach or model until it produces the desired outcome. The intention here is to show that there are parallels from which one can derive useful insights.

Planning is key to success and, in many respects, there cannot be too much of it. Time spent *upfront* is usually amply rewarded by certainty of delivery; in other words, there are no surprises. The time required to plan a change management project should not be underestimated. Unless it is taken seriously, it will not produce the desired effect and the entire approach might be needlessly discredited. Facility management can provide a mechanism for managing routine change; however, it cannot deal with wholesale change. Other ways must be found, such as outlined above. Whatever approach is taken, it is vital to consult with all stakeholders: their input is necessary and their support might well be likewise. Since implementing change generally involves alterations to organizational structure and personnel, these factors will need to be looked at both on an organizational and an individual level.

Communicating change

It is important that those involved in the changes – personnel and other key stakeholders – are informed and that they are involved in decision-making. Communication is the means by which important messages are put across and commitment is returned. Failure here will mean that strategic planning (including resources planning) and organizational development and growth will be impeded as the change process becomes stalled. People can often be influenced by education and persuasion. Education is the milder form of social influence because it can help in presenting several different viewpoints, some of which will be unbiased. In this way, the target audience is offered a choice. On the other hand, persuasion can be targeted directly at personnel conforming to one viewpoint. It can be used to get personnel to accept change such as new working methods and new technology. Other forms that are available include propaganda and indoctrination, although the former is unethical and the latter is extreme and unacceptable in a democratic society. Nonetheless, it might help to be aware of these extreme measures, if only to ensure that they are avoided.

The process view of change management discussed earlier deserves further elaboration. Clearly, not everyone will be comfortable with graphical or pictorial representations of something they see all around them in the richness of the working environment. In extreme cases, they might see a process model as a crude device that strips away all that is human about work and the workplace. In one sense they are right – models *are* abstractions of reality. To complete the exercise we need to embellish the model, portraying the new arrangement with information that will help people to understand sufficiently what is involved. No process model should, therefore, be posted as the blueprint for the future unless it is accompanied by supporting descriptions of activities, the human and other resources required to perform them, the tools that can be applied to assist in this task and the controls that will be applied to ensure that the process delivers. Communicating a complete package of information is critical to success.

Roles and responsibilities

Implementing planned change brings the change manager directly to the all-important task of protecting the budget. The budget will have presumably been set according to an accepted plan and is an especially challenging situation when the changes involve outsourced services. These will be subject to contracts in which change – sometimes referred to as variations – might be accommodated. There are a number of reasons why change can be necessary, but most significantly we should think about the circumstances where a change can lead to increased cost.

Some changes can be anticipated and resources provided for them, whilst there might be no possibility of predicting others. Circumstances can include the following:

- shifting needs and priorities within the organization;
- unforeseen requirements of external bodies;
- unforeseen conditions external to the organization;
- unforeseen conditions in the workplace;
- designers or other specialists requiring additional resources to complete work; and
- the change manager simply failing to include certain work.

Arguably, the most important point to bear in mind is that change is generally not welcomed and is distrusted. It is therefore important that changes are allowed for in terms of quality or performance, cost and time before project initiation, so that the organization is fully prepared. It is conceivable that personnel will understand and accept the need for a change. Change managers must also consider the needs of service providers. The latter should be treated even-handedly to ensure their commitment. In overall terms, certainty and speed are of the essence in change management for ensuring a smooth transition and minimal disruption in workflow (see earlier section on Transition). Ensuring the commitment of everyone affected increases the chance of success.

Innovation, research and development

Facility management is testament to the notion that change – particularly the introduction of new services and disciplines – can occur in the business world and that, consequently, there can be a positive impact upon the environment. Innovation is a process that has a close relationship with managing change. Improved ways of managing the delivery of services, some of which are outcomes from the rethinking of processes and procedures, have been covered in earlier chapters. It should be the mission of organizations to ensure that they keep abreast of important changes external to themselves, on the one hand, and to create and then satisfy new markets on the other. Increasingly, innovation is occurring as the result of formal research and development, not a process of trial and error. Recognition of facility management as multidisciplinary by nature does not therefore preclude those from a research or business development background from becoming involved. On the contrary, these are important competences that must exist within the organization or that must be accessible externally.

Innovation is not some nebulous activity performed in laboratories – it is a process for helping the organization, its end-users and the wider society to benefit from something that is new. A culture of innovation is necessary if future changes are to be faced with some confidence of success. Change management can provide the vehicle for exploiting the results of research and development. Whilst research and development is an important feature of the innovation process, it is only part (see Fig. 14.3). The first of these identifies with business objectives and the last

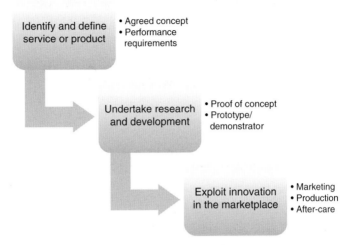

Fig. 14.3 The relationship between research, development and exploitation in the innovation process.

with the commercial exploitation of the results of both research and development. All too often, the efforts of research and development produce results that are not picked up and so they fail to be implemented. Innovation, as a process, recognizes that there must be a phase of implementation during which the results of research and development – in providing a solution to a problem identified earlier – can be successfully exploited. This usually means – if it is a matter of insourcing – that personnel will have to do things differently. They might find that their roles and responsibilities have to alter significantly. Making adjustments to exploit an innovation, be it a new product, working method or system, will involve managing change.

Research and development provides the vehicle for meeting challenges and for enabling innovation to take place; but it does not guarantee that innovations will appear. The relationship between innovation, research and development and commercial exploitation needs to be discussed, albeit briefly.

Innovation is not invention, although some things might be discovered or created by individuals in the normal course of their work; but nor is it serendipity. Innovation is when an act, such as the application of a new material or product, or the introduction of a new method, impacts positively on the environment. In other words, it is a process that enables something new or novel to be created. For innovation to succeed, it has to be formally recognized within the organization. It is not a covert activity or moonlighting on company time. In most large corporations, innovation is the process by which they are able to retain and build market share, by bringing new products and services to the marketplace before their competitors. For this to happen there has to be an organizational structure and culture that encourages innovation across the board – everyone is capable of something.

Innovation is not a department or unit, although research and development personnel might need to be co-located. There is a distinction between making everyone conscious of innovation and charging certain personnel with having to solve particular problems. No matter what money is spent on research and development, it cannot be used as a reliable indicator of an organization's propensity for innovation. Clearly, there is a relationship between the resources available to perform research and development and the chances of producing innovative products or services. In facility management – taken in the broadest sense – significant sums of money are being spent on research and development. Researchers are actively trying to find answers to questions and solutions to problems identified by their own or a sponsoring organization.

Conclusions

Transition is concerned with how the organization can control the move from one service delivery arrangement to another without impacting negatively on normal operations or business continuity. The extent to which transition is mounted will depend on a number of factors. Common amongst them is a concern for the time, resources and costs that will be involved in an environment that is subject to uncertainty and risks. Where transition is on a large scale and/or complex, the organization will face many challenges, and would be well advised to apply the full measure of checks and controls to reduce risks and increase certainty of outcomes. In contrast, a minor transition might seem sufficiently straightforward that the approach could be rather informal and without need of plans and procedures. The usual retort is that it seems like *a sledgehammer to crack a nut*. Under these circumstances, it is vital to stress that the approach should be one of scaling down rather than omitting anything – *scale it, don't skip it*.

Change appears in other, less obvious guises. It exists in the day-to-day routine of managing an organic entity that has to adjust to disturbances in the environment, which must be minimized lest they impact normal operations, thereby threatening business continuity. Change is therefore bound to be a concern and one that can be a force for good and bad. Organizations that are able to apply themselves differently and quickly might have an advantage over their competitors. However, this comes at a cost. Time and resources must be invested in planning – there can rarely be too much. Tools and techniques are available to help in the formalization of the change process. Change managers do, however, need to ensure that they involve all stakeholders from the outset. Producing a workable plan for change is no *ten-minute job*; it is the result of careful thinking that has clear objectives, which can be measured. Management of change can be seen therefore as a powerful tool in itself, as it helps the organization maintain focus on its business objectives whilst identifying and bringing about the operational transformations that will help to deliver them. As the dynamics of the workplace change, so facility management has to change to enable the organization to implement strategies that treat change as a normal feature of business life. The need for innovative thinking and practices within organizations in any sector is generally recognized. This has to include facility management, which combines many disciplines that bring their different skills and expertise to bear on solving problems to enable the quality of living and work to advance. Research and development might well be required, but not before precise needs have been identified and agreed. Some long-standing conventions and assumptions must be challenged. The organization should plan for a future that will be more onerous, more restrictive and more challenging than in the past, but retain flexibility to exercise options that allow business opportunities to be targeted and pursued.

Checklist

This checklist is intended to assist with review and action planning.

	Yes	No	Action required
1. Does the organization recognize transition as a project to be managed with the support of appropriate competence and skill in project management?	☐	☐	☐
2. Is the principle of scaling accepted in the context of the organization's approach to transition?	☐	☐	☐
3. Where transition is proposed, has a plan been prepared and has the project that it represents been appropriately resourced?	☐	☐	☐
4. Does the plan for transition and subsequent actions define the time, resources and costs involved, as well as recognizing the inherent uncertainty and risks?	☐	☐	☐
5. Has a mobilization plan been prepared to cover the winding down and phasing in/ramping up of service delivery by different service providers or the in-house team, where appropriate?	☐	☐	☐
6. Have affected stakeholders been involved, or will they be involved, in the process of signing off satisfactory service delivery following transition?	☐	☐	☐
7. Have responsibilities been properly transferred, or will they be transferred, following transition?	☐	☐	☐
8. Are after-action reviews planned?	☐	☐	☐
9. Has the organization decided how it will deal with lessons learned in transition?	☐	☐	☐

	Yes	No	Action required
10. Is there an explicit methodology for managing change in general?	☐	☐	☐
11. Is this methodology transparent, i.e. does it make the plan for change explicit and will it enable stakeholders to buy into it?	☐	☐	☐
12. Are major change projects given special status, i.e. do they have separately identified resources and time-plans?	☐	☐	☐
13. Is there a communication network for adequately disseminating and gathering information with respect to proposed changes?	☐	☐	☐
14. Are there policies and/or procedures for dealing with variations to the implementation of a planned change?	☐	☐	☐

15 Information Management

Key issues

The following issues are covered in this chapter.

- Information is the lifeblood of facility management; without it, the organization is not in control of its facility assets and is unlikely to be able to account for them reliably. Managing information is a key factor contributing to successful facility management.

- When facility assets are delivered, so too are information assets. The organization should, however, avoid a situation where information and data for operations and management are delivered all at once at hand-over – there must be phased handover to allow assimilation, training and induction to take place in a controlled manner.

- Information management needs to be in place before a new or refurbished facility is delivered – it cannot be an afterthought. An information deliverables list with an information handover plan should be prepared by the facility asset delivery team.

- An information management strategy and policy should be prepared to support the procedure for collecting, analysing, storing, updating, communicating and controlling information and data relating to the facility.

- A facility handbook should be prepared to hold information and data required for the safe, correct and efficient operation of the facility. The handbook should cover legal, commercial, financial, technical and managerial information and data. Wherever possible, it should be in digital form so that it can be more easily kept up to date.

- *As-built* and *as subsequently altered* information should be incorporated in the facility handbook together with a building logbook or equivalent.

Total Facility Management, Fourth Edition. Brian Atkin and Adrian Brooks.
© 2015 John Wiley & Sons, Ltd. Published 2015 by John Wiley & Sons, Ltd.

- Building information modelling (BIM) has opened up opportunities for organizations to maintain an up-to-date representation of the facility in digital form that integrates geometry and spatial relationships with the quantities and properties of facility assets (i.e. components and systems) and the spaces they occupy.

- Most progress in BIM is likely to be made on new-build projects, but opportunities for retrospective action applied to existing facilities are likely to follow. It will be necessary, however, to weigh the benefits of BIM against its cost.

- A computer-aided facility management (CAFM) system should be utilized for the purpose of controlling information that falls under the umbrella of facility management. It should support data exchange with the organization's building information models (BIMs) and ERP system, where either is present.

Introduction

The efficient and effective management of information and data are necessary for the organization in order to comply with various obligations and duties, as well as to be able to derive optimal use and benefit from the facility. The breadth of information to be managed can be substantial and demands a structured approach to its collection, analysis, storage, updating, communication and control. The starting point is to understand the various types of information and data that are needed for the day-to-day management of the facility throughout its life cycle. Ownership and management of a facility brings with it the responsibility for its safe, correct and efficient operation, which extends to the well-being of occupants and other end-users. These undertakings go beyond concerns about the technical aspects of the facility to cover myriad issues for which there are specific responsibilities and accountabilities. Information and data needed for these purposes might be found in different parts of the organization; in some cases, information might be unavailable. Knowing which information and data have to be managed is vital and can prove challenging.

Knowledge about the facility has real value; moreover, the cost of delivering the asset in the first instance includes the cost of producing and managing information and data. In the case of a new facility, information assets are delivered alongside the physical asset. The relationship between the two has to be defined if the facility is to be delivered as promised, capable of being operated safety and correctly, and serving its intended purpose well into the future. This will need to be incorporated alongside other tasks in the project schedule so that the facility manager is adequately prepared for the start-up of operations. The delivery of a service is also the delivery of information. In managing a facility, we need to know about the spaces to be serviced, the services to be performed and the actual performance of those services. Moreover, it is no longer enough to report on what has been done; organizations and service providers are looking for ways to anticipate demands to optimize their approach to facility management. Technology is increasingly providing the tools for these purposes, in particular computer-aided facility management (CAFM) and, more recently, building information modelling (BIM). Information has become a commodity – and a valuable one – with which to inform decisions and shape actions. It is the lifeblood of facility management, without which the organization will fail to deliver its promise to end-users – too little information and the facility management function will be starved; too much and it could be overwhelmed. Important guidance about how to manage information is available within standards. In particular, the provisions of BS 8587, which are reflected in this chapter, cover many facets of information management, not least the provision of a facility handbook.

Managing information

Information management offers benefits beyond the collection, analysis, storage, updating, communication and control of information and data. It provides an important component in the basic infrastructure for facility management. The efficient and effective use of information is the cornerstone of successful facility management, enabling forward planning that can proactively support the core business. The organization's information management in general will probably reveal the extent to which it is equipped to handle information and data for facility management purposes.

Where information management does not form an explicit part of the facility management strategy, it should be incorporated at the next available opportunity; that is, when updating the strategy. It will be necessary to ensure alignment between the information management strategy and the facility management strategy, just as it is necessary to have alignment between the latter and the organization's business strategy and business objectives. In most cases, some information and data will be shared and so it will be essential, therefore, to ensure that any updating is reflected in all three strategies so that there is no inconsistency.

Basic plan for information management

Managing information and data can seem to some people to be an almost trivial matter and undeserving of special attention. For others, effective information management is regarded as critical to the success of facility management. Furthermore, it cannot be an informal or *ad hoc* arrangement, but must be properly planned and integrated into the organization's processes, activities and systems. As a minimum, an information management plan should be prepared so that information management processes, activities and systems can be implemented effectively. Once a plan has been prepared, it will be necessary to keep it up to date so that it continues to reflect current requirements and those anticipated in the near future. This is not so much a matter of keeping abreast of developments in technology, but a case of monitoring changes in legislation to ensure that the plan remains fit for purpose and enables the organization to remain compliant.

The plan needs to include a definition of the information management process as it concerns the organization's interests in, and responsibilities for, the facility, the functions or activities defining the process, the information flows between those functions or activities and the controls that have to be applied. The use of an ICT-based methodology and tools for designing, developing and implementing information systems is recommended so that changes can be tested and their likely impact determined before they are implemented. Policies and procedures concerning the use of ICT-based systems, where they exist, should be taken into account when preparing the plan. Those functions or activities that are subject to statutory or other regulatory oversight need to be identified, with details included in the plan.

Information and decision-making

Information management is often misunderstood and regarded as another term for document management; it is a means to inform, influence and implement actions in the workplace and, unlike document management, is dynamic and increasingly digital. However, it is not just a matter of technology. Information management can provide an organization with an edge over its competitors. Having information ahead of events is a key to success and survival. In the context of facility management, information can be used to control the use of resources and determine whether or not they have been spent judiciously. Having information that can be relied upon is a fundamental precept of management and one that will improve the quality of decision-making.

Traditionally, information tended to follow events and was often incomplete and inaccurate due to the lack of a systematic means for handling it. The conventional view was that information was all much the same and could be treated as such. An accounting mentality prevailed, with action more as a reaction to problems that arose. Facility management could not be more different; if it is to support the core business, it has to be ahead of events. Information required to make a decision about what to do tomorrow must to be at hand today – timeliness is paramount. Given that condition, it is realistic to expect information to be incomplete and less than accurate. What is important is that a decision can be made. Compliance with statutory requirements, on the other hand, requires time to produce complete, accurate information; it is not possible to finish something one day and attest to it fully the next day. People also expect to receive what they are promised and within reasonable time and for nothing to be missing. When considering information and data for a particular purpose, it is necessary therefore to think about its completeness, accuracy and timeliness. To do otherwise could waste resources or stall decision-making.

In the above simple examples, we should accept that to regard all information as if it was the same, regardless of need, application or context, is plainly wrong. In accepting this principle, it must follow that information systems that do not differentiate between types of information or need are not unlikely to provide sufficient support for the organization. In this regard, four aspects of information management deserve attention:

1. processes;
2. resources;

3. technology; and
4. policies and standards.

Information and processes

If they are to deliver information to support the facility management function, processes have to be defined. A close coupling between business processes and the facility management process is therefore essential; otherwise, the basic tenet that facility management is there to support the core business is contradicted. For this reason, it is advisable to model or map primary processes to include facility management. Instead of being separate – that is, a stand-alone function – facility management should be integrated into the organization's business processes (see Figure 15.1).

Atkin and Björk (2007) have described an approach where the functions within facility management form an integral part of the organization's business processes and cannot be separated from them. The usual means for portraying a business process or system is an information model or map prepared in accordance with a recognized standard such as *IDEF0*, in which inputs, controls, outputs and mechanisms relating to functions are modelled simultaneously in a hierarchy of detail. Each lower-level function in the hierarchy can be potentially broken down into a further level of detail to create a workflow model – in accordance with the *IDEF3* standard – where task sequences and decisions are captured. When used in combination, *IDEF0* and *IDEF3* provide a powerful means for analysing and improving information processes and the systems that are based upon them.

Process models are part of the analysis and design of many industrial methods. In facility management, the use of process modelling is relatively rare, but is not without examples and proponents. Process models can provide facility managers with a means to define decision-making and determine improvements to their

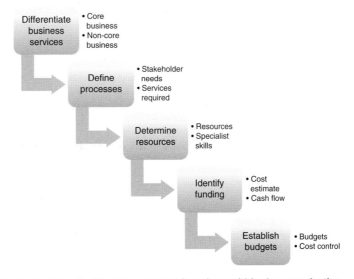

Fig. 15.1   Embedding facility management functions within the organization.

current procedures and practices. The implication is that the design of processes should precede the drafting of procedures. Since procedures tend to focus on specific areas, it is essential that they are contextualized and supported by the correct information and appropriate controls.

A hierarchical process model that portrays the broader context and that is explicitly top-down is more likely to be inclusive than a set of procedures that have been assembled from different sources, no matter how well developed. Concentrating on devising the best procedures without taking account of the underlying processes is ultimately likely to result in inferior outcomes. This situation highlights the paradox in current thinking about best practices, where the summation of all best practices is naturally expected to yield improved efficiency and fewer wasted resources and missed deadlines. Yet it might obscure simpler, more effective means for achieving success in service delivery. A process model can provide transparency and a means for sharing an understanding of what is needed and how it might be accomplished. In this way, decision-making can be shared and questioned in an attempt to define the basis of fit-for-purpose procedures, which can then be operationalized with the support of ICT.

Resources are the means by which information is captured, processed and exchanged. In Chapter 10, we discussed ICT infrastructure as part of a specialist service, along with some of the considerations associated with it. Additionally, it is important to recognize that different personnel are needed to provide the service and to support it in use. These might seem to be one and the same; however, providing a service is not enough – personnel must be able to perform their work efficiently and effectively. The cost of implementing an information system to support facility management could be equal to the cost of the initial investment in the system or perhaps greater.

Technology is the classic *moving target*. It is never going to be possible to stay at the forefront unless substantial funds can be committed and, frankly, for many organizations that is not a good use of money. Individuals can easily justify buying a new computer for personal use and might have to answer to no one; however, the organization must adopt a rational and cost-conscious approach to any purchase. Even so, it is unlikely that the technology needed to support the facility management function would be significant by corporate standards. The demands placed on central ICT services by the facility management function should present few if any concerns.

Policies and standards are in a sense two sides of the same coin: policies strive for internal order and consistency, whilst standards aim for commonality and interoperability. Standards can be mandatory, but many are not. The facility management strategy will lay the ground for applying policies followed by procedures that comply with relevant standards. The intention is not to put a brake on the organization; on the contrary, policies and procedures are there to help it deliver reliable services through a more certain process.

Factors for success

Information has to be accurate, reliable, up-to-date and complete for most applications. Often, this is far easier said than done. As we have observed above, it is not simply a matter of processes or technology; much also depends on resources in the form of people and finance, guided by standards and policies. Taken together, these four aspects can help the organization succeed in its facility management, because the approach complements that taken to corporate management.

Other factors contributing to success include:

- access by personnel at the appropriate level to information needed in their work;
- seeing information as an asset to be exploited through sharing internally and externally in commercial arrangements with others; and
- assuring privacy, security, authenticity and integrity of information.

The above could easily apply to almost any kind of organization. In the context of facility management, personnel have to be kept informed of matters that affect them in the workplace – HSSE is an obvious example. The facility manager also needs to be able to use information about the facility in dealings across the organization and in contractual arrangements with others externally, subject to matters of privacy and security. An organization that takes these matters seriously will benefit from the more effective management of information resources and systems that:

- adds value to the services delivered to end-users;
- reduces risk exposure;
- reduces the costs of business processes and service delivery; and
- stimulates innovation in internal business processes and service delivery.

Information categories

Information is not, as we have implied, one homogeneous mass. To understand its nature and thus appreciate its value, we can consider two distinct categories.

1. *Structured data* – pieces of information held digitally in databases and used to support operations. They cover details about the facility, end-users, service providers, suppliers and other resources inside and outside the organization.
2. *Unstructured data* – typically, non-digital forms of images, drawings, contracts and paper documents generally.

The obvious implication is that, in time, all information will be captured digitally, as only in this way can it be fully utilized. Information that is non-digital is difficult to share and risks being lost. Even so, steps have to be taken to assure the integrity and protection of digital data.

Information auditing

An ever-present function is that of auditing. All organizations are subject to some form of audit and most will have to observe statutory checks for compliance. The perception is that audits are used to uncover some irregularity or malpractice, which is true; however, the practice of information auditing has wider benefits. In the context of facility management, information auditing is used to:

- inform the facility management strategy;
- check that the strategy aligns with business objectives;
- define facility-related information needs;
- maintain a searchable inventory of information;
- identify information deficiencies and surpluses;
- measure the cost and value of information; and
- exploit the potential of information internally and externally.

Information about how well, or not, the facility is supporting the core business is knowledge that has a value. Once it has been analysed and contextualized, information can be a ready source of knowledge. The cost of its collection and processing can, however, be significant so it is important to know if information is being handled needlessly, such as might occur where too many key performance indicators (KPIs) are being reported. KPIs should be, by definition, the significant few and not the trivial many. Reporting on every aspect of operations might seem to be putting senior managers firmly in control, but they have to know what to do with the information.

Information management strategy

For larger organizations, an information management strategy is advisable. This should set out the general requirements for collecting, analysing, storing, updating, communicating and controlling information and data. The sources of information and data, processes, functions or activities and the levels of authority for the purpose of access will need to be identified. The facility's manual of authorities can be used to define levels of authority, approvals and access to information and data. Inevitably, there will be many interfaces between the organization and external bodies. Therefore, the information flows between the respective parties will have to be controlled. As with all strategies, the information management strategy should avoid delving into the details of activities or functions and information flows.

The information management strategy should reflect the principle of inclusiveness by taking into account the needs of existing and anticipated end-users, especially those of disabled people and others with equalities-related needs. One fairly common weakness in strategy formulation is to underplay the importance of human resources in general and the need for training of personnel in particular. Adequate provision for these requirements should be set out in the information management strategy and detailed in the policy and procedures guiding implementation. ICT-based systems and equipment have to be accessible by all personnel, including disabled people, and those with underdeveloped levels of ICT literacy. The different modes and formats of communication and information required to support inclusiveness and any training of personnel must therefore be taken into account.

Information management policy

An important link between the information management strategy and information management procedures at the operational level is provided by the information management policy. Procedures will be framed by policies that reflect the organization's standing on HSSE and CSR, amongst other matters. In this connection, it will be necessary to identify affected stakeholders in order to take account of their legitimate interests, and how those interests should be prioritized. Any applicable legislation or codes of practice should be identified and reflected in the information management policy.

Information management procedures

If implementation is to work, procedures governing the implementation of policy will have to be drafted. Amongst the many requirements for managing information will be those aimed at ensuring that personnel work within the information system and do not maintain their own copies and versions of information and data on local or removable storage. The facility handbook (see the later section on The facility handbook) is intended to encourage personnel to work within the system; but is only valid for as long as it is regarded a vital tool of information management. The form, structure and content of the facility handbook must be amenable to digital storage and retrieval, as well as printing, where necessary, on a controlled basis. Content must be capable of being updated easily and also on a controlled basis. Existing arrangements for document storage and version control in the organization are likely to have a strong bearing on the ways in which information and data relating to the facility are managed. A normal requirement is to prepare detailed procedures for personnel with responsibility for data gathering and entry into ICT systems, not least to assure security and protection of data.

Information security and data protection

Security and protection have grown in importance to the extent that the organization will need to be very clear about how it manages information and data. A strict policy and associated procedure for securely storing information and data have to be maintained. Specifically, documents and records should be held in a location that has controlled access and systems for preventing damage to the condition and integrity of information and data (e.g. fire prevention). Duplicate copies of all records are best kept in a location away from the facility to which they relate and should be accessed only when absolutely necessary. Without proper controls, there is the danger that records could be duplicated, creating an immediate problem from lack of version control and data inconsistency. The task of ensuring that duplicate records remain current is easy to solve when all information and data are digital. It is more difficult with paper copies. A further concern is the existence of legislation covering data protection and *freedom of information*. Access to information will therefore have to be on a controlled basis, with a clearly defined procedure for dealing with requests. For these reasons, a risk assessment should be undertaken before determining the arrangements for the secure storage of information and data. The manual of authorities should cover access levels and responsibility for granting or withdrawing permissions.

Roles, responsibilities and accountabilities

A common concern when managing information is about defining *who does what*. The roles, responsibilities and accountabilities of personnel involved in managing the facility and information relating to it are best captured in a responsibility assignment matrix (i.e. a RASCI chart) and incorporated within the information management policy on a general level, and within any procedure where individual tasks are defined. In practical terms, the functions or activities defined in the information management process should be listed with their assigned responsibilities and accountabilities. Other roles, such as personnel to be consulted or informed and those who are required to act in support, have to be included. Where external bodies are involved in managing the facility, including the delivery of services and supplies, details should be similarly recorded. The facility handbook can be used for this purpose.

The facility handbook

Information and data are required for a wide range of purposes and needs, some of which have been discussed. One long-standing concern is fragmentation of information and data; another is redundancy of data and version control. Managing these requirements can be achieved through the creation of a facility handbook incorporating legal, commercial, financial, technical and managerial information that can be made available to personnel with appropriate permissions. The handbook is a means for capturing and making available the information and data required to sustain the facility's operations into the future, as well as a means for demonstrating compliance. It can be paper-based, digital or a combination of the two. Increasingly, the handbook is becoming digitally based; however, some information, such as that contained within legal documents, might have to be preserved on paper. Doing so does not mean that digital copies cannot or should not be produced and incorporated in the handbook. In fact, scanned copies would be desirable – more so, if they are searchable.

If handled properly, the facility handbook will be a major resource in facility management. A variety of formats and structures are possible; however, it is likely to prove helpful to users of the handbook if the information management strategy, policy and procedure form the introduction, perhaps in a summarized form. As for the main body of the handbook, this could be broken down into the following sections:

- legal;
- commercial;
- financial;
- technical; and
- managerial.

In general, the handbook should contain information that is likely to assist the facility manager, and other senior managers, in the safe and correct operation of the facility: it would not normally be appropriate for end-users. Instead, information should be extracted and incorporated into a facility user guide (see the section below on The facility user guide) so end-users can gain the maximum benefit from their use of the facility, as well as ensuring they are aware of their own responsibilities. Since the facility user guide is a subset of the facility handbook, then any changes to the information in the former should result from updates and changes to the information within the latter. It will be essential to ensure consistency across the two documents. As a matter of practicality, end-users (or at least some representative group amongst them) should be involved in compiling and updating the facility user guide so that it addresses – as opposed to assuming – their needs. This aspect is particularly important in regard to the needs of disabled people and others with equalities-related needs. In general, it might be appropriate to offer awareness-building for end-users so that they are able to derive the most benefit from the facility user guide and, hence, the facility.

The facility user guide

The guide should typically cover matters of a practical nature, such as the internal environment (including controls), stairs, lifts/elevators, security system, emergency procedures, environmental management (including energy saving, water conservation and waste management), ground transportation, training and induction (BSRIA, 2011). The aim should be to make end-users aware of the part they can play in ensuring that the facility is safe and comfortable, as well as providing advice on how to deal with any concerns and incidents that might arise. For these reasons, the facility user guide needs to be drafted from an end-user's perspective.

Information and data

Information and data take many forms and should be classified to align with requirements including those of corporate accounting policy and procedures. Two of the more common issues in information management are data redundancy and dispersed or stand-alone systems. To guard against these issues, the use of any existing cost and management accounting system ought to be considered. Centralized cost and management accounting does, however, bring with it the possible fragmentation of information and data, not least concerning the facility handbook. In fact, the extent of ICT support for information management is likely to have some impact upon the controls that can be applied to the sharing of information and data.

Facility management deals with routine, day-to-day changes such as moving objects (e.g. furniture and equipment) and temporary arrangements. More significant changes need to be organized as projects (see Chapter 14). Where facility management involves the delivery of minor capital projects, additional controls are likely because of wider stakeholder interests and the collaborative nature of project teamwork. This kind of work should not be confused with a project for the delivery of a facility. In any event, a distinction should be drawn between information and data that are related to facility assets and those that are related to projects. Where the facility is subject to a project for its delivery, the requirements for managing information are covered by standards, processes and procedures linked to BIM. For other projects, certain information and data might need to be handled separately from others. Such a situation occurs with financial data because it represents capital expenditure (CAPEX) as opposed to operational expenditure (OPEX). Sometimes the distinction has to be drawn between organizational approval – that is, a matter for the business to determine as it sees fit in meeting its targets – and corporate approval; that is, an executive decision involving financial commitment. It is necessary to ensure that authorization for expenditure is correctly defined. Some information might be shared amongst many parties at the operational level, whereas other data might have to be restricted to senior managers. The manual of authorities should make clear *who can have access to what*, as well as recording details of *who can authorize what*.

Nature of information and data

So far, we have discussed information and data in general terms. There are innumerable types of information and data in regard to a facility and some classification or differentiation is necessary. The terms *information* and *data* differentiate between structured data, from which meaning can be derived by the person receiving it, and raw or unstructured data, such as statistics, facts and transactions. Similarly, *documents* and *records* differentiate between structured information that is exchanged between people and systems (i.e. documents) and information that is created, received and maintained (i.e. records). Information and data can also be considered in terms of their required degree of accuracy, completeness and time-criticality, as discussed earlier. Failure to draw these distinctions can result in wasted resources, missed deadlines and penalties, as well as compromising HSSE. Some information, for example, might be required urgently so that a timely decision can be taken even though it might not be possible to collect everything or for it to be completely accurate. These kinds of situations routinely present themselves when a decision has to be taken without delay and that will affect future actions. Senior managers often find themselves in this position. Any delay in decision-making could prove costly and so it is essential to make a decision based on the best possible information available at the time. When reporting on financial matters – for example, the compilation of annual accounts – information and data must be both accurate and complete. Since it takes time to collect and consolidate such information and data, a reporting period is normally allowed for submission of finalized accounts.

Legal information

One overriding consideration when referring to legal information is to recognize that the *law is the law*. Compliance is not optional and, generally, for good reason. It will be necessary, therefore, for the organization to be very clear about the extent to which it is required to maintain and retain legal documents and records about its facility. This applies especially in cases where the facility is subject to multi-tenant occupation and where details of the separate tenancies should be recorded in the facility handbook. These will need to include the layout of the facility, on all levels, indicating the boundaries between the different tenancies and any other information that helps to define entitlement. Written agreements and contracts could also be considered as falling under the umbrella of legal information, although they have a commercial aspect to them. Original documents, including leases and tenancy agreements, should be securely stored away from the facility and protected against fire, flood or other damage. Copies of documents, in whole or in part, should be captured in the handbook as scanned copies if possible.

Where there is any assignment or sub-letting of any part of the facility, details pertaining to control over management of the facility, such as rights of access and inspection, need to be captured in the handbook. Where the facility is the subject of a green lease, policies and procedures intended to conserve resources should be coordinated to optimize outcomes. Green leases make use of incentives to align the parties – primarily landlord and tenant– within the terms of a lease agreement towards sustainable business practices that involve, for example, conservation of resources and waste elimination, while helping to maintain a safe and productive internal environment.

It is possible that, depending on jurisdiction, legal requirements will apply to the admissibility of digital information and data relating to the facility and associated storage and access conditions. It will also be necessary to identify and inform relevant parties of any legal requirements applying to the retention and maintenance of records, registers, information and data. The holding of asset registers (see Chapter 12) is an especial requirement in many jurisdictions and may well require comprehensive information and documentary evidence to be maintained.

In many cases, approvals and permits of one kind or another will apply to the facility because of the nature of the processes and activities carried out within it. Details should be captured in the handbook. Sometimes, for reason of a change to normal operations, such as extended hours of operation, it will be necessary to seek additional permissions; in these cases, the details should be added to the handbook. Personnel might also be required to provide evidence of their competence, skill or formal qualification to show that they are capable of safely and correctly operating the facility and the plant, equipment and systems within it. Again, details need to be recorded in the handbook.

Details of inspections and testing are likely to form part of statutory compliance and should, therefore, be captured too. They include information on:

- personal well-being;
- protection of personal property;
- energy-saving measures;
- water conservation;
- recycling of waste products and materials; and
- protection of building fabric and finishes.

HSSE will likely impose various requirements and, amongst them, risk and hazard assessments will be typically encountered. It will be essential, therefore, to record the details in the handbook. Where a health and safety file has been prepared under legislation covering design and construction, it must be incorporated so that it is available to the facility manager. Provision should be made in the handbook to cross-reference any other information relating to HSSE matters, to avoid error and for ease of access. Information has to be provided for disabled people and others, who might have equalities-related needs or concerns and who are visiting the facility. Such information has to be made available in advance of, and upon, arrival at the facility to explain access, movement and emergency evacuation procedures. All provisions should be reviewed periodically to ensure that they remain up to date.

Legislation relating to the employment of personnel and other obligations and duties, including those associated with any transfer of employment to another organization, will require detailed records to be kept. It is highly advisable that, where transfer of employment is contemplated, every step is documented. The transfer of employment is a complex area and one that might well require legal advice to be sought.

Commercial information

Commercial information covers such matters as valuations of the real estate comprising the facility and its contents, insurance policies and market data. Details should be captured in the facility handbook, where disclosure would not compromise commercial interests. A plan for conducting and incorporating valuations of the facility for the purpose of insurance needs to be arranged so that its current value is known at any time. Wherever practicable, these valuations should be maintained in the handbook. Where the facility is subject to assignment or sub-letting, the basis of the agreement and schedule of charges will need to be recorded, updated as necessary following increases or decreases in charges. Details of any other matter that reflects a third party's commercial interest in the use of the facility needs to be recorded. One example is a permission granted to a third party, for instance, allowing advertising signs to be affixed to an external wall. In some cases, amenities such as a health or fitness club or coffee shop might be shared in a multi-tenanted facility.

SLAs should be incorporated in the handbook. A distinction should be drawn between those that arise from assignment or sub-letting and those that are required for the overall management of the facility.

Financial information

The extent to which financial information relating to the facility is part of corporate cost and management accounting, including processes, procedures and systems, will have to be determined. In cases where there is a division between practices designed for corporate purposes and those specifically for facility management, the interfaces between the functions or activities and the roles and responsibilities to be exercised will have to be defined. As noted earlier, the use of a manual of authorities can help in clarifying arrangements and responsibilities.

It might be impractical or unnecessary to expect or suggest changes to corporate cost and management accounting to accommodate the requirements for facility information management. It is, however, critical to control information flows and correctly undertake functions or activities, noting that they might be governed by regulations or accounting standards.

The cost of operating the facility is essential information and how it is collected, analysed and presented is important. Usually, a code of accounts will be in place to enable control over commitments and expenditure against individual and group cost items and their associated budgets. The extent to which corporate financial systems extend to the procurement of facility-related services and supplies will need to be ascertained. Details of such systems, including applicable policy and procedures, should be summarized in the handbook.

Existing corporate financial arrangements are likely to override any that might apply to non-core business processes; that is, facility management. In most cases, it is necessary to incorporate details of financial systems, policy and procedures within the handbook, so that the extent of financial systems and the information and data they handle is properly documented. Transparency and auditability are central to this concern. While budgets might be confidential to personnel with specific levels of authority, provision for this information should be made within the handbook as a matter of good practice. The question of whether budgetary information should be recorded too or held elsewhere will have to be answered. If held elsewhere, reference to its location and the level(s) of authority required to access will need to be recorded.

The rationale for including budgetary information within the handbook is to enable account to be taken of forecasted and actual costs and other relevant data for the delivery of services. Facility managers are normally responsible for providing estimates of the cost of services for successive financial years, so that provision can be made to meet future commitments and expenditure. Financial planning and control cannot be effective if cost data are unavailable. Furthermore, budgets should be determined in light of actual and forecasted costs.

Details of orders placed and contracts awarded should be recorded in the handbook. The following information is typical of that required for control purposes:

- purchase (or order) number and date;
- name of the service or supply;
- name of the service provider or supplier;
- normal contact details;
- escalation contact details;
- reference number or code for uniquely identifying a transaction;
- contract sum or monetary value of a purchase order;
- basis of price (e.g. fixed or variable/reimbursable);
- term of the contract or order;
- apportionment of costs to financial years;
- details of incentives or penalties;
- budget allocated;
- statement of whether or not the budget is likely to be exceeded; and
- authority for approval.

The basis of cost accounting policy and procedures should be noted in the handbook. Consideration should be given to the inclusion of costs relating to approved expenditure and the work items and service provisions to which these relate. It should be possible for an auditable trail of transactions to be made available to authorized persons; otherwise, reference should be made to the location of this information. Generally, it is unnecessary to duplicate cost accounting systems and procedures to cover facility management where the former are provided for the organization as a whole. In cases where a particular process, system or procedure is established for the core business, then reference to that arrangement might be sufficient.

Information and data on the performance of services and the work items they comprise should be measured and recorded. The scope and degree of breakdown of this information should be defined in SLAs, and ought to be sufficient to enable comparisons to be made at predetermined intervals for the purpose of establishing progress against targets based on the use of KPIs. Performance data should be cross-referenced to work items and the services and/or contracts of which they form a part. Consideration should be given to portraying the results of comparisons and other analyses in graphical form, so that trends or other patterns can be easily detected. The use of a facility management dashboard should be considered and the recording of summary information from it on a regular basis, perhaps monthly.

The form and content of the reports required for financial purposes and for supporting the day-to-day management of the facility should always be specified. Wherever practicable, the capabilities of any ICT-based systems used in this connection should be configured to avoid manual entry or duplication of data. ICT-based systems should be capable of allowing *ad hoc* queries to be performed on the database and for reporting to be customized to suit system end-user requirements.

As a general requirement, reporting should enable easy comprehension of the current status of facility management in terms of expenditure against commitments and approved budgets, accompanied by any indication of over-expenditure or significant under-expenditure. Reporting has a prominent role in forecasting total expenditure against current commitments as well as identifying over-expenditure. ICT-based systems should be implemented in order to support the requirements of corporate accounting policy and procedures.

Technical information

The safe and correct operation of the facility will rely on considerable technical information and data, which has to be kept up to date. The starting point for considering technical information and data is the facility's *as-built* information covering its design and construction and any subsequent changes to either (i.e. *as subsequently altered*). As-built information should be incorporated into the facility handbook. This should involve, principally, plans showing the layout of the facility on all levels, including basic measurements, and indicate:

- points of entry and exit, including means of escape;
- toilets and changing/locker rooms;

- lift/elevator and escalator access;
- temperature control points;
- break-glass fire alarm activation points;
- fire extinguishers and hose reels;
- first-aid boxes; and
- reception and helpdesk, where located on-site.

The requirements for providing as-built design information should be considered in the wider context of BIM – see the earlier section and the later section on Building information models. In the case of a new or refurbished facility, a certificate of making good defects or a similar record confirming the remedying of defects is ordinarily produced and should be incorporated within the handbook. Doing so will provide a ready answer later as to whether a particular defect was present at handover or not.

The operating procedures for the facility in general – and, specifically, in regard to building services engineering installations and other systems not forming part of the processes of the core business – should be described. Information should be recorded in the handbook alongside, or as part of, details incorporated from either the building logbook or the building manual. Particular attention should be drawn to critical systems within and outside the facility and requirements in this regard. Periodic reviews of this information will determine if this information is up to date, as it is important to minimize disruption and avoid loss of business continuity in the event of any breakdown or failure. The requirement for periodic condition surveys should be considered as a means for keeping information up to date.

The condition of the facility in terms of its structure, fabric, building services engineering installations, finishes, fittings and furnishings should be recorded and updated as and when changes occur or are first observed. Industry-wide standards exist in many countries for managing, specifying and delivering building services engineering maintenance. Reference to these standards can be useful when framing tendering requirements and, later, during operation and use when benchmarking the costs of service delivery. The standards specify tasks that need to be performed and their frequency in order to keep physical assets in the optimal operational condition. The frequency of surveys should be planned in conjunction with planned maintenance or other periodic work (see Chapter 12). It is important to maintain a current understanding of the condition of the facility as far as is practicable. Additionally, the means for notifying relevant stakeholders as to conditions that might affect them or about which they have an interest should be agreed and recorded. It is important to ensure that nothing could prevent necessary information from being made available to those with the authority to view it.

In the case of a new or refurbished facility, assessments and reports covering the facility's environmental impact should be incorporated within the handbook. This should be cross-referenced to information about the facility's *as-built information* or any subsequent updating of it. An appropriate methodology for systematically reviewing the environmental performance and impact of the facility throughout its operation and use should be determined. Any relevant legal requirements affecting data collection, reporting and display of information relating to the facility's energy performance should be identified and recorded in the legal section of the handbook. For instance, energy performance certificates and/or display energy certificates might be required, together with the standard or rating system adopted and details of:

- energy consumption by type of space and/or activity;
- energy consumption by type of fuel or renewable source;
- carbon (dioxide) equivalent (CO_2-eq) emitted per square metre per annum;
- actual CO_2-eq emissions compared to target emissions;
- energy-saving practices; and
- energy generation, where applicable.

Where any aspect of the management of the facility necessitates the preparation of a method statement or procedure, details should be incorporated in the handbook. When deciding whether information within a method statement or procedure should be fully detailed or summarized, consideration should be given to the extent and frequency of use. Procedures that are necessary for the day-to-day operation of the facility should be readily available and, ideally, should be accessible via the organization's intranet, or other means of internal communication, at locations within the facility based on the activities to which they relate, and/or circulated to affected personnel in printed form.

Certain method statements are required under legislation, for example HSSE, and it is important that these are readily accessible at all times. Cross-referencing these with other HSSE information in the handbook is vital. Other statements and procedures might not be referred to so frequently and could be archived until required. Under such circumstances, it is important to know what information is held and where, together with the arrangements for gaining access and, if applicable, the level of authority required.

Communication of information by the most efficient and effective means depends on factors such as the size and complexity of the organization and the extent to which ICT-based systems are embedded in work practices. The most appropriate means for communicating information effectively and facilitating action should be identified irrespective of ICT-based systems. In other words, it is better not to assume that placing information on the organization's intranet solves the problem of communication.

The question of whether or not service specifications should be incorporated in full in the handbook has to be addressed. Performance-based specifications – that is, output specifications – tend to be more concise than prescriptive specifications. Depending on the extent of specifications, it might be acceptable to summarize the main requirements within the handbook. Any process or activity that could pose a risk for users of the facility should be highlighted. The question of how information about such risks might be made readily available to persons likely to be affected will need to be answered. Again, it is wrong – even dangerous – to assume that placing important information on the organization's intranet will solve the problem of communication.

Managerial information

Information and data required for the safe, correct, effective and cost-efficient day-to-day operation of the facility has been largely covered under the previous sections. A more strategic view of operations is also needed and is something that is usually shared amongst senior managers, including the facility manager. A chart showing the organization in terms of its functional areas, the relationship between them and lines of communication should be incorporated in the handbook. Details of the human resources required to be allocated to functional areas should be included, as far as is practicable with regard to matters such as security and commercial sensitivity. In particular, personnel with responsibility for HSSE must be identified and their details, such as those for use in case of emergency and matters relating to security, should be recorded.

Arrangements for maintaining appropriate levels of security and the well-being of end-users should be outlined and incorporated in the facility handbook. Details of surveillance operations, including the use of CCTV or other means of observation, should be outlined, together with arrangements for contacting external bodies in the event of a breach in security or other incident. Where areas are reserved within the facility for the detention of individuals, the arrangements, responsible persons and their contact details should be recorded. Most facilities do not require any special areas or services for the detention of individuals, other than those designed exclusively for this purpose. Exceptions include stadiums, some major commercial developments and facilities serving the needs of vulnerable people. Security in this context is a specialist function and the services, as well as information about them, would be subject to regulatory oversight.

In the normal course of managing a facility, it is necessary to make end-users aware of matters such as operating hours, arrangements for out-of-hours working, appropriate and inappropriate behaviour, individual responsibilities and actions in the event of an incident or emergency. Details of these requirements should be recorded in the handbook and made available to all occupants and, where appropriate, other users of the facility, including those visiting for short periods perhaps of a few days or weeks. Consideration should be given to communicating these details via the organization's intranet and circulating them in printed form.

Arrangements for dealing with visitors to the facility should be outlined and recorded in the handbook. In addition to matters required under statutory obligations and duties – for example, those relating to HSSE – visitors should be provided with appropriate means of identification and information about their responsibilities whilst in the facility – see above. Arrangements in regard to auxiliary aids and assistance procedures should also be recorded. The procedure for dealing with incidents, accidents and other emergencies, including arrangements for the evacuation of disabled people, should be recorded and communicated via the organization's intranet and circulated in printed form, including posting on noticeboards in locations where they can be easily viewed.

A helpdesk should be maintained to assist end-users in gaining the maximum benefit from their use of the facility. The helpdesk might be a physical arrangement in so far as it has a location that is accessible to occupants and other users, or it might be a virtual arrangement. Whichever arrangement is adopted, details should be provided within the handbook and communicated to all users via the organization's intranet and circulated in printed form. Details of the support that the helpdesk is intended to provide should be outlined and cross-referenced to other sections of the handbook. The extent to which the helpdesk function extends beyond dealing with general inquiries and other day-to-day matters will have to be determined. In cases where the helpdesk function extends, for example, to the direct management of emergency repairs and reactive maintenance, information sufficient to document policies and procedures should be incorporated in the handbook. Routine requests for assistance or other support in regard to day-to-day operations should be channelled through the helpdesk and logged.

The extent to which matters relating to quality control are covered by, and incorporated in, the handbook rather than by the quality system has to be agreed (see Chapter 11). It is important that there is no loss of consistency between control over the performance of facility management and quality control of core business processes. Details of the arrangements for maintaining consistency should be incorporated in the handbook.

In the case of a new or refurbished facility, a post-implementation review (sometimes referred to as a post-construction review) should be undertaken during the first few months of occupation. A further review should be undertaken within one year of construction. These reviews should identify the extent to which the facility satisfies the requirements in terms of its design, construction and operability. Details of the reviews should be fed back to the designer or design team and other key stakeholders and a summary recorded in the handbook, together with any actions that have been agreed.

During the early years of occupancy of a facility, it is important to monitor performance, deal with any problems and questions from occupants and other users, undertake post-occupancy evaluations (POE) and discuss, act upon and learn from the outcomes (see Chapter 11). Details of evaluations should be summarized in the handbook. Consideration should be given to communicating this information via the organization's intranet or circulating in printed form.

Details of the performance of service providers and/or in-house teams in delivering services should be measured, analysed and reported (see Chapter 11). Summary information should be incorporated in the handbook, which should be kept up to date, to enable periodic comparisons to be made and trends to be detected.

Provisions for accommodating vehicles and bicycles should be incorporated in the handbook. Details should include the number and location of car parking bays for occupants and visitors and the location of bicycle racks. Where car parking provision falls outside the curtilage of the facility, provisions should be likewise incorporated. Account should be taken of any information that is required from vehicle users as a condition of parking; for example, proof of valid insurance cover. Information on public transport connections should also be recorded in the handbook.

Effective and cost-efficient facility management relies on having information and data on the cost of services and utilities, including energy use. Internal comparisons of performance are a starting point, but to be more effective a comparison of the cost of providing the facility and services with a facility elsewhere should be considered. Benchmarking costs and other performance-related data should be implemented as a routine practice undertaken at intervals to reveal where action is necessary to correct and/or improve performance (see Chapter 11). Significant amounts of quantitative and associated qualitative data might be collected and analysed on a regular basis to help with this requirement. Targets for improvement should be recorded in the handbook to enable comparison to be drawn with actual performance in general and the cost of providing services and the consumption of energy in particular.

Facility management deals with routine changes such as space efficiency, the way in which space is used and the services that are required to support activities in those spaces. Details of changes to the way in which space is used and the services that are required should be recorded in the handbook. In cases where changes involve adaptation or extension to the existing structure or fabric of the facility, details should be used to update the *as-built* information, plans for maintenance and other work that might be affected.

The extent of information and data required for supporting business continuity in the event of an incident or other emergency affecting operations should be established. Similar consideration should be given to the information and data required to maintain or re-establish support services of the kind covered by facility management in the event that the core business has to be temporarily relocated. Contingency plans to cover the above eventualities should be incorporated in the handbook and periodically reviewed.

Information and data collection

Information and data are required for a variety of purposes and might exist as complete or partial documents and records. It is necessary, therefore, to determine the extent of information and data that has to be managed given its intended purpose and the requirements that have to be satisfied. Clearly, information and data have first to be recorded, implying that if they have not already been collected, then they should be. It is important to keep in mind that a primary deliverable is the provision of a facility handbook and, therefore, its collation of information and data is needed to provide a complete and accurate account of the requirements for the safe and correct operation of the facility, as a minimum.

The nature of information management is such that some information and data can be collected regularly, almost as a continual operation, whereas other information and data will have to be collected at intervals. Cycles of information and data collection should be determined having regard to the purpose of the activity and the requirements defined in the information management strategy, policy and procedures.

As-built *information*

It is important to recognize that whilst *as-built* information is essential for the safe and correct operation of the facility, it is equally important to ensure that any subsequent changes are also captured and recorded. For this reason, information can be differentiated in terms of:

- *as-built* information, which should have been prepared before the handover of the facility (e.g. construction details, plans, elevations, sections and other perspectives showing the location of building services engineering installations); and
- *as subsequently altered* information, which needs to be retained during the operational phase (e.g. details of defects, maintenance, alterations and redecoration).

Drawings

Whilst design information has traditionally been shown on drawings – either paper-based or digital – the increasing use of ICT means that data models rather than flat drawing files are held. Drawings can, therefore, be generated from almost any perspective on demand. They should include *as-built* and *as subsequently altered* information that includes (Richards, 2010):

- A location or neighbourhood plan, showing the position of the facility and the site in relation to its surroundings.
- The site plan, showing the facility and any external engineering installations; for example, drainage runs and incoming public utilities.
- General arrangement plans of each floor and the roof, to a scale not normally greater than 1:50.
- Elevations and sections.
- Foundation plans and details, together with available soil investigation reports.
- Structural plans and sections, including information relating to design parameters, such as permissible superimposed loadings on floors.
- Structural details, such as structural steel connections and concrete reinforcement drawings and bending schedules; these are particularly important when pre-stressed or post-stressed forms of structure have been used.
- Details of the construction of external wall elements and roofs, including insulation materials and vapour barriers.
- Materials that might be injurious to health and safety.
- Locations of waste systems.
- Locations of essential intake and shut-off of utilities (i.e. water, electricity, gas and telecommunications).

All drawings, including those used in design and construction, should be verified against the *as-built* facility. Where a discrepancy is found, full details should be recorded and the affected drawing(s) should be labelled *as subsequently altered*. The latter term should also apply to any further changes that occur during the operational life of the facility. Accurate information must available at any time, and for some kinds of facility this will be a legal requirement.

Specifications and schedules

The records of the facility should similarly include *as-built* and *as subsequently altered* information covering the specification of:

- all materials incorporated – for example, name and type of cladding profile, mix of concrete, species and grade of timber;
- materials with properties that could prove injurious to health and safety;
- all plant, machinery and equipment, including manufacturers' trade literature, manuals and instructions for installation, operation and maintenance; and
- methods of work used during construction that are specific to a particular system, such as the assembly of prefabricated components.

All specifications and supporting information, including those used during construction work, should be verified against the *as-built* facility. Where a discrepancy is found, details must be recorded and the affected specification changed to show it as having been subsequently altered and the date on which that was done.

Information handover

In the case of a new facility, the design and construction team must provide *as-built* information and other documentation in digital form required for the safe, correct, efficient and cost-efficient operation of the facility. The format of this information should be agreed with the asset delivery team, together with the timing of information handover. To assist in this process, an information handover plan should be prepared during the design phase by the designer or other party with responsibility assigned for this task. Doing so will enable adequate preparation and training to be arranged in advance of commissioning, handover and start-up of the facility. The deliverables should be defined in the information handover plan, including their timing and the format in which they are to be provided. Progress in delivering this information needs to be shown in the project schedule for the new facility.

Data drops

Within the life-cycle phases of the design, construction and operation of a facility are points at which information and data are required to be delivered for the purpose of BIM. In the case of a new facility, these points coincide with decision gates in a phase-gated process for delivery of the asset and involve deliverables known as *data drops*. These data drops should be planned and aligned with the organization's business processes and facility management, so that the latter is capable of receiving the necessary inputs. The extent to which the evolving model aligns with, and satisfies, functional requirements can be assessed at these data drop points. Any discrepancy or divergence between requirements and the information in the model should be communicated with the designer or other party responsible for design development and/or BIM management.

Building information models (BIMs)

BIMs offer many advantages due to the integration of information and data across the life-cycle phases of the facility. For owners, the availability of unambiguous spatial information and component details, amongst other information, provides a vital baseline for operations and maintenance. In the case of an existing facility, the retrospective application of BIM should be considered, since it benefits the management of the facility over the medium to long term. In particular, BIM supports the capture of geometry, spatial relationships, geographical information and the quantities and properties of assets (i.e. components and systems) as well as the spaces in which they are placed. A useful, practical overview of BIM is to be found in Race (2012).

BIMs overcome shortcomings in the traditional handover of *as-built* information on paper by providing a digital version of the facility that is both dynamic and easy to update. Under the traditional approach, static information in the form of drawings and specifications is not always adequately coordinated. Moreover, changes might not be recorded so that, over time, the drawings and specifications that once represented the *as-built* facility are no longer valid. The creation of a model provides information and data about the physical attributes of the facility. In turn, the model establishes a baseline for facility management, including the management of subsequent changes to the facility. Over time, the model can provide a rich history of the facility, which has a value in future business decisions and, if the need arises, when disposing of the facility. The PAS 1192-2 standard has defined a number of maturity levels – from Level 0 to 3 – to help in understanding the technology and application of BIM. Distinguishing between the levels enables the organization to recognize its current maturity, as well as pointing to the changes that are required to achieve the next level. Level 1, for instance, signifies the use of managed 2D or 3D computer-aided design (CAD) systems in collaborative work involving standard data structures and formats, whilst commercial data are managed by stand-alone systems. Level 2, on the other hand, signifies a managed 3D environment involving separate-discipline BIM tools with attached data; whilst commercial data are managed by an ERP system integrated through means of proprietary interfaces or bespoke middleware.

Standards and protocols for BIM

It is important that the organization recognizes and adheres to accepted standards for BIM; in particular, the definitions and protocols that govern the structuring of information and data. In the case of a new facility, it is necessary to anticipate information deliverables; that is, data drops within the information handover plan and the expectations of designers and other interests in terms of the information and data that they require to undertake their work as part of the progressive development of the design and the model.

For asset delivery teams, information for facility management purposes appears to represent something of a dilemma. For the most part, teams have tended to leave the collection of operations and maintenance data until after handover, because they have not known what to include. In the BIM community, there is still debate as to who should be responsible for the delivery of facility management information, how much extra work is involved and how much it all costs. The expectation is that the data set required for facility management will become a by-product (with extension) of the information required for construction. Exactly what information is needed for facility management is, however, for the organization to specify.

BuildingSMART is the international body responsible for creating and maintaining the Industry Foundation Classes (IFC) specification that provides, amongst other things, support for asset and facility management functions. The IFC data model is an open, neutral and standardized specification for BIMs. It represents a common data schema that makes it possible to hold and exchange data between different proprietary software applications. An IFC model view definition (MVD) defines a subset of the IFC schema that is needed to satisfy one or many exchange requirements. The scope of this view or data set is to define IFC content for exchange between AEC applications and CAFM and computerized maintenance management system (CMMS) applications (see Figure 15.2).

The organization should anticipate and, where appropriate, plan for the need to exchange information about its facility using the Construction Operations

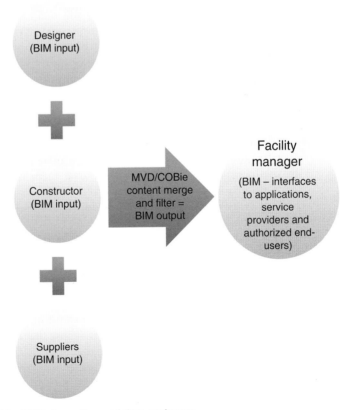

Fig. 15.2   BIM information and data exchange.

Building information exchange (COBie). Together, the MVD and COBie assist in defining a standard structure and minimum data fields to support facility management. The resultant FM Handover MVD and COBie can be viewed as *suitcases* for facility management information and data. They enable efficient transfer of critical model content to the facility manager. They are not, however, the same thing. The FM Handover MVD captures geometry and relevant data sets, whereas COBie is a means for transferring information gathered during design and construction. For a review of BIM from a facility owner's perspective, see Eastman *et al.* (2011).

COBie is general enough that it can be used to document both building and infrastructure assets, yet it is simple enough to be transmitted using a spreadsheet. It is a means for sharing structured information, which can be extracted automatically from an *as-built* model or populated manually. The COBie data set is intended to contain information about managed assets; that is, facility assets that involve significant scheduled maintenance with consumable parts that require regular inspection.

The use of models for design and construction can reduce the work required to pull together facility management data. However, difficulties exist in validating the FM data set against the *as-built* facility. Part of the task is to verify that the constructor actually installed what was originally specified. On the upside, equipment vendors can contribute by including standardized COBie data sets with their equipment submittals. PAS 1192-2 sets out a standard linear, phase-gated process for ensuring that the necessary information is exchanged at given points in the design and construction workflow, which is, in turn, reflected in the designer's digital plan of work in the form of data drops.

As noted, responsibility for producing the data set for facility management seems to divide the AEC community. Nonetheless, the idea is that the asset delivery team creates it jointly. Architects can start with their room/space and level data; then it can go to the building services engineers, who enter details of the equipment that fits inside those rooms/spaces. Finally, the constructor adds commissioning and start-up data, which have been supplied by product manufacturers in a predefined form. While all of this could be done after handover of the facility, it is more efficient to have each party enter and verify its own data from source during design, construction, testing and commissioning.

The practical difficulty that multiple layers of data cannot be captured in a single IFC can be avoided through the use of a COBie spreadsheet. A single COBie spreadsheet is capable of being imported into most application software. One implication of COBie is that it shifts facility management data collection costs from OPEX to CAPEX. There could be worthwhile savings by delegating the task to the asset delivery team instead of having the facility manager gather and organize data after handover. Those that are demanding COBie aim to reduce expenditure and leverage digital asset data created by others during design and construction. Government bodies are beginning to leverage the value of digital asset information and require delivery of specific asset information to be represented on handover in a particular structured fashion *and* in an open format. The PAS 1192-3 standard, which specifies the information required for the operational phase of facility assets using BIM, will increase the opportunities for organizations and their facility managers to integrate more asset- and service-related data than ever before. CAFM and CMMS vendors have not been slow to respond to this initiative.

Retrospective BIM

The application of BIM to an existing facility has much to offer in terms of capturing facility information, managing asset registers and logging maintenance and service data, although it can be expensive to set up. Nonetheless, the benefits and costs of retrospectively applying BIM should be explored. Where no digital model exists for the facility, it would require comprehensive survey data to create the *as-built* model. Newer and less expensive technology for capturing survey and condition data will encourage their creation and management.

Systems and interfaces

Facility management covers a diverse range of functions or activities, some of which are performed manually whilst others are aided by computer. The use of ICT in this regard should be defined and cover both manual and computer-aided processes, as well as interfaces to other electronic systems and, where relevant, external bodies. Consideration should be given to the preparation of an information map to show functions or activities, both manual and computer-aided.

Computer-aided facility management (CAFM)

Managing the use of space can be a major feature of facility management, with planning for different uses increasing demands on resources at all levels. For some, the extent of change can be a priority and, as discussed in Chapter 14, change can be regarded as entirely normal. Having tools available to plan and explore the impact of changes can represent a significant productivity boost for the organization that has to routinely redeploy resources to meet shifting demands and needs in the workplace.

The original concept of CAFM stems from developments that combined space planning and 3D CAD to support the planning and monitoring of physical space and the activities within it. These graphics-based systems model both the geometry and attributes of three-dimensional spaces. Many CAFM software packages are based on a CAD front-end (e.g. Autodesk's AutoCAD and Bentley), linked to a relational database back-end such as Microsoft SQL or the open-source package, MySQL. Typically, the database contains non-graphical attribute data of the spaces and objects associated with them. The database can be searched and reports generated to suit user needs. Moreover, major CAD vendors have BIM tools (e.g. Autodesk Revit Architecture, Graphisoft ArchiCAD and Bentley Architecture). Histories of changes can be mined to provide insights into patterns of use that can help us understand social interaction and networks. These are important for creating workplaces that enhance end-user experience and provide the organization with highly effective spaces. Nowadays, CAFM tends to be applied to any computer-based system for supporting the management of a facility.

Linking scheduling software to the database of a CAFM system to handle the time dimension creates what is known as 4D CAD, which can be used to plan, schedule and optimize changes. The advantage is that proposals for change can be tried and tested in the computer before they are made. Other dimensions, such as cost and energy performance, can be added to provide further modelling of the facility and conditions within it. The collective term for this technology is nD CAD. As time passes, CAFM and building management systems (BMS) will converge. Ultimately, facilities will be modelled digitally in a single system from inception, with the impact of design on operations closely scrutinized. Information will no longer be handed over in the conventional sense, as the model will evolve through the different phases over the project life cycle. Owners already have to demonstrate to planning authorities the environmental and other impacts that their new facility will create. The rest is mostly incremental development.

Where the facility is existing, the use of a proprietary CAFM system can go a long way to providing the organization with control over its facility. A typical CAFM system might cover:

- budgetary and other financial controls;
- cost accounting;
- the asset register;
- condition-based monitoring of assets;
- early detection of problems and rapid fault reporting;
- operational plans, including the frequency of functions or activities to be performed;
- risk and hazard assessment;
- identification of any relevant statutory and other regulatory requirements;
- permits to work;
- PPE equipment issued and returned;
- planned maintenance – actual maintenance completed versus planned;
- reactive maintenance;
- change management;
- job orders and other requisitions for goods and services;
- job logging, prioritization and tracking (including backlog);
- energy use and carbon dioxide equivalent (CO_2-eq) emitted per annum;
- resource consumption and productivity measures;
- analysis of work undertaken to identify trends;
- import/export of COBie information;
- space planning and space utilization;
- workstation location and furniture management;
- performance indicators for the delivery of services;

- end-user experiences of services delivered;
- exception reporting for management purposes; and
- audit trail of system transactions.

A CAFM system should be selected that is capable of interrogation in real time with minimum latency. Interoperability with the organization's ERP system should be key consideration in any decision to implement CAFM.

Conclusions

Information management is essential to the safe, correct, efficient and cost-effective operation of a facility. Information is needed to control and measure the performance of the facility and the services delivered within it. When facility assets are delivered, so too are information assets; however, the delivery of information should be phased ahead of the start-up of the facility. Information assets have a value into the future, because they will grow with the use of the facility, helping to ensure that senior managers are informed by the *right information at the right time in the right format*. Information management therefore amounts to much more than reporting on events; it is used to make sure that facility management works ahead of events as far as possible in anticipating the organization's needs and end-user requirements. Information management is the glue that holds facility management together. In the case of a new or refurbished facility, a procedure needs to be in place for collecting, analysing, storing and updating information and data before handover and start-up of the facility. An important vehicle for supporting this requirement is the facility handbook, which provides the means for collating legal, commercial, financial, technical and managerial information and data. The handbook should preferably be digital. *As-built* and *as subsequently altered* information forms an important element of the technical section of the handbook, together with the contents of the building logbook or equivalent. It is, however, recognized that most organizations are more concerned with existing facilities and so the handbook can provide the means for integrating information and data about a facility, which can then be kept up to date. Historically, 3D CAD technology has been used to model the use of space, as well as to enable new facility designs to be scrutinized for compliance with building codes and energy performance requirements. However, greater strides forward are likely through the development of BIMs, supported by specifications and guidance, enabling an up-to-date digital model of facility assets to be maintained across the life-cycle phases. The availability of international standards (i.e. IFC and COBie) for describing and supporting data exchange will quicken the use of BIMs. As progress is made with respect to new and refurbished facilities, where BIMs are increasingly being mandated by governments, attention will begin to turn towards existing facilities. The ongoing development CAFM will help to support data exchange between BIMs, asset information models and ERP applications.

Checklist

This checklist is intended to assist with review and action planning.

	Yes	No	Action required
1. Does the organization regard information about its facility as of strategic, as well as operational, importance?	☐	☐	☐
2. Is there an information management strategy for facility management?	☐	☐	☐
3. Has the facility management function been defined explicitly in the form of a process model or map?	☐	☐	☐
4. Has an information audit been undertaken to determine the value of information and any deficiency in its provision?	☐	☐	☐
5. Is there a policy of capturing comprehensive digital information and data on the facility?	☐	☐	☐
6. Are there procedures for collecting, analysing, storing, updating and reporting information and data relating to the facility?	☐	☐	☐
7. In the case of a new or refurbished facility, is the handover of information for facility management defined according to a plan or schedule?	☐	☐	☐
8. Is there a facility handbook?	☐	☐	☐
9. Has *as-built* and *as subsequently altered* information been incorporated in the facility handbook?	☐	☐	☐
10. Has a facility user guide been prepared?	☐	☐	☐
11. Is the organization aware of the benefits of BIM and the changes in legislation mandating its use?	☐	☐	☐

		Yes	No	Action required
12.	In the case of a new or refurbished facility, have steps been taken to exchange data using a recognized protocol such as COBie?	☐	☐	☐
13.	Where applicable, has responsibility for managing BIM during the design and construction of a new or refurbished facility been defined?	☐	☐	☐
14.	In the case of an existing facility, has the application of BIM been evaluated in terms of cost and benefits?	☐	☐	☐
15.	Is use being made of available CAFM technology for managing the facility?	☐	☐	☐

Appendix A

Glossary

accommodation strategy
objective assessment of the space requirements of an organization and how these will be satisfied – see also space management

activities
tasks that are needed to complete deliverables (EN 15221-5:2011)

adaptability
possibility of changing characteristics such as volume, function or space in order to meet new demands or needs (BS 8536:2010)

added value
tangible gain from a decision, action or procedure that exceeds its monetary equivalent; for example, a specified service might be performed at its most economical cost yet still provide further benefit from, say, the manner in which end-users' other needs are satisfied – see also best value

agency
employment of personnel through a specialist or general recruitment agency; they provide variable standards of selection expertise, personnel support and training, and end-user support

as-built information
expression of the design, its working detail, construction works and/or installations, functions, operations and maintenance needs of a facility in a form suitable for use in managing that facility (BS 8536:2010)

asset
item, thing or entity that has potential or actual value to an organization (ISO 55000: 2014)

Total Facility Management, Fourth Edition. Brian Atkin and Adrian Brooks.
© 2015 John Wiley & Sons, Ltd. Published 2015 by John Wiley & Sons, Ltd.

asset cost breakdown
itemization of the capital cost of a facility asset in terms of its constituent parts (BS 8587:2012)

asset management
coordinated activity of an organization to realize value from assets (ISO 55000: 2014)

asset register
collection of records holding information about facility assets in terms of their manufacturer, vendor, make, model, specifications, date of acquisition, initial cost, maintenance costs and requirements, accumulated depreciation and written-down value (BS 8587:2012)

attitude survey
means for measuring the perceptions, expectations and experiences of people for the purpose of objective analysis

BACnet
data communication protocol for building automation and control networks

basis for design
information and data concerning the required function, form, layout, specification and operation of a facility, amongst other matters (BS 8536:2010)

benchmarking
process of measuring performance (including price) of facility services and comparing the results internally and/or externally (EN 15221-1:2006); method for comparing the performance of the leading organizations in a market segment (ISO/IEC 29155-1:2011)

best value (for money)
relationship between cost/price and quality that is optimal for a given organization or customer; not to be confused with lowest price

breakdown maintenance
operation of restoring an item to fulfil its original function after a failure in its performance

briefing
process of identifying and analysing the needs, aims and constraints (the resources and the context) of the client and the relevant parties, and of formulating any resulting problems that the designer is required to solve (ISO 9699:1994)

briefing plan
coordinated set of actions for preparing and developing the brief and supporting documentation (adapted from BS 8536:2010)

buildability
degree to which the design of a planned building assists its construction and utilization (BS 8536:2010)

building energy management system (BEMS)
optimizing the use of energy in a building or other facility that relies on sensing of, and control over, spaces and the environmental conditions within them

building fabric
elements and components of a building other than furniture and engineering installations (BS 8210:2012)

building information modelling (BIM)
process of designing, constructing or operating a building or infrastructure asset using electronic object-oriented information (PAS 1192-2:2013)

building intelligence
characteristic of a building that has been subject to technological enhancement and that is capable of some degree of sensing and control in anticipation of, and response to, end-user requirements – see also intelligent building

building logbook
operations and maintenance information used to improve energy management within a building or other facility (adapted from BS 8587:2012)

building maintenance
work, other than daily and routine cleaning, necessary to maintain the performance of structure, fabric, components and building services engineering installations

building management system (BMS)
computer-aided control systems, including hardware and software, to collect and monitor parameters and performance data of plant, equipment, systems and elements either at source or remotely and to enable corrective action to be initiated (BS 8210:2012)

building manual
historical log of a building's operation and maintenance, and record of refurbishments and alterations, to meet the requirements of building regulations (BS 8587:2012)

building services engineering
mechanical and electrical installations, including heating, ventilating and air-conditioning (HVAC), transportation, electrical power, lighting, fire protection, security and communication systems

business continuity
capability of the organization to continue the delivery of products or services at acceptable predefined levels following a disruptive incident (adapted from ISO 22300:2012)

business continuity management
holistic management process that identifies potential threats to an organization and the impacts to its business operations and which provides a framework for building organizational resilience to safeguard the interests of its key stakeholders, reputation, brand and value-creating activities (adapted from ISO/IEC 27031:2011)

business infrastructure management
support system required by an organization to enable it to do business

business process re-engineering (BPR)
fundamental rethinking and radical redesign of business processes to bring about dramatic improvements in performance

CAFM
see computer-aided facility management system

carbon emissions
polluting carbon substances released into the atmosphere

carbon footprint
net amount of greenhouse gas emissions and their removal, expressed in CO_2 equivalents (adapted from ISO 16759:2013)

carbon management
reducing the impact of carbon dioxide (CO_2) emissions on the planet, as part of a global warming mitigation strategy based on carbon capture and storage

carbon metric
measure of the weight of carbon dioxide equivalent (CO_2-eq) emitted per square metre per annum (based on GHG emissions over a 100-year period) expressed as kg CO_2-eq/m²/annum by type of facility

client
organization that procures facility services by means of a facility management agreement (EN 15221-1:2006)

code of accounts
classification system used to uniquely identify each element in a breakdown of work or cost

competent person
person, suitably trained and qualified by knowledge and practical experience, and provided with the necessary instructions, to enable the required task(s) to be carried out correctly (BS 9999:2008)

compliance audit
selection of adequate and proportionate security controls to protect information assets and give confidence to interested parties

computer-aided facility management system (CAFM)
systems, applications and tools that automate functions needed to support the core business in its efficient and effective use of facilities (from BS 8210:2012)

computerized maintenance management system (CMMS)
system specifically designed to enable the planning, organizing, directing and controlling of forward maintenance programmes and to collect and collate historical data on the performance of assets so that the most effective maintenance strategy is selected under actual performance and environmental conditions (adapted from BS 8210:2012)

condition-based maintenance
operations that are based on the results of condition monitoring of plant, equipment and elements to avoid loss of function or failure

condition monitoring
act of measuring and recording data from operating parameters using either human senses or instrumentation to verify plant and equipment condition and trends (BS 8210:2012)

contingency planning
activity designed to take account of conditions or events whose occurrence or effect is uncertain and which would likely result in a change to the agreed plan (from BS 8892:2014)

continual improvement
process of challenging current levels of achievement or performance in order to raise outputs from a recognition that today's performance might not be enough to meet tomorrow's needs; recurring activity to enhance performance (ISO 22300:2012)

contracting out
often referred to as outsourcing, where work is undertaken by an external body as opposed to being carried out in-house (i.e. insourced)

control
comparison of actual performance with planned performance, analysing variances and taking appropriate corrective and preventive action as needed (ISO 21500:2012)

corporate real estate management
discipline and practice of making a financial return from real estate without changing the core business

corporate social responsibility policy
statement of the measures taken by an organization to act as a good citizen and to further society's interests in a sustainable future (BS 8536:2010)

corrective action
action to eliminate the cause of a detected non-conformity (ISO 14001:2004)

corrective maintenance
maintenance carried out after fault recognition and intended to put an item into a state in which it can perform a required function (EN 13306:2010)

co-sourcing
combining insourcing and outsourcing

cost contingency
sum added to a cost estimate to cover conditions or events whose occurrence or effect is uncertain and which would likely result in additional cost (BS 8892:2014)

critical activities
activities that have to be performed in order to deliver the key products and services that enable an organization to meet its most important and time-sensitive objectives (adapted from BS 25999-1:2006)

critical environment
area or location that, in the event of its non-availability, would have a significant negative impact upon an organization's business processes and activities (adapted from BS 8210:2012)

critical path
longest planned sequence of activities (or tasks) in a network (BS 8892:2014)

critical success factor
attributes of a service that determine whether or not its objectives and priorities have been met

custodial services
range of services in the management of persons subject to official control under the terms of relevant criminal justice legislation

customer
organizational unit that specifies and orders the delivery of facility services within the terms and conditions of a facility management agreement (EN 15221-1:2006)

cyber-agent
autonomous or semi-autonomous, internet-based application used to initiate, monitor and control a process

data drop
data that are deliverable at a defined gateway in a phase-gated process (adapted from BS 8587:2012)

data elements
basic units of information that are quantifiable and measurable (BS 8587:2012)

data integration
principle that data are entered once only into a computer-based system, enabling more than one application to share those same data

de-layering
removing supervisory or management grades within an organization where there is no real or perceived benefit from their continuance; the effect is to flatten the hierarchy to bring senior managers closer to the customer

deliverable
product or service as an outcome of a process

demobilization
phase to transfer facility services back to the client or to a new facility management service provider, as specified in the facility management agreement (EN 15221-2:2006)

design brief
statement that describes the purpose and required functions and performance of a facility, product or service; also a stage in the design phase (BS 8536:2010)

design briefing
process of translating the organization's business and functional requirements (as instructions and information) into the design of a facility

design development
transitional phase where the basis of the design progresses towards the production of detailed design information (BS 8536:2010)

disaster recovery
planning of operations to take account of circumstances that would pose a significant threat to the organization's continuation in the event of an incident – see also risk management

document
fixed and structured amount of information that can be managed and interchanged as a unit between users and systems (ISO 29845:2011)

document management
control over the generation, distribution, storage and archiving of information, usually taken to mean the use of a computer-based system for this purpose

down-cycling
process of converting waste materials or products into new materials or products of lower quality and/or reduced functionality

downsizing
reducing the scale of an operation or process to a level in keeping with the demands placed upon it

due diligence
comprehensive, proactive process to identify the actual and potential negative social, environmental and economic impacts of an organization's decisions and activities over the entire life cycle of a project or organizational activity, with the aim of avoiding and mitigating negative impacts (ISO 26000:2010)

element
functional part of a building or other facility (BS 8210:2012)

emergency maintenance
immediate corrective work to be carried out to restore correct function and to avoid the consequences of failure

empowerment
providing personnel (and others under one's control) with the ability to make decisions that will affect their own work and personal development; synonymous with effective delegation

end-user
recipient of facility-related services (BS 8572:2011); person receiving facility services (EN 15221-1:2006)

energy audit
measurement of the amount, rate and cost of energy consumed in operating a facility in order to achieve acceptable conditions – it usually contains a comparative element

environmental audit
assessment of the extent to which a system or organization conforms with legislation and practices designed to protect the environment

environmental impact
any change that may be adverse or beneficial to the environment, wholly or partially resulting from any aspect of construction works, parts of works, processes or services and related to their life cycle (adapted from ISO 15392:2008)

environmental policy
overall intentions and direction of an organization related to its environmental performance, as formally expressed by top management (ISO 14001:2004)

environmental protection
taking steps to ensure that the consequences of actions, operations and processes do not harm or in any way pose a threat to the ecosystem

external envelope
roof and façade, including openings

external stakeholder
individual or group outside an organization having an interest in the activities of that organization (BS 8572:2011)

facilities management
see facility management

facility
tangible asset that supports an organization (EN 15221-1:2006)

facility asset performance
requirements in terms of measurable outcomes for meeting organizational goals (adapted from BS 8210:2012)

facility audit
determining the extent to which the provision of an existing facility matches needs within an organization – see also accommodation strategy and space management

facility handbook
organized collection of documentation covering the operation of a facility (BS 8536:2010)

facility information management
organized set of activities designed to gather, manipulate, store and retrieve information about a given facility

facility maintenance
work needed to maintain the performance of the building structure, fabric and components, and engineering installations (BS 8210:2012)

facility management
integration of processes within an organization to maintain and develop the agreed services that support and improve the effectiveness of its primary processes and activities (adapted from EN 15221-1:2006)

facility management agreement
written or oral agreement stating the terms and conditions for provision of facility services between a client and an internal or external service provider (EN 15221-1:2006)

facility management brief
document for embodying the facility-related services required by an organization and used to inform the design, construction, commissioning and operations process

facility management contract
legally binding facility management agreement between different legal entities (EN 15221-1:2006)

facility management contractor
organization that contracts to provide facility services and is accountable for the contract's performance (adapted from EN 15221-1:2006)

facility management service provider
organization that provides the client with a cohesive range of facility services within the terms and conditions of a facility management agreement (EN 15221-1:2006)

facility manager
person responsible for the facility management team, who is the single point of contact for the organization on the strategic level; this person leads the facility management team, ensures quality and continual improvement and conducts strategic projects and tasks (adapted from EN 15221-4:2011)

facility manual
see building manual

facility planning
phase within facility management for examining the case for a changed or new facility and the subsequent planning of design and construction

facility-related service (facility service)
service supporting the primary activities of an organization, delivered by an internal or external provider (BS 8572:2011)

feasibility study
means for establishing the economic viability, performance and acceptability of the design and other measurable parameters of a facility (BS 8536:2010)

flawless start-up
fault-free commencement of operations (BS 8587:2012)

framework agreement
formal arrangement between an organization and two or more service providers establishing the terms of contracts to be awarded in a given period

functional approach
approach to facility management that focuses on integration of individual services to attain the required output (EN 15221-2:2006)

functional brief
interpretation of the statement of needs in the form of recommendations (provisions) for the design of the facility (BS 8536:2010)

gateway
key assurance or decision point in a process (BS 8536:2010)

green lease
use of incentives to align parties towards sustainable business practices within the terms of a lease agreement (BS 8587:2012)

handover
act of passing responsibility for, and control over, a facility to the owner or operator following testing and commissioning (BS 8536:2010)

hazard assessment
identification of a potentially dangerous or threatening occurrence and its subsequent assessment – see also risk assessment

health, safety, security and environment (HSSE)
services protecting the facility from external dangers or internal risks and protecting assets and the health and well-being of the people and providing a safe and sustainable environment (adapted from EN 15221-4:2011)

helpdesk
point of contact for requesting information and action in response to a facility-related need; it does not have to be a physical location, but can, for example, be an online service

human resources management (HRM)
function that takes account of the needs, motivations and welfare of people in order to help them realize their potential

IDEF
Integrated DEFinition, where *IDEF0* is the international standard for modelling business processes and *IDEF3* is the standard for workflow

incentivization
practice of including incentives in an arrangement or system in order to motivate the parties within it; often, but not always associated with a specified reward, which might be monetary

inclusive design
design that seeks to include everyone, irrespective of needs, circumstances or identity

Industry Foundation Classes (IFC)
model to describe construction data based on a platform-neutral, open-file format specification to support interoperability

information handover plan
statement of intentions and timings for the delivery of information assets (BS 8587:2012)

information management
processing and storage of information in a controlled manner (BS 10008:2008)

information management plan
statement of intentions for the collection, maintenance, updating, communication and control of information and data (BS 8587:2012)

informed client function
individual or group within an organization with expertise in procurement, designated to act as the client or customer in a procurement transaction (BS 8892:2014)

in-house
occurring within the organization

initial investment costs
costs incurred before taking a facility into use; for example, planning, design, construction and legal costs and the cost of incentives such as rent-free periods; sometimes referred to as upfront costs

insourcing
delivery of a service by one part of an organization to another (BS 8892:2014)

installation
system or items of plant and equipment having the function of a facility or part thereof; also the act of installing (BS 8536:2010)

integrated facility services
set of facility services that interact with each other (EN 15221-1:2006)

intelligent building
facility that affords a high level of support for its users through the use of technology and a design that takes account of the inevitability of change

intelligent client/customer
see informed client function

internal stakeholder
individual or group within an organization (BS 8572:2011)

interoperability
digital exchange of data between different systems or applications and the use of those data

key performance indicator (KPI)
measure that provides essential information about the performance of facility services delivery (EN 15221-1:2006)

letter of intent
note or memorandum setting a clear intention to take a certain course of action or enter into a formal agreement (EN 15221-2:2006)

life cycle
consecutive and interlinked evolutionary stages of the object under consideration, until it reaches the end of its life (adapted from BS 8544:2013)

Likert scale
psychometric scale used in questionnaires that assumes that the strength/intensity of experience is linear; that is, on a continuum from 'strongly agree' to 'strongly disagree'

logistics
services concerned with the transport and storage of goods and information and with improving the relevant processes (EN 15221-4:2011)

maintenance audit
process in which a competent person surveys all assets to determine maintenance requirements, so that the assets continue to perform their intended function

maintenance management
process of ensuring that the most effective and efficient maintenance programme is formulated and delivered to ensure that assets continue to perform their intended function (BS 8210:2012)

maintenance manual
technical instructions intended to preserve an item in, or restore it to, a state in which it can perform a required function (EN 13460:2009)

maintenance plan
structured and documented set of tasks that include the activities, procedures, resources and the timescale required to carry out maintenance (EN 13306:2010)

maintenance policy
statement of organizational requirements in terms of regulations and standards to be observed (BS 8210:2012)

maintenance programme
arrangement of maintenance tasks in terms of their sequence, durations and resource requirements (BS 8210:2012)

maintenance strategy
statement of the organization's approach to maintenance management (adapted from BS 8210:2012)

managed budget
arrangement where a contractor takes responsibility for the payment of all suppliers and provides a consolidated invoice at the end of each month; the fee is related to the contractor's own resources as deployed

management of change
process of anticipating and planning for changes within an organization in response to the business environment, to ensure that it continues to meet its objectives

managing agent
specialist who acts as the organization's primary professional advisor on facility management

managing contractor
single organization to manage individual service providers

manual of authorities
document containing the authorities and authority holders within an organization relating to its business, functions and legal entities (BS 8587:2012)

metric
measure, quantitative or qualitative, of relative achievement of a desired performance characteristic; for example, percentage of work complete and output per unit of time – see performance indicator

milestone
point on a timeline, a time-plan or a schedule that indicates a noteworthy event (adapted from BS 8892:2014)

mobilization
phase to establish and implement all resources, systems, data and procedures prior to taking full responsibility for the facility services to be delivered as specified in the facility management agreement (EN 15221-2:2006)

norm
standard, model or pattern regarded as typical

office automation
integration of office activities by means of an information processing system (ISO/IEC 2382-1:1993)

offshoring
business decision to replace domestically delivered service functions with imported services produced in another country

open book
transparent exchange of relevant information between the client and the facility management service provider (EN 15221-2:2006)

operability
capability of being put into use or practice (adapted from BS 8536:2010)

operating level agreement (OLA)
agreement between the informed client function and a service provider that embodies more detailed aspects of service delivery than are found in service level agreements

operational carbon
weight of carbon dioxide equivalent (CO_2-eq) attributable to the operational phase of a facility (BS 8536:2010)

operational phase
use or occupancy phase in the life cycle of a facility (from BS 8536:2010)

operational plan
organization's statement of actions intended to achieve a specific business goal(s) (BS 8210:2012)

operational strategy
overall approach to managing the production or use of a facility (BS 8572:2011)

operator
organization responsible for the day-to-day operation of a facility (BS 8536:2010)

outcome
end-result of a process, such as the delivery of a product or service (BS 8536:2010)

outsourcing
placing one or more services in the hands of an external service provider; that is, a contractor; also referred to as contracting out

owner
individual or organization owning or procuring a facility; this can refer to both existing and prospective owners (BS 8536:2010)

partnering
cooperative method of working with service providers to enable both parties to share in the benefits arising from the pursuit of continual improvement

penetration test
examining the functions of a data processing system to find a means of circumventing computer security (ISO/IEC 2382-8:1998)

performance
ability to fulfil required functions under intended use conditions or behaviour when in use (from ISO 15392:2008)

performance-based payment (system)
method of payment based on agreed output criteria (EN 15221-2:2006)

performance indicator
measured or calculated characteristic of a service to show the status or level of performance at a defined time (adapted from EN 15221-3:2011) – see also key performance indicator (KPI) and metric

permit-to-work
documented procedure that authorizes certain people to carry out specific work within a specified time-frame, setting out the precautions required to complete the work safely, based on a risk assessment

phase-gated process
model of production in which progression is subject to satisfying criteria at defined decision gateways

planned maintenance
maintenance organized and carried out with forethought, control and the use of records to a predetermined plan, based on the results of condition surveys

planned preventive maintenance
maintenance carried out at predetermined intervals or according to prescribed criteria and intended to reduce the probability of failure or the degradation of the functioning of an item (BS EN 13306:2010)

post-implementation review
study of the effects of a system after it has reached a stabilized state of operational use (ISO/IEC 2382-20:1990)

post-occupancy evaluation (POE)
process of evaluating a building or other facility in a systematic and rigorous manner after it has been built and occupied (BS 8587:2012)

primary activities
activities that constitute the distinctive and indispensable competencies of an organization in its value chain (EN 15221-1:2006)

primary process(es)
process, identified by an organization, as essential to the provision of a service or product in its value chain, direct to its customers (BS 8572:2011)

process
interrelated or interacting activities that transform inputs into outputs (adapted from ISO 9000:2005)

procurement
process that creates, manages and fulfils orders and contracts relating to the provision of goods, services and engineering and construction works or disposals, or any combination of them (adapted from ISO 10845-2:2011)

procurement policy
generic policy applying to all procurements of the procurer and that informs all subsequent stages of the procurement process (BS 8534:2011)

procurer
individual or body responsible for procuring goods or services (BS 8572:2011)

project brief
summary of the requirements for the definition of a project, including the development of its design (BS 8536:2010)

project execution plan
statement of the intentions and arrangements for the implementation of a project; that is, its construction work, and supporting activities and processes (BS 8536:2010)

project execution strategy
high-level statement of the intentions and arrangements for a project (BS 8536:2010)

provision
functional, operational or end-user requirement (demand and/or preference) in relation to a facility (BS 8572:2011)

public–private partnership (PPP)
arrangement where the public sector enters into an arrangement with the private sector to create an asset or service for public benefit, such as education, healthcare or transportation

quality
degree to which a set of inherent characteristics fulfils requirements (from ISO 9000:2005) – synonymous with performance

quality circle
opportunity for personnel of different grades to meet informally, sometimes outside working hours, to discuss ways of improving the performance of their tasks and the effectiveness of their decision-making

radio frequency identification (RFID)
device containing readable data concerning the properties of the object to which it is attached – sometimes referred to as a tag

reactive maintenance
see unplanned maintenance

real estate
land along with anything affixed to the land, such as buildings (adapted from EN 15221-4:2011)

record
information created, received and maintained as evidence and information by an organization or person, in pursuance of legal obligations or in the transaction of business (ISO 15489-1:2001)

reliability centred maintenance (RCM)
systems-based methodology used to determine maintenance tasks necessary to ensure that a facility asset or system continues to function in order to fulfil its purpose as designed in its present operating context (BS 8210:2012)

remedial work
redesign and work necessary to restore the integrity of building fabric and components to a standard that will allow the facility to perform its original function

residual life
period during which a material or component might reasonably be expected to continue to fulfil its present function, provided that it is routinely maintained

right-sizing
establishing the most appropriate structure and resourcing for an organization – see also downsizing

risk and opportunity register
record of identified risks and opportunities, including results of assessment/analysis and planned responses (from BS 8892:2014)

risk assessment
overall process of risk analysis and risk evaluation (BS 6079-3:2000)

risk management
systematic application of policies, procedures, methods, and practices to the tasks of identifying, analysing, evaluating, treating, and monitoring risk (BS 6079-3:2000); coordinated activities to direct and control an organization with regard to risk (ISO 31000:2009)

safe system of work
formal procedure that results from a systematic examination of a task to define safe methods to ensure that risks are minimized

scenario analysis
structured technique used to build different descriptions of how the future might be

schedule
plan of tasks and their times with the resources required to achieve defined objectives (from BS 8892:2014)

schedule contingency
time added to a schedule to cover conditions or events whose occurrence or effect is uncertain and which would likely result in delay (BS 8892:2014)

scope creep
uncontrolled changes or continual growth in a project's scope

scope of work
design, construction work and/or installation, testing and commissioning, handover and start-up activities necessary to deliver an operational facility (BS 8536:2010)

separate company
reconstitution of the in-house facility management team into an independent entity, with the objective of expanding its business by gaining contracts from other organizations

serviceability
capability of a facility, building or other constructed asset, or of an assembly, component or product thereof, or of a movable asset, to support the function(s) for which it is designed, used or required to be used (adapted from ISO/TR 21932:2013)

service level
complete description of requirements of a product, process or system, with their characteristics (EN 15221-3:2011)

service level agreement (SLA)
agreement between the client or customer and the service provider on performance, measurement and conditions of services delivery (EN 15221-1:2006)

service provider
organization that is responsible for the delivery of one or more facility services (EN 15221-1:2006)

service specification
requirements of a given service expressed as work to be undertaken or performance to be achieved

shell and core building
base building elements such as structure, envelope and fit-out of common areas (BS 8536:2010)

sick building syndrome
condition affecting the users of buildings that disappears after they stop using the building and that cannot be attributed to a specific factor

Six Sigma
sample of a statistical population or a technique for improving end-user satisfaction, profitability and competitiveness through a focus on the end-user by the disciplined use of facts, data and statistical analysis

smart device
piece of equipment that performs specific tasks and is controlled by a user interface; increasingly, a sensor and controller that can sample, measure and communicate data, enabling an appropriate response in an electromechanical system

smart homes
housing in which technology is used to support the occupants and other users – see also intelligent building

sourcing
delivery of facility services from within or outside the organization

space (accommodation)
services for the provision of accommodation, such as design and build, acquisition or renting of accommodation, including its administration, management and disposal (adapted from EN 15221-4:2011)

space management
process by which best use is made of available space matched to needs

space utilization
measure of whether and how space is being used (BS 8587:2012)

stakeholder
person, group or organization that has interests in, or can affect, be affected by or perceive itself to be affected by, any aspect of the project (ISO 21500:2012)

stakeholder impact analysis
method for evaluating the influence that stakeholders possess in regard to an organization, facility or project (BS 8536:2010)

statement of needs
expression of the objectives and needs of an individual or organization and the extent to which they are likely to be satisfied by a facility (BS 8536:2010)

steady state
stable operation and use (BS 8536:2010)

strategic fit
degree to which an organization is matching its resources and capabilities with opportunities in the external environment

structured data
information and data in digital form that can be searched and archived

subcontractor
organization engaged by a facility management service provider to perform a specific portion of a facility service (adapted from EN 15221-2:2006)

supplier
provider of a facility service or a product (EN 15221-1:2006)

support processes
workflow of activities not designated as primary activities (non-core activities) (EN 15221-4:2011)

sustainability
state in which components of the ecosystem and their functions are maintained for both the present and future generations (ISO 15392:2008)

sustainable development
development that meets the needs of the present without compromising the ability of future generations to meet their own needs (ISO 15392:2008)

sustainable space provision
appropriate and affordable space requirement of an organization (BS 8587:2012)

technical solution
design of the structure, fabric, building services installations or fit-out of a facility (BS 8536:2010)

tenant
individual or business that has temporary possession of, or pays rent for, real estate owned by another party (adapted from EN 15221-4:2011)

total cost of ownership (TCO)
direct and indirect costs of a product or system over its lifetime

total facility management (TFM)
single entity that takes responsibility for delivering all (or almost all) facility services

totally serviced workplace
serviced and fully operational facility, enabling users to begin or resume work immediately

total productive maintenance (TPM)
systematic approach to improving maintenance effectiveness, which operates at the tactical level and which normally builds on successful implementation of strategic approaches such as reliability centred maintenance

total quality management (TQM)
holistic approach to quality improvement in all life-cycle phases

transition
activities for migrating agreed-upon knowledge, assets, liabilities, systems, processes and people from the client to the provider in order to create the desired delivery capability, and the reverse situation (adapted from ISO 37500: 2014)

transition management
process for accomplishing transition (BS 8892:2014)

transition planning
activity of preparing for transition (BS 8892:2014)

triple bottom line
accounting framework with three dimensions – social, environmental and financial; also called the three Ps – people, planet and profits

unplanned maintenance
reactive maintenance that is carried out in response to functional failures of plant, equipment, systems or elements

unstructured data
information and data in non-digital form, such as photographs and drawings, being held on paper

up-cycling
process of converting waste materials or products into new materials or products of better quality and/or greater environmental value

workplace
services related to the working environment; for example, furniture, equipment and tenants' fit-out (EN 15221-4:2011)

workplace productivity
extent to which the working environment (surrounding an individual) contributes towards or detracts from the amount and/or quality of work undertaken

zero carbon

minimization of carbon emissions through energy efficiency, using micro-generation and low- or zero-carbon energy technology to move towards energy self-sufficiency

zero-sum (game)

situation in which a gain by one party is matched by an equal loss by the other party

Appendix B

Prevention of fraud and irregularity

Definitions

Fraud might be defined as the use of deception with the intention of obtaining an advantage. Corruption is the giving or receiving of money, goods or services for favours provided. The risks of fraud and corruption can be reduced by awareness of their nature and good procurement practice. Fraud should be deterred. Prevention is always preferable to detection and strong preventive controls should therefore be applied.

Risks

Facility services have long been considered to carry a high risk of fraud, corruption and other irregularity. The frauds can take a number of forms, some involving collusion with the organization's personnel or agents.

One fraud risk is the *ringing* of contracts, whereby a group of service providers conspires to form a ring for submitting tenders – ostensibly in competition but, in fact, having arranged amongst themselves which firm will bid the lowest. Even the lowest tender will be overpriced. The aim of the ring will be to win the majority of the contracts available and share them.

Frauds can be perpetrated in the execution or pricing of work for new contracts. This can take a variety of forms, from failure to perform to specification, to deliberate falsification of suppliers' invoices or timesheets leading to overpayment for services. Maintenance contracts also provide opportunities for a service provider to claim for more work than has been done, with or without collusion.

The pricing of contracts not let by competitive tender carries the risk that costs might be deliberately overstated. This can be a particular problem in *cost plus* contracts and in small-value non-competitive contracts, which can add up to large amounts of expenditure over time.

Particular care needs to be taken about the acceptance of gifts, hospitality and other benefits, and to ensure that there is no conflict of interest in the award of contracts.

Total Facility Management, Fourth Edition. Brian Atkin and Adrian Brooks.
© 2015 John Wiley & Sons, Ltd. Published 2015 by John Wiley & Sons, Ltd.

Key principles of control

There are a number of basic principles of control to minimize the risk of fraud in the procurement of services.

Separation of duties

Duties should be separated to ensure that no individual has control over the award and procurement process for contracts. For example, there should be a separation of duties between ordering the work, certification and authorization of payments. Failure to separate duties is one of the most common elements of fraud in this context.

The organization should also ensure that all personnel are aware of the risks of fraud, and of their responsibilities for reporting any fraud or suspicions of fraud to the appropriate level of management. One option is to set up an internal fraud helpline.

Authorization

All transactions or specified activities should be approved or sanctioned by a manager or other responsible person before they are undertaken. Limits for these authorizations should be specified. Authorization seeks to ensure that proper responsibility is taken for all transactions and activities. Authorization should ensure that delegated limits are complied with, as well as providing independent scrutiny and consistency in the procurement process.

Competitive tendering

Contracts should normally be let by competition. A decision not to use competitive tendering should require a higher level of authority.

Regular supervision

There should be positive supervision of the procurement process, including regular and unannounced checks of transactions. In addition, managers should carry out pre-commitment checks to confirm the need for the service, and that the type of contract is appropriate and the estimated costs are realistic.

Record-keeping

Appropriate records must be kept to enable every decision and transaction to be traced through the system. The requirement to keep proper records is an important deterrent to fraud.

Documentation

Standard documentation, in the sense of being uniform and consistent, can help to enforce conformity with procedures and legal requirements.

Budgetary control

Budgetary control matches resources and costs to responsibilities for objectives and outputs. Managers should be fully accountable for the achievement of their objectives and targets. Budgets should be closely linked to planning and review procedures to ensure that the proposed expenditure is essential. This will help to minimize the risk of fraud.

Indicators of fraud

The following might indicate the occurrence of fraud in the tendering and award of contracts for services:

- Contracts that do not make commercial sense.
- Contracts that include special, but unnecessary, specifications that only a favoured supplier could meet.
- Consistent use of single-source contracts.
- Split ordering to circumvent contract conditions or thresholds for tendering.
- Service providers who are qualified and capable of tendering, but who do not do so for no apparent reason.
- Unusual patterns of consistently high accuracy in estimating tender costs – this is used to deflect the attention of auditors and senior managers, who tend to look for adverse rather than favourable variances.
- Withdrawal, without obvious reason, of the lowest tenderer, who might then go on to become a subcontractor of a high tenderer.
- Patterns in tenders from a group of firms; for example, fixed rotation of the lowest tender.
- A service provider tendering substantially higher on some tenders with no logical cost justification.
- Tender prices appearing to drop whenever a new tenderer submits a bid.
- Obvious links between service providers tendering for the works; for example, companies sharing the same address, and having the same directors, managers and professional advisors.
- Acceptance of late tenders.
- Disqualification of a suitable tenderer.
- A change in a tender after other tenders are opened, often by the drafting of deliberate mistakes into the initial tender.
- Poor documentation of the contract awarding process.
- Suppliers awarded contracts disproportionate to their size.
- Contracts awarded to service providers with a poor performance record.
- Unexplained changes in contract shortly after award.
- A successful tenderer repeatedly subcontracting work to companies that submitted higher tenders.
- A consistent pattern of the same winners and losers (from the tender lists).
- Undue patronage, by consistently favouring one firm or a small number of firms over others.
- Close personal relationships between personnel and suppliers.

Table B.1   Risks and controls in the award of contracts.

Activity	Risk	Control
Scoping of contract	The contract specification is written in a manner that favours a particular supplier.	Use a contract panel consisting of technical, end-user and purchasing representatives to ensure that more than one person is involved in drawing up the specification.
Contract documentation	The conditions of the contract are changed to accommodate a favoured supplier and/or exclude competitors who cannot meet the varied conditions.	Use standard contract conditions and specifications. Any variations to be approved by senior managers.
Setting evaluation criteria	Original evaluating criteria are changed after the receipt of submissions to ensure that favoured suppliers are shortlisted.	Use evaluation criteria as agreed by the contract panel prior to tendering. Where public procurement directives apply, state evaluation criteria in advance.
Selection of tenderers	The selection of a group of tenderers with a view to ensuring that the favoured tenderer will win.	Selection by panel against clearly defined and objective criteria; where applicable, in accordance with the requirements of public procurement directives.
Tendering	Contract rings – repeat orders using narrow source list. Links between service providers – uncompetitive tendering.	Firms should be selected by someone other than personnel commissioning the work. Widen the sourcing list by the introduction of new firms and examine tender records for a pattern of pricing and tenderers who have been awarded contracts. Check for links in names, addresses and telephone numbers plus tendering partners.
Tender evaluation	Collusion to ensure that the favoured supplier is chosen.	Technical and commercial evaluation to be carried out independently by the contract panel.
Post-tender negotiations	Modification of the favoured supplier's tender to ensure that it is successful.	Where necessary, identify reasons for negotiation and negotiate with a minimum of two suppliers.
Single-source procurement	Overstating of prices.	Competitive tendering and advance purchase planning. Tight budgetary control and a comprehensive system of price checking.

Tables B.1 and B.2 show the risks of which the organization should be aware, and suggested control factors that can be used to minimize risk.

Declarations of interests

Personnel at all levels should be required to declare any personal interests in proposed contracts, and appropriate administrative arrangements to facilitate this should be put in place. Relevant *personal interests* for this purpose could include not only financial interests but also interests such as membership of public bodies

Table B.2   Risks and controls in the management of contracts.

Activity	Risk	Control
Contractual correspondence	Altering terms and conditions to suit a favoured supplier.	Contract terms and conditions will be the procurement team's responsibility and may not be altered without approval from senior managers.
Contract management	False claims for work not carried out or exaggerated claims for actual work done.	Clear audit trail with written records. Authorization of changes, by senior managers, to original document. Site checks, random and systematic.
Claims negotiation	Assisting the service provider to justify claims.	Claims negotiation should be carried out using professional advisors.
Certification of completion	Inadequate certification might lead to overpayments or payment for work not carried out.	Clear separation of duties between ordering the work, certification and authorization for payment. Ensure that certified documents are not returned to the originator.
Authorization	Contract splitting to keep contract values under an individual's authorized financial limit.	The splitting of contracts should not be allowed unless authorized by senior managers. Checks and sampling should be established to detect this.
Acceptance of documentation to support claims	Documentation has been modified or fabricated.	Act on original documents. Do not accept copies/faxes. Do not accept use of correction fluids without obtaining satisfactory explanation for any amendments.
Supervision	Payment for work not done and duplication. Failure to monitor daywork on site. Duplication of names on more than one return or *ghost-workers*. Work paid for under one contract and provided in a different format on another contract. Lack of separation of duties, failure to report gifts and hospitality or other conflicts of interest.	Good site supervision and audit of site diary. Look for similar work in same location and enforce contract management controls. Separate duties; ensure that hospitality rules are formulated and understood; have a clear conduct and discipline code, including conflicts of interest and penalties; take disciplinary action against personnel who fail to declare a conflict of interest.
Security of documents	Duplication and manipulation of accountable documents.	Restricted access to accountable documents, such as works and stores orders, tender documents and claim forms. Serial numbering should be used.

or closed organizations. The duty to decline would also extend to the interests of persons closely connected with them, such as his/her spouse/partner and the close family of the individual or of the spouse/partner.

The organization will need to handle such a declaration with sensitivity so as not to impair good working relationships with suppliers or service providers.

Risks and controls

A formal request to the tenderer to sign to the effect that no fraud or corrupt practice has occurred when developing the tender could be introduced at prequalification acknowledgement stage or at submission of a proposal or tender. This has two effects:

- *Deterrent* – the service provider is alerted to the fact that the organization is aware of the risk of fraud and will be on the lookout for any evidence that it has occurred.
- *Protective* – it ensures that should something fraudulent come to light there can be no excuse that the service provider was not aware of the policy of the organization.

Adapted from *Estates and buildings procurement: prevention of fraud and irregularity in the award and management of contracts* (HM Treasury, 1996) and updated in light of practical experiences.

Appendix C

Risks involved in outsourcing

Planning to outsource

- Are the objectives for outsourcing correctly identified?
- Is the service to be outsourced adequately scoped and defined?
- Have the direct and indirect costs of delivering the outsourced service been adequately calculated?
- Will adequate competition be generated from credible service providers?
- Does the outsourced management team have the right number and mix of skills?

Shortlisting of prospective service providers

- Are there appropriate evaluation criteria?
- Are there adequate safeguards against corruption or bias in the evaluation?
- Is there sufficient expertise on the evaluation team?

Negotiating contracts

- Have end-user requirements been translated into business requirements?
- Are measures of service provider performance defined?
- Are appropriate penalties for unsatisfactory service provider performance included in the contracts?
- Is the organization's contract protected against the service provider making excessive profits?
- Are the contingency plans that would apply in the event of disasters defined?
- Are there adequate safeguards against the commercial failure of the service provider?
- Are termination arrangements specified?
- Are there adequate safeguards to protect the confidentiality of data?
- Are there appropriate arrangements for the control of assets?

Total Facility Management, Fourth Edition. Brian Atkin and Adrian Brooks.
© 2015 John Wiley & Sons, Ltd. Published 2015 by John Wiley & Sons, Ltd.

- Are there plans for transferring the employment personnel in an orderly fashion, where this applies?
- Is adequate audit access provided for in the contracts?

Tender evaluation

- Have the evaluation criteria been tested thoroughly?
- Have the service provider's price proposals and their experience in delivering equivalent business been tested thoroughly?
- Are there safeguards against corruption or bias in the selection of service providers?
- Is there sufficient expertise in the evaluation teams?
- Are there safeguards against the possibility of legal challenge by service providers?

Contract award

- Are there adequate skills in the negotiating team?
- Is the significance of contract terms properly assessed?
- Are there safeguards against disruption to existing business prior to the handover of responsibility to the successful service providers?

Contract management

- Are there adequate arrangements to manage the contracts after award, including performance monitoring and price-control mechanisms?

Adapted from *Information Technology Services Agency: Outsourcing the Service Delivery Operations* (NAO, 1996) updated in light of practical experiences.

Appendix D

Contract provisions

Contractual approach and terms

The contract should normally be for a period of three to five years. The organization might consider the option of extending by one or two further years. It should ensure that contract documentation is consistent with the specification.

The contract should include provisions for:

1. The organization (as employer) to retain ownership of, and access to, all relevant records and knowledge.
2. The arrangements for another service provider to take over the service at short notice in the event of the financial failure of the incumbent service provider.
3. The handling of changes in the organization's requirements.
4. Full disclosure of all data by means of open-book accounting, which gives the organization access to the service provider's premises, systems, books and records.
5. The organization's right to check the qualifications and competences of the personnel who the service provider proposes to use and to approve any appointment beforehand.
6. Requiring the service provider and any subcontractors to have in place a quality system.
7. Contingency arrangements.
8. The arrangements for the transfer of assets at the start and end of the contract.
9. The mechanisms for dispute resolution.
10. The arrangements for handover to a succeeding service provider at the end of the contract.

If the contract involves a one-off transfer of assets to the successful tenderer, it should include a clawback provision to allow the organization to share the

Total Facility Management, Fourth Edition. Brian Atkin and Adrian Brooks.
© 2015 John Wiley & Sons, Ltd. Published 2015 by John Wiley & Sons, Ltd.

benefit if the service provider then sells them on. The contract should contain clear and precise terms that:

(a) Detail the service levels and performance standards that the service provider is required to meet.
(b) Define the performance monitoring arrangements and the associated information requirements.
(c) Link payment to performance.
(d) Detail any remedies in the event of a default of whatever nature.

The organization might wish to guarantee the expected workload for the first few years of a contract, in order to generate enough interest from potential tenderers. If transfer of employment applies,[1] the contract should stipulate that, at the end of the contract, the existing service provider will have to provide other tenderers with information about personnel who would transfer to them under this arrangement.

The contract should set out the pricing regime:

- A fixed price for items or tasks that can be defined fully.
- A variable price for those which cannot.
- Arrangements for sharing savings.

The payment structure should provide the service provider with an incentive to perform well, for example by:

- Paying nothing until the required performance standards are met.
- Making subsequent payments dependent on the continued meeting of these standards.
- Structuring payments to provide incentives to improve performance.
- Making good identified failures at the service provider's cost.
- The recovery of costs incurred by the organization in rectifying poor performance.
- The removal of particular services from the service provider.
- In exceptional circumstances, the right to terminate the contract.

The organization should require appropriate third-party protection in the form of parent or associated company guarantees, performance bonds and evidence of the appropriate insurance cover.

The organization should normally reserve the right to terminate the contract in the event of a change in the controlling interest in the service provider. Moreover, the contract should ensure that the service provider cannot assign any part of the contract to a third party without the organization's agreement. Contracts should be consistent internally and with each other, yet flexible enough to cope with any approved changes in end-user requirements over the course of the contract.

---

[1] In Europe, EC Directives are applicable to all EU member states and prescribe policy and procedures covering the transfer of personnel. In the UK, the relevant legislation is the Transfer of Undertakings (Protection of Employment) Regulations 2006 (TUPE), as amended by The Collective Redundancies and Transfer of Undertakings (Protection of Employment) (Amendment) Regulations 2014.

General conditions of contract for the provision of services:

1. Definitions.
2. Services.
3. Recovery of sums due.
4. Value-added tax (VAT).
5. Bankruptcy.
6. Inclusion and equalities.
7. Transfer, sub-letting and subcontracting.
8. Corrupt gifts and payments of commission.
9. Drawings, specifications and other data.
10. Use of documents and information.
11. Disclosure of information.
12. Law.
13. Arbitration.
14. Security measures.
15. Approval for admission to government premises and information about work-people (a condition that would not apply outside the public sector).
16. Observance of regulations.
17. Safety.
18. Accidents to service providers' servants or agents.
19. Special health and safety hazards.
20. Liability in respect of damage to property.
21. Service provider's property.
22. Intellectual property rights.
23. Patents.
24. Default.
25. Insurance.
26. Duty of care.
27. Design liability.
28. Personal injury and loss of property.
29. Hours of work.
30. Service provider's organization.
31. Break.
32. Facilities provided.
33. Duration of contracts.
34. Variation of requirement.
35. Contract documents.
36. Amendments to contracts.
37. Monitoring and liaison meetings.
38. Price.
39. Price fixing.
40. Lead-in costs.
41. Payment.
42. Payment of subcontractors.
43. Availability of information.
44. Transfer of responsibility.
45. Quality assurance.

Appendix E

Typical sections of an SLA

1. Definitions.
2. Services.
3. Value-added tax (VAT).
4. Subcontracting.
5. Resolution of dispute.
6. Default.
7. Duty of care.
8. Hours of work.
9. Occupation of premises.
10. Agreement holder's organization.
11. Break.
12. Facilities provided.
13. Terms of agreement.
14. Variation of requirement.
15. Agreement documentation.
16. Amendments to agreement.
17. Monitoring and liaison meetings.
18. Price.
19. Extensions.
20. Allocation of costs.
21. Transfer of responsibility.

Total Facility Management, Fourth Edition. Brian Atkin and Adrian Brooks.
© 2015 John Wiley & Sons, Ltd. Published 2015 by John Wiley & Sons, Ltd.

Bibliography

Standards

British Standards

BS 8210:2012, *Facilities maintenance management – Guide.*

BS 8536:2010, *Facility management briefing – Code of practice.*

BS 8544:2013, *Guide for life cycle costing of maintenance during the in use phases of buildings.*

BS 8572:2011, *Procurement of facility-related services – Guide.*

BS 8587:2012, *Guide to facility information management.*

BS 8892:2014, *Transition management of facility related services – Code of practice.*

BS 10008:2008, *Evidential weight and legal admissibility of electronic information – Specification.*

BS 11000-1:2010, *Collaborative business relationships – A framework specification.*

BS 18004:2008, *Guide to achieving effective occupational health and safety performance.*

European Standards

EN 12973:2000, *Value management.*

EN 13306:2010, *Maintenance – Maintenance terminology.*

EN 13460:2009, *Maintenance – Documentation for maintenance.*

EN 15221-1:2006, *Facility management – Terms and definitions.*

EN 15221-2:2006, *Facility management – Guidance on how to prepare facility management agreements.*

EN 15221-3:2011, *Facility management – Guidance on quality in facility management.*

EN 15221-4:2011, *Facility management – Taxonomy, classification and structures in facility management.*

EN 15221-5:2011, *Facility management – Guidance on facility management processes.*

EN 15221-6:2011, *Facility management – Area and space measurement in facility management.*

EN 15221-7:2012, *Facility management – Guidelines for performance benchmarking.*

Total Facility Management, Fourth Edition. Brian Atkin and Adrian Brooks.
© 2015 John Wiley & Sons, Ltd. Published 2015 by John Wiley & Sons, Ltd.

EN 15331:2011, *Criteria for design, management and control of maintenance services for buildings.*

EN 60300-3-11:2009, *Dependability management – Application guide – Reliability centred maintenance.*

International Standards

ISO 9000:2005, *Quality management systems – Fundamentals and vocabulary.*

ISO 9004:2009, *Managing for the sustained success of an organization – A quality management approach.*

ISO 10001:2007, *Quality management – Customer satisfaction – Guidelines for codes of conduct for organizations.*

ISO 10002:2004, *Quality management – Customer satisfaction – Guidelines for complaints handling in organizations.*

ISO 14001:2004, *Environmental management systems – Requirements with guidance for use.*

ISO 15392:2008, *Sustainability in building construction – General principles.*

ISO 15686-1:2011, *Buildings and constructed assets. Service life planning – General principles and framework.*

ISO 15686-2:2012, *Buildings and constructed assets. Service life planning – Service life prediction procedures.*

ISO 15686-10:2010, *Buildings and constructed assets. Service life planning – When to assess functional performance.*

ISO 22301:2012, *Societal security – Business continuity management systems: Requirements.*

ISO 22313:2012, *Societal security – Business continuity management systems: Guidance.*

ISO 31000:2009, *Risk management – Principles and guidelines.*

ISO 37500:2014, *Guidance on outsourcing.*

ISO 55000:2014, *Asset management – Overview, principles and terminology.*

ISO 55001:2014, *Asset management – Management systems – Requirements.*

ISO 55002:2014, *Asset management – Management systems – Guidelines for the application of ISO 55001.*

ISO/IEC 27001:2013, *Information technology – Security techniques – Information security management systems – Requirements.*

Publicly available specifications (precursors to British Standards)

PAS 1192-2:2013, *Specification for information management for the capital/delivery phase of construction projects using building information modelling.*

PAS 1192-3:2014, *Specification for information management for the operational phase of assets using building information modelling.*

References

Aaltonen, A., Määttänen, E., Kyrö, R. & Sarasoja, A.-L. (2013) Facilities management driving green building certification: a case from Finland. *Facilities*, 31(7/8), 328–42.

Alexander, K., Atkin, B.L., Bröchner, J. & Haugen, T. (eds) (2005) *Facilities Management: Innovation and Performance*. Spon, London.

Aronoff, S. & Kaplan, A. (1995) *Total Workplace Performance: Rethinking the Office Environment*. WDL Publications, Ottawa.

Atkin, B. & Björk, B.-C. (2007) Understanding the context for best practice facilities management from the client's perspective. *Facilities*, 25(13/14), 479–92.

Barrett, P.S. & Baldry, D. (2003) *Facilities Management: Towards Best Practice*, 2nd edn. Blackwell, Oxford.

BCO (2013) *Occupier Density Study*. British Council for Offices, London.

BSRIA (2009) *The Soft Landings Framework – for Better Briefing, Design, Handover and Building Performance In-Use*. BG 4/2009. BSRIA, Bracknell.

BSRIA (2011) *Building Manuals and Building User Guides*. BG 26/2011. BSRIA, Bracknell.

CABA (2002) *Technology Roadmap for Intelligent Buildings*. Continental Automated Buildings Association and National Research Council, Ottawa.

Carbon Trust (2007) *Building Controls: Realising Savings through the Use of Controls*. CTV032. Carbon Trust, London.

CIBSE (2006) *Building Log Book Toolkit*. TM31. CIBSE, London.

Clements-Croome, D. (ed.) (2000) *Creating the Productive Workplace*. Spon, London.

CoreNet (2012) *Corporate Real Estate Industry Portfolio Data: Economic and Buying Influence Indicators*. CoreNet Global, Inc., Atlanta, GA.

Eastman, C., Teicholz, P., Sacks, R. & Liston, K. (2011) *BIM Handbook: a Guide to Building Information Modeling for Owners, Managers, Designers, Engineers and Contractors*, 2nd edn, John Wiley, London.

Eriksson, P.E., Atkin, B.L. & Nilsson, T. (2009) Overcoming barriers to partnering through cooperative procurement procedures. *Engineering, Construction and Architectural Management*, 16(6), 598–611.

Gadde, L.-E. (1996) *Supplier Management in the Construction Industry: Working Papers*. Chalmers University of Technology, Gothenburg.

Total Facility Management, Fourth Edition. Brian Atkin and Adrian Brooks.
© 2015 John Wiley & Sons, Ltd. Published 2015 by John Wiley & Sons, Ltd.

Hofstede, G. (1991) *Cultures and Organisations: Software of the Mind – Inter-Cultural Cooperation and its Importance for Survival.* McGraw-Hill, New York.

HM Treasury (1996), *Estates and Buildings Procurement: Prevention of Fraud and Irregularity in the Award and Management of Contracts.* DAO letters, 17/96. Treasury Officer of Accounts team (TOA), HM Treasury, London.

Hon, C.K.H., Hinze, J.W. & Chan, A.P.C. (2014) Safety climate and injury occurrence of repair, maintenance, minor alteration and addition works: a comparison of workers, supervisors and managers. *Facilities,* 32(5/6), 188–207.

Kaplan, R.S. & Norton, D.P. (1996) *The Balanced Scorecard: Translating Strategy into Action.* Harvard Business School Press, Boston, MA.

Kelly, J., Male, S. & Drummond, G. (2004) *Value Management of Construction Projects.* Blackwell, Oxford.

Koivu, T., Tukiainen, S., Nummelin, J., Atkin, B. & Tainio, R. (2004) *Institutional Complexity Affecting the Outcomes of Global Projects.* Working paper, VTT, Espoo, Finland.

Leibfried, K.H.J. & McNair, C.J. (1994) *Benchmarking: a Tool for Continuous Improvement.* HarperCollins, London.

Leiringer, R. (2003) *Technological Innovations in the Context of Public–Private Partnership Projects.* Doctoral thesis, Department of Industrial Economics and Management, The Royal Institute of Technology (KTH), Stockholm.

NAO (1996) *Information Technology Services Agency: Outsourcing the Service Delivery Operations. Report by the Comptroller and Auditor General, National Audit Office.* HMSO, London.

Olander, S. & Atkin, B.L. (2010) Stakeholder management – the gains and pains. In: *Construction Stakeholder Management,* 15 (eds. E. Chinyio & P. Olomolaiye), 266–75. Wiley-Blackwell, Oxford.

Pande, P.S., Neuman, R.P. & Cavanagh, R.R. (2000) *The Six Sigma Way.* McGraw-Hill, New York.

Pennycook, K. (2001) *Effective BMS – a Guide to Improving System Performance.* BSRIA, Bracknell.

Purdey, B. (2013) Occupant stimulus response workplace productivity and the vexed question of measurement. *Facilities,* 31(11/12), 505–20.

Race, S. (2012) *BIM Demystified.* RIBA Publishing, London.

Richards, M. (2010) *Building Information Management. A Standard Framework and Guide to BS 1192.* BIP 2207. BSI, London.

Rostron, J. (ed.) (1997) *Sick Building Syndrome: Concepts, Issues and Practice.* Spon, London.

SMG (2006) *Space Management Project: Summary.* 2006/42, UK Higher Education Space Management Project, Space Management Group, University of Westminster, London.

Tan, Y., Shen, L., Langston, C., Lu, W. & Yam, M.C.H. (2014) Critical success factors for building maintenance business: a Hong Kong case study. *Facilities,* 32(5/6), 208–25.

Thompson, P. & Warhurst, C. (eds) (1998) *Workplaces of the Future.* Macmillan, Basingstoke.

Wikberg, F., Olofsson, T. & Ekholm, A. (2014) Design configuration with architectural objects: linking customer requirements with system capabilities in industrialized house-building platforms. *Construction Management and Economics*, 32(1–2), 196–207.

Williams, S. (2002) *Managing Workplace Stress.* John Wiley, London.

Wong, K. & Fan, Q. (2013) Building information modelling (BIM) for sustainable building design. *Facilities*, 31(3/4), 138–57.

INDEX

References to figures are given in italic type. References to tables are given in bold type.

3D CAD, 324, 327
4D simulation, 328
accident(s), 198
  book, 89, 90
  causes, 76, 93
  prevention, 74
  reporting, 89, 139
  response procedures, 285, 319
  zero accidents policy, 88, 139
accommodation strategy, 48, 332
  see also space strategy
accounting, 17, 53, 114, 138, 171
  cost, 239
  open-book, 112, 114, 136–138,
    161, 179, 363
  policy, 316
  see also budgets; cost; financial
    appraisal
action research, 294
activities, 4–7, *6*, 332
adaptability, 24–25, 32, 262, 332
added value, 73, 94, 184, 332
aerospace industry, 229–231
agency personnel, 103, 108, 110,
  116, 169, 332
air conditioning, 251
air quality, 75–76
annual review, 104, 140, 163
  maintenance strategy, 221, 223,
    227, 237

approved persons, 48
as subsequently altered information,
    234–235, 239, 258, 316,
    322–323
as-built information, 32, 316–317,
    321–322, 324, 332
asbestos, 88, 224, 253
asset(s), 186–187, 332
  management, 2, 239, 333
  register, 237–238
assistance procedures, 319
attitude surveys, 103, 333
audits, 50–53
  compliance, 168, 335
  information, 307–308
  market, **48**, **49**, 52–53, 140
  portfolio and space, 50–51
  resources, 52–53
  services, 52–53
  skills, 241
Autodesk AutoCAD, 327
autonomous agents *see* cyber-agents

BACnet, 236, 267, 333
Balanced Scorecard, The, 213
barcodes, 256, 259
basis for design, 27, 32, 333
benchmarking, 8, 193, 208–209,
    216, 230, 321, 333
  best practice and, 209–210

Total Facility Management, Fourth Edition. Brian Atkin and Adrian Brooks.
© 2015 John Wiley & Sons, Ltd. Published 2015 by John Wiley & Sons, Ltd.

best value and, 12, 44
clubs, 53, 140, 212
continual improvement and, 210
cost estimation and, 210
excessive, 45
facility management, **49**, 212–214
informed client function and, 8
maintenance and, 223
outsourcing and, **49**
partnering and, 176, 209
process, 210–212
space efficiency and, 25, 51
standards and, 317
see also performance targets
Bentley, 327
best practice, 12, 109, 209–210,
    218, 306
awareness of, 44, 126, 151
continual improvement and, 210
facility management benchmarking
    and, 212
human resources management, 55
performance measurement and,
    193, 200, 212–213, 214
practices inconsistent with, 112,
    113, 118
procurement policy and, 124
service specifications and, 134, **135**
best value, 3, 6–8, 12–13, 59, 333
cooperation and, 16
facility management strategy, 45,
    51, 54
maintenance, 222, 224, 226, 227
ownership models, 44
partnering, 176, 178, 182, 188–190
performance management,
    199–200, 210, 216
procurement, 127, 134, 138,
    140, 141, 145
risk and, 4, 7
service delivery, 98, 103, 106,
    118, 148, 159, 160
space management, 25
see also cost
best-in-class comparators, 211, 212
beta test, 168
bicycles, 320

BIM *see* building information models
Bluetooth, 260
bonds, 185, 364
BOOT contracts, 181
BOT contracts, 30–31, 181
BPR, **49**, 335
breakdown maintenance, 229, 333
BREEAM, 35, 250
briefing, 26–27, 333, 348
functional brief, 31–32
plans, 333
budget
approval, 283
best practice and, 44
business case and, 27
contingency costing, 284
contract cost and, 148
cuts, 6, 123
financial review, 197–198
fixed, 30
indicative, 29
information management, 315–316
levels, 66
managed, 97, 110, 112–113, **116**,
    117, **117**, 345
public-private partnerships (PPP), 30
service delivery and, 52, 57
space servicing and, 51
transition, 276, 279, 282–283,
    288, 296
see also accounting; financial
    appraisal
build operate and transfer (BOT)
    contracts, 30–31, 181
buildability, 334
building
automation, 243, 267, 333
energy management systems (BEMS),
    242, 251, 259, 265, 334
fabric, 313, 334
information models (BIM), 34,
    266, 303, 324–325, 334
retrospective, 327
standards and protocols, 324–325
intelligence, 164, 170, 334
see also intelligent buildings
logbooks, 231–232, 240, 334

building (*cont'd*)
management systems, 236, 328
manuals, 232, 317, 334
modular, 262, 264, 267, 270
obsolescence, 260–261, 266
services engineering, 15, 34, 175,
222–223, 233–235, 317, 334
BuildingSMART, 325
bundled services, **10**, 104, 115
buried services, 259
business
context, 44–45
continuity, 23, 154–155, 162, 238,
276–277, 321, 334
disruption, 147, 148
maintenance and, 15, 221,
223, 240
management, 2, 154–155,
280, 291, 335
service delivery and, 289
transition and, 255, 273, 274,
276–277, 298
core *see* core business
non-core, 6–7, 51–52, 54, 100, 105,
165, 180, 315
objectives, 27, 46, 99–100, 292–293
change management and, 271,
275, 293
cooperation and, 16, 177
CREM and, 21
environmental management
and, 271
facility management strategy and,
18, 42, 43, 48, 50, 54, 99–100
innovation and, 297, 298, 303
maintenance and, 221–222, 223,
225, 226, 239, 240
performance management and, 58,
64, 67, 159, 199–201, 215, 216
risk and, 7
stakeholder engagement and, 149
plan, 6, 48–49, 50, 180, *293*
processes, 52, 78, 99–100, 122,
305, 315, 320
re-engineering (BPR), **49**,
293, 294, 335
strategy, 6, 21, 42, 45–46, 48, 50, 57, 303

cables, 259
CAD, 324, 327–328
CAFM, 302, 303, 305, 325, 327–329
call centres, 71, 74
car parking, 320
carbon
emissions, 27
equivalent, 31, 32, 35, 36, 249
footprint, 13, 27, 32, 248–249, 335
management, 29, 35, 335
metric, 335
operational carbon, 346
targets, 262–263
zero, 248, 262, 354
case studies
aerospace corporation, 229–231
global consultancy, 80–82
cashflow, 163
catering, 194
cellular offices, 81
change
communication, 295
control, 160–161, 274–275, 288
management, 3, 14, 17, 292–294, 345
communication, 295
organizational change, 292–293
roles and responsibilities,
295–296
routine change, 292
transition process, 275–276
see also transition
manager, 279, 294–296, 298
process, 274, 289, 293–295
cleaning, 132, 134–137, **136**, 174,
194, 197, 205
client, 8–9, 335
organisation *see* informed client
function
public sector, 182–183
representatives *see* managing agent
climate
change, 243
exterior, 51
indoor, 236, 259–260, 269
clinical systems, 169
co-sourcing, 6, 7, 14, 104, 337
COBie, 325–326

codes of accounts, 315, 335
collaborative relationships, 174–179
    see also partnering; public-private
        partnerships
commercial information, 314
commissioning, 39, 234, 252, 267,
        323, 326, 342
    briefs and, 26, 29–34, 340
    tender process and, **358**
communication, **49**, 74, 295, 319
    change, 295
    failure, 230
    horizontal, 71, 73
    ICT and, 151, 254, 257
    information management and,
        302, 303, 308, 318
    inter-departmental, 31
    interpersonal, 65
    managerial, 48, 319
    obstruction, 76, 79
    plan, 39, 221
    with service providers, 56, 102,
        126, 138, **138**, 153, 156
    space planning and, 83
    stakeholder, 276
    structure, 23
    systems, 233, 255, 300
    upward, 47, 71
    wireless, 259, 269
communities, 262–263
competence
    core, 16–17, 21, 64–65, 104, 167
    stripping, 189
competent persons, 85, 87, 91,
        335, 344
competition, 45, 73, 127, 174, 361
    for goods and services, 100
    partnering and, 176, 189
    for resources, 243
    for talent, 63, 66
    see also tendering
competitive advantage, 7
competitiveness, 21, 71, 82, 125, 140,
        151, 215, 351
compliance audits, 168, 335
computer-aided design (CAD), 324,
        327–328

computer-aided facility management
        (CAFM), 302, 303, 325,
        327–329
computerized maintenance
        management system
        (CMMS), 230–231, 238,
        241, 325, 336
concessionaire, 233
concessions, 30, 35, 181
condition surveys, 223, *225*, 226,
        227, 317, 327, 336, 347
conflict, 93, 94
    avoidance, 47, 143, 149, 208
    resolution, 81
conflicts of interest, 9, 114, 125,
        149, 159, 166, 359
constructability, 13
construction
    specifications, 222, 323, 324
    subcontracting, 185–186
Construction Operations Building
        information exchange
        (COBie), 325–326
contingency planning, 87, 104,
        280, 283–284, 286–287,
        290, 336, 361
continual improvement, 44, 71,
        138, 174, 210, 289, 336
    commitment to, 126, 159, 178,
        193, 217
    contract administration and, 161
    culture of, 56, 165, 231, 291
    definition, 336
    environmental management
        system, 246
    facility manager and, 216, 341
    partnering and, 209
    performance management and,
        193, 199, 200
    targets and, 189
continuing professional development
        (CPD), 10, 18, 60, 65–66, 109
contracting out *see* outsourcing
contracts, 102, 139
    administration, 144, 155, 156,
        161, 163, 286
    annual review, 140

contracts (*cont'd*)
  award, 55, 123, 125, 142, 144–145,
    146, 153
    budget and, 283
    requirements, 362
  conditions, 143, 156, 357, 358
  cost control, 158
  documentation, 10, 358, 363
  management, 3, 5, 7, *8*,
    125, 155–161
  negotiation, 55, 143
  partnering, 177
  payment, 157
  pre-contract meetings, 141
  procurement, 139
  public-private partnerships,
    181–182
  review, 148, 161
  standard forms, 132, 144, 177
  sum, 108, 157, 158, 197, 226, 282, 315
  transition, 280–281
  see also tenders
cooperative arrangements *see*
    partnering
core business, 6, 293
  facility management and, 4, 6, 13,
    147, 148, 182, 213, 320
  information management and,
    303, 304, 305, 308, 316
  non-core business and, 6, 6, 52,
    54, 100
  outsourcing, 105
  service levels and, 200
  stress and, 94
  transition management, 152, 321
core competence, 16–17, 64
corporate
  governance, 10, 122
  real estate management (CREM),
    17, 21, 337
    see also real estate management
  social responsibility (CSR), 11, 27,
    29, 34, 124–125, 128, 130, 221
    definition, 336
    sustainability and, 242, 247–248
corrective action, 336
corrective maintenance, 229, 337

cost
  analysis, 50
  benefit analysis, **49**
  direct, 105, 108, 116, 175, 274,
    282, 283
    transition management, 274,
      282, 283
  estimation, 34–35
    benchmarking and, 210
    contingency, 284
    direct costs, 108
    outsourcing, 108
    transition, 282–283
  indirect, 98, 105, 108–109, 111,
    115, 119, 175
    transition management, 274,
      282–283
  life-cycle *see* cost, whole-life
  operational, 13, 24–25, 27, 30–31,
    35, 79, 246, 249
  price and, 53
  value for money, 12–13
  whole-life, 32, 35–36, 142, 182,
    249, 261, 264
    maintenance and, 221, 225
CPD, 10, 18, 60, 65–66, 109
credit reference agencies, 129, 152
critical activities, 122, 337
critical environments, 229, 237, 337
critical path, 281, 284, 337
critical success factor (CSF), 46,
    64, 100, 125, 173, 199–200,
    210–211, 337
cross-culture, 47–48
culture
  organisational, 4–5, 7, 60, 72, 73, 198
    of continual improvement, 56,
      165, 178, 231
    of innovation, 296, 297
    poor, 94
    service providers, 129–130
  regional and national, 45, 47–48, 51
custodial services, 93, 170–171, 337
customer charters, 151
customers, 337
  end-users and, 184
  external, 89, 99, 106, 149, 181, 187

internal, 106, 149–150, 162
service providers, 166
services, 12, 80, 166
as stakeholders, 247
see also end-user
cyber-agents, 257, 258, 267, 337

data, 307
capture, 197
protection, 309–310
data drops, 323–324, 326, 337
data elements, 338
DBFO contracts, 181
de-layering, 24, 71, 293, 338
deadlines, 281–282
debt finance, *183*, 184, 185
deliverables, 338
delivery logistics, 258
demobilization, *123*, 147, 274,
    286–288, 338
design
    brief, 23, 27, 28–29, 30
    briefing, 2, 20, 41, 193–195,
        221, 252, 338
    change control, 35–36
    development, 35–36
    evaluation, 32
    facility management
        briefing and, 26–34
    for operability, 20–21
design and build contracts, 21,
    185, 371
design, build, finance, operate
    (DBFO) contracts, 181
detainee care, 171
development (and research), 76,
    296–298
digital divide, 265
disabled people, 15, 50, 60, 67, 89,
    101, 319
    inclusive design and, 25, 31, 32,
        50, 129
    information requirements, 62,
        308, 311, 314
    legislation covering, 15, 62
disaster recovery, 23, 168, 169, 339
discounting, 112

dispute resolution, 125
disruptive change, 292
documents, 338
    management, 258, 304, 338
    tracking, 258
downsizing, 24, 46, 71, 293, 339
drawings, 33, 322
drug testing, 171
duties
    contractual, 156, 178
    corporate social responsibility
        and, 130
    human resources planning, 61
    logbook and, 231
    separation of, 10, 356, **359**
    service providers, 92, 139
    statutory, 15, 36, 87, 171, 199,
        285, 319

e-tags, 258
    see also RFID tags
e-tendering, 141
education
    change communication, 295
    end-users, 252, 268
    facility management, 9, 17,
        65–66, 109
    skills development, 10, 18,
        56, 60, 64, 109
efficiency gains, 54, 179
electronic data interchange (EDI), 257
embedded technology, 244, 259,
    265, 267
emergency maintenance, 229
empowerment, 63, 66, 67, 71, 73, 339
end-users, 137
    internal customer as, 149
    public-private partnerships, 184
    satisfaction, 3–4
        informed client function and, 8–9
    service, 106
        quality assessment, 202–203
    service review, 196
    stakeholders as, 101–103
energy
    consumption, 243, 250, 262, 263
        design and, 32, 266, 269

energy (*cont'd*)
  prediction, 249
  records of, 238, 318
  services installations and, 233,
    236, 251, 254
costs, 251, 260
efficiency, 32, 35, 228, 248,
    250–251, 270, 334
  building energy management,
    242, 251
  see also zero carbon
management systems, 242,
    251, 259, 265, 334
performance, 34, 35, 232, 242,
    250–251, 319, 328–329
certificates, 318
saving, 249, 250, 271, 311
  see also sustainability
engineering services, 15, 175
enterprise resource planning, 197–198
environmental factors, 68, 83, 223
  see also climate
environmental performance, 246,
    250, 317
  intelligent buildings, 253–255
European Bank for Reconstruction and
    Development (EBRD), 185
European Investment Bank (EIB), 185

facility handbook, 31, 33–34, 309,
    310–311, 340
  see also building manual
facility maintenance *see* maintenance
facility management
  analysis, *8*, 43, *48*, 50, 50–53,
    54, 57
  approaches, 7
  benchmarking, 212–213
  brief, 20, 26, 29–30, 40, 41, 194, 340
  contract, 341
  dashboard, 206–207
  definition, 5–6
  implementation, 9, 12, 43, *48*, **49**,
    55–56
  origins, 4–5
  scope, 2, 5, 6
    creep, 101

of services, 54, 99, 103–104, 119,
    120, 161, 165, 278
service provider *see* service
    providers
strategy, 43–44, 98, 104, 221,
    222, 246
  business context, 44–45
  cross-cultural, 47–49
  drivers and constraints, 45–46
  formulation, 48–50, 100, 193
  human resources and, 59
  implementation, 55–6
  information management
    strategy and, 303
  maintenance and, 219, 221, 222
  outsourcing and, 161, 171
  procurement and, 122, 126
  solution development, 53–54
  stages, 12
  techniques and tools, **49**
facility manual *see* building manual
facility planning, 13, 18, 19–41, 341
  as-built information, 32–33
  design briefing, 26–34
  design development, 35–36
  feasibility study, 34–35
  operability, 13
  real estate management, 21–23
  serviced workplaces, 22–23
  space efficiency, 25
  space management, 23
  space utilization, 24–25
  stakeholder impact, 38–39
  sustainability, 24–26
  work environment, 74–78
feasibility studies, 34–35, 341
financial
  appraisal, 128–129, 197–198
  controls, 18, 156, 171, 198, 213,
    276, 283
    maintenance, 226–227, 239
  information, 314–315
  management, 17
  objectives, 221
fire precautions, 90–91, 235
first aid, 90
fitness for purpose, 13, 35, 226

flawless start-up, 20, 34, 341
flexibility
    design, 24, 25, 32
    ICT use, 74
    management, 30
    real estate, 262
    service assessment and, 205
    service contracts, 121, 124, 136,
        159, 162, 182
    service delivery, 96, 105, 106,
        107–108, 113, 114, **116**
    service providers, 167
    space utilization, 78, 81, 82,
        260–262
    strategy, 46
    working patterns, 7, 72, 74, 80,
        87, 115, 246
        division of labour, 230
forensic services, 168, 171
framework agreements, 139, 177, 341
fraud, 9, 355–360
freedom of information, 125, 309–310
functional brief, 20, 27, 31–32, 341

gain-sharing, 177, 179, 190
Gantt chart, 281–282
gateways, 342
governance, 279–280
government aid, public-private
        partnerships, 185
GPS, 259
Graphisoft ArchiCAD, 327
green agenda, 248
    see also sustainability
Green Deal, 250–251
green leases, 34, 313, 342

hand-arm vibration syndrome
        (HAVS), 88
handover, 342
    see also commissioning
hard issues, 5
hazards, 91, 92–93, 238, 280, 285, 342
health, safety, security and
        environment (HSSE), 85,
        87–88, 286, 342
    briefing, 285

change management and, 293
compliance, 89, 152, 163, 233
fire precautions, 90–91
incentives and, 139
inclusivity and, 129
information management, 152,
        307, 309, 312, 314, 318, 319
legislation, 124, 237, 318
maintenance and, 220, 221, 224,
        231, 233
noticeboards, 89
policies, 27, 128, 129, 309
procurement and, 129
reporting, 89–90, 198
responsibilities, 125
risk assessment, 91, 92–93
    see also risk, assessment
training, 90
zero accidents, 88, 139
health-care services, 164, 169–170, 259
    telecare, 268–270
healthy living, 265–266
heating, 76, 107–108, 233, 236, 334
helpdesks, 106, 121, 153, 161, 175,
        317, 319–320, 342
    ICT, 166, 167
homeworking, 72, 81, 82
hot-desking, 21, 23, 78, 80
hotelling, 78
housing, 265–266
    multi-storey, 266–267
    quality, 267
human resources, 73–74, 342
    management, 3, 5, 14–15, 17,
        59–60, 155, 214
        access, inclusion and equality, 62–63
        employment obligations, 62
        empowerment, 63
        job competences and skills, 63–64
        performance appraisal, 64–65
        personal development, 65–66
        talent management, 63
    managers, 171
    performance review, 198–199
    planning, 60–61
    strategy, 73
HVAC, 233, 236, 334

ICT *see* information and
    communications technology
IDEF, 305, 342
IFC, 325–326, 329, 342
in-house provision *see* insourcing
incentives, 9, 125, 132, 138, 148, 315, 342
  HSSE performance and, 139
  individuals, 64
  service providers and suppliers,
    159, 173, 174–175, 189
  sustainability and, 264, 313
inclusive design, 25, 31, 32, 50,
  129, 269, 270
indemnities, 172–173, 191, 285
Industry Foundation Class (IFC),
  325–326, 342
information
  audits, 307–308
  categories, 307
  handover, 291, 323, 343
  management, 15, 302–303, 343
    budgets, 315–316
    commercial information, 314
    data collection and, 321
    drawings, 322–323
    financial information, 314–315
    health, safety, security and
     environment (HSSE), 152,
     307, 309, 312, 314, 318, 319
    legal information, 312–313
    managerial information, 319–320
    plans, 303–304, 343
    policy, 309
    processes, 305–306
    security, 309–310
    strategy, 308–309
    success factor, 306–307
    technical information, 316–318
    see also facility handbook
  systems, 164, 165, 169, 227,
    304, 306, 309
information and communications
  technology (ICT), 5, 51, 64,
  121, 137, 151, 166–167, 316
  applications, 167–168
  benchmarking and, 209
  budget management and, 112

change management and, 17, 293, 294
design information, 322
financial reporting and, 316
homeworking and, 72, 81
household access, 265, 268
information management and, 64,
  109, 209, 304–305, 308, 311, 318
infrastructure, 167
interconnectivity, 267
maintenance management,
  230, 231
performance management, 50,
  94, 151, 206
performance reporting, 192, 206
performance testing, 168–169
procurement and, 122, 125
productivity and, 69, 70, 74, 82
re-engineering, 24, 26
resource audit and, 52
resource planning and, 56
security and, 168–169, 197
service level agreements (SLA), 172
service providers, 164
skills, 65
space utilization and, 24, 51, 260, 261
strategy, 54
support personnel, 306
see also computer-aided facility
  management (CAFM)
informed client function, 4, 55, 61,
  109–110, 126, 147, 216, 343
  scope, 8
  service level agreements and, 133
innovation, 17, 296–298
  service provision, 131, **131**, **142**, 205
  technological, 72, 100
insourcing, 1, 148–151, 342, 343
  costs, 108, 109, 167, **214**
  job functions, 67
  outsourcing and, 98, 110, 140,
    162, 188
  service delivery, 148, 162
  training and, 60
  transition and, 55, 273, 274, 277,
    285, 286, 297
  see also co-sourcing
inspections, 313

insurance, 143, 144, 171, 172–173, 186, 191, 285–286, 314
  proof of, 89, 320, 364
  public-private partnerships (PPP), 186
intelligent buildings, 236, 243–244, 253–254, 270, 343
  see also buildings, intelligence
intelligent client *see* informed client function
internal rate of return (IRR), 249
internal stakeholders, 36–37
International Facility Management Association, 5
international standards, 2, 65, 105, 329, 368
internet, 254, 257, 267, 337
interoperability, 238, 306, 329, 343
interpreter services, 171
intranets, 206, 254, 318–320
invention, 297
inventory, 33, 238, 241
  management, 255, 256, 257, 308
irregularity 61, 9, 307, 355, *see also* fraud
ISO *see* international standards

job
  competences and skills, 63–64, 66, 67
  satisfaction, 63, 72–73, 79
  security, 71, 72

key performance indicator (KPI), 192, 193, 199–200, 202–203, 316, 343
  environmental management, 246
  facility management strategy and, 54
  identification, 209, 217, 318
  in-house team, 156
  maintenance planning, 223, 226, 239
  performance management and, 193
  personal appraisal and, 64–65
key roles, 15–16
knowledge
  management, 263
  work, 69, 71, 74, 261

landscape design, 171
law, 171

Leadership in Energy and Environmental Design (LEED), 35, 250
learning
  curves, 287
  lifelong, 64
    see also continual improvement
leases, 21–22
  green, 313, 342
legal issues
  advice, 186, 312–313
    public-private partnerships (PPP), 186
  challenges, 362
  entities, 184, 341, 345
  information, 33, 232, 301, 310, 312–313, 317–318, 329
  responsibilities and obligations, 16, 62, 130, 199, 232, 245, 317–318, 322
  support functions, 80, 137
  title, 16
legislation, 264
letters of intent, 344
life-cycle
  assessment, 246
  costs *see* whole life costs
  monitoring throughout, 265
  perspective, 20
  phases, 26, *26*, 323, 324, 328, 329, 353
    operational, 346
  risks, 92
  tracking, 258–259
  value chain, 256
lighting, 76
Likert scale, 196, 344
logbooks, 231–232
logistics, 258, 268, 344

maintenance
  clinical systems, 169
  contracts, 158, 355
  management, 5, 15, 21, 219–241
    see also computer-aided maintenance management
  manuals, 236–237, 344
  methods, 227–231

maintenance (*cont'd*)
  planned preventive, 158, 200, **202**,
    205, 227–231, 265, 347
  plans, 222–227, 344
  policy, 221–222
  reliability centred, 228–229, 349
  special equipment, 158
  specialized, 106
  strategy, 221, 344
  unplanned, 158, **203**, **204**,
    229–230, 240, 353
  vehicle, 57, 177
managed budget, 97, 110, 112–113,
    116, 117, **117**, 345
management
  change *see* change management
  of contracts, 3, 5, 7, 8, 125, 155–161
  information *see* information
    management
  maintenance *see* maintenance
    management
  operational, 47, 197, 205–206
  organizational levels, 46–47
  real estate *see* real estate
    management
  strategic, 46
  tactical, 46–47
managerial information, 319–320
managing
  agents, 97, 110–115, 126, 139, 345
  contractors, 97, 111–113, **116**,
    117, 345
manuals
  of authorities, 124–125, 308, 310,
    312, 314, 345
  maintenance, 236–237, 344
manufacturing, 265
market
  audit, **48**, **49**, 52–53, 140
  testing, **49**, 98, 118, 140
mass customization, 260, 266
mentoring, 56
menu of prices, 114
metrics, 292, 345
Micro-Scan*fm*, 212–213
Microsoft SQL, 327
milestones, 100, 122–123, 281, 286, 345

mission
  critical services, 166, 172
  critical systems, 166, 169
mixed economy, 7
  see also co-sourcing
mobilization, 7, 8, 141, 142, 152–155,
    284, 286–288, 345
  periods, 144, 147, 148
  plans, 163, 274, 286–287, 299
modular building, 260, 261, 262,
    264, 267, 269, 270
morale, 45, 71–72
motivation, 17, 65, 73, 98, 133, 154
multi-skilled personnel, 109, 230
multinational organizations,
    44–45, 47–48
MySQL, 327

nanotechnology, 259
national owner-operators, 44
neighbours, 37, 245
networks, 166, 167
  automation and control, 236,
    267, 333
  sensor, 259–260
  social, 328
  virtual private, 72, 254
  wireless, 259
non-core business, 6–7, 51–52, 54,
    100, 105, 165, 180, 315
  see also support services
noticeboards, 89

obsolescence, 260–261, 266
occupational health, 88–89
office
  automation, 254, 345
  design, 77–78
    case study, 80–82
    open-plan, 78–80, **136**
  work, 71
offshoring, 104–105
  see also outsourcing
open-book accounting, 112, 114,
    136–138, 161, 179, 346, 363
open-plan offices, 78–80, **136**
operability, 13, 346

operating level agreements (OLA), 133, 346
operational carbon, 346
operational management, 47
  service assessment, 205–206
  service review, 197
operational phase, 250, 256, 346
operators, 16, 346
  public-private partnerships (PPP), 185–186
opportunities, **10**
optimization, **49**
option evaluation matrix, 116–118, **116**
out-of-office working, 72
  see also teleworking
outcomes, 346
output specification, 134, 188, 191, 318
outsourcing, 7, 14, 98–99, 149, 151–152, 277, 346
  business objectives and, 99–100
  control, 109
  cost estimation, 108
  facility management strategy and, **49**, 54, 55
  flexibility, 107–108
  health-care services, 164, 169–170
  human resources and, 59, 62, 71
  ICT, 166–169
  informed client function and, 8
  insourcing and, 188
  market testing, 140
  markets for facility-related services, 117–118
  option evaluation matrix, 116–118
  professional services, 171–172
  recruitment services, 171–172
  relationship with service provider, 106
  risks, 114, 122, 172–173, 285, 361–362
  service delivery, 109–115
    managed budget, 112–113
    managing agents, 110–111
    managing contractor, 111–112
    total facility management, 113–114
  service provision attributes, 105–106

service uniqueness, 106–107
single versus multiple services, 115–116
sourcing policy, 104
transition to/from, 55, 273, 276, 280, 285
see also insourcing; public-private partnerships (PPP)
overheads, 112, 140, 150
owner-operators, 44–45
owners, 16, 21–22, 346

partnering, 16, 109, 165–166, 176–178, **176**, 191, 230, 346
  benchmarking, 209
  performance appraisal, 178
  risk, 178–179
  see also public-private partnerships (PPP)
passive systems, 31, 253, 260, 266–267
patient transport services, 169
payments, 52, 112, 157–159
  approval, 124
  contractual, 125, 156, 286
  fraud prevention, 356
  ICT support, 168
  performance-related, 63, 138, 156, 163, 363
  public-private partnerships (PPP), 187
  service providers, 61, 153
penalties, 125, 132, 139, 202, 312, **315**, **359**
  financial malpractice, 283
  for legislative violation, 9, 202, 240
  performance-based, 125, 139, 148, 361
  service level agreements, 121, **138**, 148
  turnaround contracts, 228
penetration tests, 172, 346
performance
  appraisal, 64–65, 158–159, 201–205, 347
    partnering, 178
  bonus payments, 63, 138, 156, 163, 363
  management, 14, 139–140, 193–194

performance (*cont'd*)
  benchmarking, 208–209
  see also benchmarking
  critical success factor, 199
  data collection, 203
  facility management dashboard,
    206–207
  human resources, 198–199
  key performance indicator (KPI),
    193, 199–200
  post-implementation reviews,
    194–195
  quality and, 194
  service reviews, 196–198,
    197–198
  measurement, 61, 78, 94, 132,
    160, 194, 202, 224
  see also key performance
    indicator (KPI)
  objectives, 64
  reporting, 205
  specification, 134
  targets, 134–135
  see also benchmarking
performance-based systems, 136,
    318, 347
permits-to-work, 92, 108, 232,
    237, 239, 285, 347
personal development, 65–66
personal protective equipment (PPE),
    91, 239, 328
personnel (agency), 103, 110, 169, 332
PEST, **49**
pipes, 259
planned preventive maintenance,
    227–231, 347
planning *see* facility planning
planning and scheduling, 56, 93,
    227, 294
policy-making, 46–47
pollution, 75, 196, 245
post-implementation reviews,
    194–195, 291, 320, 347
post-occupancy evaluation (POE),
    291, 320, 347
power/interest matrix, 38, *38*
PPE, 91, 239, 328

PPP *see* public-private partnerships
pre-contract meetings, 121, 141,
    144, 146, 154
price, 53
primary activities, 347
private sector organizations, 10–11
procedure, 134
process modelling, **49**, 295,
    305–306, 330
procurement, 14, 122–123, 348
  assessment criteria, 130–131
  best value, 102
  brief, 29
  centralized versus decentralized,
    123–124
  collaborative, 174
  consortium, 177
  contracts, 139
  corporate social responsibility, 130
  cultural fit, 129–130
  financial appraisal, 128–129
  financial close, 142–145
  fraud and irregularity, 355–360
  local versus national service
    providers, 127
  new facility, 20, 21
  performance measurement, 139–140
  policy and procedures, 124–125, 348
  process, 122–123
  public, 105, 125, 141, **358**
  public-private partnerships, 181
    see also public-private
      partnerships
  requests for information (RFI),
    127–128
  requests for proposals or tender,
    131–133
  service level agreements, 137–138
    see also service level agreements
  service specifications, 131–132,
    133–137
    see also service specifications
  services, 43, 56, 110
  strategy, 98, 102, 118, 276
  tender competitions 140-1, *see also*
    tendering
  see also outsourcing

product life-cycle tracking, 258–259
productivity, 24, 83, 101, 102, 108,
        198, 247, 353
    change and, 293
    communication and, 74
    ICT and, 168, 254, 327
    measurement, 69–70, 200, 239, 328
    morale and, 71–72
    nature of work, 70–72
    organization, 73
    performance and, 148
    rewards and, 72–73
    stress and, 93–95
    working arrangements, 78–80, 230
    workplace environment, 45,
        73–74, 254
        design issues, 77–78
        internal climate, 75–76
        sick building syndrome, 76–77
professional services, 171–172
progress reporting, 288
project
    brief *see* briefing
    execution strategy/plan, 29, 348
    management, 273, 275, 281
provision, 348
public procurement, 105, 125, 141, **358**
public sector organizations, 11, 165,
        176, 180, 190, 365
    outsourcing, 14
    tendering procedure, 121, 132
    see also public-private partnerships
        (PPP)
public-private partnerships (PPP), 30,
        165–166, 179–183, 190, 348
    bondholders, 185
    construction contractors, 185
    contracts, 181–182
    debt finance, 185
    end-users, 184
    equity providers, 184–185
    facility management, 187–189
    financial advice, 186
    government aid, 185
    insurance, 186
    issues, 189
    legal advice, 186

partnership categories, 180–181
    build, operate and transfer
        (BOT), 181
    payment, 187
    procurement, 181
    project company, 184
    public sector clients, 182–183
    regulatory bodies, 183–184
    risk, 188–189
    specialist advice, 186
purchase orders, 108, 143, 162, 197,
        282, 283, 316
purchasing, 17, 245, 287
    split responsibility, 9, 37, 357
    utility supplies, 12, 177
    see also procurement

quality
    assurance, 52, 215
    control, 320, 348
        performance and, 194
        thresholds, 134, 134–135
    systems, 215–216
questionnaires, 92, 101, 103, 127,
        195, 211, 213, 344

radio frequency identification (RFID)
        tagging *see* RFID
radiology, 169
re-engineering, **49**, 335
reactive maintenance, 229, 349
real estate
    acquisition, 21, 39, 53, 351
    management, 21
        flexibility, 260–263
        ownership versus renting, 21–22
        serviced workplaces, 22–23
        space management, 23
recovery (disaster/incident), 23,
        168, 169, 339
recruitment, 17, 59, 63, 150
    services, 171–172
    see also agency personnel
redundancy (employment), 62
redundancy (engineering)
    data, 310, 311
    supply chain, 9

regional facilities owner-operators, 44
regulatory bodies, 183–184
  compliance review, 199
reliability centred maintenance
    (RCM), 228–229, 349
remedial work, 349
reprographics, 205
request for information (RFI),
    127–128, 141–142
research and development, 296–298
research findings, 34, 72
resources, 306
  audit, 52–53
responsiveness
  to change, 243, 254–255, 271
  to service failure, 107–108
retraining, 17, 59, 65
retrofitting, 250, 260, 266
reward, 72, 138, 178
  allocation, 9, 10
  extrinsic and intrinsic, 72
  performance-related, 60, 64, 66,
    72–73, 94, 133, 159, 202
    inappropriate, 139
  sharing, 165, 177
  specification, 121
RFID tagging, 255–260, 270, 349
  second-generation, 257
risk, **8–9**, 55, 349
  allocation, 101
  analysis, 49, 189, 276
  assessment, 18, 39, 89, 90, 91,
    92–93, 349
    change control and, 160
    high-priority services, 107–109
    ICT services, 168, 309
    indemnity and, 172, 189
    permit-to-work and, 232, 347
    procurement and, 122
    service mobilization, 154
    space audit, **49**
    transition, 276–277, 284, 285
    zero accidents policy and, 88
  best value and, 4, 7
  downside, **8**, 39
  exposure, 22, 119, 169, 189,
    261, 280, 290, 307

fire, 90
life cycle, 92
management, 186, 349
mitigation, 55, 191, 335
outsourcing, 4, 114, 122, 172–173,
    285, 361–362
partnering arrangements, 178–179
proposals for tender and, 132–133
public-private partnerships (PPP),
    188–189
sharing, 12, 107, 165, 177
specialist services, 172–173
transfer, 188–191
upside, **9**, 39
routine change, 292
running costs *see* operational costs

safe systems of work, 285, 344
safety *see* health, safety, security and
    environment (HSSE)
safety management, 86, 236, 255
satellite centres, 72
satellite communications, 254
satisfaction rating, 65, 200, 204
Scandinavia, 45, 264
scenario analysis, 277, 350
scope creep, 101, 103, 350
scope of work, 32, 350
security, 32, 52, 77, 93–95, 170, 319
  building access, 285
  building intelligence and, 164, 254
  information and communications
    technology (ICT), 164, 166,
    168–169, 170, 197, 346
  information management and,
    309–310, **359**
  protection of individuals, 93
  reporting, 197, 198, 205, 212
  RFID tags and, 254, 260
  service providers, *175*, 210
  systems, 233, 235, 236, 243, 251, 311
  see also health, safety, security and
    environment (HSSE)
self-delivery, 114
sensor combinations, 259
sensor networks, 259–260
service concepts, 261

service delivery, 148–149
  bundled, 10, 104, 115
  change control, 160–161
  collaborative, 174–176
  contract administration, 161
  insourcing, 150–151
  mobilization, 152–153
    plan, 153–154
  partnering, 176–178
  performance reviews, 159–160
  post-implementation review, 289
service level agreements (SLA),
    101–102, 120–121, 137–138,
    145, 316, 350
  changes to, 192, 199
  contract review, 161
  customer charters, 151
  division of responsibilities, 162
  drafting, 55, 137–138, 145, 171,
    172, 190, 223
  facility handbook and, 314
  failure, 173
  ICT services, 166
  performance management, 148,
    192, 193, 197, 199
  performance monitoring, 163,
    201–205, 216, 316
  rationale for, 133, 165
  review, 161, 199, 290
  sections, 366
  security systems, 170
  service specifications and, 133–134
  specialist services, 172
  stakeholder engagement,
    101–102, 170
service providers, 92, 341, 350
  communication with, 56, 102,
    126, 138, **138**, 153, 156
  duties, 92, 139
  failure, 9, 129
  flexibility, 167
  HSSE and, 129
  incentives, 159, 173, 174–175, 189
  local versus national, 127
  partnering *see* partnering
  payments, 61, 153
  relationships between, 111

  relationships with, 9, 10, 15, 55,
    65, 103, 146, 173–176
  expertise, 164
  operational review, 161
  outsourcing and, 106
  subcontractors, 113
  see also partnering
request for information (RFI),
    127–128
secondary *see* subcontracting
selection, **49**, 111, 118
  see also tendering
subcontracting by, 113, 154
service specifications, 101–102,
    131–132, 133–137, 145,
    199, 318, 350
  changes to, 160, 192, 199
  content, 135–136
  fraud and, **357**
  output, 318, 188
  performance management, 109,
    134–135, 148, 163, 192
  performance monitoring, 201, 289
  SLAs and, 137, **138**
  stakeholder engagement, 170
  tender evaluation and, 141
serviced facilities, 22–23
services audit, 51–52
shell and core building, 351
sick building syndrome, 69, 76, 76–77,
    84, 351
single point of responsibility, 21, 98,
    114, 115
Six Sigma, 193, 215, 351
skills
  audits, 241
  development, 10, 18, 56, 60, 64, 109
  profile, **49**, 52
smart
  control *see* buildings, automation
  homes *see* intelligent building
  sensors, 244
  systems, 258–260
  tagging *see* RFID
social infrastructure, 94, 275
soft issues, 5, 16, 171, 186
Soft Landings Framework, 34

software, 124, 167, 254, 325
CAFM, 327–328
COBie, 324–325
open-source, 256
planning and scheduling, 56
see also building management
systems; ICT
sourcing policy, 104
space, 24–26, 30–33, 351
efficiency, 23–25, 50, 80, 321
management, 23, 39, 51, 351
utilization, 24–26, 41, 51, 61, 78,
205, 239, 351
space strategy, 50, 53
special-purpose vehicle (SPV), 184
specialist services, 172
specialization, 165–166
specifications, 33
construction, 222, 323, 324
information management, 324,
326, 368
service *see* service specifications
speed of response, 105–107, 124
stadiums, 170
stakeholders, 149
benchmarking and, 51
classification, 37–38
communication with, 85, 212, 221
consultation, 28, 54, 56, 62, 274
documentation and, 232
as end-users, 101–103, 120
engagement, 11
external, 37
gold-plating, 9
identification, 36–38, 41
impact assessment, 38–39
internal, 36–37
outsourcing, 102–103
public-private partnerships,
182–187
see also customers; end-users
statement of needs, 27–28, 30,
31, 34, 351
steady state, 290, 352
strategic fit, 27, 29, 252
strategic implementation, 55–57
strategic management, 46

strategy formulation, 48–49
stress, 45, 71, 73
-related illness, 69, 86
productivity and, 93–95
sick building syndrome and, 76–77
structured data, 307, 312, 352
subcontracting, 111–114, 128,
143–144, 152, 352, 365, 366
by service providers, 154
design and construction, 185–186
fraud and, 357
supplier relationships, 125, 205,
231, 250, 267, 268
supply chain, 231
agreements, 112–113
costs, 113, 152
redundancy, 9
requirements, 152
support processes, 352
surveillance, 319
survey questionnaires, 75, 82, 101,
103, 195–196, 203–204, 333
surveys (condition of building), 223,
226, 227, 317, 347
sustainable development, 25,
244–245, 352
sustainability, 13–14, 18, 243–245,
270, 352
communities, 262–263
corporate social responsibility and,
130, 247–248
environmental management,
245–246
environmental performance, 250–251
policies, 29
space provision, 24–25, 352
see also energy management
SWOT analysis, **49**
synergies, 21

tactical management, 46–47
teamworking, 9, 10, 71
telecare, 169, 268–270
teleconferencing, 148
teleworking, 72, 78–79
health-care services, 169–170,
268–269

tenancy agreements, 312–313, 352
tendering, 111, 146
  assessment, 62
  best value, 12–13
  competitions, 140–141
  conflicts of interest, 149
  contract award, 139
  documentation, 62
  e-tendering, 141
  evaluation, 141–142, **358**
  fraud and, 357–358
  frequency, 139
  market testing, 140
  negotiation, 143
  procedures, 121, 132
  requests for, 132–133
  requirements, 317
  two-envelope system, 141
  see also contracts
time zones, 74, 169
top-down approach, 43, 77, 294, 306
total cost of ownership (TCO), 142,
    167, 221, 225, 227, 352
total facility management (TFM),
    45, 61, 97, 98, 113–115,
    117, 352
  example SLA, **138**
  problems, 113–114
total productive maintenance (TPM),
    227, 229, 353
total quality management (TQM), 353
tracking
  building occupants, 254
  materials, 258
  objects, 256, 257, 259, 265
training
  facility management, **9**, 17
  fire wardens, 90
  health and safety, 90, 129
  in-house personnel, 10
  procurement, 43
transaction costs, 22, 112, 152
transition, 275–276, 353
  actions, 279–280
  after-action reviews, 291–293
  contracts, 280–281
  costs, 282–283

budget approval, 282
  governance, 279–280
  innovation, 296–298
  insurance, 285–286
  mobilization, 286
  planning, 294–295, 353
  provision phase-in, 288–289
  readiness, 284–285
  roles and responsibilities, 295–296
  service delivery, 289
  sign-off, 290
  timescales, 281–282
  transfer of responsibilities, 290–291
  transition control, 276–277
  types, 277–278
  uncertainty management, 283–284
  see also change management
transportation, 177
triple bottom line, 244–245, 353
TUPE, 364

uncertainty management, transition,
    283–284
unconventional working, 78–79
universal footprint, 78
unstructured data, 307, 312, 353
utility supply, 175–176

value
  best *see* best value
  engineering, 102
  management, 102, 193, 367
  for money, 4, 7, 12, 177
vehicles
  accommodation, 320
  fleet management, 189
  maintenance, 57, 177
vendor lock-in, 167, 189, 228
vibration, 76
videoconferencing, 254
virtual
  office, 23, 72
  private networks, 70, 254, 260
VoIP, 254

water conservation, 243, 251–252,
    271, 311

whole-life carbon, 248–249, 261
winter, 107–108
work done, 160
work environment, 68, 70, 73–75,
   83, 94, 245, 353
   design issues, 77–78, 155
work equipment, 91
work outstanding, 160
workers' rights, 62, 95
workflow, 74, 141, 257, 258, 296,
   305, 326, 342
working hours, 72

working time, 287
workplace
   design, 17, 262
   productivity *see* productivity
   serviced, 5, 19–20, 22–23, 39, 80,
      98, 260
   strategy, 68, 72, 79, 83
workstations, 22, 76, 78, 79, 239, 254, 328

zero accidents, 88, 139
zero carbon, 248, 262, 354
zero-sum game, 282, 354

Keep up with critical fields

Would you like to receive up-to-date information on our books, journals and databases in the areas that interest you, direct to your mailbox?

Join the **Wiley e-mail service** - a convenient way to receive updates and exclusive discount offers on products from us.

Simply visit www.wiley.com/email and register online

We won't bombard you with emails and we'll only email you with information that's relevant to you. We will ALWAYS respect your e-mail privacy and NEVER sell, rent, or exchange your e-mail address to any outside company. Full details on our privacy policy can be found online.

www.wiley.com/email

WILEY